ALESSANDRO AND DOMENICO SCARLATTI

COMPOSER RESOURCE MANUALS
(VOL. 34)

GARLAND REFERENCE LIBRARY
OF THE HUMANITIES
(VOL. 1125)

GARLAND COMPOSER
RESOURCE MANUALS
General Editor: Guy A. Marco

1. *Heinrich Schütz* by Allen B. Skei
2. *Josquin Des Prez* by Sydney Robinson Charles
3. *Sergei Vasil'evich Rachmaninoff* by Robert Palmieri
4. *Manuel de Falla* by Gilbert Chase and Andrew Budwig
5. *Adolphe Adam and Léo Delibes* by William E. Studwell
6. *Carl Nielsen* by Mina F. Miller
7. *William Byrd* by Richard Turbet
8. *Christoph Willibald Gluck* by Patricia Howard
9. *Girolamo Frescobaldi* by Frederick Hammond
10. *Stephen Collins Foster* by Calvin Elliker
11. *Béla Bartók* by Elliott Antokoletz
12. *Antonio Vivaldi* by Michael Talbot
13. *Johannes Ockeghem and Jacob Obrecht* by Martin Picker
14. *Ernest Bloch* by David Z. Kushner
15. *Hugo Wolf* by David Ossenkop
16. *Wolfgang Amadeus Mozart* by Baird Hastings
17. *Nikolai Andreevich Rimsky-Korsakov* by Gerald R. Seaman
18. *Henry Purcell* by Franklin B. Zimmerman
19. *G. F. Handel* by Mary Ann Parker-Hale
20. *Jean-Philippe Rameau* by Donald Foster
21. *Ralph Vaughan Williams* by Neil Butterworth
22. *Hector Berlioz* by Jeffrey A. Langford and Jane Denker Graves
23. *Claudio Monteverdi* by K. Gary Adams and Dyke Kiel
24. *Carl Maria von Weber* by Donald G. Henderson and Alice H. Henderson
25. *Orlando di Lasso* by James Erb
26. *Giovanni Battista Pergolesi* by Marvin E. Paymer and Hermine W. Williams
27. *Claude Debussy* by James Briscoe
28. *Gustav and Alma Mahler* by Susan M. Filler
29. *Franz Liszt* by Michael Saffle
30. *Ludwig van Beethoven* by Theodore Albrecht
31. *Franz Joseph Haydn* by Floyd K. Grave and Margaret G. Grave
32. *Felix Mendelssohn* by Donald Mintz
33. *Edgard Varèse* by Anne F. Parks
34. *Alessandro and Domenico Scarlatti* by Carole F. Vidali
35. *Henricus Isaac* by Martin Picker
36. *Guillaume de Machaut* by Lawrence Earp
37. *Edward Elgar* by Christopher Kent

ALESSANDRO AND DOMENICO SCARLATTI
SCARLATTI
A Guide to Research

Carole F. Vidali

GARLAND PUBLISHING, INC. • NEW YORK & LONDON
1993

Library of Congress Cataloging-in-Publication Data

Vidali, Carole Franklin,
 Alessandro and Domenico Scarlatti : a guide to research / by Carole F.
Vidali.
      p.   cm. — (Garland reference library of the humanities ; vol. 1125)
(Composer resource manuals ; vol. 34)
   Includes discographies and indexes.
   ISBN 0–8240–5942–5 (alk. paper)
   1. Scarlatti, Alessandro, 1660–1725—Bibliography.   2. Scarlatti,
Domenico, 1685–1757—Bibliography.   I. Title.   II. Series.   III. Series:
Garland composer resource manuals ; v. 34.
ML134.S218V5   1993
016.78'092'2—dc20   93–16636
                                                                         CIP
                                                                         MN

Printed on acid-free, 250-year-life paper
Manufactured in the United States of America

GARLAND COMPOSER RESOURCE MANUALS

In response to the growing need for bibliographic guidance to the vast literature on significant composers, Garland is publishing an extensive series of research guides. This ongoing series encompasses more than fifty composers; they represent Western musical tradition from the Renaissance to the present century.

Each research guide offers a selective, annotated list of writings, in all European languages, about one or more composers. There are also lists of works by the composers, unless these are available elsewhere. Biographical sketches and guides to library resources, organizations, and specialists are presented. As appropriate to the individual composer, there are maps, photographs or other illustrative matter, glossaries, and indexes.

ALESSANDRO AND DOMENICO SCARLATTI: A GUIDE TO RESEARCH

PREFACE *A DUE*

When one considers the enormous body of literature, several complete editions, numerous critical reports, yearbooks, etc. which exist for Johann Sebastian Bach and George Frederick Handel, it is difficult to understand why nothing remotely comparable exists for either Alessandro Scarlatti or his more famous son Domenico.

What literature there is about these two composers overlaps to a certain degree; however, their lives and contributions are different enough to merit separate books. This is, indeed, what I have written although the two books contained herein (referred to in the text as Book I and Book II) are connected through cross references. Each "book" has its own preface, introduction, and indices.

The author's aim is to guide a beginning researcher (defined here rather broadly to include musicology students, performers, and music teachers) in obtaining information about the two composers (their lives, milieu, and works) which is historically significant, accurate, up to date, representative of different viewpoints, or illustrates unresolved research problems. A further aim is to provide information about available modern or facsimile editions and recordings as it is through these that the music comes alive.

The question of performance practice has

been addressed in Section III, 1 of both books; references to reviews of modern performances appear in Section III, 2.

Many indices and bibliographies were used to identify Scarlatti materials, chief among them the *Music Index*; the *International Inventory of Music Literature* (known as *RILM*); *Doctoral Dissertations in Musicology* (most recent edition by Cecil Adkins, 1984); *Dissertation Abstracts International* and lists of foreign dissertations including: Richard Schaal's *Verzeichnis musikwissenschaftlicher Dissertationen* (Bärenreiter, 1963; suppl., 1974) with annual supplements in *Die Musikforschung* (German); Paul Doe's compilation in various issues of the *Royal Musical Association. Research Chronicle* (English); and Rostirolla's *Bibliografia delle tesi di laurea* in the *Nuova rivista musicale italiana* 21 (1987), 656-700 and its supplement *Le tesi in storia della musica... 1976/77 - 1987/88* by Giulio D'Amore in *NRMI* 22 (1988), 741-781 (Italian).

Carole Franklin Vidali

Syracuse, New York

April 1992

ACKNOWLEDGMENTS

This project could not have been completed without the assistance of a number of friends and colleagues. Deserving of special mention for her unflagging interest and willingness to share her expertise, information and materials is Hermine W. Williams of Clinton, New York. Also most helpful were Don Seibert, Music Librarian and Dorcus MacDonald, Head of the Interlibrary Loan Department of Syracuse University's Bird Library; Michael Ochs, Head, Loeb Music Library, Harvard University; and Charles Lindahl, Reference Librarian, Sibley Music Library, Eastman School of Music. I much appreciate the generous lending policies of schools rich in Scarlatti materials such as Cornell University and Vassar College which made available out-of-print and difficult to obtain materials. The encouragement of Guy A. Marco and Marie Ellen Larcada, editors at Garland Publishing, is gratefully acknowledged. I also wish to thank my family for their support during these months, especially my husband Gianfranco for assisting with the technical aspects of indexing on the computer and my mother Dorothy Franklin for her role in caring for my two young children during the final stages of my research.

ABBREVIATIONS

AMS   American Musicological Society

DA   *Dissertation Abstracts International.* Ann Arbor, Mich.: University Microfilms, 1952-

MGG   *Die Musik in Geschichte und Gegenwart.* Ed., Friedrich Blume. Kassel: Bärenreiter Verlag, 1949-1967.

MS   Manuscript (or MSS: manuscripts)

NG   *New Grove Dictionary of Music and Musicians.* Ed., Stanley Sadie. London: Macmillan, 1981.

NGIBM   *New Grove Italian Baroque Masters.* New York: W. W. Norton, 1984

NRMI   *Nuova rivista musicale italiana*

RAI   Radiotelevisione Italiana

RILM   *Répertoire internationale de littérature musicale.* v.1-. 1967-.

RISM   *Répertoire internationale des sources musicales.*

UMI   University Microfilms International

UTET   Unione Tipografia Editrice Torinese

BOOK I

CONTENTS

Preface   xvii

Introduction   xix

I. Life and Works   3

    1a. Biographies, Biographical
        Articles, Conference Proceedings   3
    1b. Letters and Documents   10
    2. Scarlatti Family   13
    3. Cultural and Aesthetic Background   18
        General   18
        Florence   24
        Naples   26
        Rome   32
    4. Scarlatti's Relationship to
        Handel and Other Composers   38

II. Studies of the Music   45

    1. Vocal Music   45
        Cantatas   45
        Church Music   55
        Madrigals   64
        Operas: History   65
        Studies of Specific Operas   88
        Oratorios: History   102
        Studies of Specific Oratorios   109
        Serenatas   115

    2. Instrumental Music
        Keyboard Music   119
        Other Instrumental Music and   123
        Instrumental Style

III. Performance Background   129

      1. Performance Practice   129
          General Guides or Bibliographies   130
          Baroque Period (with bearing on
          Scarlatti)   131

      2. Modern Performances   143
          Performance Reviews   144
          Church Music   144
          Operas   145
          Oratorios   153

 IV. Sources   157
      Alessandro Scarlatti Worklists,
      Catalogs, etc.   159
      General Catalogs, Articles,
      Bibliographies and Directories
      of Sources   165

  V. Scarlatti's Works in Modern Edition   171
      or Facsimile

      1. Vocal Music   171
          Cantatas; Cantata Collections   171
          Suppl.: Unpublished Cantata
          Editions in Dissertations   182
          Church Music   185
          Suppl.: Unpublished Church Music
          Editions in Dissertations   191
          Madrigals   192
          Operas   193
          Operas, selections: Arias, Duets,
          Overtures (Sinfonias), etc.   197
          Oratorios and Large Sacred Works   202
          Serenatas   204

      2. Instrumental Music   205
          Orchestral & Chamber Music   205
          Keyboard Music   210

 VI. Discography:
      Alessandro Scarlatti on Record   213
          Introduction   213
      1. Vocal Music   214
          Arias   214
          Cantatas   215

Church Music   221
Madrigals   225
Operas   225
Oratorios and Large Sacred Works   228
Serenatas   230

2. Instrumental Music   231
Concertos   231
Keyboard Music   233
Chamber Music   234

Index of Authors   235

Index of Names   241

Index of Compositions   249

PREFACE

Although a number of 20th century music historians have written of his genius, Alessandro Scarlatti is one of the most underrepresented major composers of his era in terms of literature, modern editions, and performances. There is no thematic catalog or critical edition of all the works nor even a single collected edition of his over 600 authenticated cantatas.

The present volume focuses on recent books, articles, and dissertations which have contributed significantly to our understanding of the composer, his work, and milieu. The majority of the entries were selected from the literature of the last two decades up to c1985; however, an attempt was made to include earlier studies of major importance or historical significance as well as major articles, etc., published within the last few years. Certain items were not available to the author but were considered too important to exclude; they are identified as "not seen." When a published abstract or other information was found for any of these (e.g., in RILM or DA), it is cited.

A separate worklist has not been included as others (the most recent in *NGIBM*, item 430) are readily accessible; however, some corrections and additions to the *NGIBM* list encountered in the course of work on this book have been noted. There is a greater need for a current list of modern editions of Scarlatti's works. *NGIBM* cites only a few of these beyond the incomplete collected editions of the operas and oratorios. Thus, a substantial part of this volume is devoted to lists of the

works (principally in complete form) in modern
or facsimile edition. A number of Scarlatti's
cantatas and church music compositions
unavailable in published editions have been
identified in unpublished doctoral
dissertations.

The author has also sought to provide a
selective discography of the composer's works
including relatively recent issues and
reissues. For more information on this, see
the "Introduction" to section VI.

INTRODUCTION

As we survey the life and works of
Alessandro Scarlatti from the perspective of
the 90s, we can state with a certain degree of
confidence that the major outlines have been
sketched, many of the details clarified, and
some of the errors made by past historians
laid to rest. A number of scholars have
contributed to this understanding in our
century. Foremost among them are Edward J.
Dent, whose groundbreaking studies formed the
basis for all subsequent Scarlatti research
(item 6, etc.), and Alfred Lorenz whose study
of the early operas was a milestone in the
history of Scarlatti scholarship (item 205).
The early researches of Prota-Giurleo, Fienga,
Dotto, and Tiby all helped to fill in
important biographical details (see items 31-
33, 9, 8, and 38, respectively).

More recently, Mario Fabbri's study of the
correspondence between Scarlatti and Prince
Ferdinando de Medici (item 19), Roberto
Pagano's biographies, (items 16 & 34), Frank
Walker's "Additional Notes" (appended to the
reissue of Dent's Scarlatti biography), and
encyclopedia articles by Edwin Hanley (items
13-14 & 133), Malcolm Boyd (item 3) and Donald
J. Grout (item 12) have helped contribute to
the picture of the composer's life that is now
generally accepted.

Although the major events in Scarlatti's
life and information relating to some
performances of his works have been
documented, our knowledge of the music itself
is still very limited. In 1968, Jack Westrup
(item 256) wrote:

> *In any other country [than Italy] a composer as celebrated as Alessando Scarlatti would by now have been commemorated in a series of volumes incorporating at least all the surviving operas and oratorios.... In fact very little has been done since Edward Dent published his pioneering volume in 1905....*

Since Westrup's reproof, only one additional volume in Lino Bianchi's oratorio series has been issued bringing the total number to 5. Although an excellent set of facsimile editions, *The Italian Oratorio 1650-1800* (Garland Publishing, 1986-) edited by Howard E. Smither, has recently appeared, no Scarlatti volumes are among them. With regard to Scarlatti's operas we are more fortunate. Nine volumes in a notable series, *The Operas of Alessandro Scarlatti*, were issued under the general editorship of Donald J. Grout before his death. These editions are exemplary in terms of their scholarship, clarity, and introductory notes (additional critical notes on each are available from the Isham Memorial Library, Department of Music, Harvard University). Only one additional volume has come out since, this issued by the Harvard University Department of Music. Several other new and facsimile editions of operas by Scarlatti have appeared very recently (see Section V, 1), but all the published scores taken together still do not equal even half of the surviving operas nor a quarter of those actually written.

With the cantatas we confront even greater lacunae. Edwin Hanley's superb dissertation, a monumental study of Scarlatti sources and attributions combined with a thematic catalog that includes a mine of information, is unique in the literature. That it has never been published is only one of the puzzles encountered in the field of Scarlatti studies. Hanley has documented over 600 cantatas for which attributions are reasonably certain as well as more than 100 others less reliably attributed to him. Thus, Scarlatti appears to have been the most prolific cantata composer of the Italian

Baroque.   It is not only numbers, however,
that command the attention of music scholars;
there is general agreement that Scarlatti's
cantatas represent his best work and the
epitome of the genre.   They also illustrate
every stage of his development as a composer.
This having been said, it is at the very least
odd that there has been no attempt in all
these years to come out with a complete
edition of these works.

Recently Malcolm Boyd has selected and
introduced a collection of 29 Scarlatti
cantatas in facsimile (see Section V, 1), the
largest number available to date in a
published source.   Modern editions exist
(including several edited by Boyd), but these
are few in relation to Scarlatti's enormous
output.   Supplementing the published sources
are a number of editions included in
dissertations and theses.   Fifty-five of these
have been included here in Section V, 1; a
number of others (not included in the present
volume) exist in masters theses.

A number of research problems need further
attention.   Some of these are: to learn more
about the Scarlatti hand in order to further
identify which works are autograph, which
copies; to identify the copyists; to identify
some of the works to which arias in
collections belong; to match up librettos
(which rarely include the composers' names)
with unidentified scores; to reassess the
composer's contributions to comic opera
(scenes/ intermezzos) and their influence on
instrumental music; to provide an overview of
his operatic style and changes in it; to
examine Scarlatti's and other contemporary
composers' treatment of the same text; and to
provide scholarly editions and/or facsimiles
for the serenatas, remaining oratorios,
cantatas (as mentioned above), and
theoretical/pedagogical works.

Book I

Alessandro Scarlatti

LIFE AND WORKS OF ALESSANDRO SCARLATTI

1a. Biographies, Biographical Articles, Conference Proceedings

1. Badura-Skoda, Eva. "Ein Aufenthalt Alessandro Scarlattis in Wien im Oktober 1681." *Die Musikforschung* 27 (1974): 204-208.

   Presents documentation for Scarlatti's visit to Vienna in 1681 and additional information taken from the account books of the court of Leopold and Empress Eleonora. According to Grout (item 194) Scarlatti was present there for performances of *Gli equivoci nel sembiante* during Carnival, the only time it is certain that he left Italy. Strohm (item 436) gives the performance place as Linz, not Vienna, though the libretto was printed in the latter city.

2. Ballola, Giovanni Carli. "Alessandro Scarlatti." *Musica (Kassel)* 20 (1966): 255-258.

   Speaks of the lack of Scarlatti sources (both with regard to the number of important monographs and the number and quality of published editions). Summarizes conceptions of the composer fostered by writers in the field of seventeenth- and eighteenth-century music. Discusses the book of Mario Fabbri which contains transcriptions of the surviving correspondence between Scarlatti and Prince Ferdinando de' Medici (item 19).

3. Boyd, Malcolm. "Alessandro Scarlatti; I. La vita, II. Le opere teatrali, III. Le cantate da camera, IV. Musica sacra e strumentale." In *La Musica; enciclopedia storica*. Ed. by Alberto Basso. Turin: UTET, 1966-1971. Vol. 4 (1966), pp. 127-157. Port., facs., mus.

An accurate and detailed account of the
composer's life followed by a rather in-depth
discussion of Scarlatti's works. Catalog of
works on pp. 138-156 (presented in a clear,
readily accessible format), but no MS sources
or library locations cited; list of editions;
and bibl., pp. 156-157 -- all now superseded
by item 12.

4. *Celebrazione del terzo centenario della nascita di Alessandro
    Scarlatti*. [Naples]: RAI, 1960. 89 pp. Ports.,
    illus.

Frequently   cited,   rare   collection   of
tercentenary essays by G. Confalonieri, F.
Nicolini, M. Labroca, F. de Filippis, and U.
Prota-Giurleo (items 68, 78, 28, 10 and 32,
respectively).   Includes reproductions
of the frontispiece of the libretto   for *Gli
equivoci del sembiante* (1679, Rome; 1680, Naples) in
the library of St. Cecilia Academy, Rome;
portraits   of   Alessandro   (two   by   unknown
artists) in the Licea, Bologna, and Naples
Conservatory and one of Domenico (by an
unknown artist) at Naples Conservatory; the
Concert   italien print in which Domenico is
represented;   and   a   possible   portrait   of
Flaminia by Solinema in the Toulouse Museum.

5. *Colloquium Alessandro Scarlatti Würzburg 1975*. Her-
    ausgegeben von Wolfgang Osthoff und Jutta
    Ruile-Dronke (Würzburger Musikhistorische
    Beiträge, 7) Tutzing: Hans Schneider, 1979.
    v and 258 pp. ISBN 3-7952-0260-4.

Collection includes an introduction by
Osthoff and seven addresses presented at the
Colloquium   of   the   Gesellschaft   für
Musikforschung upon the 250th anniversary of
the composer's death. Transcriptions of
discussions following each paper raise a
number of interesting issues. Individual
contributions cited as items 114, 170, 174,
196, 216, 229, and 315.   Pages 217-58:
supplement containing 15 musical examples; pp.

215-16 contain an index to these. Review in *Rivista italiana di musicologia* (1980): 269-275 by Maria Antonella Balsano.

6. Dent, Edward J. *Alessandro Scarlatti: His Life and Works*. London: Edward Arnold Ltd., 1905. 2nd rev. ed., new impression with preface and additional notes by Frank Walker. N.Y: St. Martins Press, 1960. xii and 252 pp. Port. Reprint of 1960 ed.: St. Claire Shores, MI: Scholarly Press, Inc., 1976. ISBN 0-403-01541-3 and Irvine, CA: American Biography Service, Inc., 1988. Port.

The pioneering study (and, amazingly, still the only comprehensive book-length study in English) of the composer's life, works, and musical style. Though dated, it is still indispensable due to the author's sophisticated insights and his early examination of original documents and manuscripts and as a point of reference for most later studies. Numerous musical examples. Emphasis more on opera and vocal works than instrumental and keyboard music. "Catalogue of Extant Works"; genealogical table of the original edition omitted. Index. Updated by Walker's "Additional Notes," pp. 233-248.

7. _____. "Alessandro Scarlatti." *Royal Musical Association, London. Proceedings* 30 (1903-1904): 75-90.

Speech given to the Association and discussion which followed. Presents some of the ideas which appeared afterward in his book (item 6); principally an examination of the chamber cantatas and operas. Ascribes Scarlatti's lack of popularity in modern times (versus the popularity of Corelli) to the complexity of his music. Discussion reveals how little others knew of Scarlatti's style at this time.

8.   Dotto, Paolo. "Gaspare Alessandro Scarlatti,
         il Palermitano." *Musica d'oggi* 17 (1935): 383-
         386.

      A frequently cited brief, yet scholarly,
      article which took issue with some of the
      prevailing ideas of the day concerning the
      composer (e.g., place of birth, teachers) and
      cited documentary evidence from the archives.
      Dotto was the first to determine Scarlatti's
      exact date of birth through examination of the
      parish registers in Palermo in 1926.

9.   Fienga, Pasquale. "La véritable patrie et la
         famille d'Alessandro Scarlatti." *Revue
         musicale* 10/3 (Jan. 1929): 227-236.

      Early biographical study of Alessandro and
      his family based on documents in the Vatican
      Archives, Rome. Corrected some of the errors
      fostered by various earlier studies, e.g.,
      Francesco Florimo's *La scuola musicale di Napoli e i suoi
      conservatorii.*   (item 76) and Francois Joseph
      Fétis' *Biographie universelle des musiciens...* (2nd ed.
      Paris, 1889). Established the facts concerning
      Alessandro's marriage and the birth of his
      first child Pietro Scarlatti.

10.   Filippis, Felice de. "Il sepolcro di Alessandro
         Scarlatti nella chiesa di S. Maria
         Montesanto." In *Celebrazione del terzo centenario...*
         (item 4), pp. 69-79.

      Description of the composer's sepulchre and
      the chapel of S. Cecilia in which it is
      located. Gives text and description of the
      three paintings that decorate the walls as
      well as reproductions of a painting of S.
      Cecilia and of the original and later
      (inscribed in 1958 by the Association
      Alessandro Scarlatti) epigraphs.

11.   Grossi, Genaro. "Alessandro Scarlatti." In

Domenico Martuscelli's *Biografia degli uomini illustri del Regno di Napoli*, Vol. 6. Naples: N. Gervasi, 1813-1822.

The first important biography of A. Scarlatti appears in this book according to Dent; nevertheless, full of errors or exaggerations. Contains engraved portrait of the composer, possibly after Solimena. For reproduction, see item 16, plate opposite page 64.

12.   Grout, Donald J. "Alessandro Scarlatti." In *The New Grove Italian Baroque Masters*. N.Y.: W. W. Norton, 1984. pp. 209-231 and pp. 241-243. ISBN 0-333-38235-8 (hardback); ISBN 0-333-38236-6 (pbk).

The best and most recent introduction to the composer and his work and for most undergraduates the most accessible. Written in English, with the most up to date bibliographies and worklists currently available. Pp. 232-240 written by Edwin Hanley. Worklist (pp. 244-262) and bibl. (pp. 263-267) by Malcolm Boyd. This article is an updated version of the article which first appeared in *The New Grove Dictionary of Music and Musicians* (1980).

13.   Hanley, Edwin. "Scarlatti, Alessandro." *Enciclopedia della musica*. Ed. by Claudio Sartori. Milan: G. Ricordi and C., 1963-1964. Vol. 4 (1964), pp. 132-137.

A superb write-up of the life of Scarlatti with corrections of the errors of some early historians and an in-depth examination of Scarlatti's style: its formation, development, the principles which guided it, its reception, etc. List of works and short bibl., pp. 136-137.

14.   _____. "Scarlatti, Pietro Alessandro Gaspare."

Die Musik in Geschichte und Gegenwart. Ed. by
Friedrich Blume. Kassel: Bärenreiter
Verlag, 1949-1967. Bd. 11 (1963), Cols.
1482-1506. Cols. 1486-1498: list of works.
Cols. 1503-1506: editions and bibl.

Detailed account of Scarlatti's life and
works reflects Hanley's impeccable scholarship
and particular concern to clear up false or
unproven reports about the composer
perpetuated in the literature. Contains the
most accurate and complete list of his works
to be published in an encyclopedia before *NG*
(updated in *NGIBM*, item 430) though no MS
sources are cited. Mentions a greater number
of modern editions than *NGIBM*; however, the
latter was able to include more recent
publications. List of cantatas incorporates
the work of his thesis and updates it.

15.   Holmes, William C. "Lettere inedite su
      Alessandro Scarlatti." In *La musica a Napoli
      durante il seicento* (item 77), pp. 369-378.

Author reports on newly found documents
relating to the life and artistic career of
the composer between 1700 and 1703 in the
Archivio di Stato, Florence, and the Archivio
Albizzi (now in the private library of the
Guicciardini family of Florence). A series of
letters written almost entirely in Naples help
clarify aspects of the composer's life and of
musical life in Naples. The majority of the
letters were written to Albizzi by Giovanni
Battista Salomoni, a friend from Florence who
was the granducal envoy to Naples at the
beginning of the 1700s. Fifteen letters are
identified and their general contents
outlined. They include references to
Scarlatti's daughter Flaminia, to his operas
Tito Sempronio Gracco and another (unidentified)
which may be *Turno Aricino*, as well as to his
travels, etc.

* Nicolini, Fausto. "Alessandro Scarlatti a Napoli." In *Celebrazione...*, pp. 19-50. Cited as item 78.

16. Pagano, Roberto, Lino Bianchi, and Giancarlo Rostirolla. *Alessandro Scarlatti*. Turin: Edizioni RAI (ERI), 1972. 612 pp. "Biografia" by Pagano, pp. 5-233. Bibl., pp. 237-244. Review in *Music and Letters* 54 (1973): 474-475.

    Pagano's biography, which is fully documented, amply illustrated, and more comprehensive than any previously written, constitutes the major written contribution to this important but rare volume designed for private distribution. Its special strength is the wealth of detailed information on the social and cultural milieu of the composer (particularly during the early years in Sicily and Naples and during periods in the composer's life for which biographical data are scarce). See items 275 and 435, respectively, for comments on the contributions by Lino Bianchi and G. Rostirolla.

17. Pagano, Roberto. "Alexander Scarlatti, civitatis Panormi." *Conservatorio di musica Vincenzo Bellini, Palermo, annuario 1960-61* (1962): 11-.

    Not seen.

* _____. *Scarlatti; Alessandro e Domenico: due vite in una*. Cited as item 30.

* Prota-Giurleo, Ulisse. *Alessandro Scarlatti "il Palermitano"*.... Cited as item 31.

18. Ronga, Luigi. "Motivi critici su Alessandro Scarlatti." *Rivista musicale italiana* 56 (1954): 125-140.

Discussion of Scarlatti's melodic and
harmonic style, the individuality with which
he set cantata texts, his critics' faulty
judgements based primarily on analysis of
isolated examples which were compared with
theoretical writings.   No references to
specific musical examples.

*   Salazar, Adolfo. "Los Scarlatti...." Cited
       as item 34.

*   Talbot, Michael, and Colin Timms. "Music and
       the Poetry of Antonio Ottoboni (1646-1720)."
       Cited as item 101.

1b. Letters and Documents

*   Della Seta, Fabrizio. "La musica in Arcadia
       al tempo di Corelli." Cited as item 90.

19.   Fabbri, Mario. *Alessandro Scarlatti e il Principe
       Ferdinando de' Medici*. Florence: Leo S. Olschki
       Editore, 1961. 124 pp.   (Historiae musicae
       cultores biblioteca, 16)   ISBN 88-222-1637-
       7.

Monographic study of Scarlatti's life and
relationship to Ferdinando de' Medici during
the 30-year period, 1683-1713.   Includes
transcriptions of all the known correspondence
between Ferdinando and the composer and
excerpts from other documents (including the
Regole per principanti).   Author states that c60
letters survive; a number were lost,
especially from 1690 to 1702. Pages 58-61
include references to Domenico and
Ferdinando's letter recommending Domenico to
the Venetian Alvise Morosini. See "Ausgabe" in
Hanley's *MGG* article (item 14) for other
publications containing selected letters of
the composer. Chapter 3 is a discussion of the
music "per il tempo di penitenza e di tenebre"
(see item 155).

20. Kirnberger, Johann Philipp. *Die Kunst des reinen Satzes in der Musik*. Berlin and Königsberg, 1776–1779. Facs. reprint: Hildesheim: Georg Olms, 1968. 2 vols. in 1. Bd. 2, 3rd Abteilung, pp. 143–162.   Pp. 163–175: motet *Laetatus sum* by Scarlatti.

Contains the German translation of Scarlatti's *Discorso sopra un caso particolare in arte*, April 1717, which survives only in this form, the original manuscript having been lost (mentioned by Fétis and later in *Gli Scarlatti* as having once been in the Biblioteca del Conservatorio di San Pietro a Maiella, Naples, and containing 28 pp. in folio with 12 musical examples). Important theoretical document which gives detailed defense of principles for treating dissonances in strict counterpoint as well as Scarlatti's beliefs regarding individual artistic freedom. See also item 22.

21. Llorens Cisteró, José M. "Las dedicatorias de los manuscritos musicales de la Capella Sixtina." *Anuario musical (Barcelona)* 11 (1956): 59–90.

Pp. 71–72 give the Latin text of a dedication to a Mass in 5 voices (which corresponds to Scarlatti's *Messa Clementina*) as it appears in the autograph manuscript (184,f2, corresponding to no. 193 Cappella Sixtina). Composer cited as Alessandro Scarlatti. Addressed to Clement XI.

22. López-Calo, José. "L'intervento di Alessandro Scarlatti nella controversia sulla Messa Scala Aretina di Francisco Valls." *Analecta musicologica* 5 (1968): 178–200 (Studien zür Geschichte der italienische Musik, 5).

Summary of the controversy between two Spanish composers over the use of dissonance (defended by Valls on grounds of artistic liberty). Includes extracts of writings by participants in the dispute and parts of the

text of Scarlatti's intervention (the
Discorso...) in Kirnberger's translation (item
20). Describes unsuccessful search for the
original MS referred to by Fétis (*Biographie
universelle des musiciens...*, , 2nd ed, vol. 7, p.
430).

23. *Musikhandschriften in Basel aus verschiedenen Sammlungen.*
    *Katalog der Ausstellung im Kunstmuseum Basel vom 31. Mai bis
    zum 13. Juli 1975.* Hrsg. von Tilman Seebass.
    Basel: Kunstmuseum Basel/ Basler
    Berichthaus, 1975. 99 pp. Bibl.: pp. 95-
    96; Namenregister: pp. 97-99.

    Exhibition included two Scarlatti autographs
    (from unidentified   private collections in
    Basel): 1) a letter of Alessandro Scarlatti
    written March 7, 1693, in Naples (cited in
    brackets by the editor as being addressed to
    Cardinal Ottoboni) and possibly enclosed as a
    cover letter with the 2nd part of the oratorio
    La Giuditta [i] (first Roman performance, 1695,
    with additions): Cat. # 10, p. 34 (see also
    items 94, 283, 301, and 436 for discussion of
    authorship of the libretto); and 2) MS of
    cantata "Su la sponda del mare," formerly in
    the private library of Fortunato Santini: Cat.
    #11, p. 34 (facsimile of opening page
    reproduced on p. 13).

*   Scarlatti, Alessandro. *Discorso di musica sopra un
    caso particolare in arte...*, *1717* (see items 20 and
    22).

*   _____. *Per accompagnare il cembalo o organo...1715.*
    In the British Library, London (BM Add.
    14244, fol 40a). Excerpts in item 268 and
    item 344, p. 812. (Part of the *Regole...*, see
    below).

*   _____. *Le regole per principianti.* c1715. In the
    British Library, London (BM Add. 14244, fol.
    13a, 38r-43v and 31517, fol. 35-38n) and the

Biblioteca dell'Abbazia, Montecassino,
Italy: Codex 126 D4. Also appears in
opening pages of other MSS of the toccatas
including the Higgs MS *Toccate per cembalo per ben
principiare a sonare, et al nobile portamento delle mani*.... at
Yale (see items 318, 324, 437). Brief
excerpts in items 19, 35, and 344.

Scarlatti's comments on fingering and rules
for figured bass realization.

24. Winternitz, Emanuel. *Musical Autographs*.
     Princeton: Princeton University Press, 1955.
     Notes. Vol. 1: text; bibl. Vol. 2: facs.,
     plates. Illus., mus. exs.

     Vol. 2, plates 15, 16, and 17 show
     facsimiles of excerpts from Alessandro
     Scarlatti's autographs of *Quante le grazie son*
     (1703), cantata in e for alto and continuo;
     "Aria per camera: Cerca, cerca nel cor" (1706)
     (Coll. Ac. Filarmon. Bologna); and *La Griselda*
     (1720) (Collec. London, B.M.). Vol. 1, pp.
     53-55, contains commentary on these examples.

2. Scarlatti Family

25. Dent, Edward J. "New Light on the Scarlatti
     Family." *Musical Times* 67 (1926): 982-983.

     A summary of the discoveries made by Prota-
     Giurleo (item 31) regarding the Scarlattis.

26. Dietz, Hanns-Bertold. "A Chronology of
     Maestri and Organisti at the Cappella Reale
     in Naples 1745-1800." *American Musicological
     Society. Journal* 25 (1972): 379-406.

     Discussion of musical life in Naples during
     the second half of the eighteenth century
     based on documents in the Archivio di Stato,
     Naples. References on pp. 386-387 to Pietro
     Filippo Scarlatti, a son of Alessandro who was
     "organista ordinario" at the Cappella from

1712 to 1750, the year of his death.
Chronology supplements that of Giacomo Leo,
which covered the first half of the century
(*Leonardo Leo, musicista del sec. XVIII e le sue opere musicale*.
Naples, 1905).

*   Donato, Giuseppe. "Su alcuni aspetti della
        vita musicale in Sicilia nel seicento."
        Cited as item 73.

27.   Fienga, Pasquale. "Giuseppe Scarlatti et son
        incertaine ascendance directe." *Revue musicale*
        13 no. 123 (Feb. 1932): 113-119.

        Attempts to determine whose son Giuseppe
        Scarlatti actually was based on surviving
        documents including baptismal records, etc.

*   _____. "La véritable patrie et la famille
        d'Alessandro Scarlatti." Cited as item 9.

28.   Labroca, Mario. "L'esempio e l'insegnamente
        su una grande famiglia." In *Celebrazione...*
        (item 4), pp. 51-56.

        Author attempts to convey something of the
        ambience that surrounds a family for whom
        music making is a way of life, the focal point
        of its existence.

29.   Ligi, Bramante. "La cappella musicale del
        Duomo d'Urbino." *Note d'archivio* 2 (1925): 1-
        369.

        Chapter 6, pp. 133-136, presents documents
        relating to the appointment and residence of
        Pietro Scarlatti as maestro di cappella at
        Urbino; he remained from Feb. 1705-Oct. 1708.
        A. Scarlatti visited there in 1707.

30.   Pagano, Roberto. *Scarlatti; Alessandro e Domenico: due*

vita in una. Milan: Arnoldo Mondadori Editore, 1985. 494 pp.

A biography written in the style of a novel yet containing scholarly apparatus (footnotes, index of names). No bibliography. Explores the cultural background of the various locations in which the composers were active, the relationship between father and son, etc. By the author of the most recent and extensive biography of Alessandro Scarlatti to date (item 16). Includes new biographical data on Domenico (see also items 22 and 23, Book II).

*   Pascual, Beryl Kenyon de. "Domenico Scarlatti and His Son Alexandro's Inheritance. "*Music and Letters* 69 (1988): 23-29. Notes, App. Cited as item 24 in Book II.

31.   Prota-Giurleo, Ulisse. *Alessandro Scarlatti "il Palermitano" (la patria e la famiglia)*. Naples: privately printed, 1926. 42 pp.

A pioneering study based on newly discovered documents at Naples which corrected many earlier errors concerning the Scarlatti family and A. Scarlatti, in particular (e.g., that his birthplace was Palermo, not Trapani), and provided other information about the family. Includes transcriptions of some of the original documents cited. Review in *The Monthly Musical Record*, Nov. 1926.

32.   _____. "I congiunti di Alessandro Scarlatti." In *Celebrazione...* (item 4), pp. 56-67.

Discusses the activities of the less famous musical members of the Scarlatti family: Anna Maria and her daughter (by Nicola Barbapiccola) Giuseppina; Melchiorra, Francesco, Giuseppe, and Tommaso.

33. _____. "Notizie intorno ad Anna Maria
    Scarlatti (1661-1703)." *Archivi d'Italia e rassegna
    internazionale degli archivi; periodico della Bibliotheque des
    Annales Institutorum* (Rome). 2nd ser. Vol. 27
    (1960): 351-371.

    Not seen.

34. Salazar, Adolfo. "Los Scarlatti (una ilustre
    familia musical)." *Nuestra musica* 3 (Oct.
    1948): 231-240 and 4 (Jan. 1949): 5-15.

    Vol. 3 (pp. 231-236) contains a discussion
    of the Scarlatti family's contributions to
    music, mentioning later musicians bearing the
    Scarlatti name active in Spain and summing up
    what was then known about the Scarlatti family
    (with references to Fétis, Fienga, Dent, et
    al.). Vol. 4 (pp. 5-15) contains a general
    biographical overview of Domenico followed by
    a discussion of the keyboard instruments then
    in use, their terminology, characteristics,
    etc.

*   Sartori, Claudio. "Gli Scarlatti a Napoli."
    Cited as item 217.

35. *Gli Scarlatti (Alessandro - Francesco - Pietro -Domenico -
    Giuseppe); note e documenti sulla vita e sulle opere. Raccolti in
    occasione della settimana celebrativa (15-21 settembre 1940-
    XVIII)*. Siena: Libreria Editrice Ticci,
    1940. 92 pp.

    Brief commentaries on the works performed
    during the week-long celebration which
    included performances of Alessandro's *Il trionfo
    dell'onore* (see item 271) and Domenico's *Stabat
    Mater* as well as various instrumental and vocal
    pieces; on the Scarlatti family and Domenico
    (by Sebastiano A. Luciani); and on Alessandro
    (by Luigi Ronga, an earlier version of item
    18). Also contains section of Scarlatti
    "curiosities" with excerpts and facsimile
    reprints from documents among which are the

"Avvertimento" from the original edition of
Domenico's *Ezercizi*, the first page of his
autograph *Miserere*, excerpts from Alessandro's
Regole per principianti, a diagram of his hands (from
the I-Nc MS *Toccate per cembalo*), and the
frontispiece and an aria from his *Narciso* as
well as the "Contributo a un catalogo delle
opere teatrali di Alessandro Scarlatti
esistenti nelle biblioteche italiane" by
Emilia Zanetti and Claudio Sartori (item 438)
and a list of "Opere, Oratori e Cantate" by
Ugo Rolandi.

36. Solar Quintes, Nicolas A. "Documentos sobre
     la familia de Domenico Scarlatti." *Anuario
     musical* (Madrid) 4 (1949): 137-154.

     Traces the Scarlatti family genealogy to the
     present century in the person of Eduardo
     Scarlatti, author of books on the history of
     the theater, living in Portugal at the time
     this article was written. Documents relating
     to Domenico quoted (including some from his
     residence in Spain and Portugal).

37. Springer, Hermann. "Das Partiturautograph con
     Giuseppe Scarlatti's bisher verschollener
     Clemenza di Tito." *Beitrage zum Bibliotheks-und
     Buchwesen P. Schwenke... gewidmet.* Berlin, 1913. pp.
     257-261. Mus. ex.

     Not seen.

38. Tiby, Ottavio. "La famiglia Scarlatti; nuove
     ricerche e documenti." *Journal of Renaissance and
     Baroque Music* (1947): 275-290.

     Searched parish registers of Palermo and
     published results in this article. Identified
     the birthplace of Alessandro's father Pietro
     and the birthdates of 7 of the 8 children.

39. Walker, Frank. "Some Notes on the Scarlattis."

Music Review 12 (1951): 185-203.

Some of these notes are reprinted in Dent's
book (item 6, pp. 233-248). Divided into 11
sections. Discusses family including
information on Alessandro's father, sister
Anna Maria, and sons Domenico and Francesco,
etc.

3. Cultural and Aesthetic Background

General

40. Buelow, George J. "Music, Rhetoric and the
    Concept of Affections: A Selective
    Bibliography." *Music Library Association. Notes* 30
    (1973-1974): 250-259.

    Cites both primary and secondary sources
    containing information on rhetorical
    principles in music as well as general works
    on rhetoric and oratory.

41. _____. "Rhetoric and Music." In *New Grove
    Dictionary of Music and Musicians*. Ed. by Stanley
    Sadie. London: Macmillan, 1980. Vol. 15,
    pp. 793-803. ISBN 0-333-23111-2.

    Good introduction to the relationships
    between music and rhetoric; includes
    discussion of the Affections and musical
    figures illustrating the concept.

42. Burney, Charles. *General History of Music from the
    Earliest Ages to the Present Period*. With critical and
    historical notes by Frank Mercer, 2 vols.
    London, 1935. Reprint, N.Y.: Dover, 1957.
    Vol. 2, 1098 pp. (Original ed.: London,
    1776; 2nd ed., corr. and rev., 1789).

    Based on his travel diaries, Burney's
    history was one of the earliest to cover the
    Baroque and pre-classical periods. Vol. 2
    contains many references to Alessandro

Scarlatti and his works and several to Domenico. Comments regarding Alessandro mostly favorable; respected for his learning (counterpoint, harmony, melody) as well as for the beauty of his melodies though regarded as having a "severe style." Burney provides examples, references, conversations, excerpts from scores in his possession. Pp. 629-663 include a discussion of 35 cantatas with 4 pages of musical examples.

43. _____. *Present State of Music in France and Italy*. Reprinted as Vol. 1 of *Dr. Burney's Musical Tours in Europe* with title *An Eighteenth-Century Musical Tour in France and Italy*. Ed. by Percy A. Scholes. London: Oxford University Press, 1959. xxxv and 328 pp. Index in Vol. 2. (Original ed.: London, 1771; 2nd ed., 1773).

References to Alessandro Scarlatti in both volumes; includes Jomelli's high opinion of the church music and Hasse's remarks that Scarlatti was the greatest master of harmony in Italy. References to Hasse as student of Scarlatti in 1725, to Quantz's meeting with Hasse and Scarlatti, and to the scores (including MS copies) Burney received as gifts from various acquaintances.

44. Cecchi, Emilio, and Natalino Sapegno. *Storia della letteratura italiana*. Milan: Garzanti Editore, 1967-1968. 9 vols.

Massive, multi-volume history of Italian literature. Extensive bibliographies with brief annotations which serve to place the works cited in historical perspective. Numerous plates, index. Vol. 5: *Il seicento*. Vol. 6 (1968) *Il settecento*. Vol. 9 (1967) contains name index for set.

45. Corte, Andrea Della, ed. *Satire e grotteschi di musiche e di musicisti d'ogni tempo*. Turin: UTET, 1946. 917 pp.

Pp. 243-248 contain a satirical poem by the
Venetian critic Bartolomeo Dotti regarding the
scandals of women opera singers and Alessandro
Scarlatti's opera *Mitridate Eupatore*. Also
includes satires of Lodovico Adimari relevant
to Alessandro. Gives the Italian text by G.
Gigli of Domenico Scarlatti's opera *La Dirinda*.

46.   Cowart, Georgia. *The Origins of Modern Musical
       Criticism: French and Italian Music, 1600-1750*. Ann
       Arbor: UMI Research Press, 1981. 381pp.
       (Studies in Musicology, 38) ISBN 0-8357-
       1166-8. Mus. exs., notes, bibl., index.

       Interesting background on the eighteenth
       century disputes over French and Italian music
       and the aesthetic credos which championed
       reason on the one hand and the senses on the
       other.

*   Della Corte, Andrea. See Corte, Andrea Della.

47.   Donadoni, Eugenio. *A History of Italian Literature*.
       5th ed. Vol. 1. Trans. by Richard Monges.
       N.Y.: New York University Press, 1969. xiii
       and 361 pp. Index in Vol. 2.

       A good general history of Italian
       literature. Chap. 6: "The Seventeenth
       Century" includes a discussion of Giovanni
       Battista Marini and Chap. 7: "The Eighteenth
       Century," a description of Arcadia.

*   Galliard, John Ernest. See under Raguenet,
       Francois.

48.   Hearder, Harry, and Daniel Phillip Waley, eds.
       *A Short History of Italy from Classical Times to the Present
       Day*. Cambridge: Cambridge University Press,
       1963. 263 pp.

       Chapter 5 discusses "The Centuries of

Foreign Despotism," including the Spanish domination: 1513-1713 and the eighteenth century.

49. Jannaco, Carmine. *Storia letteraria d'Italia. Il seicento*. Reprint of 2nd rev. ed. 1966. Milan: Casa Editrice Dr. Francesco Vallardi, 1973. xvii and 775 pp.

A massive history of Italian literature of the 1600s covering all genres. Includes extensive bibliographical notes for each chapter as well as a greatly expanded and updated bibliographical supplement covering publications since 1966. Discussions of Baroque concepts, esthetics, poetics, historiography, etc., and problems relative to each topic.

50. Lee, Vernon [Violet Paget]. *Studies of the Eighteenth Century in Italy*. 2nd ed. London: T.Fisher Unwin, 1907.

Early chatty history of the period which includes the author's own inimitable opinions and evaluations of notable figures and events. Frequently cited source of information on Crescimbeni and the Arcadian reforms. Much of the information on Scarlatti now known to be inaccurate.

51. Montanelli,Indro,and Roberto Gervaso. *L'Italia del seicento (1600-1700)*. Milan: Rizzoli, 1969. Bibl., index.

A readable documented history of the period. Includes a chronology of main events.

52. Quazza, Guido. "L'Italia e l'Europa durante le guerre di successione." In *Storia d'Italia*. Vol. 2. Pp. 779-931. 2nd ed. Turin: UTET, 1965. Plates, maps, bibl. note.

Provides historical background for the early part of the eighteenth century.

53.   Raguenet, Francois. *A Comparison between the French and Italian Musick and Operas* (Paris, 1702; London, 1709). Trans. from the French and ed. with notes by Oliver Strunk. In *Musical Quarterly* 32 (1946): 411-436.

An important early source for the study of eighteenth-century performance history, musical aesthetics, and cultural politics. Original anonymous English translation attributed to John Ernest Galliard. Numerous flattering references in the translator's footnotes to A. Scarlatti and his works performed in England (including *Pirro* and the cantatas). Pro-Italian stance foreshadowed the disagreements which later escalated into the "*guerre des bouffons*."

54.   _____. *A Comparison between the French and Italian Musick and Operas...* with *A Critical Discourse upon Operas in England....* London, 1709. Reprint: Farnborough, Hants; England, 1968. xii and 86 pp. SBN (GB) 576 28446.7.

Facsimile of Raguenet's essay in the original English translation (possibly by John Ernest Galliard) and the translator's own *Critical Discourse*, which contains information on Italian works performed in England including Scarlatti's *Pirro* and his arias for *Thomyris* and *Clotilda*. Original located in Cambridge University Library.

55.   Salvatorelli, Luigi. *A Concise History of Italy from Prehistoric Times to Our Own Day*. N.Y.: Oxford University Press, 1940. Trans. from the Italian by Bernard Miall. 688 pp. Bibl., index of names.

Chapter 15 "Italy under the Spanish Domination," pp. 415-457 contains a detailed discussion of politics with references to the cultural situation.

56. Schumann, Reinhold. *Italy in the Last Fifteen Hundred Years: A Concise History*. Lanham, Maryland: University Press of America, 1986. 397 pp. ISBN 0-8191-5628-0. Chronology, reading lists, index.

Gives background history of the periods relevant to Scarlatti.

57. Testi, Flavio. *La musica italiana nel seicento*. 2 vols. Milan: Bramante Editrice, 1970-1972 (Storia da Sant' Ambrogio a noi). Vol. 1: 493 pp. Notes, plates, bibl. (pp. 469-481), index of names. Vol. 2: 501 pp. Bibl.: pp. 477-90, index of names.

Vol. 1 is a discussion of melodrama. Vol. 2 examines chamber works, the oratorio, church music, instrumental music, theory, and musical costume.

58. Valsecchi, Franco. *L'Italia nel seicento e nel settecento*. Turin: UTET, 1967 (Società e costume; panorama di storia sociale e tecnologica, 6) 889 pp. Extensive bibl.

Provides a panoramic view of life in Italy during the seventeenth and eighteenth centuries. Amply illustrated.

59. _____. *L'Italia nel settecento dal 1714 al 1788*. Verona: Mondadori, 1959 (Storia d'Italia, 7) Maps, plates, extensive bibl., chron., geneal. tables for the ruling families. Name index; index to plates and figs. (over 500).

Although most material deals with the period after Scarlatti's death, the volume provides

some background on the earlier eighteenth-
century political and cultural setting.

60. Wilkins, Ernest Hatch. *A History of Italian Literature*.
Rev. by Thomas G. Bergin. Cambridge:
Harvard University Press, 1974. 570 pp.
Apps. and index: pp. 525-570.

Readable history of Italian literature.
Includes discussion of Baroque literature and
description of Metastasian texts. Appendix 2,
a list of English translations and books in
English dealing with Italian literature.

61. Zanetti, Roberto. *La musica italiana nel settecento*. 3
vols. Busto Arsizio: Bramante Editrice,
1978. 1615 pp. (consecutively numbered).
Bibl., indices, notes.

Detailed history of eighteenth-century
Italian music organized by genre. Chapters on
the theater and the oratorio, in particular,
contain extensive discussion of Alessandro
Scarlatti and his contemporaries. Lengthy
bibliographies (with some typographical errors
and omissions) and index of names in Vol. 3.
Notes contain useful information.

Florence

62. Cochrane, Eric. *Florence in the Forgotten Centuries 1527-
1800*. Chicago and London: University of
Chicago Press, 1973.

Book IV, "Florence in the 1680s," provides
an insight into that place and time.

63. De Angelis, Marcello. "Ferdinando de' Medici:
l'"Orfeo" dei principi." In *Il giardino d'Europa.
Pratolino come modello della cultura europea*. Milan:
Mazzotta, 1986.

Not seen.

64. _____. "Il teatro di Pratolino tra
    Scarlatti e Perti; il carteggio di Giacomo
    Antonio Perti con il principe Ferdinando de'
    Medici (1705-1710)." *Nuova rivista musicale italiana*
    21 (1987): 605-631.

    Explores the reasons (esthetic and personal)
    behind Ferdinando's change of heart regarding
    Scarlatti's work and his patronage of Perti
    instead (especially after the performance of *Il
    gran Tamerlano* in September 1706). Notes the
    important information regarding the theatrical
    customs of Ferdinando's court in the 1700s,
    which can be gleaned from a study of the
    correspondence between Ferdinando and both
    Scarlatti and Perti. Includes a transcription
    of the complete surviving correspondence
    between Perti and Ferdinando published here
    for the first time in one place.

65. Fabbri, Mario. "Firenze." In *Enciclopedia dello
    spettacolo*. Ed. by Silvio and Sandro d'Amico.
    Vol. 5, pp. 371-395. Rome: Casa Editrice le
    Maschere, 1958. Bibl.

    Robert and Norma Weaver wrote (item 225)
    that with this article the "real productivity
    and character of Florentine opera [was]
    revealed for the first time in an important
    general reference."

*   _____. *Alessandro Scarlatti e il Principe Ferdinando
     de'Medici*. Cited as item 19.

*   Weaver, Robert Lamar. See items 225, 226, and
     227.

Naples

66. Bianconi, Lorenzo, and Renato Bossa, eds.
     Musica e cultura a Napoli dal XV al XIX
     secolo (*Quaderni della rivista italiana di musicologia*, 9)
     Florence: Olschki, 1983. 384 pp. ISBN 88
     222 3202 X.

*   Borren, Charles Van den. *Alessandro Scarlatti et
     l'esthétique de l'opera napolitaine.* Cited as item 224.

*   Bossa, Renato. *Musica e cultura a Napoli....* Cited as
     item 66.

67. Ciapparelli, Pier Luigi. "I luoghi del teatro
     a Napoli nel seicento le sale <private>."
     In *La musica a Napoli durante il seicento* (item 77),
     pp. 379-412.

     Documents the history of the sites in which
     theatrical performance (in its broadest sense,
     including festivals, masques, etc.) took place
     in Naples during the 1600s: the private palace
     gardens, courtyards, and salons. Extensive
     notes refer to primary and secondary sources.
     Includes quotations from contemporary diaries,
     etc., that describe various events as well as
     8 plates which reproduce floor and garden
     plans and prints. Fig. 8, which depicts the
     open-air celebration organized July 26, 1685,
     for the name day of the queen of Spain,
     Donn'Anna, reveals how the palace theater
     looked before the earthquake of 1688. A
     discussion of that theater shows that it was
     intended exclusively for *spettacoli.*

68. Confalonieri, Giulio. "Alessandro Scarlatti e
     la cultura musicale Napoletana." In
     Celebrazione... (item 4), pp. 7-18.

     An intelligent examination of Scarlatti's
     relationship to Naples. Criticizes some of
     the common hypotheses regarding Scarlatti's

early life (his teachers, reputation as the founder of the Neopolitan School, influences by Neopolitans such as Provenzale, etc.). Shows that the early influences were Roman and Venetian.

69. Confuorto, Domenico. *Giornali di Napoli dal MDCLXXIX al MDCIC*. Ed.by N. Nicolini. 2 vols. Naples: L. Lubrano, 1930.

Accounts of everyday life in the city from 1679-1699; news reports, court circulars, society columns, gossip, etc., all contained in them. Mention of volcanoes, earthquakes, plague.

70. Coniglio, Giuseppe. *I vicerè spagnoli di Napoli*. Naples: Fausto Fiorentino Editore, [1967] (Collana di cultura napoletana, 16)   398 pp. Lengthy bibl.

History of the Spanish viceroys including Gaspar de Haro, marchese del Carpio (pp. 316-322) and Luigi Francesco de la Cerda, duke of Medinaceli (pp. 336-347), who were Scarlatti's patrons. Description of each viceroy's character, the practical problems he confronted, and methods he used to attempt to solve them.

71. Croce, Benedetto. *History of the Kingdom of Naples*. English trans.by Frances Frenaye. Ed. by H. Stuart Hughes. Chicago: University of Chicago Press, 1970.   xxiv and 260 pp. ISBN 0 226 12080 5 and 0 226 12081 3 (pbk). Chronology, index.

Based on 6th ed. (1965) of Croce's *Storia del regno di Napoli* (Bari: Laterza, 1925). Classic history; explores the relationship between the classes and analyses events and institutions.

72. Dietz, Hanns-Bertold. "Sacred Music in Naples during the Second Half of the 17th Century."

In *La musica a Napoli durante il seicento* (item 77),
pp. 511-527.

Points out some of the features in the
church music of Veneziano (a student of
Provenzale) which were characteristic of
contemporary Neopolitan opera as represented
by Alessandro Scarlatti.

73. Donato, Giuseppe. "Su alcuni aspetti della
     vita musicale in Sicilia nel seicento." In
     La musica a Napoli durante il seicento (item 77) , pp.
     567-623. Notes, plates (graphs), chronology
     of Sicilian musical editions of the
     sixteenth and seventeenth centuries, and
     chronology of musical works (theatrical)
     performed in Sicily to the year 1700
     (including Scarlatti's operas).

     Examines Sicily's musical, especially
     operatic, links to Naples, during the 1600s.
     Discusses the activities of a travelling
     performing group known as the *Musici
     Accademici Sconcertati*; the close ties between
     the noted Roman singer Marc'Antonio Sportonio
     (active in Sicily) and the Scarlatti family;
     and the Sicilian performance of Scarlatti's *La
     Rosmene o vero L'infedeltà fedele*, which the
     author maintains was performed in 1688 (the
     same year as the Naples performance and two
     years after the Roman premiere) rather than
     1683 as was previously thought.

74. Doria, Gino. *Storia di una capitale. Napoli dalle origini al
     1860*. Naples, 1963. 5th ed., rev.: Milan:
     Ricciardi Editore, 1968. xv and 281 pp.
     Index of names.

     Readable history of the city of Naples
     including the period of the Spanish
     domination. Cites such details as the number
     of inhabitants, however, goes beyond a mere
     recitation of facts.

75. Fabris, Dinko. "Generi e fonti della musica
     sacra a Napoli nel seicento." In *La musica a
     Napoli durante il seicento* (item 77), pp. 415-454.
     Mus. exs., notes, table.

     A study of sacred music written for the
     common people and for the aristocrats in
     Naples during the 1600s. Identifies the
     genres, the churches which had a musical
     chapel or important organist, etc. Reference
     to Alessandro Scarlatti's Mass dated 1690 as
     perhaps the only sacred work definitely
     attributable to Scarlatti's Neopolitan
     sojourn. Table: "Il repertorio della musica
     sacra a Napoli nel seicento," includes a
     reference to Scarlatti's *Madrigali spirituali* of
     1690.

76. Florimo, Francesco. *La scuola musicale di Napoli e i
     suoi conservatorii*. 4 vols. Naples: Morano, 1880-
     1882 [1883]. 215; 472; 650; xxiv and 610 pp.

     An often-cited early history of music in
     Naples in which the author attempted to
     provide an overview of the various regional
     "schools," a history of the 4 Neopolitan
     conservatories (with biographies of its
     important teachers and students), and a
     chronology of all operas produced there from
     1651 to 1881 with information as to the
     theaters, librettists, composers, performers,
     etc. See items 187, 197, and 230 for a
     discussion of the use of the terms Neopolitan
     school and Neopolitan opera. Vol. 3 contains
     indices to names referred to in each of the 4
     vols.

77. *La musica a Napoli durante il seicento. Atti del convegno
     internazionale di studi Napoli, 11-14 aprile 1985.* Ed. by
     Domenico Antonio D'Alessandro and Agostino
     Ziino. Rome: Edizioni Torre d'Orfeo, 1987
     (Miscellanea musicologica, 2) xii and 730
     pp. Index of names by Jania Sarno. Illus.,
     mus. exs., tables, facs., graphs, bibl. and
     content notes.

Contains lengthy scholarly papers on seventeenth-century Neopolitan vocal (sacred and secular) and instrumental music as well as musical theater. Explores institutional aspects of music in Naples and its relationship to Sicily. Several important papers focus on Scarlatti and a number of others contain relevant information on the composer and/or his family. Selected individual papers cited as items 15, 67, 72, 73, 75.

78. Nicolini, Fausto. "Alessandro Scarlatti a Napoli. Appunti." In *Celebrazione...* (item 4), pp. 19-50.

Presents a more or less year-by-year description of events related to Scarlatti's opera and serenata productions at Naples based primarily on accounts of Confuorto (item 69), Bulifon, and Croce (item 180) with notes on the librettists Francesco Antonio Tullio and Sebastiano Biancardi (Domenico Lalli).

79. _____. *L'Europa durante la guerra di successione di Spagna con particolare riguardo alla città e regno di Napoli*. Naples: Presso la R. Deputazione, 1937-39. 3 vols. Vol. 1, 550 pp. Notes, index, analytical index (by region and author of dispatches), which outlines various dispatches in chronological order and gives page refs. Covers May 1700-Feb. 1701. Vol. 2, 580 pp. Notes and indices as above for period Mar.-July 1701.

Provides a day-by-day chronicle of news and goings-on during the war of the Spanish succession based on various ambassadorial dispatches.

80. Perrúcci, Andréa. *Dell'arte rappresentativa premeditata ed all'improvviso*. (Naples, 1699). Ed. by Anton Giulio Bragaglia. Florence: Edizioni Sansoni Antiquariato, 1961. 275 pp. Intro.

and bibl. notes.

Modern edition of this valuable eighteenth-
century Neopolitan comic opera librettist's
treatise on the method of "predisposed
improvisation" practiced in the *Commedia
dell'arte*.

81. Robinson, Michael. "The Governors' Minutes of
    the Conservatory S. Maria di Loreto,
    Naples." *Royal Musical Association. Research Chronicle*
    10 (1972): 1-97.

    Study of one of the four conservatories
    founded in the sixteenth century for the care
    of orphans. During the seventeenth century
    accepted paying boarders for instruction in
    music. Pp. 36ff. give background on the
    school, its daily functioning and politics,
    etc. Training ground for Neopolitan
    composers. A. Scarlatti elected Maestro di
    Cappella in 1689 but stayed only briefly.

82. Viviani, Vittorio. "Napoli." In *Enciclopedia
    dello spettacolo*. Rome: Casa Editrice La Maschere,
    c1954. Vol. 7, pp. 1007-1024. Bibl.

    Good overview of theater in Naples including
    the Settecento and Ottocento.

83. _____. *Storia del teatro napoletano*. Naples: Guida
    Editori, 1969. 971 pp.

    A lengthy history of Neopolitan theater from
    ancient to modern times. Chap. 5: information
    on seventeenth-century dialect comedy in
    Naples; Chap. 6 on Andrea Perrucci, librettist
    for many comic intermezzos; Chap. 7 on
    Alessandro Scarlatti. The author rejects the
    view shared by many contemporary music
    historians that Scarlatti represents the
    epitome of the Baroque rather than a
    forerunner of the Enlightenment; believes that
    this is a misrepresentation and distortion.

Rome

84. Ademollo, Alessandro. *I teatri di Roma nel secolo
     decimosettimo*. Reprint of 1888 ed. Bologna:
     Forni, 1969. xxviii and 283 pp.
     (Bibliotheca musica Bononiensis, sezione
     III, N. 12)   Apps. (7) and index of names
     and notable things.

     Covers period 1604–1699. Based on archives,
     diaries, memoirs, *avvisi*, letters, etc.   No
     bibliography,   though   footnotes   included.
     Interesting   information   on   theatrical
     celebrations including *feste, fuochi artificiali*, etc.
     App. 7 a chronological list of sacred drama in
     the time of Innocent XII with title, composer,
     poet, dedication, place, year, etc.

85. Andrieux, Maurice.   *Daily Life in Papal Rome in the
     Eighteenth Century*.   Trans. by Mary Fitton.
     London: George Allen and Unwin, 1968.   223
     pp.   American ed., N.Y.: Macmillan, 1969.
     Plates, index, bibl.

     Account of daily occurrences and rituals in
     the papal city.   Written in a popular style,
     though documented.

86. Bossa, Renato.   "Corelli e il cardinal
     Benedetto Pamphilj; alcune notizie."   In
     *Nuovissimi studi Corelliani. Atti del terzo congresso
     internazionale (Fusignano...1980)*, pp. 211–218.
     Florence: Leo S. Olschki, 1982   (Quaderni
     della revista italiana di musicologia, 7)
     ISBN 88 222 3096 5.   "App.," pp. 218–222.
     "Discussione," p. 223.

     Corrects some errors the author found in
     Montalto's studies (see items 97 and 98),
     including several details relating to A.
     Scarlatti.   The appendix contains the text of
     a   document   (Biblioteca Casanatense, Rome:
     misc.   1360/22),   which   describes   the
     celebration held in Rome in honor of the
     return to health of King Louis XIV of France.

87. Cametti, Alberto. *Cristina di Svezia , l'arte musicale e gli spettacoli teatrali in Roma*. Rome, 1911 (Nuova antologia, 16, ott. 1911). 18 pp. Reprint with bibl. notes and identification of historical sources in *Annuario della R. Accademia di S. Cecilia* (Rome) (1930-1931): 38ff.

Provides information about the singers and composers (including Scarlatti, Corelli, and Pasquini) in the Queen's service and the musical performances she presented or promoted.

88. _____. *Il Teatro Tordinona poi di Apollo*. 2 vols. Tivoli: Arti Grafiche Aldo Chicca, 1938 (Atti e memorie della R. Accademia di S. Cecilia, Rome) 669 pp. Plates, bibl., indices.

Fundamental study of this theater (one of the two public theaters in seventeenth-century Rome). Vol. 1 a detailed, documented history of the theater from its beginning in 1671 through its various destructions and rebuildings to its final demise in 1889; gives information on its milieu, its performances, and its various patrons, composers (including Scarlatti), etc. Plates, bibl., and list of author's other publications. Vol. 2 a chronology of the performances (1671-1697 and 1733-1888) and indices of works; dances; composers; poets; concertmasters, etc.

89. Compagnino, Gaetano, and Giuseppe Savoca. "Cristina di Svezia e il suo circolo." In *Il settecento: l'arcadia e l'età delle riforme*, pp. 45-47 (Letteratura italiana Laterza, 6/32) Ed. by Carlo Muscetta. Bari: Laterza, 1973. Bibl., p. 74.

Brief but illuminating summary of Christina's life and the role the Arcadian society (formally established only after her death) with its many regional offshoots played in the unification of Italian literary style

during the eighteenth century. Excellent
bibliography.

90. Della Seta, Fabrizio. "La musica in Arcadia
    al tempo di Corelli." In *Nuovissimi studi
    Corelliani. Atti del terzo congresso internazionale
    (Fusignano...1980)*, pp. 123-150. Florence: Leo
    S. Olschki, 1982 (Quaderni della revista
    italiana di musicologia, 7) ISBN 88 222
    3096 5.

    Contains documents (sonnets) of Alessandro
    Scarlatti (Terpandro) from the Arcadian MSS
    (located I-Ra: Rome: Biblioteca Angelica) and
    other information about the Arcadians and
    their music during this period.

91. Durante, Sergio. "*La Guida Armonica* di Giuseppe
    Ottavio Pitoni; un documento sugli stili
    musicali in uso a Roma al tempo di Corelli."
    In *Nuovissimi studi Corelliani. Atti del terzo congresso
    internazionale (Fusignano...1980)*, pp. 285-326.
    "Discussione," p. 327. Florence: Leo S.
    Olschki, 1982 (Quaderni della revista
    italiana di musicologia, 7). ISBN 88 222
    3096 5.

    Discusses the Roman musician Pitoni (who
    served as organist and *maestro di capella* for
    cardinal Pietro Ottoboni at S. Lorenzo in
    Damaso), his relationship to Corelli, and his
    Guida which is unique as a source of
    identifying works now dispersed or anonymous
    (e.g., arias from the opera *l'Arsate* which he
    attributes to Scarlatti). In it Scarlatti is
    grouped with Giovanni Bononcini, Stradella,
    Perti, Corelli, and Pasquini as a composer in
    the *sesto stile*.

92. Gaye, Vera M. *L'opera critica e storiografica del
    Crescimbeni*. Parma: Ugo Guanda Editore,
    1970. 104 pp. Bibl., pp. 101-104.

    A concise introduction to the life and works

(all editions) of Crescimbeni, including a
description of the Arcadian society of which
he was a founder and prime mover (and of which
A. Scarlatti, Corelli, and others were
members).

93.   Marx, Hans Joachim. "Die *Giustificazioni della casa
      Pamphilj* als musikgeschichtliche Quelle."
      Studi musicali 12 (1983): 121-187. Pp. 142-187:
      transcription of the *Giustificazioni* (documents
      from the private archive of the Doria-
      Pamphilj family), dated 1697-1709.

      A very important study in which the author
      attempts to provide a detailed description--
      rather than a summary which was all that was
      available previously in published form--of the
      contents of part of the *Giustificazioni* (covering
      the years 1677-1709 with the exclusion of
      Benedetto's Bolognese years: 1690-93).
      Extends from the beginning of the cultivation
      of music at Benedetto's court until Handel's
      departure from Rome. Article includes
      numerous references to Alessandro Scarlatti
      and his relationship to this patron.

94.   _____. "Die Musik am Hofe Pietro Kardinal
      Ottobonis unter Arcangelo Corelli."
      Analecta musicologica 5 (1968): 104-177
      (Studien zur italienish-deutschen
      Musikgeschichte, 5).

      The fundamental study of Cardinal Ottoboni
      and his music. Based on previously
      undiscovered records in the Fondo Ottoboni of
      the Vatican Library. Includes household
      accounts, list of names (including Scarlatti),
      and other similar material from the years
      1689-1713. See also Hansell article (item
      331).

95.   Moberg, Carl-Allan. "Christina och musiken."
      Dansk-Aarbog for musikforskning 5 (1966-1967): 168-
      171.

Not seen.   RILM abstract 1975 #744.

96.   Montalto, Lina.   "Arcangelo Corelli
      nell'ambiente musicale romano   fra il 1671
      e il 1713."   *Rivista musicale italiana* 56 (1954):
      241-246.

      Discusses patronage of the Roman circle of
      composers which included Corelli and A.
      Scarlatti.

97.   _____.   *Un mecenate in Roma barocca, il Cardinale
      Benedetto Pamphilj (1653-1730)*.   Florence: Sansoni,
      1955.

      The most in-depth study of this Roman patron
      of the arts and A. Scarlatti's first
      influential and generous benefactor; based on
      the author's researches in the Archivio Doria-
      Pamphili, Rome.

98.   _____.   "Fra virtuosi e musici nella corte
      del Card. Benedetto Pamphilj."   *Rivista
      italiana del dramma* 5 (1941): 83-97, 193-209.

      An early investigation into the Pamphili
      family, its passionate patron of the arts,
      Benedetto, and the Roman cultural milieu
      during the latter half of the 1600s and the
      first decades of the 1700s.   Based on the
      author's research in the private archives of
      the Doria-Pamphili family, Rome.

99.   Montesi Festa, Hilda.   *Cristina di Svezia*.   Milan:
      Fratelli Treves   Editori, 1938.   274 pp.

      A biography of Christina written in literary
      style.   Describes events in the Queen's life
      from her birth to her death.   Chapter 9 begins
      coverage of her Roman stay.   Based mainly on
      seventeenth- and eighteenth-century MSS or
      printed editions, especially those of the
      Swedish historian Arckenholz and the works of

Carlo de Bildt, a Swedish minister to Rome, published c1899-1908.

100. Russo, Rosario. "Cristina di Svezia." In *Enciclopedia italiana*. Vol. 11 (1931), pp. 971-972. Rome: Istituto Giovanni Treccani, 1929-1939.

An interesting summary of Christina's life, with short bibliography of early published references.

101. Talbot, Michael, and Colin Timms. "Music and the Poetry of Antonio Ottoboni (1646-1720)." In *Händel e gli Scarlatti a Roma* (item 38 in Book II), pp. 367-438. Pp. 397-438: "Catalogue of Antonio Ottoboni's *Poesia per musica* and Its Musical Settings;" p. 438: index of composers named in the catalogue.

Reveals Antonio Ottoboni as "a key figure in the interchange of culture between Venice and Rome over a period of 30 years or more." Establishes Antonio Ottoboni as the author of the text of Scarlatti's *Cain* oratorio. Identifies the works (including cantatas) by A. Scarlatti with texts by A. Ottoboni.

*   Timms, Colin. See under Talbot, Michael.

102. Valesio, Francesco. *Diario di Roma*. Ed. by Gaetana Scano with Giuseppe Graglia. Milan: Longanesi & C., 1977-1979. 6 vols. xxv and 641 pp.; 877 pp.; xi and 950 pp.; 1145 pp.; xi and 930 pp.; 655 pp. Notes, indices, bibls., docs.

The surviving volumes of Valesio's diary (dating from Aug. 9, 1700 to Mar. 10, 1711 and Dec. 24, 1724 to Mar. 27, 1742) provide a daily chronicle of events in eighteenth-century Rome among which are a number of references to musical performances given by the aristocratic families. Contains references to Alessandro Scarlatti and other persons with the Scarlatti name (e.g., an Abate Scarlatti). The gap in coverage, unfortunately, eliminates the possibility of finding documentation regarding Domenico's Roman activities.

4. Scarlatti's Relationship to Handel and Other Composers

* Bianchi, Lino. "Dall'oratorio di Alessandro Scarlatti all'oratorio di Händel." In *Händel e gli Scarlatti a Roma*, pp. 79-91. Cited as item 274.

103. Bossa, Renato. "Le *Sonate a quattro* di G. A. Avitrano (1713). In *La musica a Napoli durante il seicento* (item 77), pp. 307-322. Mus. exs., table.

Author states that Scarlatti's *Salve Regina* in g minor for soprano, 3 violins, and continuo preserved at the Archivio musicale ...dei Padri Filippini, Naples and in a more recent copy at the library of the Conservatorio di Musica S. Pietro a Maiella, Naples, may have been a kind of prototype or archtype for certain of Avitrano's sonatas for 3 violins and basso continuo (organ).

104. Celletti, Rodolfo. "Il virtuosismo vocale nel melodramma di Haendel." *Rivista italiana di musicologia* 4 (1969): 77-101.

Discussion of the influence of the Italian style and A. Scarlatti and Steffani, in particular, on the development of Handel's operatic vocal style. Author sees influences in the extension of vocal ranges, higher tessitura, longer vocalizing passages, and more varied figures.

* Collins, Michael. "L'orchestra nelle opere
  teatrali di Vivaldi." Cited as item 179.

105. Crain, Gordon Ferris, Jr. "The Operas of
     Bernardo Pasquini." Ph.D. dissertation,
     Yale University, 1965. 2 vols. 552 pp.
     UMI order # 65-15-026. Vol. 1: Text, 217
     pp., app., bibl.; Vol. 2: Catalogue
     (thematic and analytic) of surviving
     authenticated operas, xiii and 317 pp.,
     index.

     Examines the datable operas of Pasquini
     (1672-1693) written during the height of opera
     activity in Rome during the patronage of Queen
     Christina of Sweden. Concludes that in some
     respects these anticipate the changes in style
     and taste that culminated in Alessandro
     Scarlatti (sharper differentiation between
     aria and recitative styles and functions, more
     arias, tonal harmonic orientation). Appendix
     in Vol. 1, pp. 195-211, a chronological survey
     of operas represented in Rome during four
     decades of the seventeenth century; includes
     citations to other dramatic works by Pasquini
     and to operas and oratorios of A. Scarlatti.
     Bibl., pp. 212-17. Vol. 2, pp. 291-317,
     contains an alphabetical index of arias and
     ensembles (including balli, intermezzi, and
     sinfonie) with references to the thematic
     index.

* Dean, Winton. "Handel and Alessandro
  Scarlatti." Cited as item 181.

* Dixon, Graham. "Handel's Music for the Feast
  of Our Lady of Mount Carmel." Cited as
  item 153.

106. *Francesco Gasparini (1661-1727). Atti del primo convegno
     internazionale (Camaiore, 29 settembre-1 ottobre 1978)*
     (Quaderni della Rivista italiana di
     musicologia, 6) Florence: Leo Olschki,

1981.   341 pp.   ISBN 88 222 2988 6.

Contains a number of papers which refer to
Alessandro Scarlatti as a friend of Gasparini,
one who acquired his knowledge of opera
composition in the same way (rewriting earlier
works), one who was classed by researchers in
various "schools" with problematic results,
etc. Engaged in a contest with Scarlatti in
which both produced cantata settings of *Andate o
miei sospiri*. Both worked for the Portuguese
ambassador to Rome, c1724; both wrote arias
for Pasticcios, e.g., *Thomyris Queen of Scythia*
(1707) and *Clotilda* (1709).

107. Gianturco, Carolyn. "Evidence for a Late
      Roman School of Opera." *Music and Letters* 56
      (1975): 4-17.

Discusses Roman opera as represented chiefly
by Pasquini and Stradella; probable that these
composers most influenced A. Scarlatti's
earliest operas. Mentions difficulty in
studying late seventeenth-century Roman opera
due to "almost complete lack of printed scores
or modern editions." Works of Pasquini and
Melani are similar to the "style and structure
of Scarlatti's earliest operas...." A number
of operas by these composers are based on the
same librettos.

108. Harris, Ellen T. *Handel and the Pastoral Tradition*.
      London and   N.Y.: Oxford University Press,
      1980.   292 pp. ISBN 0-19-315236-3.   Bibl.,
      index.

Chapter 2, "The Pastoral in Italy," gives
valuable background on the history of the
pastoral and Arcadia; pp. 37-56 deal
specifically with Alessandro Scarlatti's
cantatas and operas and his relationship to
Handel and the Arcadia circle.

109. _____. "The Italian in Handel." *American
      Musicological Society Journal* 33 (1980): 468-500.

Tables, mus. exs.

Compares the style of Scarlatti's cantatas and Handel's Italian cantatas; concludes that Handel's music does not reflect A. Scarlatti's vocal style as held by Dent, et al. Stylistic approaches "widely divergent." Response by J. Merrill Knapp and reply by Ellen T. Harris in *JAMS* 34 (1981): 366-369.

110. Kirkendale, Ursula. "The Ruspoli Documents on Handel." *American Musicological Society. Journal* 20 (1967): 222-273, 516.

Major review of literature related to Handel's Italian years and new documentation from the Fondo Ruspoli in the Archivio Segreto Vaticano. Examines the question of what music Handel could actually have heard from 1707-1709, including music by Alessandro and Domenico Scarlatti.

*   La Via, Stefano. "Un'aria di Händel con violoncello obbligato e la tradizione romana." Cited as item 333.

111. Lindgren, Lowell.. "Le opere drammatiche *romane* di Francesco Gasparini (1689-1699)." In *Francesco Gasparini (1661-1727). Atti del primo convegno internazionale* (item 106), pp. 167-182.

Discussion of the Roman theatrical works of Gasparini and their relationship to the work of other contemporaries including A. Scarlatti.

112. Mayo, John Stanford Miles. "Handel's Italian Cantatas." Ph.D. dissertation, University of Toronto, 1977. Bibl.

Study of Handel's 70 works for solo voice and continuo and 25 for voice and instrumental ensemble written 1706-1709. States that the

later cantatas show an increasing awareness of
the Italian style of A. Scarlatti among
others. Compares works by Handel and
Scarlatti which use the same text.

113. ____. "Zum Vergleich des Wort-Ton-Verhält-
nisses in den Kantaten von Georg Friedrich
Händel und Alessandro Scarlatti." In *G. F.
Händel und seine italienischen Zeitgenossen*, pp. 31-44.
Ed. by Walther Siegmund-Schultze. Halle-
Wittenberg : Martin-Luther-Universität, 1979
(Wissenschaftliche Beiträge, 8).

Explores the stylistic and thematic
relationships between Handel's and Scarlatti's
settings of the same cantata texts: *Ah che
purtroppo è vero, Filli adorata e cara, Fra tante pene, Ne' tuoi
lumi, Nel dolce tempo*, and *Qualor l'egre pupille*.
Concludes style of declamation in recitatives
similar, but Scarlatti wrote more varied
harmonies.

114. Strohm, Reinhard. "Alessandro Scarlatti und
das Settecento." In *Colloquium Alessandro
Scarlatti Würzburg 1975* (item 5), pp. 153-167.
Anhang: pp. 164-167. Discussion: pp. 168-
176. Trans. into English by the author as
"Alessandro Scarlatti and the Eighteenth
Century" in his *Essays...* (item 115) without
the app. and discussion.

Examines Scarlatti's influence on Italian
vocal music of the eighteenth century.
Contemporary tastes and dissemination of
operas indicate a rapid decline in influence
c1710. Comparison of Scarlatti's techniques
and text settings with those of Pollarolo,
Handel, and Hasse. Appendix includes complete
edition of a newly discovered *Salve Regina*
(c1720) [Ex XIII, pp. 240-250] in the
Bayerische Staatsbibliothek, Munich (MS Coll.
Mus. Max. 92).

115. _____. *Essays on Handel and Italian Opera*. London: Cambridge University Press, 1985. x and 303 pp. Notes, bibl., index. ISBN 0-521-26428-6. Review in *Musical Quarterly* 72 (1986): 119-123 by Paul Henry Lang.

Strohm's essays including items 114 and 116 are presented here in English for the first time. They contain interesting background on the culture and politics of Rome during Handel's sojourn there, a time when Alessandro and Domenico Scarlatti were also part of this milieu.

116. _____. "Francesco Gasparini le sue opere tarde e Georg Friedrich Handel." In *Francesco Gasparini (1661-1727) Atti...* (item 106), pp. 71-83. Trans. into English by the author as "F. Gasparini's Later Operas and Handel" in his *Essays...* (cited as item 115), pp. 80-92.

Examines influence of Gasparini and other contemporary Italians including A. Scarlatti and Corelli on Handel's operatic and instrumental style.

117. _____. "Hasse, Scarlatti, Rolli." *Analecta musicologica* 15 (1975): 221-257 (Studien zur italienisch-deutschen Musikgeschichte, 10) Mus. exs., notes.

Study of a group of arias (partly arrangements of arias from A. Scarlatti's *La Griselda*) written by Hasse c1727-29 for private performances in Neopolitan salons. Musical examples from each composer presented side by side to facilitate stylistic comparisons. Hasse's settings shown to be far different in style from those of Scarlatti. Includes list of *Arie da camera* and other individual pieces copied by an anonymous Neopolitan c1730 preserved in the Biblioteca del Conservatorio di Musica "Giuseppe Verdi," Milan, Archivio

Musicale Noseda, including the aria "Luce mia bella," a setting from Act 2, scene 7 of *La Griselda*, probably by Scarlatti. The "Notenbeispiele" give music examples (in open score) from a number of Scarlatti arias from *La Griselda* in the Noseda archive.

118. Zanetti, Emilia. "Haendel in Italia."
     Approdo musicale 3/12 (1960): 3-73.

     Information on Rome during Handel's early stays in Italy and his relationship to the Scarlattis, Corelli, etc. Not seen.

119. _____. "La presenza di Francesco Gasparini in Roma. Gli ultimi anni 1716-1727." In *Francesco Gasparini (1661-1727). Atti del primo convegno internazionale* (cited as item 110), pp. 259-319.

     Provides a critical chronology and documents related to the second and last Roman period of Gasparini; contains numerous references to A. Scarlatti.

II

STUDIES OF THE MUSIC

1. Vocal Music

Cantatas

120. Allenson, Stephen Mark. "Theory and Practice in the Arcadian Cantatas of Alessandro Scarlatti, 1703-1706." Ph.D. dissertation in progress, Royal Holloway, London.

121. Berry, Corre. "The Secular Dialogue Duet: 1600-1900." *Music Review* 40 (1979): 272-284.

Pages 278-279 contain a brief discussion of the formal characteristics of two of Alessandro Scarlatti's 2-voice cantatas with dialogue texts: *Lisa del foco mio* and *Ahi, che sarà di me*.

122. Boyd, Malcolm. "Form and Style in Scarlatti's Chamber Cantatas." *Music Review* 25 (1964): 17-26. List of works suppl. Dent's catalog (item 6).

Often-cited discussion of Alessandro Scarlatti's chamber cantatas. Boyd's division of the cantatas into two stylistic/formal periods (pre-1697 and post-1697) has been criticized by Freund (item 130). See also Hanley's comments in *NGIBM*, pp.236-237. Hanley's thematic index and catalog (item 134) was, apparently, not available to the author at the time this article was written as it is not cited.

123. ____. "Introduction." In *Cantatas by Alessandro
     Scarlatti 1660-1725*. N.Y.: Garland Publishing,
     1986. pp. [vii-x].

     Brief introduction to Scarlatti's cantatas
     in general and to those specifically chosen
     for this collection.

124. Caraci, Maria. "Le cantate romane di
     Alessandro Scarlatti nel Fondo Noseda." In
     Händel e gli Scarlatti a Roma (item 38 in Book II),
     pp. 93-112.

     Detailed description of the 59 cantatas (65
     counting titles existing in more than 1 copy)
     in this major Scarlatti collection. Author
     discusses the copyists' hand, the problem of
     trying to arrive at a chronology (even a rough
     chronology) in order to trace the development
     of the composer's style in this genre,
     previous attempts at a chronological outline,
     difficulties in ascertaining whether dates
     which appear on the MSS are composition or
     copying dates, etc. Refers to Emanuel
     d'Astorga as the single true successor to
     Scarlatti in terms of his use of audacious
     harmonies and "bizzarrie."

125. Collins, Leo Wilkie Jr. "Alessandro
     Scarlatti: Solo Cantatas for Bass." D.M.A.
     dissertation, Boston University, 1960. [iv]
     and 206 pp. Bibl., pp. 94-99. App. A:
     Sources of the MSS, pp. 100-102. App. B:
     Original text and side by side trans., pp.
     103-119. App. C: Transcription with basso
     continuo realization, pp. 121-206.

     Attempts to classify the bass cantatas
     according to Schmitz's (item 146) style
     divisions and using Schmitz, Dent, and the
     author's own observations, summarizes the
     style characteristics in the cantatas of the
     three periods. Chapters 4 and 5 contain an
     analysis of each cantata in the study.
     Includes modern performing edition of 9 solo

cantatas for bass voice (see Section V, 1 for titles).

126. Damuth, Laura. " Interrelationships Between the Operas and Datable Cantatas of Alessandro Scarlatti." Ph.D. dissertation in progress, Columbia University. Cited in *Doctoral Dissertations in Musicology*, ed. by Cecil Adkins, p. 123. Philadelphia: American Musicological Society, 1984.

127. Daw, Brian Allan. " Alessandro Scarlatti's Cantatas for Solo Soprano and Continuo, 1708-1717." Ph.D. dissertation, University of Southern California, 1984. ix and 445 pp. Bibl.: pp. 437-445. Transcriptions: pp. 147-436. Order: Micrographics Dept., Doheny Library, University of Southern California, Los Angeles, CA.

A study of the 27 reliably attributed (see item 134) cantatas for solo soprano and continuo from Scarlatti's mature style. Examines features in common and ways of reconstructing continuo realizations similar to those the composer may have written. Analytical overview and discussion of special features of selected cantatas. Includes transcriptions of the 27 (with modern clefs, critical notes, etc., but no realization of the continuo) based on film copies of the original manuscripts. Chapter 1 provides an overview of the 783 known cantatas with tables surveying formal structures, key areas, time signatures, etc. Chapter 2 includes author's continuo realization of "Solo il dolore" from *Lontananza crudele, deh perché?*"

128. Dent, Edward J. "The Italian Chamber Cantatas." *Musical Antiquary* 2 (April-July 1911): 142-153 and 185-199.

Excellent historical overview including superb insights into Scarlatti's style.

129. Edmunds, John. "Chamber Cantatas: The Mastery
     of Alessandro Scarlatti." *Tempo*. New Series
     42 (1956-1957): 24-30.

     An appreciation of the cantatas by an
     American composer who was for 2 years a fellow
     of the Italian government. Edmunds edited a
     collection of the cantata arias as well as one
     of Venetian *arie antiche*; these editions were used
     in 2 recitals for the BBC and the Italian
     Institute given by Peter Pears and Ilse Wolf
     and selections were recorded on Deutsche
     Grammophon by Nell Tangeman.

130. Freund, Cecilia Kathryn Van de Kamp.
     "Alessandro Scarlatti's Duet Cantatas and
     Solo Cantatas with Obbligato Instruments."
     Ph.D. dissertation, Northwestern University,
     1979. 2 vols. 740 pp. UMI order #7927341.

     Reviews bibliographical research on
     Scarlatti's cantata repertoire to date;
     emphasizes that only Hanley (item 134) has
     developed valid criteria for establishing
     authenticity. Studies all the cantatas
     presently attributed to Alessandro Scarlatti
     scored for 2 voices with continuo (c100) and
     for 1 or 2 voices with added instruments.
     Discusses texts (mostly anonymous) in relation
     to seventeenth-century lyric poetry. Seven
     authenticated dated cantatas by Scarlatti
     representative of the changes in his style
     between 1692 and 1725 analysed in detail and
     related to the other cantatas. Suppl. vol.
     includes the texts of 6 representative
     cantatas discussed in the main volume and
     transcriptions of 7 representative cantatas
     (see Section V, 1 for titles), as well as a
     catalog of primary sources and a bibliography
     of articles and books. Due to space
     limitations performance practice and problems
     were not dealt with.

131. _____. "Evaluating the Bibliographical
     Sources for Alessandro Scarlatti's Cantata

Repertoire." Typescsript. Available from the author, 618 Hull Terrace, Evanston, IL 60202.

Not seen. According to citation in *A Checklist of Music Bibliographies and Indexes in Progress and Unpublished*, 4th ed., ed. by Dee Bailey (Ann Arbor: Music Library Association, 1982), Freund evaluates catalogs of the composer's cantatas compiled by Edward J. Dent, Paul Strüver, Edwin Hanley, and Giancarlo Rostirolla (items 6, 147, 134, 435, respectively).

132. Gialdroni, Teresa M. "Francesco Provenzale e la cantata a Napoli nella seconda metà del seicento." In *La musica a Napoli durante il seicento* (item 77), pp. 125-154. 5 apps., notes, mus. exs.

A study of two collections of Provenzale's cantatas. Refers to the rather widespread use of popular song motives by composers of the period and their use by Provenzale in place of the aria in some of his cantatas. Cites Scarlatti's use of the popular song *La bella Margherita* in Act II, scene 1 of *Gli equivoci in amore* (Rome, 1690): the cantata of Lesbo.

133. Hanley, Edwin. "(Pietro) Alessandro (Gaspare) Scarlatti: 6. The Cantatas". *The New Grove Dictionary of Music and Musicians*, ed. by Stanley Sadie. London: Macmillan, 1980. Vol. 16, 556-557. Reprinted in *NGIBM*, pp. 233-238 as "Alessandro Scarlatti." Other Works, II. "Cantatas."

Most up-to-date summary of current knowledge of Alessandro Scarlatti's chamber cantatas.

134. _____. "Alessandro Scarlatti's Cantate da Camera: a Bibliographical Study." Ph.D. dissertation, Yale University, 1963. 546 pp. UMI order #74-7897.

The most reliable study of sources and
attributions of the Scarlatti chamber
cantatas. Supplemented by the author's lists
in *MGG* and *New Grove* (items 14 and 133).
Approximately 3000 manuscripts (95% of those
extant) examined (most in European archives).
Explores authenticity of attributions (through
systematic comparison of MSS) and reviews
earlier catalogs of the cantata repertory.
Thematic index of all known chamber cantatas
with performance media, dates (when
established), authors of texts, sections, MS
sources (if known) with library and call
number. Incorporates all listings from
previously published catalogs, references,
etc., which can be authenticated. Items not
included appear without index number and with
explanation of exclusion. Supplants Dent's
catalog. 120 cantatas and many copies added.
Lists 191 dated cantatas. Availability only
through University Microfilms. An
indispensable catalog.

135. Henry, Oscar Mervine. "The Doctrine of
     Affections in Selected Solo Cantatas of
     Alessandro Scarlatti." Ph.D. dissertation,
     Ohio State University, 1963. 431 pp. UMI
     order #64-7022.

     Examines 30 chamber cantatas for solo voice
     and continuo to see whether Scarlatti used
     stereotyped formulas or techniques
     illustrative of the "Doctrine of Affections"
     as the basis for textual expression.
     Concludes that Scarlatti respected the theory
     of expression of the Doctrine as revealed in
     eighteenth-century writings but never
     permitted codified devices to limit his
     musical response to the text. App. contains
     the complete score of the 1712 version of the
     cantata *Andate o miei sospiri*.

136. Inkeles, Maryann Teresa. "A Study,
     Realization, and Performance of Unpublished
     Cantatas for Soprano and Basso Continuo ca.

1690-1706 of Alessandro Scarlatti." Ed.D.,
Columbia University Teachers College, 1977.
388 pp. UMI order #77-14,728.

An analysis of the style and interpretation
of 10 unpublished cantatas for soprano and
basso continuo by Alessandro Scarlatti. Relies
heavily on Dent (item 6). Includes a
performing edition for each (see Section V, 1
for individual titles). Discussion of
performance practice including realization of
the continuo and vocal ornamentation. Apps.
include selected cantata incipits photocopied
from MSS, a table of vocal ornaments (based
mostly on Donington (item 362), a list of the
cantatas discussed which are available on
microfilm or photocopy with locations and MS
numbers and a representative recital program.
A number of typing errors. Main contribution
is the editions although these would have
been more useful if more clearly written.

137. Kinsky, Georg. *Manuskripte, Briefe, Dokumente von Scarlatti
bis Stravinsky: Katalog der Musikautographen-Sammlung Louis
Koch*. Stuttgart: Hoffmannsche Buchdruckerei
Felix Krais, 1953. 361 pp. Index.

Page 1 describes the solo cantata Quante le
grazie son" for high voice with basso
continuo, the autograph MS of which was in
Koch's private library.

138. Lake, Mary Beth. "A Critical Edition of the
Cantata *Nel silenzio comune* by Alessandro
Scarlatti, with Historical Commentary."
Ph.D. dissertation, Michigan State, 1980.
59 pp. UMI order #8112109.

Edition based on British Library MS Add.
14163. Includes simple realization of figured
bass and substitution of modern clefs when
appropriate. Basically as it appears in MS.
Performance suggestions, critical and
editorial notes, and English translation of
text included. See Section V, 1 for edition

information.

139. Mayrhofer, Marina.   "Sei cantate napoletane di
     Alessandro Scarlatti anteriori al 1694."   In
     La musica a Napoli durante il seicento   (item 77), pp.
     155-163.

     Studies the composer's early cantatas which
     reflect   the   various   musical   problems
     characteristic of music originating in Naples
     in the 1600s and by extension in the great
     European courts and Scarlatti's solutions to
     them.   Focuses on a selection of 6 cantatas
     for voice and basso continuo dating from
     between 1690 and 1693 (MSS in the Naples
     Conservatory): *Da sventura a sventura; Il Germanico* or
     *Già di trionfi onusto; Sopra le verdi sponde che la Brenta
     superba; Ch'io scoprì il mio affetto; Di cipresso funesto;* and
     Mentre Eurillo fedele [*Su le rive del Tebro*].

140. Morris, Robert Bower.   "A Brief History and
     Survey of the Italian Solo Cantata of the
     17th and 18th Centuries, part II.   *National
     Association of Teachers of Singing. Bulletin.*   24/3
     (1968): 4, 6, 8.

     A survey of the stylistic and formal
     characteristics of the cantatas written by
     composers of the "Neopolitan school."
     Comments on vocal range and requirements,
     text, accompaniment, and other aspects of
     special interest to singing teachers and
     performers.   No bibliography or list of
     editions included although some mentioned in
     the text.   Part I of the article which deals
     with the early history appears in *NATS. Bulletin.*
     24/2 (1967): 22-27.

141. _____ .   "A study of the Italian solo cantata
     before 1750."   Mus. Ed.D. dissertation.
     Indiana University, 1955.   197 pp.   UMI
     order #14,300.

     Analysis of 80 cantatas by 18 composers

including Alessandro Scarlatti. Fourteen cantatas used as reference points. Eight reprinted here from "publications not generally available," and six "transcribed from manuscripts or...early editions...not easily readable by modern performers." Not seen; however, the amount of material covered with respect to the number of pages seems to indicate rather superficial analysis of individual works.

142. Murray, David Colden. "A Performing Edition of Alessandro Scarlatti's Chamber Cantata *Tra speranza e timore*;" Pt. I of Ed.D. dissertation, Indiana University, School of Education, 1963. American Doctoral Dissertations x 1963, p. 139.

Not seen.

* *Musikhandschriften in Basel aus verschiedenen Sammlungen....* Cited as item 23.

143. Pastore, G. A. "Nuove cantate di Alessandro Scarlatti." *Il San Carlo (Naples)* (1960): 32.

Not seen.

144. Piersall, Paul Richard. "The Bass Cantatas of Alessandro Scarlatti." D.M.A. dissertation, University of Oregon, 1971. 228 pp. UMI order #72-964.

Examination of Scarlatti's style in relation to the bass cantatas and discussion of each. Includes those with accompaniment of 2 violins and continuo; or with continuo alone. Discussion and illustration of ornamentation, continuo realization, and the singer. Performing editions of 9 of the 10 given (see Section V, 1 for individual titles) as well as locations of the MSS discussed. The latter are, however, poorly cited; some list only the city without the specific library and none indicate the MS catalog numbers. Italian texts with translation in English given; errata (actually changes made by the author,some of which are interpretive) cited.

145. Rose, Gloria. "The Italian Cantata of the Baroque Period." In *Gattungen der Musik in Einzeldarstellungen. Gedenkschrift Leo Schrade* I, pp. 655-677. Ed. by Wulf Arlt, Ernst Lichtenhahn, and Hans Oesch. Bern: Francke, 1973. Mus. exs.

Brief but informative history of the Italian cantata from the early seventeenth century; reference to Alessandro Scarlatti as among the genre's leading composers.

146. Schmitz, Eugen. *Geschichte der weltlichen Solokantate*. 2nd ed. (Reprint of 1st ed). Leipzig: Breitkopf & Härtel, 1955. 365 pp.

A. Scarlatti's cantatas discussed on pp. 145-156. Divides the cantatas into three periods: pre-1703; 1703-1708 (Roman period); 1708-1725 (Neopolitan period). Doesn't mention the composer's return to Rome in 1717-1722. Discusses Scarlatti as leading member of the "Neopolitan school" and a formative influence on Leo, Vinci, and others. This view now considered untenable.

*   Strohm Reinhard. "Scarlattiana at Yale." Cited as item 437.

147. Strüver, Paul. "Die Cantata da camera Alessandro Scarlattis." Ph.D. dissertation, University of Munich, 1923. 185 pp. 2 Beilage (suppls).

Not seen. Hanley (item 134) provides the following information. Study limited to cantatas in libraries of German-speaking

countries; 374 listed. Cantatas and copies
not in Dent's catalog added. Provided
information about autographs, doubtful works
or attributions, etc. Bibl. references.
Author examined only about a third of the
repertoire omitting most in the Santini
collection, Münster. Catalog contains errors,
such as inclusion of works by Domenico
Scarlatti.

* Talbot, Michael, and Colin Timms. "Music and
  the Poetry of Antonio Ottoboni (1646-1720)."
  Cited as item 101.

* Van de Kamp, Cecilia Kathryn. See Freund,
  Cecilia Kathryn Van de Kamp.

* Winternitz, Emanuel. *Musical Autographs*. Cited
  as item 24.

148. Zanetti, Roberto. "La cantata." In *La musica
     italiana nel settecento* (item 61), pp. 895-946.

     A. Scarlatti's cantatas surveyed, pp. 896-
     913. Divides discussion into 3 periods
     similar to Schmitz's (item 146). Gives text of
     the composer's dialect cantata *Ammore, brutto
     figlio...* and formal outlines of *Speranze mie* (1694),
     Eliotrope d'amore (1694), *Io morirei contento*, and
     Pensieri, oh Dio. Chapter less useful for its
     analysis than for its detailed citations and
     lists. Includes brief mention of the
     serenatas and a list of principal compositions
     written in the genre.

Church Music

149. Bank, Jan A. "De Kerkmuziek van Alessandro
     Scarlatti." *St. [Sint] Gregoriusblad* 80 (1956): 2-
     6.

     Primarily a bibliographical survey of

Scarlatti's masses. Includes brief comments on style. The two masses for 8 voices (in G minor and C major) cited have been proven spurious (see item 435, p. 516). Three movements from masses surviving incomplete are also possibly by a composer other than Scarlatti (see *NGIBM*, Rostirolla, etc.). Bank and Rostirolla together offer the most detailed bibliographical information despite the above-mentioned misattribution by the former.

150. Bonaventura, Arnaldo. "El *Stabat Mater* de Alessandro Scarlatti." *Revista de musica* 2 (1928): 145-149.

Discussion and appreciation of this work, which was published for the first time in 1928 in the editions by Felice Boghen (see Section V, 1). Brief references to the *Stabat Mater* of Pergolesi (and of Rossini). Article written in the general manner of program notes.

* Bonini, Eleonora Simi. See Simi Bonini, Eleonora.

151. Brandvik, Paul Allen. "Selected Motets of Alessandro Scarlatti." D.M.A. dissertation, University of Illinois, 1969. 465 pp. UMI order #70-13,252. Bibl., pp. 453-458.

Study of 16 representative Scarlatti motets which illustrate the range of styles characteristic of sacred music of the time (from stile antico to stile moderno--solo, small concertato, grand concertato--or some combination of the two). Analyses, transcribes, and edits the 16 motets (see Section V, 1). Apps. include an annotated list of all known Scarlatti motets, pp. 437-448; a list of libraries possessing Scarlatti manuscripts, pp. 449-450; and information regarding the distribution of voice groupings and instrumentation, pp. 451-452.

152. Day, Thomas Charles. "Echoes of Palestrina's
     Missa ad fugam in the 18th century." *American
     Musicological Society Journal.* 24 (1971): 462-469.

     Author maintains that Scarlatti's *Messe e Credo
     a 4 ad Canones* (SATB) *[Missa ad canonem in G]* borrows
     from Palestrina's *Missa ad fugam*. Scarlatti may
     have studied it in a collection prepared by
     Pasquini. Fux had the collection and it was
     probably copied by two of his pupils. MS of
     the Scarlatti mass in the library of the
     Conservatorio di Musica S. Pietro a Maiella,
     Naples (#38028). Mus. ex. of the Kyrie, p.
     467, indicates music common to both
     compositions.

*   Dietz, Hanns-Bertold. "Sacred Music in Naples
     during the Second Half of the 17th Century."
     Cited as item 72.

153. Dixon, Graham. "Handel's Music for the Feast
     of Our Lady of Mount Carmel." In *Händel e gli
     Scarlatti a Roma* (item 38 in Book II), pp. 29-
     48. App.

     Places Handel's music for the Feast in its
     liturgical context. Page 36 quotes from a
     letter by Curzio Vinchioni to Giacomo Antonio
     Perti which confirms that Alessandro Scarlatti
     directed the music with the collaboration of
     Domenico and possibly also Pietro Filippo
     Scarlatti.

154. Fabbri, Mario. "Il dolore e la morte nelle
     «voci in solitudine» di Alessandro
     Scarlatti." In *Scritti in onore di Luigi Ronga*, pp.
     127-144. Milan and Naples: Riccardo
     Ricciardi Editore, 1973.

     Discussion of some polyphonic compositions
     written by Scarlatti in 1708 for Holy Week
     [the *Responsori per la Settimana Santa*, SATB, SATB and
     basso continuo] with organ ad lib. Letter of
     1728 by Giovanfrancesco Becatelli shows

Scarlatti's style in keeping with the commonly
held aesthetic ideas of passion music of the
period.

155. _____. "Le musiche di Alessandro Scarlatti
«per il tempo di penitenza e di tenebre»".
In *I grandi anniversari del 1960 e la musica sinfonica e da
camera nell'ottocento in Italia*, pp. 17-32. Ed. by
Adelmo Damerini. Siena: Arti Grafiche
Ticci, 1960.

Same as Chapter 3 (pp. 99-114) in author's
Alessandro Scarlatti e il Principe Ferdinando de'Medici (item
19).

* Fabris, Dinko. "Generi e fonti della musica
sacra a Napoli nel seicento." Cited as
item 75.

156. Faravelli, Danilo. "Stabat Mater: poesia e
musica." *Rivista internazionale di musica
sacra* 4/1 (1983): 9-43. Mus. exs., bibl.

Textual analysis of the Stabat Mater
sequence with reference to musical settings by
Pergolesi and Alessandro Scarlatti, among
others. Not seen.

157. Hanley, Edwin. ["Record Review of A.
Scarlatti's *Messa di Santa Cecilia*"]. *Musical
Quarterly* 48 (1962): 548-550.

Discusses the edition used for the
performance (F. Steffin. Berlin-Wiesbaden:
Bote & Bock, 1957; see Section V, 1) and,
briefly, the performance itself. Background
remarks on Scarlatti's masses and discussion
of this particular work. For discographical
information, see section VI.

158. _____. ["Record Review of A. Scarlatti's
Stabat Mater]. *Musical Quarterly* 39 (1953): 493-

496.

Much more than a record review; the
performance aspects are dealt with only in the
final two paragraphs. Hanley discusses the
form, style, relationship to the secular
cantata, text, etc. Criticizes edition used
(probably F. Boghen's; see Section V, 1) and
cuts made by the conductor. For discographical
information, see section VI.

* Kirnberger, Johann Philipp. *Die Kunst des reinen
  Satzes in der Musik*. Cited as item 20.

159. Knapp, J. Merrill. "Händel's Roman Church
     Music." In *Händel e gli Scarlatti a Roma* (item 38
     in Book II), pp. 15-27.

Author questions J. Steele's hypothesis
(item 167) that Händel may have modeled his
Dixit Dominus on A. Scarlatti's and suggests that
Carissimi may have been a greater influence
(p. 20).

160. Krist, Esther. "Alessandro Scarlatti's *Messa
     di Santa Cecilia*." *American Choral Review* 15/3
     (1973): 3-13.

Brief survey of the progression of
Scarlatti's style of composing masses and more
detailed discussion of the *St. Cecilia Mass*
composed late in the composer's life (1720).
A very general article designed to familiarize
choral conductors, teachers, etc. with the
work.

* Llorens Cisteró, José M. "Las dedicatorias de
  los manuscritos musicales de la Capella
  Sixtina." Cited as item 21.

* López-Calo, José. "L'intervento de Alessandro
  Scarlatti nella controversia sulla Messa

Scala Aretina di Francisco Valls." Cited as
item 22.

161. Marx-Weber, Magda. "Römische Vertonungen des
     Psalms *Miserere* im 18. und frühen 19.
     Jahrhundert." *Hamburger Jahrbuch für
     Musikwissenschaft* 8 (1985): 7-43.

     Includes a discussion of A. Scarlatti's
     early *Miserere* [NGIBM i, 1680] in g for 2 choirs
     SSATB/SATB (Rome: Vatican Library Capp. Sist.
     MS 188/89). Author compares it with its
     prototype, Gregorio Allegri's *Miserere*. Also
     examines Domenico's *Miserere* in g minor and his
     Miserere in e minor), which date from between
     1715 and 1719.

162. Owens, Samuel Battie. "The Organ Mass and
     Girolamo Frescobaldi's *Fiore Musicali* of 1635;
     Music for Two Organs; Four Lenten Motets of
     Alessandro Scarlatti." D.M.A. dissertation,
     George Peabody College for Teachers of
     Vanderbilt University, 1974. 295 pp. Bibl.,
     pp. 291-292. UMI order #74-29,153.

     The third monograph contains a transcription
     of and commentary on 4 Lenten motets of
     Scarlatti (pp. 99-290). All are settings of a
     miserere text "Miserere mei Deus, secundum."
     Nos. 1, 3, and 4 are settings of Psalm 50
     (Vulgate numbering) and date from 1680, 1714,
     and 1715. No. 2 dates from 1705 and was to be
     performed with the Gradual of the Mass on Ash
     Wednesday. Each motet is preceded by a
     discussion of Scarlatti's style and an
     analysis. According to *NGIBM*, No. 3 dates
     from 1715 and no. 4 from 1721.

*   Rostirolla, Giancarlo. "Domenico Scarlatti e
     la congregazione di Santa Cecilia." Cited
     as item 38 in Book II.

163. Rye, Charles Stanton. "Editions of Selected

Motets from *Concerti Sacri*, opus 2 by Alessandro
Scarlatti (1660-1725)." D.M.A. dissertation,
University of Oklahoma, 1981. 261 pp. UMI
order #8129421.

Discussion of the set of 10 motets known as
the *Concerti Sacri*, the only sacred music by
Scarlatti published during his lifetime.
Places them in historical perspective and
discusses the complete corpus of motets as
well as evidence for dating the source
(assistance from E. Hanley). Structural
analysis of "Rorate coeli" and "Properate
fideles" and suggestions for performance.
Chapters 4 and 5 full score editions of these
motets with critical notes (see Section V, 1).
Selected bibl. of primary and secondary
sources, p. 243 and ff.; App. lists all known
Scarlatti motets, pp. 232-242.

164. Shaffer, Jeanne Ellison. "The Cantus Firmus
    in Alessandro Scarlatti's Motets." Ph.D.
    dissertation, George Peabody College for
    Teachers of Vanderbilt University, 1970.
    392 pp. UMI order #70-23,345.

    Consists primarily of analyses and
    transcriptions of 7 motets by Scarlatti
    (including 6 Psalms) which utilize cantus
    firmus techniques. Represent a range of
    styles (classified according to Karl Gustav
    Fellerer's *History of Catholic Church Music*, 1961).
    App. 1, pp. 362ff. is an annotated list of all
    known Scarlatti motets arranged alphabetically
    by title; gives type of setting, voice
    combination, date, location of MSS. See
    Section V, 1 for edition information.

*   Simi Bonini, Eleonora. "L'attività degli
    Scarlatti nella Basilica Liberiana." Cited
    as item 38 in Book II).

165. _____ . "Torna alla luce l'autografo di
    una messa di Alessandro Scarlatti." *Il flauto*

dolce 13 (Oct. 1985): 27-28. Notes, facs. reproductions.

Reports on the author's rediscovery of the parts (in her opinion, autograph) for the *Messa per il natale di Nostro Signore Gesù Cristo*, in A major (for double chorus of 9 voices, two violins, and organ, with the bass doubled by violoncello) dated December 1707 in the Capella Liberiana, S. Maria Maggiore, Rome. The original title was *Messa per il SS.mo Natale / per uso della Basilica di S. Maria Maggiore / Del Sig. Alessandro Scarlatti / Xbre 1707*. These MS parts not cited in previous catalogs of the composer's works. Other documents in the same archive show that it is highly probable that Domenico Scarlatti also took part in the performance of the mass. Brief information on the structure of the mass and the placement of the performers given. Mentions forthcoming editions of other works by Alessandro and Domenico found in the same archive.

166. Smith, Peter. "Liturgical Music in Italy, 1660-1750: Naples." In the *New Oxford History of Music* 5, pp. 391-397. Ed. by Anthony Lewis and Nigel Fortune. London: Oxford University Press, 1975.

Refers to A. Scarlatti's masses and *Stabat Mater* and comments (erroneously) that both Durante and Porpora were Scarlatti's pupils. Bibl., pp. 801-802.

167. Steele, John. "Dixit Dominus: Alessandro Scarlatti and Handel." *Studies in Music* (Australia) 7 (1973): 19-27.

Comparison of Scarlatti's concertato setting of *Dixit Dominus* [*NGIBM: Dixit* iv] (Library of the Conservatorio Giuseppe Verdi, Milan: Musica sacra manuscritta, ordine alfabetico 710) with the 1707 (Rome) setting by Handel. Suggests that the resemblance in design may indicate that Handel modeled his own *Dixit* on

Scarlatti's [see item 159 for another opinion]. Style and form of the settings discussed. MS in score and 4 accompanying part-books titled "Canto di Concerto, Alto di Concerto, Tenore, Basso." Parts exist in later copies.

*   Strohm, Reinhard. "Alessandro Scarlatti und das Settecento." Cited as item 114.

*   _____. "Scarlattiana at Yale." Cited as item 437.

168. Terni, Clemente. "«Stile e armonie» di Alessandro Scarlatti per un dramma liturgico." In *Celebrazioni del 1963 e alcune nuove indagini sulla musica italiana der XVIII e XIX secoli. Chigiana* 20 (1963): 115-154.

Examines the *Responsori per la settimana santa: Velum Templi scissum est, Omnes amici mei,* and *Vinea mea electa.*

169. Williams, Hermine Weigel. "The *Stabat Mater dolorosa*: A Comparison of Settings by Alessandro Scarlatti and Giovanni Battista Pergolesi." *Studi Pergolesiani/Pergolesi Studies* 2 (1988): 144-154. ISBN 88-221-0443-9. 13 exs. (including mus. exs.) and notes.

The only detailed and substantive study of Scarlatti's *Stabat*, the work Pergolesi's *Stabat* replaced as a setting for the annual observances of a confraternity in Naples. Gives a history of the Stabat Mater, its text structure, liturgical use, etc. and examines both the individual and shared characteristics of the above-mentioned settings.

170. Witzenmann, Wolfgang. "Zur Behandlung des *stile osservato* in Alessandro Scarlattis Kirchenmusik." In *Colloquium Alessandro Scarlatti Würzburg 1975* (item 5), pp. 133-147.

"Diskussion," pp. 148-152.

Discusses the classification and dating of Scarlatti's sacred music and clarifies the terminology used to refer to it, especially *stile osservato, stile alla Palestrina, stile antico*. Focuses on the composer's use of dissonance, analysing parts of the sacred works. Concludes they are linked to the earlier styles in substance (e.g., lack of formal or rhythmic contrasts) but different in certain respects (e.g., dissonance treatment).

Madrigals

171. Bowles, Kenneth Eugene. "Editions of the Madrigals of Alessandro Scarlatti (1660-1725)." D.M.A. dissertation, University of Oklahoma, 1987. 246 pp. UMI order #8713815.

    Not seen.

172. Jürgens, Jürgen. "Die Madrigale Alessandro Scarlattis und ihre Quellen; Anmerkungen zur Erstausgabe der Madrigale." In *Scritti in onore di Luigi Ronga*, pp. 279-285. Milan and Naples: Riccardo Ricciardi Editore, 1973.

    Primarily a discussion and outlining of the MSS sources of the madrigals which number among Scarlatti's minor works. Jürgens has edited the only complete modern edition of the madrigals (see Section V, 1) and has directed the only commercial recording of them (see Section VI). In view of this it is surprising that he hasn't discussed the performance aspects of the madrigals in either the present article or the introduction to his edition.

Operas: History

173. Abert, Anna Amalie. "Die Barockoper. Ein
     Bericht über die   Forschung seit 1945."
     Acta musicologica 41 (1969): 121-164.

     Discusses recent research on the history of
     Baroque opera and its regional schools. Some
     specific Scarlatti references. Excellent
     bibliographies.

174. Bianconi, Lorenzo. "Funktionen des
     Operntheaters in Neapel bis 1700 und die
     Rolle Alessandro Scarlattis." In *Colloquium
     Alessandro Scarlatti Würzburg 1975* (item 5), pp. 13-
     111. "Diskussion," pp. 112-116.

     Examines the choice of operas given in
     Naples up to 1700 in the context of cultural
     politics and viceregal power and discusses
     Scarlatti in this milieu. Discusses the
     function of opera and the public to whom it
     was addressed. Also presents the most up-to-
     date and complete chronology of opera
     performances in Naples from 1650 to 1706 with
     library locations of surviving librettos.
     Intended to supplement Strohm's chronology of
     opera performances in Naples, 1707-1734. See
     item 221.

175. _____, and Maria Teresa Muraro. "Il teatro
     di San Giovanni Grisostomo dal *Diario* di
     Nicodemus Tessin." In *Domenico Scarlatti. I grandi
     centenari dell'anno europeo della musica* (item 36 in
     Book II), pp. 140-152.

     Provides a vivid picture of Handel's
     relationship to Italian music and describes
     this popular Venetian theater as documented in
     Tessin's diary. [It was here that Alessandro
     Scarlatti's operas *Mitridate Eupatore* and *Il trionfo
     della libertà* were performed in 1707]. According
     to Boyd (item 3, p. 16, in Book II), Domenico
     "was no doubt at hand to assist his father in

preparing ... these works, and may even have taken part in their performance."

176. Bjurström, Per. *Den romerska barockens scenografi.* Nyhamnslage: Svenska humanistiska förbundet, 1977   (Svenska humanistiska förbundet, 88) 141 pp.

Examines scenography of the seventeenth- and eighteenth-century theater in Rome. Discusses opera productions in detail including A. Scarlatti's *Il Ciro* (1st performance, Rome, 1712). Not seen. Abstract in *RILM*.

*   Borren, Charles van den. See Van den Borren, Charles.

177. Burt, Nathaniel. "Opera in Arcadia." *Musical Quarterly* 41 (1955): 145-170. Plates.

Discussion of *opera seria* and the Arcadian reforms; the latter are identified and illustrated through a comparison of Appoloni/Cesti's *La Dori* (1663), a pre-Arcadian Baroque opera, with David/Pollarolo's *La forza del virtù* and Metastasio/ Porpora's *Siface* based on Arcadian principles.

178. Cametti, Alberto. "Carlo Sigismondo Capeci (1652-1728), Alessandro e Domenico Scarlatti e la Regina di Polonia a Roma." *Musica d'oggi* 13 (1931): 55-64.

A brief biography of Capeci, the librettist for works by, among others, Alessandro (and Domenico) Scarlatti and Handel. Pages 57-64 contain a chronological list of Capeci's theatrical works with information regarding the number of acts, dedication, printed editions, music, first performance, characters, and additional performances.

179. Collins, Michael. "L'orchestra nelle opere
     teatrali di Vivaldi." In *Nuovi studi Vivaldiani;*
     edizione e cronologia critica delle opere, Vol. I, pp.
     285-312. Florence: Leo S. Olschki, 1988.
     Tables (7).

An expansion of the study presented by
Collins at the conference *Il teatro musicale a Venezia e
a Napoli nel settecento*, Venice, September 9-11, 1985
organized by the Fondazione Cini (described in
NRMI 20 (1986): 154-157) in which the
structures of the aria accompaniments of A.
Scarlatti were compared with those of Handel
and other contemporaries (1694-1724).
Scarlatti's decline in popularity in this late
part of his career was shown to be linked
"directly and in inverse proportion to the
increase in the complexity of his orchestral
accompaniments." The present study was
presented at the meeting of the Istituto
Italiano Antonio Vivaldi, 1987. It extends the
earlier study to include the operas of Vivaldi
and, using Vivaldi and Handel as central
figures, compares the structures of their
accompaniments with those of their
contemporaries (from 1713 to 1735). Shows that
the "dominant tendency" was toward more dense
yet less intrusive accompaniments. Examines
Benedetto Marcello's *Il teatro alla moda* to see
which criticisms relating to the orchestral
writing can be applied to the composers above
and which works of the period he approved of.

180. Croce, Benedetto. *I teatri di Napoli, secolo XV-XVIII.*
     Naples: L. Pierro, 1891. New ed. 1916; 3rd
     ed. 1926.

An important and much-quoted early history
of the theater (including musical theater) in
Naples in the years before, during, and
following Scarlatti's activity in that city.
The new "corrected" editions were cut and re-
edited.

*   De Angelis, Marcello. "Il teatro di Pratolino

tra Scarlatti e Perti...." Cited as item 64.

181. Dean, Winton. "Handel and Alessandro
     Scarlatti." In *Händel e gli Scarlatti a Roma* (item
     38 in Book II), pp. 1-14. Mus. exs.

     Author attempts to show that A. Scarlatti
     did influence Handel. While certain stylistic
     elements (such as the "contorted chromaticism"
     in Handel's early cantatas) may have derived
     from Scarlattian influence, it is impossible
     to prove a direct connection because other
     composers also wrote in a similar way.
     However, the author maintains, there is
     evidence that one Scarlatti opera (*Mitridate
     Eupatore*), and at least one type of aria for
     which Scarlatti was famous (the slow siciliano
     type in 12/8 meter used at points of great
     emotional tension) had a "decisive influence"
     on Handel's own style.

182. Degrada, Francesco. "L'opera napoletana." In
     Storia dell'opera (item 219), Vol. 1, T. 1, pp.
     237-332. Turin: UTET, 1977. Bibl., pp.
     320-332.

     The best current and comprehensive
     introduction to the subject of Neapolitan
     opera. Reviews and documents ideas expressed
     by noted scholars in the field from Dent's
     time onward and contributes his own informed
     conclusions. Considers many aspects of the
     general subject including, among others:
     terminology, theaters, management,
     conservatories, opera's social function, A.
     Scarlatti and Naples, and the intermezzo and
     comic opera in that city. Pages 291-292
     contain a discussion of Dent's article
     "Ensembles and Finales..." (item 184).

183. _____. "Origini e sviluppi dell'opera
     comica napoletana." In *Venezia e il melodramma nel
     settecento*, pp. 149-173. Ed. by Maria Teresa
     Muraro. Florence: Leo S. Olschki Editore,

1978   (Studi di musica veneta, 6).

Written   in   1975   as   a   much-abbreviated
version of the article the author was writing
for item 182. Pp. 149-162 parallel pp. 280-
290 of that article.

184. Dent, Edward J.   "Ensembles and Finales in the
     18th Century Italian Opera."   *Sammelbände der
     internationalen Musikgesellschaft* 11 (1909-10): 543-
     569; mus. exs. and 12 (1910-1911)), 112-138;
     chronological list of MS scores by Scarlatti
     and his successors in the first half of the
     eighteenth century.

     Part 1 (Vol. 11): a study of the use of
     ensembles   and   finales   in   the   earlier
     Neapolitan operas, specifically those by A.
     Scarlatti.   Concludes that Scarlatti used
     ensembles *a 4.* in the manner of an aria to
     express a single emotion rather than as a
     dramatic device to express the interactions of
     four differentiated characters. States that
     Scarlatti may have been the first to apply the
     methods of the *opera seria* quartet to comic
     illustration (in *Il trionfo dell'onore*) and that he
     progressed toward a freer and more dramatic
     treatment of comic ensembles. Questions the
     accuracy of the tradition that claimed opera
     buffa   originated   directly   from   comic
     intermezzi.

185. _____. "Italian Opera in the Eighteenth
     Century and Its Influence on the Music of
     the Classical Period." *Sammelbände der
     internationalen Musikgesellschaft* (1913): 500-509.

     Insightful examination of the role the
     Italian   aria   probably   played   in   the
     development of the eighteenth-century symphony
     and keyboard sonata.   Allusions to both
     Alessandro and Domenico Scarlatti.

186. _____.   "A Jesuit at the Opera in 1680."   In

Riemann-Festschrift, Gesammelte Studien, pp. 381-393.
Reprint of the 1909 ed. Tutzing: Hans
Schneider, 1965.

Pages 386-387 briefly discuss the
intermezzos and comic dancing from Scarlatti's
Clearco in Negroponte, *Odoardo*, and *Tito Sempronio
Gracco*. Included in a discussion of a little
book published in 1681 by an aristocratic
gentleman, probably a Jesuit, who describes in
detail an opera he supposedly attended.

*   Donato, Giuseppe. "Su alcuni aspetti della
    vita musicale in Sicilia nel seicento."
    Cited as item 77.

187. Downes, Edward O. D. "The Neapolitan Tradition
    in Opera." In *International Musicological Society.
    Report of the 8th Congress, N.Y., 1961*, pp. 277-284.
    Ed. by Jan LaRue. Kassel: Bärenreiter, 1961.

Examines term "Neapolitan school" or
"Neapolitan tradition" as referred to by music
historians from Burney to the present and
concludes its use has led to confusion rather
than clarification. Maintains that opera
history should be studied in the broader
context of general music history and style
trends. Calls attention to need for stylistic
comparisons of operas originating from
different geographic regions, including local
dialect comedies.

188. Ferrari-Barassi, Elena. "Il melodramma negli
    altri centri nei secoli XVII e XVIII." 4th
    part: "Il trionfo del melodramma." In *Storia
    dell'opera* (item 219), Vol. 1, T. 1, pp. 409-
    546. Bibl., pp. 544-546.

Discusses opera at Rome, Bologna, Florence,
and other centers of the pontifical state,
etc., during the seventeenth and eighteenth
centuries. Author suggests that however
difficult Scarlatti may have sometimes found

the city from a financial standpoint, Rome provided the milieu he needed and could not find elsewhere to develop the synthesis which shaped his style.

189. Ferrero, Mercedes Viale. "Antonio e Pietro Ottoboni e alcuni melodrammi da loro ideati o promossi a Roma." In *Venezia e il melodramma nel settecento*, Vol. 1, pp. 271-294. Ed. by Maria Teresa Muraro. Florence: Leo S. Olschki Editore, 1978 (Studi di musica veneta, 6).

Examines the Ottoboni family's ties to Venice (their city of origin) through an examination of the theatrical and operatic works dedicated to and written, transcribed, or patronized by them. Includes references to works by Alessandro Scarlatti (*Il Ciro, Il Pirro e Demetrio*), Caldara, and Gasparini and works to which Scarlatti contributed arias, etc. (*Giunio Bruto, Odoacre*). Discussion of recently discovered MS of an Antonio Ottoboni text *Giulio Cesare nell'Egito*, apparently never produced, with drawings for scenic designs by Juvarra (reprinted here). Detailed appendices serve to demonstrate this Venetian connection. See also item 101.

190. _____. *Filippo Juvarra scenografo e architetto teatrale*. N.Y.: Benjamin Blom Inc., [1963]. Florence: Olschki, 1978.

Monumental resource. Extensive collection of plates (some in color) of Juvarra's theater and stage designs, including those for A. Scarlatti's *Il Ciro*. Catalogue raisonée which locates all extant MSS, early printed editions, and librettos (known to the author) that include Juvarra's work.

191. _____. "*Heroi e comici* sulle rive dell'Eridano." In *Venezia e il melodramma nel settecento*, Vol. 1, pp. 199-235. Ed. by Maria Teresa Muraro. Florence: Leo S. Olschki, 1978

(Studi di musica veneta, 6).

Study of the sixteenth-century sources of seventeenth-century comic opera considered from the perspective of the situation at Turin. Includes references to Alessandro Scarlatti's *L'Aldimiro* which marked the reopening of the Teatro Regio after the war and *L'Emireno* (pp. 204-205).

*   _____. "Juvarra fra i due Scarlatti." Cited as item 38 in Book II.

*   Florimo, Francesco. *La scuola musicale di Napoli e i suoi conservatorii*. Cited as item 76.

192.   Freeman, Robert S. *Opera without Drama: Currents of Change in Italian Opera, 1675 to 1725*. Ann Arbor: UMI Research Press, 1981. xii and 347 pp. (Studies in Musicology, 35)   ISBN 0-8-357-1152-8.

A study of Apostolo Zeno's reforms and the development of the Italian opera libretto (1675-1725) through a detailed examination of changes in the treatment of "members of libretto families." Extensive notes and bibl. designed to supplement Grout's *A Short History of Opera*, 2nd ed. Does not include literature published after 1967.

193.   Gianturco, Carolyn.. "Il melodramma a Roma nel secolo XVII." In *Storia dell'opera* (item 219), Vol. 1, T. 1., pp. 183-233. Bibl., pp. 231-233.

Superb background and analysis of opera in Rome from its origins to the death of Innocent XII. Examines the emergence of comic elements, the influence of Spanish drama and *commedia dell'arte*, and the contribution of Cesti's music to the development of the styles of Stradella and Pasquini.

*   Green, Douglass M. See under Lazarevich,
        Gordana: item 201.

194. Grout, Donald Jay. *Alessandro Scarlatti: An Introduction
      to His Operas*. Berkeley: University of
      California Press, 1979. vii and 154 pp.
      ISBN 0-520-03682-4.

      The best introduction to Scarlatti's operas.
      Overview yet based on specifics. Original
      sources quoted, musical examples given,
      historical context and events affecting the
      composer's life related and all written in
      Grout's characteristically penetrating, witty,
      and lucid style. In-depth analysis of *La caduta
      de' Decemveri, Il Cambise, Gli equivoci nel sembiante, La
      Griselda, Marco Attilio Regno, Il Mitridate Eupatore, Il Pirro e
      Demetrio, Il Pompeo, La principessa fedele, Il trionfo dell'onore,*
      and *Il Tigrane*.

195. _____, with Hermine Weigel Williams. *A Short
      History of Opera*. 3rd ed. N.Y.: Columbia
      University Press, 1988. xxiv and 913 pp.
      Mus. exs., illus., bibl., index. ISBN 0-
      231-06192-7.

      The basic opera history. Includes
      informative overview of Scarlatti's operas
      (pp. 171-181). Suggests comparing operas of
      Scarlatti and Gasparini based on the same
      librettos. Lengthy, revised general
      bibliography and individual chapter
      bibliographies.

196. Hucke, Helmuth. "Alessandro Scarlatti und die
      Musikkömodie." In *Colloquium Alessandro Scarlatti
      Würzburg 1975* (item 5), pp. 177-190.
      "Diskussion," pp. 201-204.

      Relates the performance of Scarlatti's only
      comic opera *Il trionfo dell'onore* on November 26,
      1718, at the Teatro dei Fiorentini, Naples to
      the Neapolitan dialect comedies performed that
      year in the same theater. Describes

Scarlatti's opera as standing midway between the old opera seria and the new dialect comedy, valid in itself but without influence on subsequent comic operas.

197. _____. "Die neapolitanische Tradition in der Oper." In *International Musicological Society, Report of the Eighth Congress, New York, 1961*, pp. 253-277. Ed. by Jan La Rue. Kassel: Bärenreiter, 1961.

Outlines chief disagreements between authors from the eighteenth to the twentieth century regarding the "Neapolitan school" including objections of Rudolf Gerber and Hugo Riemann to the term. Examines history of opera in Naples, character of arias, A. Scarlatti, Leo, Vinci, and Hasse.

198. *Italian Opera Librettos: 1640-1770*. Ed. by Howard Mayer Brown. N.Y.: Garland Publishing, 1979 (Italian Opera 1640-1770, 56, Series 1) ISBN 0-8240-2655-1 (vol. 6). ISBN 0-8240-2658-6 (vol. 9).

A facsimile series which aims to make the texts of representative Italian operas of the seventeenth and eighteenth centuries available to a wider audience. Introductory prefaces by the editor. Vol. 6 includes the facsimiles of libretti of 2 Griselda operas, that of Bononcini (Milan, 1718) and Vivaldi (Venice, 1735). Vol. 9 includes the libretto of *Telemaco* by Carlo Capeci set by Alessandro Scarlatti (Rome, 1718), the source of which is the Schatz MS 9532 in the Library of Congress.

199. Kirsch, Winfried. "Zur musikalischen Konzeption und dramaturgischen Stellung des Opernquartetts im 18. und 19. Jahrhundert." *Die Musikforschung* 27 (1974): 186-199.

Examines the operatic quartet since c1750 and its use as a series of monologues at points of crisis in the plot. Also studies forerunners, among them, the "Aria a quattro" from Scarlatti's *Telemaco* and "Penza ben-ch'ho da penzare?" from his *Il trionfo dell'onore*, Act 3, Scene 12.

200. Lazarevich, Gordana. "The Role of the Neapolitan Intermezzo in the Evolution of Eighteenth-Century Musical Style: Literary, Symphonic and Dramatic Aspects, 1685-1735." Ph.D. dissertation, Columbia University, 1970. 418 pp. UMI order #73-8965.

Important study of the Neapolitan comic tradition and, especially, the intermezzo and its forerunners. Illustrates how the attempt to set comic, realistic texts to music influenced the shape of the melodic phrase and led to the use of short motives, rests, leaps, etc., influential in the development of a new pre-classical musical language. Argues that Scarlatti is the probable originator of the Neapolitan style (as manifested in later years) through his Neapolitan comic additions (authorship not certain) to Legrenzi's Venetian opera *Il Giustino* (1683-1684) [*NGIBM* cites only a prologue from that opera as possibly by Scarlatti] and through his comic scenes designed to be performed between the acts of the dialect *drammi sacri*.

201. _____ and Douglass. M. Green. "The Eighteenth-Century Overture in Naples: Introduction." In *The Symphony 1720-1840*, Series A, Vol. 1, pp. xxxiii-lxii. Ed. by Barry S. Brook. N.Y.: Garland Publishing, 1983.

Pages xxxv-xxxix deal specifically with "The sinfonia of Scarlatti and his contemporaries" and "Naples in the eighteenth century." They present a summary of the developments in Scarlatti's overtures (including the beginning of his use of the three movement type c1695), their instrumentation, and imitators, as well as an overview of musical and political

history in Naples during the eighteenth
century.

202. Leich, Karl. *Girolamo Frigimelica-Robertis Libretti (1694-1708); ein Beitrag insbesondere zur Geschichte Opernlibrettos in Venedig* (Schriften zur Musik, 26) Ed. by Walter Kolneder. Munich: Musikverlag Emil Katzbichler, 1972. 186 pp. ISBN 3-87397-028-7.

Book-length study of one of Scarlatti's librettists. Section 1: overview of the life; section 2: librettos discussed in chronological order of their appearance. Discussion of A. Scarlatti's *Il Mitridate* (pp. 114-19) and *Il trionfo della libertà* (pp. 120-128, 151).

203. Lindgren, Lowell. "Il dramma musicale a Roma durante la carriera di Alessandro Scarlatti." In *Le muse galanti. La musica a Roma nel settecento*, pp. 35-57. Ed. by B. Cagli. Rome: Enciclopedia Treccani, 1985. Notes, mus. exs., 2 apps.

An article of major importance which explores Scarlatti's close ties to Rome, its illustrious patrons of the arts and its writers. Shows that despite Scarlatti's unhappiness with the state of music in Rome (as expressed in a the well-known letter to Ferdinando de' Medici), his works were better received there for a longer period of time than in any other Italian city because the conservative taste more closely matched his own. Interesting comparison of Scarlatti's *La Griselda* (1721) and Vivaldi's *Il Giustino*. Includes the most accurate and up to date lists of Roman productions of Scarlatti's operas available in the 2 appendices: pp. 46-57. The author is currently working on a more exhaustive list of the same.

204. Lionnet, Jean. "A Newly Found Opera by

Alessandro Scarlatti." *Musical Times* 128
(1987): 80-81.

Author discovered opera score without title
or name of composer in Biblioteca Apostolica
Vaticana, Rome: MS Chigi QV66. Similar in
plot and music to *Gli equivoci nel sembiante*. Author
names it *Una villa di Tuscolo* and discusses why it
may be by Alessandro Scarlatti. Performed on
radio Feb. 5, 1987.

*   Livingston, Herbert Stanton. "The Italian
      Overture from Alessandro Scarlatti to
      Mozart." Cited as item 334.

205. Lorenz, Alfred. *Alessandro Scarlattis Jugendoper.*
     Augsburg: Benno Filser Verlag, 1927. 2
     vols. 240 pp., name and subject index; 208
     pp.

     Pioneering study of Scarlatti's early operas
     from *Gli equivoci nel sembiante* (1679) up to *La caduta
     de' Decemviri* (1697). Vol. 1 includes detailed
     commentaries on each and discussions of style,
     harmony, melody, rhythm, forms, and key
     schemes in individual arias and the opera as a
     whole (Lorenz's methods of analysis are
     considered archaic and not generally accepted
     anymore). Vol. 2 contains 401 musical
     examples (to 1700) from the operas discussed
     in Vol. 1, including 135 complete pieces
     (arias, duets, etc). Still a valuable source
     of Scarlatti's music as many examples not
     published in any modern edition. Vol. 1, pp.
     18-38, a chronological catalog of the operas .

206. _____. "Alessandro Scarlattis Opern und
     Wien." *Zeitschrift für Musikwissenschaft* (Leipzig) 9
     (1926-1927): 86-89.

     Examines performances of Scarlatti's works
     in Vienna during his lifetime including *Gli
     equivoci nel sembiante* (titled *Amor non vuol inganni*), and
     12 or more years later, the oratorios *La*

Maddalena pentita, La Giuditta, Il Sedecia, and *San Casimiro.*

207. Lowenberg, Alfred. *Annals of Opera, 1597-1940.* 2nd ed., rev. and corr. 2 vols. Geneva: Societas Bibliographica, 1955.

The standard general opera chronology; contains a number of references to performances of operas by A. Scarlatti and other members of the Scarlatti family.

208. Mamczarz, Irene. *Les intermèdes comiques italiens au XVIIIe siècle en France et en Italie.* Paris: Editions de la Centre National de la Recherche Scientifique, 1972. 684 pp. 28 plates.

Massive history of the intermezzo tracing its origins from antiquity and its evolution and flowering in the latter half of the eighteenth century. References in the text to 9 Scarlatti intermezzos which date from between 1693 and 1716. Major part of the volume consists of source lists and catalogs of MSS (by location), printed sources (by author), titles (in alphabetical order), scores and arias (by title of the work), performances to 1893 (in chronological order), librettists, composers, interpreters, etc. Scarlatti citations are not consistent from one section to another.

* Mancini, Franco. *Feste....* Cited as item 311.

209. _____. *Scenografia napoletana dell'età barocca.* Naples: Edizioni Scientifiche Italiane, 1964. 259 pp. Reprint: Rome: G. Laterza, 1977. Apps. (indices).

Major study of scenography in Naples during the seventeenth and eighteenth centuries. Numerous illustrations indexed by the chapter

in which they appear. Arranged alphabetically
by scenographer; subdivided chronologically
and then by theater. Gives title of opera,
composer, librettist, painter, stage engineer
and costumer, when possible. Appendices
include an alphabetical title index to operas
and place and name indexes. Page 52 describes
the 1696 performance of the serenata *Il trionfo
delle stagioni* by Scarlatti and Abate Paglia at the
Palazzo Reale, Naples.

210. Morey, Carl Reginald. "The Late Operas of
     Alessandro Scarlatti." Ph.D. dissertation.
     Indiana University, 1965. v and 312 pp.
     Mus. exs.: pp. 198-311; bibl.: pp. 193-197.
     UMI order #65-10,870.

     Major study of the 36 known operas composed
     by Scarlatti between 1699 and 1725.
     Commentary on each with copies of the title
     page of the librettos for the 1st performance
     and revivals; details from introductory pages
     of the libretti; a list of all known copies of
     libretti, scores, and aria collections with
     current locations. Also provides additional
     information regarding their performance,
     reports in contemporary Neapolitan gazettes,
     and discussion of notable musical details.
     Intent to give overall view of the late operas
     and clarify date of each work. Includes
     references to Scarlatti's "self-borrowings."

211. Muraro, Maria Teresa. "Il teatro Grimani a
     San Giovanni Grisostomo. Storia e documenti
     per la costruzione di un modello." In
     *Domenico Scarlatti. I grandi centenari dell'anno
     europeo della musica* (item 36 in Book II), pp.
     121-139.

     Describes the author's research on this
     famous Venetian theater and how it was used by
     Prof. Salvatore Manzella to create a scale
     model. Documents its technical characteristics
     and social and cultural functions.

212. Ohio State University, Columbus. *The Ohio State University Theatre Collection Bulletin* 11 (1964).

Entire issue devoted to studies of Filippo Juvarra and the Ottoboni theatre. Background on Juvarra (stage designer of A. Scarlatti's *Il Ciro*).

213. Piperno, Franco. "Crateo, Olinto, Archimede e l'Arcadia; rime per alcuni spettacoli operistici Romani (1710-1711). In *Händel e gli Scarlatti a Roma* (item 38 in Book II), pp. 349-366.

Discussion of the music written for carnival in Rome between 1709 and 1712 including Scarlatti's *Il Ciro*.

214. Prota-Giurleo, Ulisse. "Breve storia del Teatro di Corte e della musica a Napoli nei secoli XVII-XVIII." In *Il Teatro di Corte del Palazzo Reale di Napoli*, pp. 19-146. Naples, 1952.

Important documented source of information on composers and musicians active at the court theater in Naples during the seventeenth and eighteenth centuries, including Scarlatti. Information on the makeup of the orchestra in different decades. Criticized by Walker (in item 6, p. 241) for "inventing" certain details.

215. Robinson, Michael F. *Naples and Neapolitan Opera*. Oxford: Clarendon Press, 1972. Reprint: N.Y.: Da Capo, 1984. ISBN 0-306-76226-9. Mus. exs., bibl. of seventeenth-, eighteenth-, nineteenth-, and twentieth-century sources, index.

Excellent modern history of opera in Naples in the seventeenth and eighteenth centuries. Discussion of the background of opera's emergence in this city, the texts and music of "heroic" and comic opera and the orchestral pieces (mainly for the period after Scarlatti). Discussion of the intermezzo includes comparison between Venetian and Neapolitan types c1706.

216. Ruile-Dronke, Jutta. "Die Dacapo-Arie des frühen Scarlatti und die Entstehung des Vivaldischen Konzerttyps." In *Colloquium Alessandro Scarlatti Würzburg 1975* (item 5), pp. 117–126. "Diskussion," pp. 127–132.

Departing from Schering's view of the solo concerto and the aria of Vivaldi's time as analogous formally, the author discusses the formal relationship between the pre-1700 arias of Scarlatti and the emerging solo concerto. Detailed analysis of "Vanne a colei" from *Gli equivoci nel sembiante*.

* Sartori, Claudio. *I libretti italiani a stampa dalle origini al 1800: catalogo analitico con 16 indici.* Cited as item 455.

* _____. *Primo tentativo di catalogo unico dei libretti italiani a stampa fino all'anno 1800.* Cited as item 455a.

217. _____. "Gli Scarlatti a Napoli." *Rivista musicale italiana* 46 (1942): 374–390.

Part 1 is a discussion of Domenico Scarlatti's contributions to Legrenzi's opera *Il Giustino.* Part 2 discusses opera buffa and the Scarlattis (Alessandro, Francesco, and Tommaso). Names of the Scarlatti family often recur in the first examples of the Neapolitan dialect comedy "per musica." Francesco thought to be composer of *Petracchio scremmetore*, but possible all 15 arias of Claudia and Silvio sung in Italian were written by Alessandro as new arias or adapted from earlier operas.

218. Stalnaker, William Park, Jr. "The Beginnings
     of Opera in Naples." Ph.D. dissertation.
     Princeton University, 1968. 349 pp. UMI
     order #69-2784.

     Originally planned as a study of the operas
     of   Alessandro   Scarlatti's   immediate
     forerunners in Naples. Author discusses his
     research of this earlier period and attempts
     to ascertain when and in what circumstances
     opera was established in Naples.

219. *Storia dell'opera.* Ed. by Alberto Basso. Turin:
     UTET, 1977. 3 vols. in 6. Vol.1, T. 1:
     L'opera in Italia; Vol. 3, T. 1 and 2: *Aspetti e
     problemi dell'opera.* Mus. exs., plates, bibls.;
     indices of works and names for entire set in
     Vol. 3, T.2. See items 182, 193, 355, 373
     for individual entries.

     An outstanding history, which reviews the
     literature on each topic and presents its own
     theories or conclusions based on the available
     information.

219b. *Storia dell'opera italiana.* Ed. by Lorenzo Bianconi
     and Giorgio Pestelli. Turin: EDT Musica.
     Pt. 1 (vols. 1-3); Pt. 2 (vols. 4-6), 1987-
     1988. Review of Pt. 2 in *Music Library Association.
     Notes* 47 (1991): 784-785.

*   Strohm, Reinhard. "Alessandro Scarlatti und
     das settecento." Cited as item 114.

*   . "Hasse, Scarlatti, Rolli." Cited as
     item 117.

220.   . *Die italienische Oper im 18. Jahrhundert*
     (Taschenbücher zur Musikwissenschaft, 25)
     Wilhelmshaven: Heinrichshofen, 1979. 398 pp.
     Bibl.

Discusses 25 operas dating from 1695-1775 (issued in modern editions) which illustrate the changes that emerged in the relationship between drama and music. Scarlatti at the beginning of the spectrum when opera was still a "drama clothed in music"; examples from his *Il Mitridate Eupatore* (pp. 63-72) and *La Griselda* (pp. 73-94), the latter in conjunction with Antonio Bononcini's *La Griselda*. Excellent lengthy bibliographies.

221. _____. "Italienische Opernarien des frühen Settecento (1720-1730)." *Analecta musicologica* 16 (1976). 2 vols. 268 pp.; 342 pp.

Vol. 1: Study. Vol.2: Musical examples and catalogs. Examines the Italian opera aria of the early eighteenth century from the standpoint of compositional techniques, verse and rhythm, character, and semantics and typology. A massive study, which includes in its introduction many citations to relevant literature. Two comic arias of Scarlatti and of L. Vinci examined in Vol. 1, pp. 22-32 (mus. exs. in Vol. 2, nos. 97-99): "Vi par che siate robba?" from *Trionfo dell'onore* and "Perchè più strugga d'amor il foco?" from *Turno Aricino* (pasticcio). Vol. 2 also includes partial work lists of 31 composers including "Alessandro Scarlatti. Opern und andere dramatische Werke 1714-1728: Wiederaufführungen..."; sources for 67 pasticcio operas; and side-by-side chronological lists of opera seria repertory performed in Rome and Naples (1707-1732). Bibl. and indices.

222. Troy, Charles E. *The Comic Intermezzo: A Study in Eighteenth-Century Italian Opera* (Studies in Musicology, 9) Ann Arbor: UMI Research Press, 1979. xvi and 242 pp. ISBN 0-8357-0992-2.

Deals with the extent to which other Italian cities followed the Venetian practice of

excluding independent comic episodes from the
printed libretto (characteristic in Venice
after 1700 in historically-based librettos)
and called them intermezzos (restricted to
performance between acts). Contains very
useful tables and appendices; for example,
Table 2 is an inventory of Sächsische
Landesbibliothek, Dresden, MS 1/F/39, 1-2,
Vol. 1, which contains 10 intermezzos (or
comic episodes) by Alessandro Scarlatti.

223. Van den Borren, Charles. *Alessandro Scarlatti et
     l'esthétique de l'opera napolitaine.* Paris: La
     Renaissance d'Occident, 1921.

     Often cited but few copies available. Not
     seen.

*   Viale Ferrero, Mercedes. See Ferrero,
     Mercedes Viale.

224. Weaver, Robert Lamar. *Florentine Comic Operas of the
     17th Century.* Ph.D. dissertation. University
     of North Carolina, 1959. xii and 366 pp.

     First study of the Florentine theater from a
     wider perspective. Earlier studies more
     specific to Pergola and Pratolino. App. 2, p.
     332: list of libretti (1597-1741) (superseded
     by item 226).

225. _____. "Opera in Florence, 1646-1731." In
     *Studies in Musicology. Essays in the History, Style, and
     Bibliography of Music in Memory of Glen Haydon,* pp. 60-
     71. Ed. by James W. Pruett. Chapel Hill:
     University of North Carolina Press, 1969.

     Brief history of Florentine theaters and
     performances which took place from 1646-1731.
     Chronology of comic operas performed from
     1657-1731 superseded by item 227. Ideas of
     the author's dissertation (item 224)
     discussed.

226. _____, and Norma Wright Weaver. *A Chronology of Music in the Florentine Theater 1590-1750: Operas, Prologues, Finales, Intermezzos and Plays with Incidental Music*. Detroit: Information Coordinators, 1978. 421 pp. (Detroit Studies in Music Bibliography, 38)   ISBN 0-911772-83-9.

Most comprehensive source of information on opera performance in and around Florence for this period. Introduction includes review of the literature, illuminating discussion of problems remaining, and errors of past writings. Discussion of theaters, academies, and influential patrons, chief among them, Ferdinand de' Medici. Major part of the book consists of indexes of librettists; composers; singers and actors; other personnel (dancers, impresarios, instrumentalists, costumers, painters, etc); theaters, academies, companies, etc; and titles of works. Bibliography of books and articles; manuscripts (diaries, letters, etc. in archives); early printed editions of librettos, etc. Cites a number of A. Scarlatti's operas as well as several by Giuseppe Scarlatti. Pp. 204-206 contain a facsimile of a letter by A. Scarlatti (dated Aug 28, 1706, Rome), which accompanied a gift of *Madrigali a tavolino*.

227. Wirth, Helmut. "Gluck, Haydn und Mozart--drei Entführungs-Opernstudien." In *Anna Amalie Abert zum 65 Geburtstag*, pp. 25-35. Ed. by Klaus Hortschansky. Tutzing: Hans Schneider, 1975.

Oriental characters in operas of, among others, Alessandro Scarlatti, seen as forerunners of the exotic types in "Turkish" operas popular in Vienna from the time of the appointment of Gluck as director of the French theater.

228. Wolff, Hellmuth Christian. "Die Buffoszenen in den Opern Alessandro Scarlattis." In *Colloquium Alessandro Scarlatti Würzburg 1975* (item 5),

pp. 191-200. Anhang (identifies 10 scenes,
sources, dates, personages etc.), pp. 199-
200. "Diskussion," pp. 201-204.

Study of 10 comic scenes each from a
different opera of Scarlatti (written 1697-
1702) the music of which is contained in
Sächsiche Landesbibliothek, Dresden, MSS (Mus.
1, F, 39 I and II). Scenes display elements
of the later intermezzo in their use of 2
characters (often husband and wife) who
combine realism and farce in portraying daily
problems of love and marriage. Author of
texts not certain, possibly, the composer.

229. _____. "The Fairy-tale of the Neopolitan
Opera." In *Studies in Eighteenth Century Music
[Geiringer Festschrift]*, pp. 401-406. Ed. by H.C.
Robbins Landon. N.Y.: Oxford University
Press, 1970.

Another critique (see also items 187 and
197) of the concept of a separate "Neapolitan
school" or "Neapolitan opera."

230. _____. "Italian Opera from the later
Monteverdi to Scarlatti", and "Italian Opera
1700-1750." In *The New Oxford History of Music*,
Vol. 5 (Opera and Church Music 1630-1750),
pp. 1-72 and 73-168, respectively. Mus.
exs. Ed. by Anthony Lewis and Nigel Fortune.
London: Oxford University Press, 1975. ISBN
0-19-316305-5.

Part one includes brief discussions of A.
Scarlatti's operas (pp. 54-63) and of comic
opera (pp. 64-72). In the latter, Scarlatti's
scene buffe from *Il pastor di Corinto* and *L'Eraclea* are
commented upon. Part two includes commentary
on the various *Griselda* operas (including those
of Giovanni and Antonio Bononcini) and on the
librettist Zeno. Author believes Scarlatti's
"main contribution [to *opera seria*] was towards
the expansion of aria form and the more active
participation of a concertante orchestra in

the arias." A good overview of Scarlatti's contributions to the genre.

231. _____. *Die Venezianische Oper in der zweiten Hälfte des 17. Jahrhunderts; ein Beitrag zur Geschichte der Musik und des Theaters im Zeitalter des Barock*. Berlin, 1937. Reprint with new introduction by the author: Bologna: Arnoldo Forni, [1975] (Bibliotheca musica Bononiensis, Sez. 3, N. 48).

The pioneering study on Venetian opera by this author. Divides the librettos of Venetian operas into 3 basic categories: heroic, heroic-comic, and comic.

232. Worsthorne, Simon Towneley . *Venetian Opera in the Seventeenth Century*. London: Oxford University Press, 1968. Reprint, N.Y.: Da Capo, 1984. Apps., plates, bibl., and suppl. bibl. (Sept. 1968), index to mus. exs., general index. xii and 194 pp. ISBN 0-306-76227-7.

An excellent modern history of *seicento* opera in Venice. Chapter 9 is a useful examination of "The Place of Opera in the Modern Aesthetics of the Seventeenth Century."

*   Zanetti, Emilia and Claudio Sartori. "Contributo a un catalogo delle opere teatrali di Alessandro Scarlatti...." Cited as item 438.

233. Zanetti, Roberto. "Il teatro; Alessandro Scarlatti." In *La musica italiana nel settecento* (item 61), Vol. 1, pp. 65-129.

An excellent recent history and discussion of Scarlatti's theater works. Lengthy bibliographic notes of special value. Author regards Scarlatti as a key link between the seventeenth-century Italian Baroque style and the more cosmopolitan eighteenth-century style of the Viennese composers.

Studies of Specific Operas

L'Arione pasticcio

234. Sartori, Claudio. *"Dori* e *Arione,* due opere
     ignorate di Alessandro Scarlatti." *Note
     d'archivio per la storia musicale* 18 (1941): 35-42.

     Locates and describes 2 copies of the
     libretto of *La Dori* (Biblioteca Universitaria,
     Bologna, and Biblioteca del Conservatorio di
     Musica S. Pietro a Maiella, Naples) and two
     MSS with arias (Modena : "Per bocca del core"
     and "Non lasciarmi spera mia gradita" and
     Conservatorio   di   Musica...,   Naples:
     "Parisatide adorata").   Libretto by Apollonio
     Apolloni; 1st performed at Naples, Palazzo
     Reale, Teatro S. Bartolomeo, Jan. 18, 1689.
     Also describes MS including aria "Mio povere
     core" by Scarlatti, the only aria of Glauco,
     from the dramma *L'Arione* (Act 1 Scene 9) with
     libretto by Oreste d'Arles and arias by 27
     composers (1st performance 1694).

     Arminio. See Strohm, item 437.

La caduta de' Decemviri

235. Williams, Hermine Weigel.   "Introduction."   In
     Alessandro Scarlatti's *La caduta de' Decemviri,*
     pp. 1-23 (see Section V, 1).   Mus. ex.,
     figs. (facs. reproductions of pages from
     various MSS), pp. 24-25.

     Discusses the history of Livy's text and
     Stampiglia's   libretto,   compares   their
     treatments of the story, and summarizes the
     opera's plot.   Describes the libretto and
     surviving MSS sources, provides a brief
     performance history and discussion of
     Scarlatti's   style,   discusses   editorial
     procedures, and presents a very instructive
     look at performance practice as it relates to
     this work.

Il Ciro

236. Jones, Gaynor G.   "Alessandro Scarlatti's *Il
     Ciro.*"   *Hamburger Jahrbuch für Musikwissenschaft* 3
     (1978): 225-237   (Studien zur Barockoper)
     Ed. by H. Marx. Trans. by Magda Marx-Weber.
     Hamburg, 1978.

     Discusses   history   of   eighteenth-century
     librettos based on Cyrus themes including A.
     Scarlatti's *Il Ciro*. Calls attention to errors
     perpetuated in reference sources (e.g., that
     Pariati   was   the   author   of   the   text   for
     Scarlatti's   setting,   which   both   the   *MGG*
     "Werkverzeichnis"   (item   14)   and   Rostirolla's
     Catalogo   (item   435)   state   incorrectly.
     Discusses performance history and research
     problems.   Gives   biographical   data   on
     performers cited in libretto in the British
     Library, London.

Clotilda pasticcio

*   Lincoln, Stoddard. "J.E. Galliard and *A Critical
    Discourse.*" Cited as item 258.

Comodo Antonino

237. Rose, Gloria.   "Two Operas by Scarlatti
     Recovered." *Musical Quarterly* 58 (1972): 420-
     435.

     Describes a MS discovered in the Thibault
     collection (now located, F: Pn) containing
     arias and duets from Scarlatti's *Comodo Antonino*
     with libretto by Francesco Maria Paglia first
     performed in 1696 in Naples and another MS
     (anonymous) identified as *Fidalba e Oreste* (not in
     NGIBM worklist) probably by the composer (4
     arias definitely by Scarlatti) first performed
     in Rome in or before 1683.   Interesting not
     only for the rediscovery of parts of these
     works but also for the discussion of the
     problems inherent in trying to identify operas
     by Scarlatti among the anonymous opera scores

of the late seventeenth century and early
eighteenth century and arias by Scarlatti in
MS collections. Useful for account of the
author's methods in tracking down MSS,
references, etc., in the attempt to determine
authorship.

Il Dafni

238. Roberts, John H. "Introduction." In
    Alessandro Scarlatti's *Dafni*, pp. vii-xi (see
    Section V, 1) and cast of characters and
    synopsis, pp. xiii-xv.

    Provides information on the background and
    sources; cites Handel's borrowings from the
    opera.

239. Sartori, Claudio. "*Il Dafni* di Alessandro
    Scarlatti." *Rivista musicale italiana* 45 (1941):
    176-183.

    Examination and discussion of 3 Dafni
    librettos set by the composer (1700 Naples,
    1701 Piacenza, 1715 Jesi) with performance
    dates and places, library locations, and
    mention of two others (1709, Genoa, and one at
    Bologna). Notes the changes and similarities
    in the texts.

La Dori. See *L'Arione.*

Gli equivoci nel sembiante

240. D' Accone, Frank A. *The History of a Baroque
    Opera; Alessandro Scarlatti's "Gli equivoci nel sembiante."*
    N.Y.: Pendragon Press, 1985 (Monographs in
    Musicology, 3) ISBN 0-918728-21-5.

    D'Accone edited the score for the Harvard
    University Press series (see Section V, 1).
    The present volume gives even greater detail
    about the opera and its history and place in

the culture of its day. A performance of the opera at University of California, Los Angeles led the author to the idea of writing a performance history of the opera. 6 tables give lists of arias by type of formal structure, a chronological list of librettos (with dates and locations in archives), and a list of extant scores in MS.

241. _____. "Introduction." In Alessandro Scarlatti's *Gli equivoci nel sembiante*, pp. 1-27 (see Section V, 1).

Includes performance history and description of sources (MS and librettos), editorial procedure, and performance practice. Plot synopsis.

L'Eraclea

242. Grout, Donald Jay. "Introduction." In Alessandro Scarlatti's *Eraclea*), pp. 1-15 (see Section V, 1). Mus. exs.

Describes story, sources, editorial procedure, performance practice (ornamentation, instruments, dynamics and tempo, rhythm).

243. _____. "Opera Seria at the Crossroads: Scarlatti's *Eraclea*." In *Studia musicologica, aesthetica, theoretica, historica* [*Lissa Festschrift*], pp. 223-232. Ed. by Elzbieta Dziebowska. Cracow: Wyd. Muz., 1979.

Study of the musical and theatrical characteristics of this transitional work. Author maintains that 1700 was a dividing point in the history of Italian opera and comments that *Eraclea* characteristically looks both to the past and to the future.

The Faithful Princess. See *La Principessa fedele*

La fede riconosciuta

244. Dent, Edward J.   "A Pastoral Opera by
     Alessandro Scarlatti."   *Music Review* 12
     (1951): 7-14.

     Confirms that the Fitzwilliam Museum MS
     bound with the Ottoboni coat of arms but
     lacking a title page or composer's name is, in
     fact, by Alessandro Scarlatti and dates from
     Sept. 1710. The author matches it with the
     libretto discovered by Lorenz in the
     Biblioteca Marcelliana, Florence (which gives
     the title) extracts of which are included in
     Lorenz's *Alessandro Scarlattis Jugendoper* (item 205).
     Music of the MS in Scarlatti's hand.   Some
     interesting comments and suggestions regarding
     performance practice.

245. _____.   "*La fede riconosciuta* di A. Scarlatti."
     Rivista musicale italiana 54 (1952): 54-60.

     An Italian translation of item 244.

Fidalba e Oreste   See under *Comodo Antonino*

La Griselda

246. Grout, Donald J. (and Elizabeth B. Hughes,
     Assoc. ed.). "Introduction." In Alessandro
     Scarlatti's *Griselda*, pp. 1-11 (see Section V,
     1). Mus. exs., illus.

     Discusses Griselda as a character in early
     literature and opera, Scarlatti's *Griselda* and
     its sources as well as editorial principles
     and performance practice (instruments, rhythm,
     recitative, embellishments).

247. _____.   "The Original Version of Alessandro
     Scarlatti's *Griselda*."   In *Essays on Opera and
     English Music in Honour of Sir Jack Westrup*, pp. 103-
     114. Oxford: Oxford University Press, 1975.

Discussion of the changes made by Scarlatti
(in his own hand) in MS score BM Add. MS14168
the title page of which contains two dates
suggesting two separate performances; the
earlier is not recorded elsewhere. Changes in
eighteenth-century Italian operas
characteristically occurred when an opera was
revived or performed in another location with
different performers; these instances
generally implied changes in characters, plot,
etc. The changes in *Griselda* were made by the
composer possibly before any public
performance or following a preliminary
performance and before the official premiere.
No changes in plot, etc. Unusual in that
changes were made in the same MS rather than
in additional MSS.

248. _____. "*La Griselda* di Zeno e il libretto
dell'opera di Scarlatti." *Nuova rivista musicale
italiana* 2 (1968): 207-225.

Examination of Griselda characters in the
history of literature (from Chaucer to
Boccaccio, Petrarch, da Bergamo) and the
origin of Scarlatti's libretto. Comparison of
the text with Zeno's in relation to the
opera's structure.

249. Junker, Hermann. " Zwei *Griselda*-Opern." In
Festschrift zum 50. Geburtstag Adolf Sandberger, pp. 51-
64. Munich: Hof-Musik-Verlag von Ferdinand
Zierfuss, 1918. vi and 295 pp. Mus. ex.

Discussion of Scarlatti's settings of the
Griselda texts by Apostolo Zeno (Rome 1721)
and Pietro Torri (1723).

250. Mioli, Piero. "*Non più reggina, ma pastorella.* Sulla
drammaturgia vocale medio e tardo-barocca
nella *Griselda*, da Scarlatti a Vivaldi." In
*Nuovi studi Vivaldiani; edizione e cronologia critica delle
opere*, pp. 83-116. Ed. by Antonio Fanna and
Giovanni Morelli (Studi di musica veneta.

Quaderni Vivaldiani, 4)   Florence: Leo S.
Olschki, 1988. ISBN 88 222 3625 4. Notes,
mus. exs., tables.

Includes   a   detailed   comparison   of
Scarlatti's and Vivaldi's treatments of the
Griselda story, the first, based on a libretto
by   an   anonymous   "author,"   the   second,   by
Goldoni (both after Zeno); an examination of
the   number   of   arias,   duets,   etc.; and   of
singers' genders and voice types; the number
of   acts,   scenes,   and   personages;   the   aria
texts;   tessitura,   accompaniment,   etc.   5
comparative tables.

*   Strohm, Reinhard. "Hasse, Scarlatti, Rolli."
    Cited as item 117.

*   _____. *Die italienische Oper im 18. Jahrhundert*. Cited
    as item 220.

251. Trowell, Brian. "Scarlatti and *Griselda*."
    Musical Times 109 (1968): 527-529.

Discussion of autograph MS, Griselda story
in literature and music, performance practices
revealed   in   the   MS   and   Scarlatti's   style.
Author produced studio recording of the work
for the BBC Third Programme broadcast June 8,
1968.   Performance   score   was   edited   by   Alec
Harman.

*   Winternitz, Emanuel. *Musical Autographs*. Cited as
    item 24.

Gli inganni felici

252. Zanetti, Emilia. *Gl'inganni felici* in una
    sconosciuta raccolta d'arte [sic?] [arie] di
    Alessandro Scarlatti." *Rassegna musicale* 14
    (1941): 416-430.

Detailed discussion of a MS in three parts bound together discovered in the Biblioteca del Conservatorio di Musica S. Pietro a Maiella, Naples; the third part contains 34 arias from A. Scarlatti's opera (1699) previously thought to be lost (except for its comic scenes). Also examined are the contents of the other 2 MS parts which contain arias from *Gerone tiranno di Siracusa* and *Teodora Augusta*, as well as a few unidentified sources. Author compares the librettos and performances; concludes that *Gl'inganni felici* shows a breakaway from seventeenth-century style and a move toward a simpler, more fluid language characteristic of Scarlatti's mature style.

Marco Attilio Regolo

253. Godwin, Joscelyn. "Introduction." In Alessandro Scarlatti's *Marco Attilio Regolo*, pp. 1-19 (see Section V, 1).

Discusses background, story, sources, editorial procedure, and performance practice (rhythm, orchestra, disposition of voice parts, performance of recitatives, ornamentation).

Massimo Puppieno

254. Slim, H. Colin. "Introduction." In Alessandro Scarlatti's *Massimo Puppieno*, pp. 1-16 (see Section V, 1).

Examines story, sources, productions, performance practice (rhythm, dynamics and tempo, orchestra, continuo, ritornellos, recitatives, ornamentation), editorial procedure, and translation.

Il Mitridate Eupatore

*   Collins, Michael.   "L'orchestra nelle opere teatrali di Vivaldi." Cited as item 179.

255. Sartori, Claudio. "Un' Arianna misconosciuta:
La Laodice di Alessandro Scarlatti." *La Scala*
79 (June 1956): 41-45, 83-84. Fr., Eng.,
Ger. summaries, pp. 83-84.

Discusses the possible reasons Mitridate was
rejected by the Venetian public. Criticizes
Giuseppe Piccioli's edition and the Piccola
Scala (for not asking Piccioli to prepare a
new edition more faithful to the original text
for use in its performance).

* Strohm, Reinhard. *Die italienische Oper im 18.*
Jahrhundert. Cited as item 220.

256. Westrup, Jack Allan. "Alessandro Scarlatti's
Il Mitridate Eupatore(1707)." In *New Looks at Italian*
Opera: Essays in Honor of Donald Jay Grout, pp. 133-
150. Ed. by William W. Austin. Ithaca:
Cornell University Press, 1968.

Study of *Mitridate* based on a careful
examination of Paris Conservatory MS 22410 now
in the Bibliotheque Nationale, Paris.
Discusses Scarlatti's use of instruments and
instrumental style, his harmony,
interpretation of the work, etc. Points out
the errors and other problems with the
incomplete and altered edition by Giuseppe
Piccioli ("Ricostruzione scenica e
strumentale." Milan: Curci, 1953).

Il Pirro e Demetrio

* Galliard, John Ernest. *A Critical Discourse.* See
item 258. See also item 54.

257. Leppert, Richard. "Imagery, Musical
Confrontation and Cultural Difference in
Early 18th-century London." *Early Music* 14
(1986): 323-333, 335-338, 341-342, 345.
Notes, plates.

A close look at a series of 8 paintings by Marco Ricci, a Venetian stage painter active in London between c1709 and 1716, that seem to depict a formal rehearsal of Scarlatti's *Pirro e Demetrio*. Examines their relationship to the controversy over Italian opera represented by the two opposing political factions (Tories and Whigs). A detailed appendix discusses Ricci's scenery for London opera (including *Pirro*); the singers thought to have participated in the opera; the singers' pay and pay disputes; the Queen's Theatre, Haymarket; and opposition to Italian opera. Extensive detailed footnotes.

258. Lincoln, Stoddard. "J. E. Galliard and *A Critical Discourse* (includes transcription....)" *Musical Quarterly* 53 (1967): 347-364.

Discusses and transcribes the anonymous *A Critical Discourse on Operas and Music in England* appended to a translation of Raguenet's *Parallele...* which was published in London in 1709. Probable translator of the *Parallele...* and author of the *Discourse* is John Ernest Galliard (translator of Tosi's *Observations on the Florid Song*, London, 1742). Pages 359-361 include comments on the performance of *Pirro* at Haymarket Dec. 14, 1708, sung in Italian and in English with airs from Scarlatti's *La Rosaura* and airs by Haym (the director). Comments that the recitative much better than in operas previously performed. Airs praised as being beautiful but too long. Flaws blamed on the librettist rather than Scarlatti in most cases. The pasticcio *Clotilda* is referred to (p. 361) as having "several good airs by... Alessandro Scarlatti...[and others]." It was performed at Haymarket Mar. 2, 1709.

259. Lindgren, Lowell. "The Accomplishments of the Learned and Ingenious Nicola Haym (1678-1729)." *Studi musicali* 16 (1987): 247-380.

Based on a paper given at the international conference on "Haendel e gli Scarlatti a Roma" in June 1985 but not published with the other

papers (see item 38, Book II). Pages 265-269
discuss details pertinent to the performance
of Haym's adaptation of Scarlatti's *Pirro* for
the London stage under the title *Phyrrus and
Demetrius*.

Il Pompeo

260. Roberts, John H. "Introduction." In
     Alessandro Scarlatti's *Il Pompeo*, ix-xii (see
     Section V, 1). Cast of characters and
     synopsis, xiii-xvi.

     Gives background on *Il Pompeo* and cites
     Handel's borrowings from it.

La principessa fedele

261. Grout, Donald J. "Introduction." In
     Alessandro Scarlatti's *The Faithful Princess*, pp.
     1-8 (see Section V, 1).

     Includes description of story, sources,
     edition, music, and performance practice.

Scipione nelle Spagne

262. Confalonieri, Giulio. "Nota su *Varrone e Perricca*
     di Alessandro Scarlatti." *Immagini esotiche nella
     musica italiana. Chigiana* 14 (1957): 39-49.

     A discussion of Scarlatti's use of comic
     intermezzi between the acts of his *opere serie*
     and, specifically, *Varrone e Perricca* or *La dama
     spagnola ed il cavaliere romano (The Spanish Lady and the Roman
     Cavalier)*, four scenes performed between the
     three acts of *Scipione nelle Spagne*. Detailed
     examination of the plot, characters, and
     relationship to the main opera
     seria. Information on the manuscript which served as
     the basis for the edition used in the Siena
     performance (the first in modern times). No
     description of staging.

263. Helm, Everett. "Scarlatti and Dali (Scenes Adjusted by G. Confalonieri to Form Comic Opera *The Spanish Lady and the Roman Cavalier*." *Musical America* 81: (Oct. 1961): 22-23.

Review of the first performance in modern times of comic scenes (*The Spanish Lady and the Roman Cavalier*) that alternated between serious scenes of Scarlatti's *Scipione nelle Spagne*. Text and edition by Giulio Confalonieri. Surrealist painter Salvador Dali designed some scenes and appeared on stage. No real action; subject: wooing and winning of lady. Between love scenes, surrealistic fantasies, pictures of Dali and his work, etc. Produced by American Alvox Corporation, head Lorenzo Alvary, (Met basso) with the idea of combining the old and the new and creating a synthesis of the arts in a way never done before. Singers: Lorenzo Alvary and Fiorenza Cossotto with accompaniment by Complesso Strumentale Italiano conducted by Antal Dorati (all in eighteenth-century costume).

La Statira

264. Boyd, Malcolm. "Scarlatti's *La Statira*." *Musical Times* 111 (1970): 495-497. Mus. exs.

Discussion of the plot, music, and history of the opera which represented the earliest example of a collaboration between cardinal (Ottoboni) and composer (Scarlatti). First performed at the Tordinona, Jan. 5, 1690. Short but informative introduction to the work (first performed in England May 7, 1970, as part of the Camden Festival).

265. Holmes, William. "Introduction." In Alessandro Scarlatti's *La Statira*, pp. 1-18 (see Section V, 1)

Includes discussion of the librettist, Cardinal Pietro Ottoboni and the performance

of the opera (which both inaugurated the Roman
Carnival season in 1690 and marked the
reopening of the Tordinona theater).
Considers Statira as a character in history
and dramatic literature and comments on the
sources of the music and librettos, editorial
procedures, and performance concerns (the
orchestra, ornamentation in recitatives and
arias, and over-dotting). Gives synopsis of
the plot.

266. _____. *"La Statira" by Pietro Ottoboni and Alessandro
Scarlatti: The Textual Sources with a Documentary Postscript*.
N.Y.: Pendragon, 1983   (Monographs in
Musicology, 2)   92 pp. ISBN 0-918728-18-5.
Review in *Music and Letters* 66 (1985): 165-166
and *Musical Times* 125 (1984): 152.

Complements author's edition of the score in
the Harvard University Press series (see
Section V, 1). Detailed examination of
sources and their differences. Especially
interesting work because the autograph
libretto which survives is also a working copy
with corrections, eliminations, and insertions
made during the rehearsals of the opera by
Ottoboni in his role as stage director.
Scholarly, entertaining, and useful study
which illuminates the social and political
context of the opera's production in Rome and
reasons for Ottoboni's textual changes.

Telemaco

267. Brown, Howard Mayer. "Preface." In
Alessandro Scarlatti's *Telemaco*, [v-vi] (see
Section V, 1). "Synopsis" on [vii-viii].
Notes   (Italian Opera 1640- 1770, 23)
N.Y.: Garland Publishing, 1978. ISBN 0-
8240-2622-5.

A very brief yet useful introduction to the
work, its background, sources, etc.

*   _____, ed. *Telemaco* (facsimile of the
libretto). Cited in item 198.

Il Tigrane

268. Collins, Michael.   "Introduction."   In
     Alessandro Scarlatti's *Tigrane*, pp. 1-26 (see
     Section V, 1).

     Discusses   the   plot   and   its   origins;
     instrumental   numbers   and   accompaniments   and
     Scarlatti's use of the chorus; arias; libretto
     and   score   sources;   editorial   procedure;   and
     performance   practice   (including   vocal,
     continuo, and instrumental practice).   A plot
     synopsis is given on pp. 23-26. Page 28 gives
     the cast of characters and describes changes
     of scene.   Pages 14-15 include excerpts (in
     Collins'   translation)   from   Scarlatti's
     treatise   on   accompaniment: *Per   sonare   il
     cembalo...1715*,   specifically,   the   section   *Per
     accompagnare il cembalo, ò organo, ò altro strumento*.

269. _____.   "An Introduction to Alessandro
     Scarlatti's *Tigrane*."   In *Essays on Music for Charles
     Warren Fox*, pp. 82-102.   Ed. by Jerald C.
     Graue.   Rochester: Eastman School of Music
     Press, 1979.

     Detailed   examination   of   plot   and
     literary/historical origins.   Discusses four
     surviving MS scores derived from the Naples
     performance of 1715 and three librettos, two
     of   which   were   printed   for   subsequent
     performances in Innsbruck (1715) and Livorno
     (1716) and which differ considerably from each
     other.   Appendix outlines the singing career
     of   Nicola   Grimaldi   (the   famous   Nicolino)
     citing 1st performances primarily; arranged
     chronologically and by title of opera.   Covers
     period 1685-1730. For Collins' score edition,
     see Section V, 1.

270. Pauly, Reinhard G. "Alessandro Scarlatti's
     Tigrane."   *Music and Letters* 35 (1954): 339-
     346.

     Description of the score in the Biblioteca

del Conservatorio di Musica S. Pietro a
Maiella, Naples. Detailed directions for
staging and acting (rare in scores).
Librettist's dedication cites it as
Scarlatti's 106th stage work. Although
libretto gives the role of Tigrane to Nicola
Grimaldi (a bass) the part is written
partially in soprano clef. Score and libretto
correspond closely. Author speculates the
score is from a later performance with a
castrato, possibly Antonio Archi (Cortoncino).

Il trionfo dell'onore

* Hucke, Helmuth. "Alessandro Scarlatti und die
  Musikkomödie." Cited as item 196.

271. Mortari, Virgilio. "Considerazioni sul *Trionfo
     dell'onore* di Alessandro Scarlatti." In *Gli
     Scarlatti* (item 35), pp. 15-19.

     Comments on the opera and the author's
     "riduzione scenica" and "trascrizione" (see
     Section V, 1) used in the performance given as
     part of the Scarlatti week, Sept. 18, 1940, at
     the Teatro dell R. Accademia dei Rozzi, Siena.

* [*Una villa di Toscolo*]

* Lionnet, Jean. "A Newly Found Opera by
  Alessandro Scarlatti." Cited as item 204.

Oratorios: History

272. Alaleona, Domenico. *Studi sulla storia dell'oratorio
     musicale in Italia*. Turin: Fratelli Bocca
     Editore, 1908. xii and 452 pp. Reprint with
     different pagination: *Storia dell'oratorio musicale
     in Italia*. Milan: Fratelli Bocca, 1945.

     A history of the oratorio in Italy which
     pays special attention to its origins.
     Appendix cites documents from the archives of

the Arciconfraternita del S.S. Crocifisso
including one dated Jan 27, 1679, which refers
to the commission of a Latin oratorio from "il
Scarlattino alias il Siciliano." Volume
contains texts of various oratorios, dramatic
narratives, and dialogues.

273. Bianchi, Lino. *Carissimi, Stradella, Scarlatti e l'oratorio musicale*. Rome: De Santis, 1969.

Written by the editor of the collected
oratorios of Scarlatti (see Section V, 1),
this volume contributes little to our
understanding of the oratorios due to its lack
of musical examples and other scholarly
apparatus and its florid prose. Review by
Gloria Rose in *JAMS* 24 (1971): 485-486.

274. _____. "Dall'oratorio di Alessandro
Scarlatti all'oratorio di Händel." In *Händel e gli Scarlatti a Roma* (item 38 in Book II), pp. 79-92.

Notes that the beginning and ending dates of
Händel's Italian journey coincide with two
important events in the history of the
oratorio: the publication of Arcangelo
Spagna's *Oratorii...* (1706), which includes the
first history of the oratorio and the Roman
Oratorio del Crocifisso's decision (1710) to
stop performing Latin oratorios (a policy not
altered until 1725). It was a period of great
activity and achievement in oratorio
composition marked by major contributions by
Scarlatti (whose works dating from 1708 are
discussed) and his contemporaries, and by the
emergence of Händel's own special style
influenced by the Italian heritage.

275. _____. "L'oratorio vertice Scarlattiano"
and "Due capolavori." In Roberto Pagano, et
al. *Alessandro Scarlatti* (item 16), pp. 255-315.
Bibl.

These two chapters form the second section
of the book by Pagano et al. They give a
general survey of Scarlatti's oratorios and
describe nine in greater detail. A good
introduction which, however, discusses the
librettos more than the music.

276. Bland, Leland Dye. "The Instrumental
     Ritornello in Selected Vocal Works of
     Italian Composers ca. 1670 to 1710." Ph.D.
     dissertation. University of Iowa, 1973.
     425 pp. UMI order #73-30,900.

Chapter 4 examines the instrumental
ritornellos in works by Steffani, Pallavicino,
Caldara, and Alessandro Scarlatti among
others. Analysed according to three criteria:
the periodic return of material between vocal
sections, the integration of solo and
instrumental parts, and the key structure.
Includes analysis of examples from Scarlatti's
Agar et Ismaele esiliati, *La Giuditta* (both versions),
Cain, overo Il primo ommicidio, and *Davidis pugna et victoria*.

277. Boyd, Malcolm. "Baroque Oratorio: A
     Terminological Inexatitude?" *Musical Times* 119
     (1978): 507-508.

Review of Howard E. Smither's *History of the
Oratorio* in which Boyd praises the author's
definition of oratorio and his correction of
certain errors of the past and calls the study
"one of the most important contributions to
musicology of the decade." For challenge to
Smither's view that the oratorio was unstaged
see letters by Winton Dean: *Musical Times* 119
(1978): 653 and 668 and Victor Crowther 119
(1978): 838. See also Boyd's response in the
same journal: 119 (1978): 821 and 838 which
includes a reference to the performance of
Scarlatti's *Oratorio per la Passione*.

278. Cafiero, Rosa, and Marina Marino. "Materiali
     per una definizione de <oratorio> a Napoli

nel seicento: primi accertamenti." In *La
musica a Napoli durante il seicento* (item 77), pp. 465-
510. Notes, 2 apps.: pp. 477-510.

Mentions Scarlatti's oratorios written in
1685 and following at Naples, and identifies
them as representative of an advanced phase of
the form in which one can no longer isolate
local characteristics since the Roman models
have become so imbued into the style of the
composer.

279. Lanfranchi, Ariella and Enrico Careri. "Le
cantate per la natività della B.V.; un
secolo di musiche al Collegio Nazareno di
Roma (1681-1784)." In *Händel e gli Scarlatti a Roma*
(item 38 in Book II), pp. 297-347.

A detailed history of the musical activities
of the C.N., which, because it is the sole
Collegio still active, provides the
possibility of retracing in house the
documents and testimonies of its musical past.
Includes remarks on the oratorio *Humanità e
Lucifero* (performed in 1704, 1719, and 1725)
attributed to Pietro Scarlatti on the
frontispiece of the MS of the score at S.
Pantaleo but to Alessandro in most other
sources. The authors defend Alessandro's
authorship and present their reasons for this
belief (see p. 329, n. 7).

280. Liess, Andreas. "Materialien zur römischen
Musikgeschichte des Seicento: Musikerlisten
des Oratorio San Marcello 1664-1725." *Acta
musicologica* 29 (1957): 137-171.

Pp. 142-171: chronological list of musicians
in the service of the Oratorio San Marcello
from Fondo San Marcello, including A.
Scarlatti.

281. _____. "Die Sammlung der Oratorienlibretti
(1679-1725) und der restliche Musikbestand

des Fondo San Marcello der Biblioteca
Vaticana in Rom." *Acta musicologica* 31 (1959):
63-80.

List of librettos Alaleona cited which no
longer exist and (pp. 65-78) list of librettos
in the Fondo San Marcello (chronological by
publication date). Gives title, text, author,
composer, performance date, place of
publication ,date, and publisher. Pages 78-80
reference each item to Robert Eitner's
Biographisch-bibliographisches Quellen-Lexikon (item 447).

282. Morelli, Arnaldo. "Alessandro Scarlatti
     maestro di cappella in Roma ed alcuni suoi
     oratori; nuovi documenti." *Note d'archivio* n.s.
     2 (1984): 117-144. Illus., docs., notes.

Part one reveals new details regarding
Scarlatti's activities as maestro di cappella
at 4 Roman churches between 1678 and 1708
(including his involvement as a composer and
participant in the performance of oratorios).
Study based on documents in several Roman
archives (IRas, IRf, IRli, IRn, IRvat). Part
two restores to Pietro Ottoboni (rather than
B. Pamphili) the authorship of the libretto of
the first (Naples) *Giuditta* (see items 23, 94,
and 436, which support Morelli's argument),
and identifies Pietro as the librettist of
Scarlatti's *Cantata per l'Assunzione della Beatissima vergine*
as well. On pp. 136-144 the author quotes
extensive excerpts from the documents
consulted; p. 144 is a facsimile page of the
Ottoboni autograph libretto.

283. Pasquetti, Guido. *L'oratorio musicale in Italia*.
     Florence: Successori Le Monnier, 1906.
     xxiii and 505 pp. 2nd ed., 1914.

Account of the social and religious
background of the oratorio in Italy still
fundamentally sound. Oratorio as a literary
form examined.

284. Poultney, David George. "Alessandro Scarlatti and the Transformation of the Oratorio." *Musical Quarterly* 59 (1973): 584-601.

Summarizes the conclusions of the author's dissertation. Discussion of the transformation from the early, more text-dominated oratorio with basso continuo accompaniment to music-dominated type with instrumental accompaniment performed as concert bearing little relationship to devotion. Contains an interesting description of a typical oratorio performance in 1715 at the palace of Prince Ruspoli taken from a travel diary (translated by the author) by a German named Uffenbach. Detailed examination of *Il trionfo della gratia* (1685) illustrating the nature of Scarlatti's early texts and settings.

285. _____. "The Oratorios of Alessandro Scarlatti: Their Lineage, Milieu, and Style." Ph.D. dissertation. University of Michigan, 1968. 248 pp. UMI order #69-12,213.

In 1976 Howard Smither called this the only detailed study of Alessandro Scarlatti's oratorios; not cited by Lino Bianchi or Giancarlo Rostirolla in items 275 and 435). The first three chapters summarize information in secondary sources on the history of the oratorio to 1725. The last three, the major part of the study, examine 26 of the 40 surviving oratorios by Scarlatti with discussions of the texts, music, patrons and performances; arias; and recitatives, choruses, and instrumental numbers.

286. Schering, Arnold. *Geschichte des Oratoriums*. Leipzig: Breitkopf & Härtel, 1911. Reprint: Hildesheim: Georg Olms, 1966. 647 pp. and Anhang (texts and mus. exs.).

Provides a general acquaintance with the

history of Italian oratorio. Place index; name
and subject index.

287. _____. "Neue Beiträge zur Geschichte des
italienischen Oratoriums im 17. Jahrhundert."
Sammelbände der internationalen Musikgesellschaft 8
(1907): 49-70.

Prints two treatises of 1706 by Arcangelo
Spagna (Ottoboni's theorist and librettist) on
the oratorio. Not seen.

288. Smither, Howard E. "The Baroque Oratorio; a
Report on Research since 1945." *Acta
musicologica* 48 (1976): 50-76.

A major review article which discusses all
the relevant literature on oratorio (defined
as a work with poetic text that is sacred,
dramatic, and original, i.e., without
substantial Biblical quotations, set to music
in a style resembling opera but without
staging or action). This was, according to
the author, the dominant definition in the
Baroque era (exceptions, of course, existed).
Discussion of writings on the subject newly
published, reprinted, or in progress since
1945.

289. _____. *A History of the Oratorio. Volume 1: The Oratorio
in the Baroque Era: Italy, Vienna, Paris*. Chapel Hill:
University of North Carolina Press, 1977.
480 pp. ISBN 0-8078-1274-9 (v.1).

Besides being the first comprehensive
history of the oratorio in the English
language, Smither's three-volume *History* is a
musicological milestone comparable in its
field to William Newman's *A History of the Sonata
Idea*. It includes discussions of Alessandro
Scarlatti's oratorios (especially pp. 335-
342), which should help students perplexed by
the generalities in item 273 understand better
the composer's contribution to the genre.

Reviews in *Musical Quarterly* 64 (1978): 397-402;
Musical Times 119 (1978): 507-508; *Music Library
Association. Notes* 34 (1978): 855-857.

290. Staffieri, Gloria. "L'oratorio musicale a Roma
(1683-1713): documenti, aspetti e problemi."
Doctoral dissertation. Università degli
Studi di Roma, 1985-1986.

Not seen.

291. Wolff, Hellmuth Christian. "Church Music and
Oratorio in Italy... Italian Oratorio and
Passion." In the *New Oxford History of Music*, Vol.
5, pp. 324-350.

Good historical overview of the Italian
oratorio during the period 1630-1750. Pp.
334-337 discuss Scarlatti's oratorios
(including the *Johannespassion*). Bibl.: pp. 798-
800.

292. Zanetti, Roberto. "L'oratorio." In *La musica
italiana nel settecento* (item 61), Vol. 2, pp. 665-
786.

Pages 665-695 discuss in some detail
Scarlatti's oratorios, pp. 695-717, the
oratorios of Scarlatti's contemporaries.
Musical examples cited but the emphasis is on
description of Scarlatti's style and his
depiction of the characters' changing
emotions. Notes give much additional detail,
e.g., n674 quotes Debussy's remarks from
Monsieur Croche (Paris, 1921; It. trans. by L.
Cortese, Milan, 1945) on Scarlatti and his
Johannespassion.

Studies of Specific Oratorios

Abraham. See *Agar et Ismaele esiliati*

Agar et Ismaele esiliati

293. Bianchi, Lino. "Preface." In Alessandro
     Scarlatti's *Agar et Ismaele esiliati*, pp. v-vii with
     2 unpaged facs. pages and pp. ix-xv: list of
     characters and text. Suppl. English trans.
     of preface paged separately, pp. i-v. See
     Section V, 1.

     Discusses MS source (A-Wn) and editorial
     procedures. Reveals that some differences in
     text exist between the libretto for the 1697
     performance in Florence and the text in the
     score (from the Roman performance, 1683).

294. Garbelotto, Antonio. "Alessandro Scarlatti."
     Archivio storico siciliano 3rd ser. 10 (1959): 239-
     248.

     Discussion of Giuseppe de Todis' libretto
     for *Abraham* (as *Agar* was titled for the Palermo
     performance of 1694) set to music by A.
     Scarlatti; from a talk prepared on the
     occasion of the 300th anniversary of the
     composer's birth. Garbelotto believed *Abraham*
     to be a different work from *Agar*, although he
     was aware that the two (as well as *L'Ismaele
     soccorso*, as *Agar* was titled in the 1697
     Florentine performance) shared the same
     subject.

Cain overro il primo omicidio

295. Bianchi, Lino. "Preface." In Alessandro
     Scarlatti's *Il primo omicidio*, pp. v-ix with
     notes pp. x-xi and 2 unpaged facs. Suppl.
     English trans. of preface paged separately,
     pp. i-ix (includes notes). See Section V, 1.

     Gives a history of the autograph manuscript
     (San Francisco State University, De Bellis
     Collection) and compares it with the surviving
     Venetian and Roman librettos. Points out
     differences between the libretto and Scarlat-
     ti's setting. Edition includes transcription

of the Venetian libretto.

296. Fabbri, Mario. "Torna alla luce la partitura
     autografia dell'oratorio *Il primo omicidio* di
     Alessandro Scarlatti." *Chigiana* 23 [n.s. 3]
     (1966): 245-264.

     Study of the autograph score of the oratorio
     discovered by the author in the Frank V. de
     Bellis collection (now housed at San Francisco
     State University, California). Compares the
     text of the Venetian libretto (Biblioteca
     Vittorio Emanuele, Rome MS 35.4.D.4.43) with
     the text of the score and finds that they
     coincide almost exactly. Scarlatti did cancel
     some parts of the text (examples are cited).
     Fabbri did not believe that Ottoboni was the
     librettist, however, see item 101. Attributes
     the apparent differences in date between the
     libretto and the score to the differences in
     the Roman and Venetian calendars. Discussion
     of Scarlatti's musical setting and use of
     instrumentation to emphasize the various
     sentiments expressed in the text. This score
     is the only dated document known from
     Scarlatti's trip to Venice.

297. Rolandi, Ulderico. *"Il Cain*, sconosciuto
     oratorio di Alessandro Scarlatti." *Note
     d'archivio per la storia musicale* 13 (1936): 176-179.

     Author identifies 3 libretti of this
     previously unknown oratorio, 2 of Venetian
     (1706) and 1 of Roman (1710) origin . Roman
     libretto described in detail. Venetian copies
     located in Biblioteca Vittorio Emanuele, Rome,
     and Civico Museo Correr (Opera Cicogna). The
     last was not seen by Rolandi but by Giuseppe
     Ortolani; Fabbri could not locate it 30 years
     later. See item 296.

*   Smither, Howard E. *A History of the Oratorio. Volume 1:
     The Oratorio in the Baroque Era: Italy, Vienna, Paris*. See
     item 289.

*   Talbot, Michael, and Colin Timms. "Music and
       the Poetry of Antonio Ottoboni (1646-1720)."
       Cited as item 101.

   Davidis pugna et victoria

298. Bianchi, Lino. "Preface." In Alessandro
     Scarlatti's *Davidis pugna et victoria*, pp. v-viii
     and unpaged facs. and notes. Suppl. English
     trans. of preface, paged separately, pp. i-
     ix. See Section V, 1.

     Reference to the first modern performance in
     Rome, May 26, 1962, conducted by the author.
     Discusses the anonymous libretto from the Rome
     1700   performance   (Biblioteca   Casanatense,
     Rome) and the only known surviving score
     (located in Lyons, France).   Story of the
     oratorio precedes the text.

   La Giuditta [i] (1693)

299. Bianchi, Lino. "Preface." In Alessandro
     Scarlatti's *La Giuditta* (Naples), pp. v-viii
     with unpaged facs. and list of characters
     and text, pp. ix-xv. Suppl. English trans.
     of preface separately paged, pp. i-vi. See
     Section V, 1.

     Description   of   MS   (Biblioteca   del
     Conservatorio di Musica S. Pietro a Maiella,
     Naples) and libretto (anon., 1695; Biblioteca
     Musicale ...del Conservatorio di Santa
     Cecilia, Rome: Carvalhaes Collection) and
     editoral procedures.   See also item 301 for
     discussion of text attributions.

*   Morelli, Arnaldo. "Alessandro Scarlatti
       maestro di cappella in Roma ed alcuni suoi
       oratori." Cited as item 282.

*   *Musikhandschriften in Basel aus verschiedenen Sammlungen.*
       Katalog.... Cited as item 23.

300. Selden, Margery Stomne. "Alessandro Scarlat-
     ti's Oratorio *La Giuditta*: a Communication."
     American Musicological Society. Journal 22 (1969): 305.

     Reports the discovery of what seems to be
     the original autograph MS of this oratorio in
     Morristown [NJ] National Historical Park
     Library. Same work (with additions) as that
     represented in the MS of the Conservatorio di
     Musica S. Pietro di Maiella, Naples, upon
     which Lino Bianchi based his edition:
     Giuditta(Naples) (see Section V, 1). Originally
     part of the collection of Charles Jennens, a
     librettist for Handel. Bound in the front is a
     three page letter of advice and directions
     addressed to an unidentified Roman patron
     (which the library believes to be Pamphilii).
     The letter, dated Mar. 3, 1693, sent with part
     1 of the oratorio, seems to be in Scarlatti's
     hand and is signed by him. This suggests that
     he assisted in the preparation of the text.
     For reproduction of this letter see Pagano, p.
     256. For modern transcription of some of the
     text of the letter, see Zanetti (item 61), p.
     678; for reference to letter by Scarlatti
     which probably accompanied part 2, dated Mar.
     7, 1693, see item 23 (in which the editor
     cites the recipient as Pietro Ottoboni).
     Morelli, et al. have identified Pietro
     Ottoboni as author of the text (see item 282).

*   Selfridge-Field, Eleanor.   "*Juditha* in
     Historical Perspective...." Cited as item
     302.

La Giuditta [ii] (c1697-1700)

301. Bianchi, Lino. "Preface." In Alessandro
     Scarlatti's *La Giuditta* (Cambridge), pp. v-x
     with notes p. xi and unpaged facs. [xiii-
     xiv]. Suppl. English trans. paged separately,
     pp. i-x including notes. See Section V, 1.

     Discussion of the two Judith oratorios;
     summarizes the confusion over authorship of

the text of the earlier Judith oratorio (concluding that Pamphili wrote it; see item 282 for a different opinion), and clarifies relationship of Pietro Ottoboni to the 2nd work (with text by Antonio Ottoboni, Pietro's uncle). Describes Cambridge MS. Useful for its details regarding the two different versions of the oratorio.

302. Selfridge-Field, Eleanor. "*Juditha* in Historical Perspective. Scarlatti, Gasparini, Marcello and Vivaldi." In *Vivaldi veneziano europeo*, pp. 135-153. Ed. by Francesco Degrada. Florence: Olschki, 1980.

A study of the above composers' settings of the story of Judith (from the Apocrypha) with special attention given to Vivaldi's setting. Cites secondary sources as evidence that oratorio composition in Venice was far greater than evidenced by surviving MSS. Gives Pamphili as author of Scarlatti's *Giuditta* [i] and Naples, 1695 as the place and date of its first performance with a later performance in Rome in 1696. *NGIBM* gives 1693 as the Naples premiere.

303. Swale, David. "The 'Judith' Oratorios of Alessandro Scarlatti." *Miscellanea musicologica* 9 (1977): 145-155.

Article marks the performance of *La Giuditta* (Cambridge) at the Adelaide Festival of the Arts, March 17, 1976. Discussion of the changes in style between the earlier version (with text here attributed to Pamphili) (1693) and the later version with text by A. Ottoboni (c1697-1700). Shows movement from operatic style toward greater understanding of the dramatic and musical requirements of a non-staged production.

Johannespassion

*   Hanley, Edwin. "Current Chronicle." Cited as
        item 427.

Il martirio di S. Orsola.   See Strohm, item 437.

Il primo omicidio.   See *Cain overro Il primo omicidio*.

San Filippo Neri

304. Bosanquet, Caroline.   "Alessandro Scarlatti's
     San Filippo Neri."   *Musical Times* 101 (1960): 700.

     Author played the cello in the first modern
     performance of the work (at the Edinburgh
     Festival, August 22/24, 1960) with the Neri
     Orchestra conducted by Michael Bush.
     Performance based on the Brussels MS. Brief
     description of the work which author states
     included one of the first representations in
     music of horses' hooves. Mostly a short
     discussion of the performance, although it
     provides no clues with respect to performance
     practice.

Serenatas

305. Griffin, Thomas Edward.   "Alessandro Scarlatti
     e la serenata a Roma e a Napoli."   In *La
     musica a Napoli durante il seicento. Atti del convegno
     internazionale di studi, Napoli, 11-14 aprile 1985* (item
     77), pp. 351-368. Notes, 3 plates, app.

     Documents an active tradition of outdoor
     music (serenata) in Rome and (later) in Naples
     during a period roughly corresponding to
     Scarlatti's life. Explains the politics
     involved. Information from the *Avvisi di Roma*
     (1671-1712) of 1677 reveals that the tradition
     was well established by that date; thus, the
     youthful Scarlatti probably observed some of
     these events. References to 3 serenatas by

Scarlatti performed in Naples in 1686 and
1696. Appendix: chronological list of
Scarlatti's serenatas with title and text
incipit; performance date; libretto
information, when available; author; score
information; and location and numbers of MSS.
32 titles cited. One eliminated from *NGIBM*
list. Asterisks indicate 22 authenticated; 10
others attributed to Scarlatti in other
sources. Some of the latter can eventually be
identified from existing scores.

306. _____. "Alessandro Scarlatti's Serenata
Erminia, Tancredi, Polidoro e Pastore." M.A. thesis.
University of California, Los Angeles, 1975.

Discusses the last of Scarlatti's
approximately 25 serenatas (Naples, 1723)
which exhibits fuller orchestration than
exists in any of the operas: flutes, oboes,
bassoons, horns, and trumpets in pairs; 1st
and 2nd violins, violas, cellos, and at least
2 double basses with harpsichord. Contains
edition by the author. Not seen.

307. _____. "Giovanni Battista Operti's *Avvisi di
Napoli*: Sources for the History of Music in
Naples during the 1690s." Unpublished paper
presented at a meeting of the New York State
Chapter of the American Musicological
Society, Albany. 14 pp.

Illuminating discussion of musical events in
Naples during the last decade of the
seventeenth century. Discusses the *avvisi*
written by the ambassador from Savoy as a
source of valuable information on the music
and the cultural and political milieu in
Naples from 1692-97. Gives background for the
performances of Scarlatti's *La Teodora augusta,
Gerone tiranno di Siracusa*, and *Venere, Adone et Amore*.

308. _____. "The Late Baroque Serenata in Rome
and Naples: A Documentary Study with

Emphasis on Alessandro Scarlatti." Ph.D. dissertation. University of California, Los Angeles, 1983. 904 pp. Illus., worklist, apps., bibl., indices. UMI order # 84-08,809.

The most comprehensive study of the late Baroque serenata in these cities. Includes an examination of the political, sociological, and theatrical background for these "large occasional cantatas... performed... to celebrate a victory..., birth of an heir," etc. The scores of 19 serenatas by Scarlatti are known and texts of 3 others have been identified in printed librettos. Griffin provides a revised list and chronology of the works. For the most current list, see item 305.

309. _____. "Nuove fonti per la storia della musica a Napoli durante il regno del marchese del Carpio (1683-1687)." *Rivista italiana di musicologia* 16 (1981): 207-228.

Major article on the performance history of outdoor *spettacoli* in Rome and Naples during the years of del Carpio's reign. Based in part on the *avvisi politici* or weekly dispatches to Rome (1671-1712) contained in 7 volumes in the Bayerische Staatsbibliothek, Munich. Del Carpio's arrival in Naples as Viceroy paralleled Scarlatti's return to that city.

310. _____. "Serenata." In *New Grove Dictionary of Music and Musicians*. Ed. by Stanley Sadie. London: Macmillan, 1980. Vol. 17, pp. 160-162.

Brief introduction to the genre by the leading expert in the field.

311. Mancini, Franco. *Feste de apparati civili e religiosi in Napoli dal viceregno alla capitale*. Naples: Edizione Scientifiche Italiane, 1968. 312 pp.

Beautifully produced, elaborately illustrated book; found in few libraries. Describes
the *feste* (numerous civil and religious
celebrations) in Naples during the years of
the Spanish viceroys and beyond and documents
the surviving graphic representations of appa-
ratuses used in them.

312. Paoli, Domenico de'. "Diana ed Endimione di
     Alessandro Scarlatti." *Rassegna musicale* 13
     (1940): 139-146. Mus. exs.

Discusses this serenata for soprano,
contralto, and four unspecified string
instruments (probably 2 violins, viola da
brazzo, and viola da gamba) discovered by the
author in 1935 in the Bibliothèque Nationale,
Paris. According to Paoli, it doesn't
correspond exactly to the Montecassino MS
cited by Eitner. Dent assigned it to 1680-
1685. Notable for its stylistic unity, "solo"
string parts, and because use of the
harpsichord as a continuo almost superfluous.
In this sense seems to be an example of
soloistic four-part string writing 30 years in
advance of the composer's *Sonate a quattro*.

313. Povoledo, Elena. " Gian Lorenzo Bernini,
     l'elefante e i fuochi artificiali." *Rivista
     italiana di musicologia* 10 (1975): 499-518.

Examines and interprets the significance
(political, sociological, and iconological) of
two festivals with fireworks held in Rome in
1651 and 1662, respectively ; these were
arranged by two Roman ambassadors and directed
by Bernini. The article includes a list of
literary and iconographic sources (seventeenth-century imprints) related to the *feste*
and *fuochi artificiali* that occurred in Rome between
1637 and 1681 and a bibliography. Provides a
historical context for the performance of
later outdoor entertainments of this nature,
including the serenatas of Alessandro
Scarlatti.

2. INSTRUMENTAL MUSIC

Keyboard Music

314. Apel, Willi. "Alessandro Scarlatti." In his
History of Keyboard Music to 1700, pp. 699-703.
Trans. and rev. by Hans Tischler.
Bloomington: Indiana University Press, 1972.
xviii and 878 pp. Mus. exs. ISBN 253-13790-X

Surveys keyboard music by the composer.
Discusses aspects of his style in *Toccate per
cembalo* housed at Yale University (formerly in
the private collection of C. M. Higgs).

315. Doderer, Gerhard. "Eine unbeachtete Quelle zu
Alessandro Scarlattis Orgelmusik." In
Colloquium Alessandro Scarlatti Würzburg 1975 (item 5),
pp. 205-211.

Description of five short organ pieces
identified as *Sonate per organo del Sigr. Alessandro
Scarlatti* in MS MM60 Reservados at the University
Library of Coimbra, Portugal. Attribution
uncertain, but may be correct, since in the
same MS other folios contain some compositions
which have been identified as Scarlatti's.
Pages 207-211: "Inhaltsverzeichnis"; pp. 210-
211 include incipits for the 5 pieces.

316. Esteban, Julio. "On the Neglected Keyboard
Compositions of Alessandro Scarlatti."
American Music Teacher 18/3 (1969): 22-23.

Discusses the musical value of the toccatas
and suggests Scarlatti was possibly the first
to use perpetual motion and bravura style
characteristic of the modern toccata (see item
314 for more accurate, historically-based
commentary on this point). Mentions the
toccatas written for didactic purposes "per
bene principiare a sonare" in which Scarlatti
included a system of symbols for fingering as
well as some innovations in form in Toccatas
4-7.

317. Humber, Ingrid. "A Structural Analysis,
     Interpretive Discussion, and Performance of
     Ten Selected Keyboard Compositions of
     Alessandro Scarlatti: As Contained in MS
     8802 of the Conservatorio 'Giuseppe Verdi'
     in Milan." Ed.D. dissertation. Columbia
     University Teachers College, 1986. 276 pp.
     UMI order #8620368.

     Structural analysis of 7 unsigned keyboard
     compositions (2 sonatas and 5 toccatas from
     the Milan MS). Author had to establish
     authenticity. Compares these toccatas with
     the 5 signed toccatas from the Yale MS.
     Provides an edition of the 7 pieces and
     discusses unnecessary changes in earlier
     editions. Suggests utilization by teachers
     who wish to include works by A. Scarlatti in
     their students' repertoire.

318. Lee, Patricia Ann Taylor. "The Keyboard Style
     of Alessandro Scarlatti as Evidenced in Two
     Manuscripts from the Library of the School
     of Music, Yale University." M.A.
     dissertation. Yale University, 1959.

     Includes a detailed study of the "Higgs
     Manuscript" (see ed. by J. S. Shedlock) and
     the "Yale Manuscript" containing four toccatas
     (included as the first 4 pieces in the edition
     by Gerlin, see Section V, 2). Not seen.
     (Summarized by Strohm in item 437).

319. Lindley, Mark. "An Introduction to
     Alessandro Scarlatti's *Toccata prima*." *Early Music*
     10 (1982): 333-339.

     A discussion of the *Toccata prima* in G major in
     relation to Scarlatti's designated fingering.
     An abridged edition of the *Toccata* by the
     author included in the article. Suggests that
     use of early fingerings such as these in
     performance will greatly alter the sound of
     these and other Baroque pieces.

*   Lippmann, Friedrich. "Sulle composizioni per
        cembalo di Gaetano Greco." Cited as item 73
        in Book II.

320. Pestelli, Giorgio. "Haendel e Alessandro
     Scarlatti. Problemi di attribuzione nel MS
     A. 7b.63. Cass. della biblioteca del
     Conservatorio Nicolo Paganini di Genova."
     Rivista italiana di musicologia 7 (1972): 103-114.

     Discussion of 5 works MS indicates are by
     Alessandro Scarlatti including a Toccata in G
     major, a Fuga (to follow) and 3 pieces without
     titles (all Lento). Author suggests that
     Mainwaring's account of the encounter between
     Handel and Scarlatti referred to Alessandro
     rather than Domenico as has been generally
     thought.

321. _____. "Corelli e il suo influsso sulla
     musica per cembalo del suo tempo." *Nuovi studi
     corelliana. Atti del secondo congresso internazionale,
     Fusignano, 5-8 settembre 1974.* Ed. by Giulia
     Giachin. *Quaderni della Rivista italiana di musicologia* 4
     (1978): 37-51 and "Discussione," pp. 52-53.

     Examines the relationship of certain
     passages and figures in the violin writing of
     Corelli to the keyboard music of Alessandro
     and Domenico Scarlatti and other Baroque
     keyboard composers. Concludes that Corellian
     influence stronger in the harpsichord works of
     Domenico Scarlatti than in those of his
     father.

322. _____. "Le toccate per strumento a
     tastiera di Alessandro Scarlatti nei
     manoscritti napoletani." *Analecta musicologica*
     12 (1973): 169-192 (Studien zur
     italienisch-deutschen Musikgeschichte, 8).

     Study of the cembalo and organ works of the
     composer contained in MSS of the Naples
     Conservatory. Identifies them, describes their

characteristics and analogous sources, and
proposes an edition [never forthcoming to my
knowledge] that would reunite the corpus for
the 250th anniversary of the composer's death
in 1975.   Pestelli comments that the only
edition of quality accessible at that time was
Vol. 13 of *I classici musici italiani*: *Primo e secondo libro di
toccate*, 10 toccatas from MS 9478, ed. by Gerlin
and Sartori. (See Section V, 2).   App.:
Incipits of Scarlatti toccatas in manuscript
in the Biblioteca del Conservatorio di Musica
S. Pietro di Maiella, Naples.

323. Sartori, Claudio. "Appendice." In *Primo e
     secondo libro di toccate del signor Cavaliere Alessandro
     Scarlatti*, pp. 133-154. Ed. by R. Gerlin. (See
     Section V, 2).

     "Bibliografia," pp. 139-143 includes de-
     scription of MS sources of all the keyboard
     works.

324. Shedlock, James S.   "The Harpsichord Music of
     Alessandro Scarlatti." *Sammelbände der
     internationalen Musikgesellschaft* 6 (1904-1905): 160-
     178.

     An important examination and discussion of
     the *Toccate per cembalo per bene principiare a sonare, ed al
     nobile portamento delle mani....* Included in MS then
     owned by C. M. Higgs now at Yale University
     (see also items 318 and 437). Some historical
     information no longer valid. Facsimile and
     musical examples. Relationship of the music
     to   that   of   Scarlatti's   contemporaries,
     including Handel, Corelli, Pasquini and to
     that of his son, Domenico, examined.   See
     Section V, 2 for edition by author.

*   Strohm, Reinhard. "Scarlattiana at Yale."
     Cited as item 437.

*   Taylor Lee, Patricia. See Lee, Patricia
      Taylor.

Other Instrumental Music and Instrumental Style

325. Abraham, Gerald, ed. *New Oxford History of Music*.
     Vol. 6. *Concert Music (1630-1750)*. Oxford and
     N.Y.: Oxford University Press, 1986. xxi
     and 786 pp. Bibl. and index by David
     Blackwell. ISBN 0-19-316306-3.

     Includes discussion of Scarlatti's influence
     on the use of certain concertante style
     elements in arias and on the type of 3
     movement overture (sinfonia) adopted for the
     later solo concerto and classical symphony.

326. Alton, Edwin H. "The Recorder Music of
     Alessandro Scarlatti (1660-1725)." *Recorder
     and Music Magazine* 4/6 (1973): 199-200.

     Brief descriptions of the known works for 1-
     3 flutes (recorders) accompanied by strings
     and/or basso continuo. Provides MS locations
     and identifies modern editions.

327. Anderson, Nicholas. "Restraint and Discipline:
     The Roman Conception of Arcadia." In
     *Nuovissimi studi Corelliani. Atti del terzo congresso
     internazionale (Fusignano 1980)*, pp. 269-284.

     Includes brief discussion of the tendency
     toward merging instrumental and vocal
     techniques apparent in the music of the Roman
     circle with references to Scarlatti's specific
     contributions. Mus. exs. from his serenata *Il
     giardino d'amore*.

328. Bettarini, Luciano. "Appunti critici sulle
     sette sonate per flauto e archi di Alessandro
     Scarlatti." *Chigiana* 25 (Nuova serie 5)
     (1968): 239-246.

Stylistic survey of 7 sonatas (1725) by A.
Scarlatti taken from MS collection of 32
sonatas (by Scarlatti et al.) in the
Biblioteca del Conservatorio di Musica S.
Pietro di Maiella, Naples. Parts are
detached; not autograph but probably
eighteenth-century copies. Score recopied
exactly from the parts (possibly in the
nineteenth century); gives date 1725. May
have been among the last works of the composer
if not the last. Possibly written for Quantz
who had come to Italy. No other known
compositions by Alessandro Scarlatti for
[transverse] flute. Not cited by Hanley in
MGG (item 14); cited in *NGIBM*.

*   Bland, Leland Dye. "The Instrumental
       Ritornello in Selected Vocal Works of
       Italian Composers ca. 1670 to 1710." Cited
       as item 276.

*   Carse, Adam. *History of Orchestration*. Cited as
       item 353.

*   _____. *The Orchestra in the XVIIIth Century*. Cited
       as item 354.

*   Collins, Michael. "L'orchestra nelle opere
       teatrali di Vivaldi." Cited as item 179.

329. De Lage, Joseph Ovide, Jr. "The Overture in
     Seventeenth Century Italian Opera." Ph.D.
     dissertation. Florida State, 1961. 239 pp.
     UMI order #61-5636.

     Examines *Settecento* opera overtures by
     prominent composers of the Roman and Venetian
     schools as well as 2 works of A. Scarlatti and
     the role such overtures played in the
     development of instrumental music. Appendix B
     includes 15 complete overtures, most
     previously unpublished. Chapter 5 discusses

Scarlatti's works to 1698.

330. Dent, Edward J. "The Earliest String
     Quartets." *Monthly Musical Record* 33 (1903):
     202-204.

     Identifies Scarlatti's four "Sonate a
     quattro" for "due violini, violetta e
     violoncello senza cembalo" located by the
     author in the Santini collection, Münster, as
     the first extant string quartets. Traces
     other MS copies arranged as the *VI Concertos in 7
     Parts*; discusses the form of each movement of
     the four Sonatas (derived from Corelli's
     "Sonate da Chiesa"); provides musical
     examples; and comments on the minuets as
     forerunners of Beethoven's scherzos.

331. Hansell, Sven Hostrup. "Orchestral Practice
     at the Court of Cardinal Pietro Ottoboni."
     American Musicological Society. Journal 19 (1966): 398-
     403.

     Abstract of paper read in Chicago at the
     Nov. 1965 Midwest Chapter meeting of AMS.
     Discussion of material in the account books of
     Pietro Ottoboni (Archivio Barberini in the
     Biblioteca Apostolica Vaticana, Rome). Reveals
     the nature of orchestras (change in make-up
     from 1690-1720 and 1720-). Information on
     terminology used for instruments; orchestral
     personnel (payment, etc.); use of keyboard
     accompaniment; and other matters relevant to
     the performance practice and socio-economic
     context of musicians (among them Scarlatti)
     patronized by Ottoboni.

332. Hell, Helmut. *Die neapoletanische Opersinfonie in der
     ersten Hälfte der 18. Jahrhunderts*. Tutzing: Hans
     Schneider, 1971 (Münchner Veröffentlich-
     ungen zur Musikgeschichte, Bd. 19) 623 pp.
     Mus. exs., bibl., index.

     Massive study which examines the opera

sinfonias of the composers indicated. Also
gives a history of the Italian opera overture
from Monteverdi through the Neapolitan opera
composers of the first half of the century and
discusses the influences their music may have
had on the development of the symphony and the
Mannheim school. Appendix includes incipits
for instrumental works of the above composers
(including sinfonias and overtures to vocal
works).

333. La Via, Stefano. "Un'aria di Händel con
     violoncello obbligato e la tradizione
     romana." In *Händel e gli Scarlatti a Roma*, (item 38
     in Book II), pp. 49-71.

     Focuses on Handel's use of the violoncello
     in aria accompaniment (especially for
     expressive purposes), the prominence of the
     cello in Roman artistic circles, and the role
     assigned to the cello in the compositions of
     Handel's predecessors and contemporaries
     (principally F. Amadei, A. Stradella, and N.
     Haym though A. Scarlatti is also mentioned).
     Mus. exs.

*   Lazarevich, Gordana and Douglass M. Green.
     "The Eighteenth-Century Overture in Naples."
     Cited as item 201

334. Livingston, Herbert Stanton. "The Italian
     Overture from Alessandro Scarlatti to
     Mozart." Ph.D. dissertation. University of
     North Carolina, 1952. iii and 343 pp.:
     text; 198 pp.: mus. exs.

     Pp. 32-42 discuss Scarlatti. Analysis of
     forms of the opera overtures for *La caduta; Il
     prigioniero fortunato; L'Eraclea; Il Mitridate Eupatore; Il Ciro; Il
     trionfo dell'onore; Marco Attilio Regolo; La Griselda*.

335. Pecman, Rudolf. "Alessandro Scarlatti: a
     Predecessor of Joseph Haydn in the Genre of

the String Quartet." In *Haydn Studies: Proceedings
of the International Haydn Conference, Washington, D.C.,
1975*, pp. 456-459. Ed. by Jens Peter Larsen
et al. N.Y.: W. W. Norton, 1981.

Scarlatti's *Quattro sonate a quattro* published
1740, 15 years after the composer's death,
represented a transitional stage in the
development of the string quartet. Although
the viola part was not yet strictly
independent, by replacing the continuo with
four individual string melodies, the composer
foresaw the potential for independent
instrumental compositions. Style still that
of the concerto grosso with solo/tutti
passages; difference between chamber and
orchestral style not clearly established as it
is in Haydn's quartets (except for his early
ones).

336. Stowell, Robin. "Pyron's Progress: 17th and
     18th Century Cello Music Discoveries." *Strad*
     94 (1983): 42-43.

     Reviews the *Three Sonatas for Two Cellos*, c1700 (MS
     Noseda coll. Biblioteca del Conservatorio
     "Giuseppe Verdi," Milan) possibly by
     Alessandro Scarlatti [not cited in *NGIBM*;
     cited by Rostirolla as of uncertain
     attribution] printed for the first time in
     their original form in Grancino Editions'
     Early Cello Series no. 4. See Section V, 2.
     In 4 movements: slow, fast, slow, fast.
     Edition includes an excerpt from Corelli's
     ornamentation of his Opus 5 as a guide for
     embellishment.

337. Talbot, Michael. "The Concerto Allegro in the
     Early Eighteenth Century." *Music and Letters* 52
     (1971): 8-18 and 159-172.

     Author challenges the theory that concertos
     were originally associated with the church or
     court and sinfonias with the opera house as
     Arthur Hutchings (*The Baroque Concerto*), and

others have stated. Terms concerto and
sinfonia began replacing sonata as titles for
heavily scored pieces at the end of the
seventeenth century. Use of the term sinfonia
as overture to a theatrical work, a thing
apart. Otherwise can't explain the *12 Sinfonie di
concerto grosso* (sinfonias for large ensemble) by
A. Scarlatti which were, like many
contemporary concertos, in part patterned
after conventional sonata models with 4 or 5
movements.

*   Via, Stefano La. See La Via, Stefano.

III

PERFORMANCE BACKGROUND

1. Performance Practice

Although much has been learned about the performance practice of the seventeenth and eighteenth centuries in general during the past several decades, many problems remain to be resolved. This is especially true in relation to the performance practice appropriate to the individual works of a given composer such as Alessandro Scarlatti. What may be appropriate for one composer's works may not be right for another's, even when they are contemporaries. Further, even when considering several works by the same composer one cannot always simply assume that one should follow the same procedures. As Hermine Williams writes in the "Introduction" to her edition of Scarlatti's *La caduta de' Decemviri* (see item 235, p. 23) with respect to the use of the cembalo in continuo accompaniment: "Lacking ...[enough] information, one might be tempted to apply principles of performance practice that are indicated in some of the other operas by Scarlatti, but what might be valid for one opera may not be valid for another."

The publications cited in the following pages include a few general guides in addition to a fairly substantial number of mainly recent articles and books on performance practice of the period selected to provide a background for the performance of Scarlatti's works. The citations range from general discussions on the performance of Baroque music to specific topics, such as figured-bass accompaniment and the embellishment of arias. For the performance of Scarlatti's theatrical works, among the most useful writings are the introductions to the individual volumes of *The Operas of Alessandro Scarlatti*, Donald J. Grout, general editor.

General Guides or Bibliographies

338. Brown, Howard Mayer, and Stanley Sadie, eds. *Performance Practice: Music after 1600* (The Norton/Grove Handbooks in Music)   N.Y.: W. W. Norton, 1990.   xi, 533 pp. Illus. (some facs.), mus. exs., notes, index. ISBN 0-393-02808-9.

A performance practice handbook which aims to address the problems confronted by both performers and musicologists.   Part I covers the Baroque era.   Includes articles by specialists   on   instruments,   voices,   pitch, tuning, keyboard fingerings, etc., as well as an extensive bibliography of treatises.

339. Jackson, Roland.   *Performance Practice, Medieval to Contemporary: A Bibliographic Guide* (Garland Reference Library of the Humanities, 790; Music Research & Information Guides, 9) N.Y.: Garland Publishing, 1988.   xxix and 518 pp.   Indices.   ISBN 0-8240-1512-6.

One of the most up-to-date guides of this sort.   Includes several references to A. and D. Scarlatti as well as other articles of general relevance for the period.   Updated through annual supplements in *Performance Practice Review*.

340. *Performance Practice Review*.   Vol. 1-   1988- Claremont, CA: Music Dept., Claremont Graduate School.

Contains articles by noted scholars.   Vol. 1 includes a 1987 and 1988 "Performance Practice Bibliography."

341. Pruett, James, and Thomas P. Slavens.
     Research Guide to Musicology. Chicago: American
     Library Association, 1985. ISBN 0-8389-0331-2.

     A readable, "user-friendly" introduction to
     some of the major sources. Discussion of the
     Baroque period, pp. 69-76; bibliography for
     Baroque music, pp. 77-78.

342. Vinquist, Mary and Neal Zaslaw. *Performance
     Practice: a Bibliography*. N.Y.: W. W. Norton,
     1971. SBN 393-02148-3. Suppl. in *Current
     Musicology* 12 (1971): 129-149 and 15 (1973):
     126-136.

     Includes references to 1131 items arranged
     alphabetically by author. Index of subjects
     (including names). Superseded by item 339.

Baroque Period (with bearing on Scarlatti)

343. Aldrich, Putnam. "The Authentic Performance
     of Baroque Music." In *Essays on Music in Honor of
     Archibald Thompson Davison*, pp. 161-171.
     Cambridge, MA: Harvard University Dept. of
     Music, 1957.

     Good general introduction to the problems
     and issues involved in attempting to recreate
     Baroque music in something like its original
     performance style.

*   Anfuso, Nella. "La vocalité italienne au
     temps de Scarlatti." Cited as item 171 in
     Book II.

344. Arnold, Frank Thomas. *The Art of Accompaniment from a
     Thorough-Bass*. London: Oxford, 1931. Reprint:
     N.Y.: Dover, 1965. 2 vols. Introduction by
     Denis Stevens. 918 pp.

     Pioneering history of the practice of
     improvising accompaniments from a figured or

unfigured bass (from the beginnings in the
seventeenth century through the eighteenth
century). Based on contemporary treatises and
prefatory comments to music scores. Includes
specific references to the practices of
Alessandro Scarlatti and translations of some
passages from his unpublished treatises "Per
accompagnare il cembalo o organo" [BM Add
14244 fol 40a] and "Regole per principianti"
[fol 13 A of the same MS].

345. Barcham, William L. "Costume in the Frescoes
     of Tiepolo and Eighteenth Century Italian
     Opera." In *Opera and Vivaldi* (item 378), pp.
     149-169

     An interesting introduction to the history
     of theatrical costume in Italy during the
     Baroque period (primarily the eighteenth
     century). Points out the problems in
     understanding their nature and what can be
     learned from studying paintings, drawings,
     stage designs, and writings of the period.

346. Barnett, Dene. "Finding the Appropriate
     Attitude: Dene Barnett in Conversation with
     Ian Parker." *Early Music* 8 (1980): 65-69.

     Interesting, informative interview with D.
     Barnett, a specialist in oratory and acting
     styles of the seventeenth and eighteenth
     centuries and instructor of performers in the
     art of gesture. Focus mainly on French style;
     says certain features applicable to Scarlatti
     and the Italian theater though to a lesser
     degree.

347. Borgir, Tharald. *The Performance of Basso Continuo in
     Italian Baroque Music* (Studies in Musicology,
     90) Ann Arbor: UMI Research Press, 1987.
     vii and 180 pp. ISBN 0-8357-1675-9.

     Deals principally with the choice of
     continuo instrument(s) in the performance of

music written, performed, and published in
Italy from 1590-1750. Author critical of the
tradition which pairs a chordal realizing
instrument with a melodic bass. See review in
Music Library Association. Notes 45 (1989): 502-503.

348. Boyden, David D. *The History of Violin Playing from Its
Origins to 1761, and Its Relationship to the Violin and Violin
Music.* London: Oxford University Press,
1965. 569 pp.

Very detailed study of the violin, its
history, technical characteristics, music,
etc. Reference to Scarlatti's use of the rare
eighth position in his *Laodice e Berenice* .

349. Brown, Howard Mayr. "Embellishing Eighteenth-
Century Arias: On Cadenzas." In *Opera and
Vivaldi* (item 378), pp. 258-276.

Discusses what can be learned on the subject
from surviving examples, specifically, those
of Hasse's wife, the noted singer Fausta
Bordoni, and those of Farinelli from a later
period.

350. _____. "Performing Practice [section] 5:
1600-1750." In *The New Grove Dictionary of Music and
Musicians*, Vol. 14. Ed. by Stanley Sadie.
London: Macmillan, 1986.

A good overview of the Baroque period and
its performance practices.

351. Buelow, George J. "A Lesson in Operatic
Performance Practice by Madame Faustina
Bordoni." In *A Musical Offering: Essays in
Honor of Martin Bernstein*. Ed. by Claire Brook and
Edward H. Clinkscale. N.Y.: Pendragon,
1977.

An article on improvised vocal ornamentation
as performed by one of the most famous prima

donnas of the early Settecento. This is
represented in a rare surviving example
discovered by the author in a work of Giuseppe
Vignati bound with 20 arias, 2 duets, and 1
quartet from Alessandro Scarlatti's *Griselda*
(Washington, D.C., Library of Congress MS:
M1500 S28 G5). Edited excerpts (a copy of the
complete aria is available from the author)
and a discussion of the nature of the
embellishments are presented. The author
suggests there may have been a major
difference between the techniques of
ornamentation employed by women singers and
those used by castrati. Remarks upon the need
for further documentation and study of the
subject of vocal ornamentation.

352. _____ . *Thorough-Bass Accompaniment According to Johann
      David Heinichen.* Berkeley: University of
      California Press, 1966. 316 pp.

A major study and translation of parts of
the 2nd edition of Heinichen's treatise *Der
General-Bass in der Composition* (Dresden: privately
printed, 1728) which included instructions for
realizing the unfigured bass of Scarlatti's
solo cantata *Lascia deh lascia al fino di tormentarmi più*.
Buelow translates the instructions *in toto* and
presents his own realization (different from
the earlier one by Schering). See Section V,
1.

353. Carse, Adam. *History of Orchestration.* N.Y.: Dover
     Publications, Inc., 1964. Unabridged and
     corr. republication of the 1925 ed. (London:
     Kegan Paul, Trench, Trubner & Co. Ltd.). xiv
     and 348 pp. ISBN 0-486-21258-0. Mus. exs.,
     index.

Discusses Scarlatti's contributions to the
history of orchestration and his writing for
strings and winds on pp. 91-105.

354. _____ . *The Orchestra in the XVIIIth Century.*

Cambridge, Eng.: W. Heffer & Sons, Ltd.,
1940. 176 pp. Reprint, 1950. Mus. exs.,
bibl., index, tables, plates.

An interesting early history of the
performance practices and make-up of the
orchestra during this period but few
references to Alessandro Scarlatti.

355. Celletti, Rodolfo. "La vocalità: il
settecento 1) Le opinioni di Pier Francesco
Tosi 2) Il vocalismo in Alessandro
Scarlatti 3) La vocalità Handeliana 4) Da
Porpora a Hasse 5) La vocalità nell'opera
buffa del primo settecento." In *Storia
dell'opera* (item 219), Vol. 3, T.1, pp. 43-
71.

Detailed discussions of: 1) the *bel canto* style
of singing especially with respect to the
change of vocal registers as described in
Tosi's treatise (item 381); and 2) the vocal
styles of Scarlatti and his younger
contemporaries.

356. Collins, Michael. "Cadential Structures and
Accompanimental Practices in Eighteenth-
Century Italian Recitative." In *Opera and
Vivaldi* (item 378), pp. 211-232.

Examines the subject in relation to
contemporary treatises including Tosi,
Heinichen, and Gasparini (see items 381, 352,
and 368, respectively) and Alessandro
Scarlatti's manuscript "per sonare il
Cembalo," etc. Cites numerous musical examples
by Scarlatti and his contemporaries. Comments
on Sven Hansell's work (see item 371) and
provides additional documentation pertinent to
the subject.

357. Covell, Roger. "Voice Register as an Index of
Age and Status in Opera Seria." In *Opera and
Vivaldi* (item 378), pp. 193-210.

Examines the assignment of certain voice ranges to certain types of characters in the opera seria and speculates about the composers' intentions in this regard.

358. Cyr, Mary. "Declamation and Expressive Singing in Recitative." In *Opera and Vivaldi* (item 378), pp. 233-257.

Discussion of recitative in Italian and French opera and the problems they pose for today's performers in terms of "speed and accentuation, addition of expressive ornaments, and a proper accompaniment." Ample references to contemporary treatises.

359. Daw, Brian Alan. "The Continuo and Its Realization." In "Alessandro Scarlatti's Cantatas for Solo Soprano and Continuo, 1708-1717" (item 127), pp. 35-63.

Discusses what can be learned and surmised about A. Scarlatti's continuo realizations from contemporary treatises and from a cantata for which Scarlatti realized the bass himself.

360. Dean, Winton. "The Performance of Recitatives in Late Baroque Opera." *Music and Letters* 58 (1977): 389-402.

Focus is Italian *opera seria* of the first half of the eighteenth century and problems of its modern revival. Stimulated by series of productions of Handel's operas. Very important examination of declamation, role of the continuo, proper performance of appoggiaturas and cadences. Critical of past studies' consideration of these points (see items 362, 382, and 371, respectively). Suggests proper performance of recitatives greatly shortens an opera's performance time.

361. Donington, Robert. *Baroque Music: Style and Performance:*

A Handbook. N.Y.: W. W. Norton, 1982. 206 pp. ISBN 0-393-30052-8.

Intended as a guide to the basics of Baroque style and as a summary of the principles underlying the music and its authentic performance. Draws much from the author's earlier *A Performer's Guide...* (item 363).

362. _____. *The Interpretation of Early Music: New Version.* London: Faber, 1975. 766 pp. ISBN 0-571-04789-0.

Basically a third edition of the volume first issued in 1963, this guide to the performance of early (chiefly Baroque) music offers numerous examples of ornamentation, etc. Well indexed; lengthy bibliography by the author (assisted by Gloria Rose).

363. _____. *A Performer's Guide to Baroque Music.* London: Faber, 1973. 320 pp. ISBN 0-571-09797-9. Mus. exs., reading list, index.

Directed at performers, including teachers and students who wish to acquire a basic knowledge of Baroque performance in the most concise and straightforward way possible.

364. _____. "A Problem of Inequality." *Musical Quarterly* 53 (1967): 503-517.

Cites examples of inequality in Italian music, including works by Alessandro and Domenico Scarlatti. Counters Neumann's view that its use is restricted to French music (see item 376, pp. 59-72).

365. Ferand, Ernest T. "Embellished Parody Cantatas' in the Early 18th Century." *Musical Quarterly* 44 (1958): 40-64.

A discussion of Francesco Durante's *Duetti/ per*

studio di maniera di cantare/ e per esercizio di accompagnare al cembalo..., parody cantatas (based on recitatives from Alessandro Scarlatti's chamber cantatas) designed for the instruction of vocal ornamentation and thoroughbass accompaniment. Also examines embellished versions of Giovanni Bononcini's *Duetti da camera,* Op. 8 and Carlo Antonio Benati's *Passi,* which provide interesting information on the ways in which da capo arias were ornamented.

366. _____. *Die Improvisation in Beispielen aus neun Jahrhunderten abendländischer Musik.* Cologne: Arno Verlag, 1956. 165 pp. English version: *Improvisation in Nine Centuries of Western Music: An Anthology with a Historical Introduction.* Cologne: Arno Verlag, 1961. 164 pp.

Numbers 27 through 31 represent embellishments and figured bass realizations of the period, including examples by Corelli, Heinichen, G.B. Bononcini, and F. Durante. Historical introduction, source references, and editorial notes relevant to each piece (including English translations of the vocal texts) provided.

367. Foreman, Edward Vaught. "A Comparison of Selected Italian Vocal Tutors of the Period ca. 1550 to 1880." D.M.A dissertation, University of Illinois, 1969. 165 pp. UMI order #M70-13,311.

Divides tutors into four major types. Discussion includes those by Maffei, Zacconi, Caccini, Durante, Tosi, Mancini, Manfredini, Aprile, Conforto, and Bovicelli. Compares their coverage concerning technical mastery of the voice and its use as an expressive instrument. Not seen.

368. Gasparini, Francesco. *The Practical Harmonist at the Harpsichord.* Ed. by David L. Burrows. English trans. by Frank S. Stillings. New Haven:

Yale School of Music, [1963]. Reissued in
1968 by Yale University Press, New Haven.

English translation of *L'armonico pratico al cimbalo*
first published in 1708 and reprinted many
times. Of particular interest for its
discussion of acciaccatura, examples of which
can be found in the works of A. and D.
Scarlatti.

* Grout, Donald J., general editor. *The Operas of
  Alessandro Scarlatti*. See individual entries
  under items 235, 241, 242, 246, 253, 254,
  261, 265, 268.

369. Haböck, Franz. *Die Gesangkunst der Kastraten*. Vol. 1
     (Ersten Notenband): *Die Kunst des Cavaliere Carlo
     Broschi Farinelli*. Vienna: Universal Ed., 1923.
     230 pp.

     Contains 25 arias and 17 excerpts with
     Farinelli's vocal ornaments. This is the only
     volume ever issued in a projected 4 volume
     set.

370. _____. *Die Kastraten und ihre Gesangkunst*. Stuttgart:
     Deutsche Verlags-Anstalt, 1927.

     A scholarly account, which discusses the
     various regional Italian singing schools in
     relation to the castrati.

371. Hansell, Sven Hostrup. "The Cadence in 18th-
     Century Recitative." *Musical Quarterly* 54
     (1968): 228-248.

     Detailed examination of recitative and
     explanation of the two ways cadences were
     generally performed in them: the "truncated"
     manner and the delayed manner. Mus. exs.,
     quotations from treatises. Criticized by
     Winton Dean (item 360) for introducing quotes
     from Gasparini related to acciaccatura.

372. Heriot, Angus. *The Castrati in Opera*. London:
     Secker & Warburg, 1956. Reprint: N.Y.: Da
     Capo, 1974. 243 pp. ISBN 0-306-706504.
     Bibl., index.

     An examination of the role of the castrati
     in Italian opera. Written in a popular style
     without the scholarly trappings of Haböck's
     studies.

*   Lindley, Mark. "Keyboard Technique and
     Articulation: Evidence for the Performance
     Practices of Bach, Handel and Scarlatti."
     Cited as item 175 in Book II.

373. Marchesi, Gustavo. "I cantanti: dalle origini
     alle soglie del romanticismo. 1) Gli
     interpreti italiani nell'epoca barocca". In
     Storia dell'opera (item 219), Vol. 3, T.1, pp.
     321-328.

     Overview of the activities of Italian
     singers of the Baroque period.

374. McClymonds, Marita P. "Preparing the Critical
     Edition: An Interview with Allen Curtis."
     In *Opera and Vivaldi* (item 378), pp. 349-357.

     Although Curtis discusses various Vivaldi
     editions, he also provides pragmatic and
     sensible suggestions for improving editions of
     early music in general. His criticisms are
     equally applicable to certain editions of
     Alessandro Scarlatti which have, in some
     cases, been prepared by the same editors that
     prepared some of the Vivaldi editions
     discussed.

375. Mendel, Arthur. "On the Pitches in Use in
     Bach's Time." In *Studies in the History of Musical
     Pitch*, pp.187-209, 210-224. Amsterdam: Frits
     Knuf, 1968. 238 pp. Reprint of *Musical
     Quarterly* 41 (1955): 332-354 and 466-480 with

"Annotations, Corrections, and Additions" (1965): pp.226-238.

Citing contemporary treatises (Tosi; Agricola, transl. of Tosi; and Doni), Mendel reveals the presence of regional differences in the tuning of keyboard instruments and the apparent lowering of pitch the farther south one traveled (thus, Venice had the highest pitch, Naples the lowest). Comments on the resultant difference in sound perceived (especially as it affected vocal pitch).

376. Neumann, Frederick. *Essays in Performance Practice*. Ann Arbor: UMI Research Press, 1982 (Studies in Musicology, 58)   321 pp. ISBN 0-8357-1351-2.

Collection of articles most of which were previously published' in major journals. Chapter 1: The Use of Baroque Treatises on Musical Performances, pp. 1-9; Chapter 2: Donington's *A Performer's Guide to Baroque Music*--a Review, pp. 11-15. (Reprint of *Musical Quarterly* 60 (1974): 658-664). See item 363. An excellent introduction to the pitfalls of applying too generally and too rigidly the statements promulgated by authors (eighteenth century and later) of treatises and performance guides. Other articles concern Neumann's controversial views on double-dotting.

377. North, Nigel. *Continuo Playing on the Lute, Archlute and Theorbo* (*Music: Scholarship and Performance*) Bloomington: Indiana University Press, 1987. xiii and 305 pp. Illus., mus. exs., app., notes, mus. list. ISBN 0-253-31415-1.

The first manual on continuo playing designed specifically for those who play these instruments. By a highly regarded lutenist who has used them in accompanying for ten years. A step-by-step guide which deals with Baroque harmony, style, technique, and

performance.   See   review   in   *Music   Library
Association. Notes* 45 (1989): 504.

378. *Opera and Vivaldi.* Ed. by Michael Collins and
     Elise K. Kirk. Austin: University of Texas
     Press, 1984. 398 pp.

     A fascinating collection of papers given at
     the Vivaldi conference in Texas. Although the
     focus is upon Vivaldi, some of the articles
     (cited here individually as items 345, 349,
     356, 357, 358, 374, and 383) are of interest
     to Scarlatti scholars as well.

379. Rangel-Ribeiro, Victor. *Baroque Music: A Practical
     Guide for the Performer.* N.Y.: Schirmer
     Books (Macmillan), 1981. 306 pp. ISBN 0-
     02-871980-8. Mus. exs., index.

     An approachable guide for performers, which,
     however, lacks specific references and
     documentation.

380. Tagliavini, Luigi Ferdinando. "L'armonico
     pratico al cimbalo." In *Francesco Gasparini (1661-
     1727). Atti...* (item 106), pp. 133-155.

     A discussion of Gasparini's thoroughbass
     treatise (item 368), its importance in
     revealing the practice of its time and place,
     and its relationship to the music of
     Gasparini's contemporaries, including
     Alessandro and Domenico Scarlatti.

381. Tosi, Pier Francesco. *Observations on the Florid
     Song....* Trans. into English by Mr. Galliard.
     London: J. Wilcox, 1742; 2nd ed 1743; 184
     pp., 6 plates. Reprint: London: William
     Reeves, 1926.

     By a singing teacher of the period, this
     treatise is important for an understanding of
     Baroque singing practice in the Italian style.

Information on technical methods, ornamentation, etc. Distinguishes between recitative
in chamber music, church, and the theater.

382. Westrup, Jack. "The Cadence in Baroque
     Recitative." In *Natalicia Musicologica Knud
     Jeppesen*, pp. 243-252. Ed. by Bjorn Hjelmborg
     and Soren Sorensen. Oslo: Norsk Musikforlag,
     1962.

     Discusses the foreshortened cadence in
     detail. Questions the frequent use of the
     delayed cadence. Quotes from theorists and
     cites examples from works by, among others,
     Scarlatti. Suggests some practical solutions.
     Criticized by Winton Dean (item 360).

383. Wynne, Shirley. "Baroque Manners and Passions
     in Modern Performance." In *Opera and Vivaldi*
     (item 378), pp. 170-178.

     A good introduction to dance performance in
     the Baroque theater with references to sources
     and suggestions for today's dancers on how to
     approach the problem of meaningfully
     recreating the prevailing styles.

2. MODERN PERFORMANCES

     In the twentieth century Scarlatti
revivals began as early as 1940 with the
weeklong celebration in Siena at which *Il trionfo
dell'onore* (among other works) was performed for
the first time since the eighteenth century.
The fifties brought revivals of *Mitridate Eupatore*
in Milan and Heidelberg, the *St. John Passion* in
New Haven and the *Saint Cecilia Mass* in Brooklyn,
New York.

     La Griselda, *L'onestà negli amori*, and *Il Tigrane* all
returned to the stage in the sixties (1960
was, of course, the 300th anniversary of the
composer's birth). Due, at least in part, to
the issuance of several volumes of Lino

Bianchi's collected edition (see Section V,
1), these years also witnessed the
rejuvenation of a number of the oratorios. *La
Giuditta* (Naples) and several other oratorios of
Scarlatti received their first modern
performances in Rome and *Il martirio di Sant'Orsola*
and *San Filippo Neri* were heard again in New York
and Edinburgh, respectively. *Cain ovvero il primo
omicidio* also received its first modern
performance at Siena in September 1966.

Works performed anew in the seventies
included the *Vespers of Saint Cecilia;* the oratorios
Davidis pugna et victoria and *La Giuditta* (Cambridge);
the operas *L'Eraclea, Gli equivoci in amore (La Rosaura),
Gli equivoci nel sembiante,* and *La Statira,* as well as
four pieces from *Comodo Antonino.*

The eighties have seen performances of
some of the oratorios (e.g., *La Giuditta* [i] in
Innsbruck (1989)) and operas (e.g., a
performance of *Gli equivoci nel sembiante* in the same
city (1988)) as well as a radio performance of
[*Una villa di Tuscolo*], a work thought to be by
Scarlatti (see item 204). With the number of
new editions now available we may be able to
look forward to further revivals in the
nineties.

Performance Reviews

Church Music

Messa di Santa Cecilia

384. Burgess, C. "Two-century-old Mass Given
     Premiere in Salt Lake City." *Music West* 16
     (May 6, 1961).

     Not seen.

385. "Scarlatti Mass Given American Premiere."
     Musical America 78 (June 1958): 19.

     Performance by the Brooklyn College Chorus

and Chorale, led by Robert Hickok with Charles
Bressler, tenor. Mason Martens edited the
score from the original MS.

386. Mitchell, Donald. "Some First Performances."
    Musical Times 97 (1956): 207.

Vespro di Santa Cecilia

387. Benary, Peter. "Luzern: Internazionale
    Musikfestwochen." *Schweizerische Musikzeitung* 110
    (1970): 304-305.

    Review of the first complete modern
    performance in Lucerne. Edition prepared by
    Hans Jörg Jans (who also prepared *Tigrane* for
    performance at Basel).

388. Seelmann-Eggebert, Ursula. "Entdeckung nach
    einem Vierteljahrtausend." *Neue Zeitschrift für
    Musik* 131 (1970): 483-484.

    Discusses the performance at the
    Internationalen Musikfestwochen Luzern (see
    also item 387). Gives performers, among whom
    were: Edward Tarr, Trumpet; Ursula Buckel,
    Soprano; chorus and Festival Strings of
    Lucerne directed by Peter Maag.

Operas

Comodo Antonino

*   Rose, Gloria. "Two Operas by Scarlatti
    Recovered." Cited as item 237.

    Not a review; Rose's article notes, however,
    the performance of 4 pieces from the opera by
    the École Normal de Musique, Paris, Salle
    Cortot, March 16, 1970.

L'Eraclea

389. Blanks, Fred R. "Mittagong." *Musical Times* 118
     (1977): 500.

     First Australian staging of an Alessandro
     Scarlatti opera; by the University of New
     South Wales Opera, dir., Roger Covell; prod.,
     Bernd Benthaak.

390. Stevens, Denis. "New York." *Musical Times* 111
     (1970): 730-731.

     Review of Ithaca performance. Use of spoken
     commentary to convey plot since no recitatives
     survive except for comic scenes.

391. Zaslow, Neil. "Ithaca." *Opera News* 34 (June
     13, 1970): 25.

     Review of Ithaca performance at Cornell
     University in honor of the retirement of
     Professor Donald J. Grout. First modern
     performance and the American premiere.
     Largely student cast; Cornell Chamber
     Orchestra, dir., Karel Husa.

Gli equivoci nel amore. (*La Rosaura*)

392. Greenhalgh, Michael. "*La Rosaura* (Opera
     Integra)." *Music and Musicians* 22 (Apr. 1974):
     50 and 52.

     Review of Feb. 9th performance by Opera
     Integra. About one third of the opera cut.
     Trans. by Jeanne Henney. Radio London taped
     for broadcast.

393. Porter, Andrew. "*La Rosaura.*" *Musical Times* 115
     (1974) 321-322.

     Review of the first modern revival; in three
     concert performances with three casts.

Hammersmith Town Hall, Feb 7-9. Performed by Addison Opera Workshop. Score of first two acts edited by Eitner in 1885; third added by directors of Opera Integra: Janet Colebrooke and Brian Galloway.

Gli equivoci nel sembiante

394. Segal, L. "Los Angeles." *Opera News* 40 (Dec. 20-27, 1975): 34-35.

Performance by UCLA Opera Workshop in conjunction with the meeting of the American Musicological Society in November. Libretto translated by Frank D'Accone; edited by Charles Speroni, Dean of the College of Fine Arts, UCLA. Photo in Grout, item 194, p. 30.

La Griselda

395. Buchau, Stephanie von. "San Francisco." *Opera News* 41 (July 1976): 37.

Review of American premiere at Berkeley. Carole Bogard in title role. Lawrence Moe, cond., with student orchestra.

396. Dean, Winton. "Radio." *Musical Times* 109 (1968): 752-753.

Review of a BBC radio (studio) performance.

397. McCredie, Andrew D. "Griselda: Kiel." *Opera* 15 (1964): 407-408.

Performance of March 29 produced by Friedrich Petzold. Wanda Busse in title role. Theodore Gress, dir. Describes sets. Photo, p. 407.

398. Müller, Paul. "Der Vater der Musikoper; Alessandro Scarlatti's *Griselda*." *Neue Zeitschrift*

für Musik 123 (1962): 337-338.

Opera presented in a German translation by
Christof Bitter; Bernhard Lonz, dir. Photo,
p. 337.

399. Porter, Andrew. "Musical Events: Flour of
Wyfly Pacience." (University of California,
Berkeley). *New Yorker* 52 (May 31, 1976): 107-
108+.

Photo from this production in Grout, item
194, p. 93.

400. Tellini, Enrico. "Naples." *Opera (Eng.)* 22
(Jan. 1971): 66-67.

Performance reviews of *La Griselda* and *Il Tigrane*
(given during the 13th Neopolitan Musical
Autumn organized by Italian radio and Azienda
Autonoma Truismo). Score revised by Hans Jorg
Jans; many cuts; speaker-related action; *Il
Tigrane* given concert performance with Paul
Esswood, countertenor, in title role. October
29, concert performance of *La Griselda* (broadcast
by BBC) with Mirella Freni in title role.

L'honesta negli amori

401. Atterberg, Kurt. "Stockholm." *Opera News* 31
(Sep. 10, 1966): 30.

Revival celebrating the 300th anniversary of
the recently restored Drottningholm Court
Theatre. With Elisabeth Söderstrom.

402. Limmert, Erich. [Hannover]. "Herrenhausen:
Scarlatti und Monteverdi." *Neue Zeitschrift für
Musik* 127 (1966): 339-340.

Discussion of the work and review of the
performance given in the Galariegebäude
Herrenhausen by the ensembles of the Royal

Stockholm Opera.

Il Mitridate Eupatore

403. Davies, Margaret E.   "Bordeaux May Vintage."
     Opera News 27 (Sept. 29, 1962): 29.

     First staged performance in France of *Il
     Mitridate*. Piccioli edition. Cond. by Glauco
     Curiel. Peter Gottlieb, baritone, in title
     role.

404. Dibb, F. "Oxford's Scarlatti." *Music and
     Musicians* 10 (Jan. 1962): 36.

*   Grout, Donald J.   [Reference to Bel Canto
     Opera Co. performance in New York, March
     1975.] See Grout, item 194, p. 75.

405. "Herrliche Bel Canto Melodik, *Mitridate Eupatore*
     von Scarlatti in Heidelberg." *Neue Zeitschrift für
     Musik* 118 (1957): 27-28.

     Brief review of Heidelberger Bühne
     performance under Paul Hager. Mentions
     premiere in Milan in May 1956 which used
     Piccioli edition and starred soprano Victoria
     De Los Angeles.

406. "*Mitridate Eupatore. Oxford University Opera Club*. *Opera
     (Eng.)* 13 (Feb. 1962): 139-140.

407. Rostand, Claude.   "French Festivals: 1962."
     Musical America 82 (Dec. 1962): 21.

     Praises Scarlatti's opera as foreshadowing
     Verdi in its "vigor and realism." Production
     staged by Roger Lalande.

408. Sadie, Stanley.   "*Il Mitridate Eupatore* at Oxford."

Musical Opinion 85 (Jan. 1962): 213.

*   Westrup, Jack. See item 256 regarding
     performance at Piccola Scala, Milan, May
     1956, in which Piccioli edition was used.

La Rosaura See *Gli equivoci in amore*

La Statira

409. Bowen, Meirion. "Camden: Shoestring
     Celebration." *Music and Musicians* 18 (July
     1970): 50.

     Praises the work and criticizes much of the
     singing, lack of movement on stage, and the
     limited stage sets (which resulted from an
     inadequate budget).

*   Boyd, Malcolm. "Scarlatti's *La Statira*." *Musical
     Times* 111 (1970): 495-497. Cited as item
     264.

410. Dean, Winton. "Camden." *Musical Times* 111
     (1970): 732.

     Detailed review of the Camden performance
     (the first in Britain) May 7-9 in the
     Jeannetta Cochrane Theatre by the London
     Chamber Opera. Critical more of the work than
     of the performance. Orchestra (string quartet
     and harpsichord with 2 trumpets for the battle
     scene) cond. by Lionel Friend. Criticizes
     staging.

411. Jacobs, Arthur. "London." *Opera (Eng)* 21 (July
     1970): 679-680.

     Review of Camden performance. London
     Chamber Orchestra at Camden Festival.
     Criticizes "plodding performance in Italian."

Il Tigrane

412. Collins, Michael. In *Essays...Charles Warren Fox*
     (cited as item 269), p. 99.

     Mentions performance by the Basel U. and
     Stadttheater in 1969 based on score prepared
     from the Naples copy under the direction of
     Hans Oesch. Performed in German translation
     except for comic scenes. Only performance
     known since one in 1716 at Livorno. Cond. by
     Paul Zelter; Countertenor, Paul Esswood.

*   Tellini, Enrico. See under *La Griselda*

Il trionfo dell'onore

413. Bollert, Werner. "Alessandro Scarlatti
     revividus." *Musica* (Kassel) 24 (1970): 38.

     Reviews performance in Berlin by the
     Berliner Kammeroper based on Mortari's
     edition.

414. Kaplan, A. "San Francisco Opera Center."
     High Fidelity/ Musical America 32 (Sept. 1982): 28-
     29 in *Musical America* section.

     At Herbst Theater by San Francisco Opera Co.
     Showcase. Used Hermine W. Williams' new
     edition, see Section V, 1 (the first
     transcription of the entire manuscript) and
     Eng. trans. by Charles Kondek. Ten of the 39
     musical numbers cut. Gives cast, directors,
     etc.

415. Koch, Heinz W.. "Freiburg: Schürfer am Werk
     (Alessandro Scarlatti: *Der Triumph der Ehre*)."
     Opern Welt 7 (July 1973): 47.

     Review of Freiburg performance April 26,
     1973 (premiere, April 22), dir. by Heinrich
     Kehm with German trans. and staging by

Wolfgang Poch. Provides list of performers, etc.

416. Lewinski, W. E. von. "Don Juan in Pisa: Alessandro Scarlatti's *Il trionfo dell'onore* bei den Schwetzinger Festspielen." *Opernwelt* 26/7 (1985): 12.

417. Limmert, Erich. "Eine Scarlatti-Uraufführung." *Musica* 14 (1960): 669-670.

418. _____. "Scarlatti's *Triumph der Ehre.*" *Neue Zeitschrift für Musik* 121 (1960): 310.

Describes the work, its staging, and performance at Hannover-Herrenhausen. Notes that it is performed for the first time in approximately its original form. Identifies performers, etc.

419. Sadie, Stanley. "Scarlatti at Cambridge." *Opera (Eng.)* 18/12 (1967): 1025-1026.

Describes workshop performance at the ADC Theatre, Oct. 18; produced by David Pountney, translation by Geoffrey Dunn; Mark Elder, cond. the University opera society. Mentions previous performances at Oxford and Birmingham.

420. _____. "*The Triumph of Honour;* Opera Viva at the New Theatre, King's College." *Opera (Eng.)* 30/9 (1979): 906-908.

Reviews the June 28 performance based on translation of Geoffrey Dunn.

Oratorios

Cain ovvero il primo omicidio

*   Fabbri, Mario. "Torna a luce la partitura
      autografia dell'oratorio *Il primo omicidio*...."
      Cited as item 296.

First modern performance at the Crypt of S.
Domenico, Siena, Sept 3, 1966. Ed. of Bruno
Rigacci and Mario Fabbri based on autograph
score in the Frank V. de Bellis Collection,
San   Francisco   State   University,   CA.
Performers included *I Virtuosi di Roma* dir. by
Renato Fasano.

*   Hicks, Anthony [Charles]. "Scarlatti." Cited
      as item 422.

Mention of performance of *Cain, ovvero Il primo
omicidio*, Nov. 1975 by the Alessandro Scarlatti
Society (dir., Anthony Bremner) "currently
concentrating on the composer's oratorios."

421. Webber, Nicholas. "Scarlatti's *Cain*." *Music
      and Musicians* 24 (Apr. 1976): 47-48.

Very negative review both with respect to
the work and its performance. Performance at
St. Martin-in-the-Fields celebrating the 250th
anniversary   year   by   the   "newly   formed"
Alessandro Scarlatti Society and its director
Anthony Bremner.

Davidus pugna et victoria

422. Hicks, Anthony.   "Scarlatti." *Musical Times* 117
      (1976): 421.

Reference to the Alessandro Scarlatti
Society performance Mar. 13th at St. George's,
Hanover Square, London, under Geoffrey Hanson;
with   soloists,   Patricia   Greig   (David),   A.
Bremner, countertenor and director of the

Society, and the Saltarello Choir. Criticized
for lack of convincing style in accompaniments.
Suggests use of Baroque instruments, etc.

423. "München Konzerte." *Oper und Konzert* 8 (July
     1970): 35.

     Not seen.

424. Wright, Peter. "David." *Music and Musicians* 24
     (June 1976): 56-57.

     Describes the work and its performance March
     13 in London (see item 422).

La Giuditta

425. "Clarion Concerts." *Music Journal* 26 (Feb.
     1968): 82.

     Very brief review of performance by the
     Abbey Singers and assisting guest artists of
     La Giuditta [i], Jan. 9 at Town Hall, New York.
     Series led by Newell Jenkins.

426. Strongin, Theodore. "New York." *American Choral
     Review* 10/3 (1968): 131. Reprinted from the
     New York Times.

     Jan. 9 concert which included performance of
     La Giuditta [i] at Town Hall with Jan DeGaetani
     as the Jewish prince briefly reviewed. Dir.,
     Newell Jenkins. Clarion Concerts Orchestra
     and Abbey Singers with assisting artists.

*   Swale, David. "The *Judith* Oratorios of
         Alessandro Scarlatti." Cited as item 303.

         Performance of 1700 (Cambridge) *Giuditta* at
         Adelaide, Australia, Festival of the Arts,
         Mar. 17, 1976 mentioned in note.

Johannespassion. Passio Domini nostri Jesu Christi
          secundum Joannem

427. Hanley, Edwin. "Current Chronicle."
     [Concerning A. Scarlatti's *Passion according to St.
     John*, performed on Dec. 29, 1952 at Yale
     University, New Haven]. *Musical Quarterly* 39
     (1953): 241-247.

     A substantive examination of the *Passion*
     performed for the first time in 250 years at a
     joint meeting of the American Musicological
     Society and the Society for Music in the
     Liberal Arts College. Not a performance
     review in the usual sense, this article
     discusses the style of the work and puts it
     into historical perspective. Oddly, for a
     composition of this magnitude, this seems to
     be the only article on the subject. Calls
     attention to the fact that the Italian passion
     has been little studied. See Section V, 1 for
     edition by Hanley.

Il martirio di Sant'Orsola

428. "Clarion Concerts Offer Novelties." *Musical
     America* 80 (Feb. 1960): 255.

     Brief description and review of first U.S.
     performance (Jan. 19) at Town Hall. Newell
     Jenkins, cond. Singers included Adele
     Addison, sop., Russell Oberlin, countertenor,
     and Ara Berberian, bass. Robert Nagel, Tpt.
     First U.S. performance. MS discovered by
     Ennemond Trillat, Conservatory of Lyons.

San Filippo Neri

*   Bosanquet, Caroline. "Alessandro Scarlatti's
     San Filippo Neri." *Musical Times* 101 (1960): 700.
     Cited as item 304.

La vergine addolorata.

*   Tellini, Enrico.   "Naples."   See under *La Griselda*.

IV

SOURCES: WORKLISTS, CATALOGS AND DESCRIPTIVE ARTICLES

The lack of a complete thematic catalog or critical edition of Alessandro Scarlatti's works poses problems for researchers and performers alike. Rostirolla's catalog (item 435) is the only published source which gives the cantata manuscript locations (and MS numbers in some cases). Hanley's unpublished dissertation, item 134 (Yale, 1967; available on microfilm from UMI) contains a thorough critical catalog of the cantatas with MS locations; it includes an analytical thematic catalog of Scarlatti's cantata repertoire that is unique in the literature . See Strohm, item 437, pp. 122ff. for comments and new information on cantata sources at Yale.

Musical incipits for the masses are given in Dent's and Rostirolla's catalogs (items 431 and 435, respectively). Incipits of some of the keyboard pieces are given in several articles (items 315 and 322) but,as Strohm justifiably notes (item 437), a thematic catalog for these works is "long deserved" and "in all the published worklists, the treatment of the keyboard music is sketchy and confused." The index in Barry Brook's bibliography of thematic indices (item 444) is useful for tracing musical incipits cited in MSS, library catalogs, etc.

As was mentioned earlier, the only collected editions of Scarlatti's works are those of the oratorios, edited by Lino Bianchi, and the operas, under the general editorship of Donald J. Grout until his death in 1987. The introductions to individual

volumes of these sets (and the supplementary
critical notes for the opera volumes available
on request from Harvard's Isham Memorial
Library) provide, with few exceptions, the
most complete information about sources for
the works represented.

For the most part, the selected work
lists, catalogs, and articles cited below
relate specifically to Scarlatti sources. It
is important to note that articles which
describe the discovery of a single Scarlatti
work in MS are usually included in the section
of the book which relates to its genre; e.g.,
a report about the discovery of an opera MS is
cited under "Opera," Section II, 1.

Scarlatti MSS are scattered throughout the
world in many public and private libraries and
archives. Published catalogs and articles
describing some of these collections exist
(though many of the former are outdated
and/or incomplete) and should be examined
along with other reference sources of a
general nature that deal with editions of
early printers and publishers, musical
instrument collections, etc. Some library
catalogs include musical incipits (e.g., the
Bibliothèque Nationale, Paris. Department des
Imprimés. *Catalogue du fonds de musique ancienne...* which
cites incipits for many of the Scarlatti
cantatas in its collection). Others,
especially journal articles, describe the
history and holdings of individual libraries
and often provide important manuscript
inventories in addition to useful information
about what is necessary to use the collection,
etc. John Glenn Paton's "Cantata and Aria
Manuscripts in the Saint Cecilia Library,"
Music Library Association. Notes 36 (1980): 563-574,
for example, cites and identifies by MS number
many individual cantatas by Scarlatti in that
archive. Still others, such as the Oxford
University, Christ Church College, *Catalogue of
Printed Music Published Prior to 1801...*, London, 1919,
which contains a number of important Scarlatti
MSS, identifies MSS for which negative

microfilms exist (from which microform copies can be supplied).

The above items illustrate some of the the types of information one can acquire from these general catalogs and articles which are too numerous to include here *in toto*. Most are listed in Vincent Duckles' and Michael Keller's invaluable *Music Reference and Research Materials*, 4th ed. (N.Y.: Schirmer, 1988).

* * *

Alessandro Scarlatti Worklists, Catalogs, etc.

430. Boyd, Malcolm. "Work-list." In article "Alessandro Scarlatti." *New Grove Italian Baroque Masters*, pp. 244-262. See items 12 and 133.

Based on the worklist in the *New Grove Dictionary of Music and Musicians*, 1980, this is the most accurate and up to date list of works available though it cannot compete in terms of detail with the earlier catalog of Rostirolla (item 435). It provides information regarding MS locations (identified by *RISM* sigla), text authorship, first performances, voices, and instrumentation. Cantata MS sources are *not* cited. Boyd and Hermine Weigel Williams assisted Donald J. Grout in the revisions which include some references to modern editions.

Following are some additions and corrections (with references to the sources of information noted); this is in no way intended to be an all-inclusive list, but rather, represents items which have come to my attention in the course of working on this book.

OPERAS

Arminio, dramma. MS of 1722 revision: US-NH. (Strohm, item 437).

Il Lismaco (of uncertain attribution; MS attrib. to B. Pasquini). MS: Dbrd-WD. (Strohm, item 436).

La guerriera costante. 4 arias attr. to Scarlatti identified by G. Rose with the conjectural title *Fidalba e Oreste* (Rose, item 237). MS: I-Vnm.

ORATORIOS, LARGE SACRED WORKS

La Giuditta (i).   Text by Pietro Ottoboni. (Strohm, item 436; Morelli, item 282; H. J. Marx, item 94).

Il martirio di S. Orsola. MS: US-NH.   (Strohm, item 437)

Cain, overo Il primo omicidio. Text by Antonio Ottoboni.   (Talbot and Timms, item 101).

CANTATAS   MS: US-NH (each cited as *unicum*). (Strohm, item 437).

Al furor che ti consiglia
Dal mio brando al chiaro lampo
Di dolore in dolor
Era un giorno Fileno
Fate, o Cieli
Lontanza e gelosia
Luci vaghe, se mirate
Lungi dal Tebro in riva
Nella febbre d'amor
Non ha un giorno di contento
(H)or che spunta nel prato
Partì l'idolo mio
Per dare pace al vostro core
Quando il fato un cor bersaglia
Restava al mesto Aminta
S'en parte sdegnato
Siete belle ancor piangenti
Son contento, non m'amate
Sul margine d'un rio cui facean
Un pensier dice alla mente

MOTETS

Stabat Mater. MS score is *not* among the holdings of the library of the Accademia di Santa Cecilia, Rome, as cited. (Hermine W. Williams from correspondence with I-Rsc).

431. Dent, Edward J. "Catalogue of the Extant Works of Alessandro Scarlatti." In *Alessandro Scarlatti* (item 6), pp. 206-232 with corrections by Frank Walker in the "Additional Notes," pp. 244-248.

    Early published catalog of MSS and librettos grouped according to genre with library locations. Does not include modern printed editions or arias in MS from unidentified operas. Gives incipits of all the masses.

*   Freund, Cecilia Kathryn Van de Kamp. "Evaluating the Bibliographical Sources for Alessandro Scarlatti's Cantata Repertoire." Cited as item 131.

432. Garbelotto, Antonio. "Contributo per un catalogo aggiornato delle opere di Alessandro Scarlatti." *Archivio storico siciliano* 3rd ser., 13 (1963): 239-344.

    A lengthy "tentative" catalog of works, librettos, iconographical sources, recordings, bibliographical sources, etc. Must be used with great caution as it contains a number of errors.

*   Griffin, Thomas. "Alessandro Scarlatti e la serenata a Roma...." Cited as item 305.

*   Hanley, Edwin. "Alessandro Scarlatti's Cantate da Camera: A Bibliographical Study." Cited as item 134.

* _____. "Scarlatti, Pietro Alessandro
  Gaspare." Cited as item 14.

* Lorenz, Alfred. *Alessandro Scarlattis Jugendoper.*
  Cited as item 205.

433. Masson, Renée M. "Inventaire des manuscrits
     (autographes et copies) des oeuvres
     d'Alessandro Scarlatti, conservés a la
     Bibliothèque du Conservatoire de Paris."
     Gazzetta musicale di Napoli 3/7-8 (July-Aug. 1957):
     112-129 and 3/10-12 (Oct.-Dec. 1957): 166-
     180.

     Catalog of Scarlatti MSS in the collection
     of the Paris Conservatory now housed in the
     Bibliothèque Nationale, Paris. October issue
     contains published corrections of Dent's list
     (see item 6). According to Boyd (item 122, p.
     26), Masson's article is "so full of mistakes
     that it serves only to aggravate the
     confusion." Not seen.

* Pestelli, Giorgio. "Appendice: Incipit delle
  toccate Scarlattiane conservate a Napoli."
  In "Le toccate per strumento a tastiera di
  Alessandro Scarlatti nei manoscritti
  napoletani" (cited as item 322), pp. 188-192.

434. Prota-Giurleo, Ulisse. "Elenco cronologico
     delle opere di Alessandro Scarlatti." In
     Celebrazione... (item 4), pp. 81-89.

     Contains lists of "Melodrammi, Feste
     Teatrali, Serenate" and "Oratorii." Differs
     on some points with the *NGIBM* "Work-list"
     (item 430), however, first section gives
     additional details for some works (e.g.,
     information regarding performers and later
     performances).

435. Rostirolla, Giancarlo. "Catalogo." In

Pagano, Robert et al. *Alessandro Scarlatti* (item 16).

A massive and comprehensive catalog of the composer's works still very useful for its wealth of detail though it has been criticized for omissions and possible misattributions. One of the few sources that lists modern editions at length; however, a number of important editions have appeared since it was published. Includes incipits for the masses and MS locations for the cantatas.

* Sartori, Claudio. "Appendice." Cited as item 323.

436. Strohm, Reinhard. "Alessandro Scarlatti." *Rivista italiana di musicologia* 11 (1976): 314-323.

Review of the Pagano, Bianchi, Rostirolla volume (cited in items 16, 275, and 435, respectively). Corrects and supplements Rostirolla's catalog (item 435) in the following categories: operas (and pasticci); serenatas; cantatas; madrigals; oratorios; masses; and motets, psalms. Useful discussion of research problems with references to research sources.

* _____. "Hasse, Scarlatti, Rolli." Cited as item 117.

437. _____. "Scarlattiana at Yale." In *Handel e gli Scarlatti a Roma...*" (item 38, Book II), pp. 113-152.

An article of major importance and usefulness for its detailed description and inventory of MSS containing works by Alessandro Scarlatti in the Yale University collections. Part 2 discusses the keyboard music especially the famous "Higgs Manuscript" (edited by Shedlock, see Section V, 2 and item

324).   Stresses   the   need   for   a   thematic
catalog and briefly discusses what putting
together a critical edition of the keyboard
works would entail.   Part 3 describes the
cantata MS holdings including Misc. Ms. 165;
Osborn Shelves, Music 22; Misc. Ms. 166; and
Osborn Shelves Music Ms. 1 and 2. Osborn 22
was not used by Hanley; it contains 13 items
attributed to Scarlatti including five unica
previously unknown. Osborn 1 and Misc Ms. 166
could not be used by Hanley either, thus
contain some items not in his catalog. Osborn
2 once owned by Charles Burney contains
"composition autographs."   Strohm discusses
all aspects of the MSS including their
history,   paper,   copyists,   bindings,   the
autographs, etc. Part 4 provides the important
information that Osborn Shelves Music 24
contains a MS of the oratorio *Il martirio di S. Orsola*
hitherto undocumented (not in *NGIBM*) and that
Misc. Ms. 75 of Roman provenance contains 6
arias, one duet, and a quartet from the 1722
setting of *Arminio*, the only known source of
Scarlatti's last operatic setting.   Part 5
mentions   late   copies   from   the   Rinck
Collection.   Appendix I gives tables of the
MSS which amount to a complete inventory and
Appendix II furnishes an alphabetical list of
texts set by the composer in the Yale MSS.

*   _____. "Werkverzeichnisse: Alessandro
           Scarlatti Opern und andere dramatische Werke
           1714-1723." In Strohm, Reinhard. "Italien-
           ische Opernarien...." (item 221), pp. 222-
           226.

438. Zanetti, Emilia, and Claudio Sartori.
     "Contributo a un catalogo delle opere
     teatrali di Alessandro Scarlatti esistenti
     nelle biblioteche italiane." In *Gli Scarlatti*
     (item 35), pp. 63-84.

     A   catalog   containing   information   on
     librettos,   scores,   and   productions   of
     Scarlatti's operas completed when conditions

limited access to resources. Works listed
alphabetically by title. Authors matched a
number of separate arias or aria collections
with the works from which they were derived by
comparing them with surviving librettos. A
number of librettos (noted for the first time)
are cited with reproductions of the
frontispiece; still a useful reference tool.

General Catalogs, Articles, Bibliographies and Directories of Sources

439. Benton, Rita, ed. *Directory of Music Research Libraries*.
RISM Ser. C, Pt. III: Spain, France, Italy,
Portugal. Kassel: Bärenreiter, 1972.

A guide to library resources in these
countries; the Spain and/or Portugal sections
have been partially updated in several
articles in *Fontes artis musicae* and *Music Library
Association. Notes*, and a major revision is
currently being planned.

440. Boyd, Malcolm. "Music Manuscripts in the
Mackworth Collection at Cardiff." *Music and
Letters* 54 (1973): 133-141.

Contents of the collection of Sir Herbert
Mackworth (1737-1791) housed in the Central
Library, Cardiff, summarized. Includes
printed and MS music, including complete
scores of Italian operas by Hasse, Capelli,
Giovanni Bononcini, Alessandro Scarlatti (*La
Statira*), etc. and vocal and instrumental works
by eighteenth-century composers. Two volumes
(MS copies) contain 18 cantatas by A.
Scarlatti among which is *Contentati mio core* for
alto and continuo not known to exist
elsewhere.

441. British Library. Dept. of Manuscripts.
Catalogue of Manuscript Music in the British Museum.
Comp. by Augustus Hughes-Hughes. London,
1906-1909. 3 vols. Reprint: London, 1964.

Vol. 1: sacred vocal music; Vol.2: secular vocal music; Vol. 3: instrumental music, treatises, etc.

An early catalog of a collection rich in Scarlatti MSS. Entries classified by form or genre so that contents of individual MSS often separated. Author indexes; title, first-line index of songs.

442. _____. *Handlist of Music Manuscripts Acquired 1908-67.* By Pamela Willets. London: British Museum, 1970. 112 pp.

Supplements Hughes-Hughes catalog (see item 441). Includes the "Additional MSS" and music MSS preserved with the printed collections of the Dept. of Printed Books.

443. British Library. Dept. of Printed Books. *The Catalogue of Printed Music in the British Library to 1980.* Ed. by Lauren Baillie. 62 vols. London: K.G. Saur, 1981- . ISBN 0-86291-300-4. Vol. 50: ISBN 0-86291-347-0 (1986)

Pages 230-236 of Vol. 50 contain a catalog of Scarlatti's printed works from the eighteenth to the twentieth centuries in the British Library collections.

444. Brook, Barry. *Thematic Catalogs in Music: An Annotated Bibliography.* N.Y.: Pendragon, 1972. [Rev. and expanded ed. forthcoming].

Includes items pertaining to Alessandro, Domenico, Giuseppe and an unidentified Scarlatti. The last is linked to the composition of a 3-act opera entitled *L'isola disabitata* included in a MS located at D-Dl (microfilm copy, CUNY Graduate Center). Music and text incipits for each number in the opera given in the MS.

445. Burney, Charles. *Catalogue of the Music Library of Charles Burney Sold in London, 8 August 1814.* Intro. by A. Hyatt King. Amsterdam: Frits Knuf, 1973. ix and 42 pp. (Auction Catalogues of Music, no. 2).

Facsimile list of Burney's music collection which contained a number of scores by both Alessandro and Domenico Scarlatti.

446. Dent, Edward J. "The Library of Fortunato Santini." *Monthly Musical Record* 34 (April 1904): 64- .

Not seen.

447. Eitner, Robert. *Biographisch-bibliographisches Quellen-Lexikon der Musiker und Musikgelehrten....* Leipzig: Breitkopf & Härtel, 1898-1904. 10 vols. Reprinted with supplements: N.Y.: Musurgia, 1947. Neuauflage: Wiesbaden: Breitkopf, 1959-1960. "2 verbesserte Auflage": Graz: Akademische Druck- und Verlagsanstalt, 1959-1960.

Now outdated in many respects (especially with regard to locations; see, however, item 457), this was until the advent of *RISM* the fundamental published reference tool for locating primary sources of pre-1800 music. Although *RISM* has begun to replace it, the published documentation for Alessandro Scarlatti that *RISM* currently provides (see items 453 and 454) is still not complete.

448. Gasperini, Guido and Franco Gallo. *Catalogo delle opere musicali del Conservatorio di M. S. Pietro a Majella di Napoli.* (Parma, 1934). Reprint: Bologna: Forni Editore, 1988 (Bibliotheca musica Bononienis, Sez. I N. 21) 696 pp. Indices of authors and names.

* *International Inventory of Musical Sources*. See *Répertoire* *internationale des sources musicales (RISM)*.

449. King, Alec Hyatt. *A Wealth of Music in the Collections of the British Library (Reference Division) and the British Museum*. London: Clive Bingley, 1983. ISBN 0-85157-330-4.

Up to date description of collections and catalogs of the British Museum and British Library containing music. Manuscripts include Scarlatti autographs of *12 sinfonie di concerto grosso*, the cantata *Ombre tacite e sole*, and, among 25 operas of Scarlatti, *La Griselda* (1721).

450. Lattes, Sergio. "Santini, Fortunato." In *The New Grove Dictionary of Music and Musicians*, Vol. 16, p. 481. London: Macmillan, 1980.

Gives a brief biography of the composer-collector with bibliography relevant to his extensive musical library (most of which is now housed in Münster).

451. McClymonds, Marita, and Diane Parr Walker. *Inventory of Librettos in North American Libraries*. Charlottesville: University of Virginia, 1987- (a *RISM* project).

Not seen.

452. Mischiati, Oscar. *Indici, cataloghi e avvisi degle editori e librai musicali italiani dal 1591 al 1798*. Florence: Leo S. Olschki Editore, 1984. 553 pp. (Studi e testi per la storia della musica, 2).

Not seen.

453. *Repertoire internationale des sources musicales (RISM)*. *Einzeldrücke vor 1800*. Bd. 7, pp. 354-356. Kassel: Bärenreiter, 1978.

Lists and locates early (pre-1800) printed

editions of some of Scarlatti's works.

454. *RISM. Musikhandschriften 1600-1800: Datenbank-Index*.
(1986 ed.) Kassel: Bärenreiter, 1986.   2
microfiches and 16 p. pamphlet (*RISM*, ser.
A, pt. II).

Manuscripts for this period were too
numerous to cite in the conventional printed
format; thus, what exists is this index on
fiche which provides access to a database with
fuller information. Citations under Alessandro
Scarlatti to date limited. One can obtain
additional information by writing Kassel (*RISM*
headquarters). *RISM* files includes items not
cited in Rostirolla (item 435): see Strohm
(item 436).

455. Sartori, Claudio. *I libretti italiani a stampa dalle origini
al 1800: catalogo analitico con 16 indici*.   Cuneo:
Bertola e Locatalli, c1990-, v.1- .

Not seen.

455a._____.   *Primo tentativo di catalogo unico dei libretti
italiani a stampa fino all'anno 1800*.   Milan:
Biblioteca Nazionale Braidense & Ufficio
Ricerca Fondi Musicali, 1973-1981.

Photocopies of cards assembled by Sartori as
a union catalog of printed Italian libretti.
Originally a RISM project. The most extensive
union catalog of Italian opera. Not seen.

456. Sonneck, Oscar G.T., comp. & ed.   *Catalogue of
Opera Librettos Printed before 1800 in the Library of Congress*.
2 vols. Washington: Government Printing
Office, 1914. Reprint: N.Y.: Johnson
Reprint Corp., 1968. 1674 pp. Facs., mus.
exs., port.

Vol. 1: title catalog; Vol. 2: author,
composer lists and aria index. Collection

includes a number by A. Scarlatti, one by
Domenico (*L'Irene*), and a number by Giuseppe,
almost entirely from the Schatz collection.
Vol. 1 includes information from the librettos
and notes by the editor.

457. Wilier, Stephen A. "The Present Location of
     Libraries Listed in Robert Eitner's
     Biographisch-bibliographisches Quellen-Lexikon."   *Fontes
     artis musicae* 28 (1981): 220-239.

     Gives the present location for most of the
     collections cited in Eitner's "Verzeichnis der
     Bibliotheks-Abjürzungen" in volume 1 of the
     Quellen-Lexikon (item 447).

ALESSANDRO SCARLATTI'S WORKS IN MODERN EDITION OR FACSIMILE

Introduction

As was noted in the preface to this book, there are few up-to-date lists of modern editions and facsimiles of Alessandro Scarlatti's works. Hanley's worklist in *MGG* includes a separate section of modern editions less circumscribed than the citations in the *NGIBM* but also, unfortunately, less current. Rostirolla's catalog has one of the largest lists of modern printed editions of the composer's works, however, some inaccuracies have been found in it (see item 436 for a supplement and corrections by Strohm). For these reasons, the focus here is upon creating a list of modern editions and facsimiles rather than on duplicating the types of source lists already available in other published literature. Note that articles at the beginning of titles are disregarded in alphabetization except for cantata editions where they are included to be consistent with the *NGIBM* worklist.

1. Vocal Music

Cantatas

Al fragor di lieta tromba. See **SERENATAS**: *Pace, amore e providenza; Al fragor di lieta tromba.*

Alfin m'ucciderete [soprano with basso continuo]. In Boyd: #18, pp. 137-146. See under Cantata Collections.

Alle troiane antenne [Didone abbandonata] [soprano with basso continuo]. In Boyd: #17, pp. 131-136. See under Cantata Collections.

Allor ch'il dio di Delo [soprano with basso continuo]. In Boyd: #14, pp. 123-126. See under Cantata Collections.

****Alme, voi che provaste* [duet for soprano and alto with basso continuo]. (Scarlatti-Durante). Ed. by F. Degrada.

Ammore, brutto figlio de pottana [Cantata in lingua napolitana] [tenor and basso continuo]. In Boyd: #24, pp. 1181-186. See under Cantata Collections.

Amor, fabro ingegnoso. In Dehn, S.W. *Theoretisch-praktische Harmonielehre.* Berlin.: Schlesinger, 1860. 2nd ed. p. 330-

****Andate, o miei sospiri (con idea humana)* [and] *(con idea inhumana).* Ed. by F. Degrada. [Rostirolla, item 435, p. 568].

Andate o miei sospiri (con idea umana). In: Choron, Alexander Étienne. *Principes de composition.* Paris: Le Duc, 1808

Andate o miei sospiri, al cor d'Irene [I] [con idea umana]. In Boyd: #26, pp. 223-228. See under Cantata Collections.

Andate o miei sospiri, al cor d'Irene [II] [con idea inumana]. In Boyd: #27, pp. 229-234. See under Cantata Collections.

Ardo, è ver, per te d'amore [soprano with flute and basso continuo]. Realisation par Raymond Meylan. Adliswil: Kunzelmann, [1981] (General Music Series GM Nr 736) Score 12 pp. and 1 part, 2 pp. Figured bass realized for harpsichord. Ed. from MS in the Naples Conservatory.

Arianna. See *Ebra d'amor....*

*Bella madre de'fiori. In: *Due Cantate...,* ed. by

Bettarini.   See under Cantata Collections.

Cantata pastorale per la nascità di nostro Signore. Christmas Cantata.   See *O di Betlemme*.

Che più farai arciero amor [duet for soprano and bass with basso continuo]. Ed. by F. Degrada. [Rostirolla, p. 568].

Clori e Dorino.   See *Che più farai arciero amor*.

Clori superba, e come mai?, excerpts: "Cruda Irene superba." In: *Cantate ad una voce, con accompagnamento di basso elaborato per pianoforte*, ed. by Alceo Toni. See under Cantata Collections.

Clori vezzosa e bella.   In: *Three Cantatas...* series ed. by Nona Pyron. See under Cantata Collections.

Correa nel seno amato [soprano with two violins and basso continuo]. Ed. by Otto Drechsler. Kassel: Barenreiter, 1974. (Concerto vocale; Bärenreiter Ed. 6459) score 24 pp. [40 pp.], and 4 parts.

First modern edition. Source: contemporary copy in Hamburg Universität, Bibliothek. 3 other MSS (London, Naples, Palermo) not consulted. Continuo realization by the editor. German translation of text. Original tempos indicated; no added dynamics. Brief commentary with performance suggestions. Review by Albert Seay in *Music Library Association. Notes* 34 (1977): 474-475.

_____. Milan: Edizioni Suvini Zerboni.

Dal bel volto d'Irene. In: *Cantate ad una voce...* ed. by Alceo Toni. See under Cantata Collections.

Didone abbandonata.   See *Alle troiane antenne*.

Dove alfin mi traeste?, excerpts: "Uccidetelo" and "Son pur ridotta". In: *Cantate ad una voce...* ed. by Alceo Toni. See under Cantata Collections.

Dunque, perchè lontano [soprano with basso continuo]. In Boyd: #20, pp. 151-154. See under Cantata Collections.

**Ebra d'amor fuggia.* *L'Arianna* [soprano with two violins and basso continuo]. Ed. by F. Degrada.

_____[soprano with two violins and basso continuo]. Hrsg. von Raymond Meylan. Frankfurt/N.Y.: Litolff Verlag/ C.F. Peters, [c1970]. score 23 pp. parts: violin 1, 6 pp.; violin 2, 6 pp., violoncello/basso continuo, 7 pp. (2 parts); cembalo, 9pp.

Sources: MS collection of cantatas, Naples Conservatory and MSS 1750-1800 in Paris. Bibliothèque Nationale. Continuo realization by Meylan (figures given.) Editorial suggestions given in small notes. Preface explains corrections. Phrasing, articulation, and dynamics are original. Italian text underlaid. German and English translations on p. 23. A clean edition. Additional performance suggestions would have helped novice performers.

Elitropio d'amor. In: *4 (Quattro) Cantate...* ed. by Tintori. See under Cantata Collections.

Entro romito speco, excerpts: "Non disperate". In: *Cantate ad una voce...* ed. by Alceo Toni. See under Cantata Collections.

**_____ [soprano with basso continuo]. Ed. by F. Degrada. [Rostirolla p.568]

Farfalla che s'aggira, excerpts: "Tenta la fuga". In: *Cantate ad una voce...*ed. by Alceo Toni. In: *Cantate ad una voce...* ed. by Alceo Toni. See under Cantata Collections.

Ferma omai, fugace e bella [alto with 2 violins, viola and basso continuo]. In Boyd #29, pp. 249-262. See under Cantata Collections.

Fermate omai fermate.   See OPERA: *La Psiche*. [Often cited as a cantata].

**Fiero, acerbo destin dell'alma mia* [duet for soprano and alto with basso continuo]. (Scarlatti-Durante). Ed. by F. Degrada. [Rostirolla, p. 568].

Fra mille semplicetti augei canori [soprano with basso continuo]. In Boyd #9, pp. 87-92. See under Cantata Collections.

Già lusingato appieno [soprano with two violins and basso continuo]. In Boyd #3, pp. 15-32. See under Cantata Collections.

Già vicina è quell'ora [soprano with basso continuo]. In Boyd #8, pp. 71-86. See under Cantata Collections.

Goderai sempre, crudele (inc). In *The Solo Song 1580-1730: a Norton Anthology*. Ed. by Carol MacClintock. N.Y.: Norton, 1973.

Ho una pena intorno. In: *Ausgewahlte Kammer-Kantate der Zeit um 1700* 3, ed. by Hugo Riemann. Leipzig: C.W.F. Siegel.

Idolo mio   See *O fileno, Filen, crudele*

***Il genio di Mitilde* [soprano with basso continuo]. Ed. by F. Degrada. [Rostirolla, p. 568].

Il rosignòlo, se scioglie il volo [I] [alto with basso continuo]. In Boyd #6, pp. 60-62. See under Cantata Collections.

_____. Includes aria, recitative, aria. In: *Study Scores of Musical Styles*, pp. 181-185, ed. by Edward R. Lerner. N.Y.: McGraw-Hill, 1968.

Il rosignòlo, se scioglie il volo [II] [alto with basso continuo]. In Boyd #7, pp. 63-70. See under Cantata Collections.

Io morireo contento. In: *4 (Quattro cantate... ed. by*

Tintori,   See under Cantata Collections.

Io son Neron, l'imperator del mondo [Il Nerone] [soprano with basso continuo].   In Boyd # 5, pp. 55-59. See under Cantata Collections.

Io son pur solo [soprano with basso continuo]. Hrsg. by Malcolm Boyd.   Kassel: Bärenreiter, [c1972].   (Concerto Vocale)   Bärenreiter ed. #6453.   Score, 12 pp; 2 parts.

Figured   bass   realized   for   keyboard instrument.   Sources: London, Royal College of Music MSS 578 and 698; Milan, Giuseppe Verdi Conservatory MS G78; Naples, Conservatory MS 34.5.3.

_____, excerpts: "Io son pur solo" and "Sono amante".   In: *Cantate ad una voce...* ed. by Alceo Toni.   See under Cantata Collections.

L'Arianna.   See *Ebra d'amor fuggia*

L'armi crudele e fiere.   In: *Three Cantatas for voice and cello...*   Series editor Nona Pyron.   See under Cantata Collections.

Lascia, deh lascia.   Gerig Av #124.   Cited in CMIP.

_____.   In: *Thorough-bass accompaniment according to J. D. Heinichen*, ed. and realized by George Buelow.   See item 352.

_____.   Ed. [sic] by Richard Jakoby. *Das Musikwerk* V. 32. Cologne: Arno Verlag, 1968; also issued singly by Arno and MCA Music, 1968.

Taken directly from Schering's edition in *Geschichte   der   Musik   in   Beispielen* without acknowledgment.   Repeats Schering's notes, editorial   indications,   and   citation (incorrect) of Scarlatti's birthdate.

_____.   In: *Geschichte der Musik in Beispielen*, pp. 378-383, ed. by Arnold Schering. Leipzig: Breitkopf, 1931.

Lascia più di tormentarmi [soprano with basso continuo]. In Boyd #2, pp. 11-14. See under Cantata Collections.

Lisa, del foco mio [Clori e Lisa] [duet for two sopranos with basso continuo]. In Boyd #21, pp. 155-164. See under Cantata Collections.

Lontan da la sua Clori [soprano with basso continuo]. Hrsg. von Malcolm Boyd. Kassel: Barenreiter, [1972] (Concerto Vocale) Score, 12 pp. and 2 parts. Bärenreiter ed. #6452.

Sources: London, British Museum MS 31509; Milan, G. Verdi Conservatory MS G78; Naples Conservatory MS 34.5.3

_____, excerpts: In: *Cantate ad una voce...* ed. by Alceo Toni. See under Cantata Collections.

Mi ha diviso il cor In: *Three Cantatas....* See under Cantata Collections.

Mitilde, mio tesor, cosi veloce In: *Historical Anthology of Music* 2, pp. 152-155, ed. by Willi Apel. Cambridge, MA: Harvard University Press, 1950.

Naqui a'sospiri e al pianto. In: *Due cantate...* ed. by Bettarini. See under Cantata Collections.

Non so qual più m'ingombra [Cantata pastorale] [soprano with two violins and basso continuo]. In Boyd #28, pp. 235-248. See under Cantata Collections.

O Fileno, Filen, crudele, ingrato. Ed. by A. Cairati. Stuttgart: Euterpe, c1928. Pl. # E.11 E. Score, 15 pp. Text in It. & Ger.

Oh di Betlemme altera povertà (Cantata pastorale per la nascita di Nostro Signore). Christmas Cantata.... Ed. by Edward J. Dent. London: Oxford University Press, 1969. 20 pp. Score. Continuo realization. English trans. underlaid with Italian text.

_____. Ed. by Edward J.

Dent. London: Oxford University Press, 1945. 14 pp.

Rehearsal edition with accompaniment and piano reduction. Italian text and English trans. underlaid.

Ombre romite e solitarie piante. In: *Allgemeine Geschichte der Musik,* vol. 3, p. 14+, ed. by August Reissmann. Munich: F. Bruckmann, 1863-65.

Ove fuor del mio seno. Ed. by J. Pittman. London: J. Lonsdale. (Gemme d'antichita, 142-143).

Pensier, che in ogni parte [soprano with basso continuo]. In Boyd #19, pp. 147-150. See under Cantata Collections.

Pensieri, oh Dio. In: *La Flora,* vol. 1, ed. by Knut Jeppesen. Copenhagen: Hansen, 1949. pp. 75-85.

Per un momento solo. With *Ove fuor...* ed. by J. Pittman.

_____ [soprano with basso continuo]. In Boyd #12, pp. 103-110. See under Cantata Collections.

Per un vago desire, excerpts. In: *Cantate ad una voce...* ed. by Alceo Toni. See under Cantata Collections.

**Poi che a Tirsi infelice* [soprano with basso continuo]. Ed. By F. Degrada. [Rostirolla, p. 568].

Poi che riseppe Orfeo [soprano with basso continuo]. In Boyd #1, pp. 1-10. See under Cantata Collections.

Prima d'esservi infedele [soprano with two violins and basso continuo]. In Boyd #4, pp. 33-54. See under Cantata Collections.

Qualor tento scoprire. In: *Armonia,* 5; ed. by A. Ritter. Magdeburg: Heinrichshofen, 1862.

Quando Amor vuol ferirmi; Cupid's Game Is Deceitful, for high voice, with the realization of the figured bass by John Moriarty from the original MS. N.Y.: R.D. Row Music Co.; C. Fischer, [1963]. 12 pp.

Cover title: Solo cantata; figured bass realized for keyboard instrument.

**Quella pace gradita* [soprano with flute, violin and basso continuo]. Ed. by F. Degrada. [Rostirolla, p. 568]

_____ [soprano with flute, violin, violoncello and basso continuo]. In Boyd #13, pp. 111-122. See under Cantata Collections.

Questo silenzio ombroso [duet for soprano and alto with basso continuo]. In Boyd #22, pp.165-172. See under Cantata Collections.

Qui vieni, ingrata Fille, excerpts: In: *Cantate ad una voce...* ed. by Alceo Toni. See under Cantata Collections.

Se amassi da dovero [l'infedeltà] [soprano with basso continuo]. In Boyd # 23, pp. 173-180. See under Cantata Collections.

Sento nel core certo dolore [soprano with basso continuo]. In Boyd #11, pp. 97-102. See under Cantata Collections.

Siamo in contesa, la bellezza ed io [soprano with basso continuo]. In Boyd: #10, pp. 93-96. See under Cantata Collections.

Solitudini amene apriche collinette. [soprano with flute and basso continuo]. Ed. by A. von Leeuwen. Leipzig: Zimmerman, c1925.

Solitudini amene [bersaglio d'empia sorte] [soprano with basso continuo]. In Boyd # 15, pp. 127-128. See under Cantata Collections.

Speranze mie, addio. [Mezzo-soprano and basso

continuo].   In: *4   (Quattro)   Cantate...*   ed.   by
Tintori.   See under Cantata Collections.

Su le sponde del Tebro.   [soprano with two violins,
trumpet, strings and basso continuo].   Kantate
für   Singstimme,   Trompete,   Streicher   und
Continuo.   Ed.   by   Bernhard   Paumgartner.
Heidelberg: Willy   Muller,   Suddeutscher
Musikverlag, 1956.   23 pp.

Preface   in German   and English.   Texts   in
Italian, German, and English with underlay in
Italian.   Score   and   b.c.   realization   by
Paumgartner.   No use   of small   notes to show
editorial   suggestions or changes.   No figures
given   for   continuo.   Measures   numbered.
Source: Florence, Luigi Cherubini Conservatory
MS D2364.   Expressive   marks,   phrasing   added
infrequently.   A   clean   edition.   Some
performance suggestions given.

_____.   In *The Comprehensive Study of
Music....*   Ed.   by William Brandt, et al.   N.Y.:
Harper's College Press, 1977.

*The Beauteous Melissa.   In *Songs of the Italian Baroque.*

**Tiranna   ingrata [baritone with two violins and
basso   continuo].   Ed.   by   F.   Degrada.
[Rostirolla, p. 568].

Tra speranza e timore [bass with violin and basso
continuo].   Ed.   by Timothy Roberts.   London,
Eng. and Fullerton, CA: Grancino Editions (ENS
4),   1986/87.   [source,   early   eighteenth-
century MS].

**Tra   verdi   piante   ombrose* [soprano   and   basso
continuo].   Ed.   by F. Degrada.   [Rostirolla, p.
568].

Troppo   ingrata   Amaranta,   excerpts: "Dimmi   qual
prova."   In: *Cantate ad   una voce...* ed. by Alceo
Toni.   See under Cantata Collections.

Vaghe selve beate, excerpts: "Godo ognor."   In:
Cantate ad una voce... ed. by Alceo Toni.   See under

Cantata Collections.

Venne ad amor desio [soprano with basso continuo].
In Boyd #16, pp. 129-130. See under Cantata
Collections.

Cantata Collections

Bettarini, Luciano, ed. *Due cantate per soprano,
archi e basso continuo*. Milan: Casa Editrice
Nazionalmusic, 1969. x and 46 pp. and parts.
Review by Gloria Rose in *Music Library Association.
Notes* 26 (1970): 832-833.

Blanchard, Roger, ed. *Airs et cantates Baroque inédits*.
For solo voice/ continuo. Vol. 4: Alessandro
Scarlatti.

Boyd, Malcolm, compiler. *Cantatas by Alessandro
Scarlatti 1660-1725*. Selected and introduced by
Malcolm Boyd (The Italian Cantata in the
Seventeenth Century, vol. 13) [Facs. of
original manuscripts]. N.Y.: Garland
Publishing, 1986. [xii] and 273 pp.; 4 pp.
"Errata" appended. ISBN 0-8240-8887-5.

Selection "chosen to represent every phase
of the composer's development...." Fine,
clear facsimiles. Brief, informative
introduction. Texts transcribed: pp. 265-273;
errata insert of #25. No. 1: *Poi che riseppe Orfeo*
(BL Additional 31511 ff 56-63v) not cited in
NGIBM; No. 25: *Al fragor...* cited as a serenata
(*Pace, amore e providenza*) in the same work.

Pyron, Nona, series ed. *Three cantatas for voice and
cello with keyboard*. London, Eng. and Fullerton,
CA: Grancino Editions, c1982. score 28 pp. 2
parts, ea. 21 pp. (Early Cello Series, 16).

Tintori, Giampiero, ed. *Quattro cantate (inedite) per
canto e pianoforte*. Milan: Ricordi, c1958. 41 pp.

Toni, Alceo, ed. *Cantate ad una voce con
accompagnamento di basso elaborato per pianoforte*. Milan:
Notari, c1920. 6 vols. in 1. (I classici della

musica italiana, 30).

Supplement: Unpublished Cantata Editions In Dissertations

Ah Mitilde vezzosa (1712), Daw, pp. 158-165

Al' pensiero miei sguardi, (1706), Inkeles, pp. 315-334

*Amo e negar nol posso (1704), Inkeles, pp. 260-266

Andate o miei sospiri (1712), Henry, Appendix

+Andate o miei sospiri (both versions) (1712), Daw, pp. 166-179 and 180-190

Appena giunse al forte campo (Oloferne), inc., Collins, pp. 121-132

Augellin vago e canoro (Ha 68) (1699), Freund, pp. 503-520

Bella quanto crudel spietata Irene (1717), Daw, pp. 191-198

*Che Sisifo infelice (1706), Inkeles, pp. 296-307

Cor di Bruto, e che risolvi?, Collins, pp. 125-132

Da quell'hora fatale (1716), Daw, pp. 199-209

Dopo lungo penar (Ha ii), Piersall, pp. 43-52 and Collins, pp. 133-139

Dov'io mi volga (1712), Daw, pp. 210-219

E come, oimè poss'io? (1714), Daw, pp. 220-230

Filli che fra gl'orrori (Ha 276) (1706), Freund, pp. 561-572

Fonte d'ogni dolcezza (1709), Daw, pp. 231-238

[H]or che di febo ascosi (Ha 511) (1704), Freund, pp. 522-559

**Il genio di Mitilde* (1711), Daw, pp. 239-252

Imagini d'orrore (1710), Freund, pp. 600-613; also, Piersall, pp. 54-71 and Collins, pp. 140-148

+*Io son Neron l'imperatore del mondo* (1698), Inkeles, pp. 163-187

La gratia, la sembianza della tua pastorella (1702), Inkeles, pp. 240-253

Lascia di tormentarmi (1709), Daw, pp. 253-263

+*Lascia più di tormentarmi* [1690] [1688= Hanley's date], Inkeles, pp. 109-119

Lasciami alquanto piangere (1716), Daw, pp. 264-273

Lasciate ch'io v'adori (1705), Inkeles, pp. 271-288

Lieti, placide e belle acque (1709), Daw, pp. 274-280

+*Lisa, del foco mio* (Ha 386) (1706), Freund, pp. 574-598

Lontananza che fai (1701), Inkeles, pp. 219-232

Lontananza crudele, deh perchè? (1713), Daw, pp. 281-289

Mentre un zeffiro arguto, Piersall, pp. 73-104

Mi tormenta il pensiero, Piersall, pp.106-120

Mia Climene adorata (1710), Daw, pp. 290-301

Nel dolce tempo in cui ritorna (1712), Daw, pp. 302-311

Nel mar che bagna al bel Sebeto il piede , Piersall, pp. 122-135 and Collins, pp. 149-154

Nel silentio comune, Lake

No, non deggio, è troppo cara (1709), Daw, pp. 312-322

O che mostro (1709), Daw, pp. 323-330

O Mitilde, fosti meco tiranna (1711), Daw, pp. 331-339

O Mitilde, o del core (1708), Daw, pp. 340-352

O voi di queste selve habitatrici (1717), Daw, pp. 353-362

Piango, sospiro, e peno (Ha 563, 2nd setting) (c1692), Freund, pp. 484-501

Queste torbide e meste onde (1717), Daw, pp. 363-375

Se vagheggio nel mattino (1709), Daw, pp. 376-388

Sopra le verdi sponde del Sebeto (1712), Daw, pp. 389-396

Sotto l,ombra d'un faggio piangente e sospirante, Piersall, pp. 137-152 and Collins, pp. 155-167

Splendeano in bel sembiante, Collins, pp. 168-178

Su le fiorite sponde, (1712), Daw, pp. 397-407

Tanto strano e l'amor mio. (1697), Inkeles, pp. 132-153

**Tiranna ingrata, Piersall, pp. 154-175

Tra queste ombrose piagge (1709), Daw, pp. 408-417

+*Tra speranza e timore*, Piersall, pp. 177-198; also Collins, pp. 179-190, and Murray.

***Tra verdi piante ombrose* (1711), Daw, pp. 418-428

Tu mi chiedi s'io t'amo (1709), Daw, pp. 429-436

Tu resti o mio bel nume, Piersall, pp. 200-218 and Collins, pp. 191-206.

Vedi, Eurilla, quel fior (Ha 761) (1725), Freund, pp. 615-645

**Vuoi ch'io spiri* (1699), Inkeles, pp. 198-210

Church Music

MOTETS

Adorna thalamum tuum Sion. "Prepare Now Your Finest Chamber" [SATB a cappella]. Ed. by Percy Young. Lat. and Eng. text. In: *Music of the Great Churches*, Vol. 3: Santa Maria Maggiore, Rome.

Audi filia, et inclina aurem (1720). "Gradual for St. Cecilia's Day" [SSA soli, SSAT chor., 2 ob., optional bass, string orch., org.]. Ed. by John Steele. [London]: Novello, 1968.

***Cantantibus organis* [sop. solo with ob., 2 violins, viola and basso continuo]. Ed. by H. J. Jans.

Caro mea vere est cibus [STB with org.]. Ed. for SATB by J. Castellini. Bryn Mawr, PA.: Theodore Presser, n.d.

Dixit Dominus (Psalm 109) [5 voices with piano or organ]. Ed. by R. Vitali. Milan: Ricordi, 1887 (Biblioteca musicale rara, 10).

Dixit Dominus [iv] [SATB soli and chorus with string orch. and org. continuo]. Ed. by John Steele. London: Novello, c1975. Score: v and 70 pp. Reviews by A.F.Carver in *Early Music* 5 (1977): 581 and Malcolm Boyd in *Musical Times* 118 (1977): 138.

See item 167 for article by Steele on this work.

Domine refugium factus es nobis. [SSATB]. Ed. by R. Ewerhart. Cologne: E. Bieler, 1961.

Est dies trophei, op.2, no. 9; motteto breve per ogni santo e santa [SATB soli, SATB chorus with 2 violins and basso continuo]. Ed. by Mason Martens. N.Y.: Leeds, 1960 (Brooklyn College Choral Series, 1001). Score 26 pp.

_____. Ed. by Carol Smith. Jenson

Publications.   Lat.   text.   Review   by   James
McCray in *Diapason* 74/2 (1983): 20.

Editorial commentary regarding the work and
performance practice.

Exaltabo te Domine quoniam.   "I Extol Thee, O Lord"
[SATB a capella].   Ed. by Paul Brandvik. Ft.
Lauderdale, Fla.: Plymouth Music Co., Inc.

Exultate Deo adjutori [SATB].   Ed. by Ernest White.
N.Y.: Music Press, c1946. (pub. pl. #MP 71-
10). Also N.Y.: Mercury Music Corp. Score 12
pp.

Brief   introductory   note.   Editor   sees
resemblance   between   Scarlatti's   and   Henry
Purcell's   harmony.   Gives   Scarlatti's
birthdate   incorrectly   as   1659.   Some
performance suggestions; tempos and metronome
markings   suggested;   use   of   modern   clefs.
Piano   part   for   rehearsal   only.   Provides
phrasing, dynamic markings, etc.

_____ [SATB].   Ed.   by   K.   Funk
and   I.   Funk.   Bryn   Mawr,   PA.:   Theodore
Presser, 1953.   Review in *Music Library Association.*
Notes 12 (1955): 645-646.

_____ [SATB].   Ed.   by   F.   Rikko.
N.Y.:   E.B.Marks, c1955. (pub. pl. # 13195).
Score 13 pp.   Review in *Music Library Association.*
Notes 12 (1955): 645-646.

Exurge Domine non prevaleat [SATB a capella].   Lat.
and Eng. text.   Ed. by Paul Brandvik.   Ft.
Lauderdale, Fla.: Plymouth Music Co., Inc.

Infirmata vulnerata, op. 2 (Concerti sacri, 3).   Ed.
by Rudolph Ewerhart. Cologne: E. Bieler, 1959.
Score 21 pp. and 3 parts. (Die Kantate, 5).

_____.   In: *Music Scores Omnibus*, I,
pp.   121-129.   Ed.   by   William   J.   Starr.
Englewood, N.J.: Prentice-Hall, 1964.

Inno   a   S.   Cecilia.   Ed.   and   rev.   by   Emilia

Gubitosi. Milan: Curci.

Intellige clamorem meum. "O Lord, I Cry Unto Thee"
[SATB a cappella]. Ed. by Paul Brandvik. Ft.
Lauderdale, Fla.: Plymouth Music Co., Inc.

**Jesu corona virginum* [4 solo voices and chorus
with instruments]. Ed. by H.J. Jans.

Laetatus sum [4 voices].   Ed. by Karl Proske.
Regensburg: F. Pustet, [c. 1855].   (Musica
Divina, 2) pp. 106-111.

Laetatus sum, revisione ed elaborazione by Emilia
Gubitosi. Milan: Curci.

Laetatus sum   [SATB].   Lucerne, Switzerland:
Edition Cron Luzern.

Laudate Dominum omnes gentes.   "O Praise the Lord
All Ye Nations" [SATTB with strings and basso
continuo]. Transcribed and ed. by Jeanne E.
Shaffer.   St. Louis: Concordia, 1973.   Score
33 pp.   Fig. bass realized for keyboard
instrument.

***Magnificat* [ii] [solo voices and chorus with
instruments]. Ed. by H.J. Jans.

Nisi Dominus aedificaverit [i]. "Vanum est". Ed. by
F. Rochlitz. Mainz: Schott, [c1840] (Sammlung
vorzuglicher Gesang-Stücke, 2) pp.44-47.

O magnum mysterium. [8 voices in two choirs SATB
SATB]. Ed. by R. Ewerhart.   Cologne: E.
Bieler, [1967]. Score 8 pp.

_____ (Sammlung religiöser Gesänge
älterer und neuster Zeit).

Salve Regina [SATB with violins and basso
continuo].   Ed.   by   Lajos   Rovatkay.
Wolfenbüttel: Möseler Verlag, c1974. Score 21
pp. (Musica italiana, 102) Figured bass
realized.

Salve Regina (Concerti sacri, op.2, no.10) [SATB

with basso continuo, violin, violoncello, doublebass]. Ed. by Mason Martens. North Hollywood, CA.: Walton Music Corp., c1964. 22 pp. Fig. bass realized for keyboard.

Salve Regina (c1720). Transcribed by Reinhard Strohm. In: *Colloquium Alessandro Scarlatti* (item 114), pp. 240-250.

**Salve Regina* [sop. with violins and basso continuo]. Ed. by G. Pannain.

Stabat Mater. [2-part women's chorus, SA with 2 violins and basso continuo]. Melville, N.Y.: Belwin Mills.

_____. [SA with 2 violins, viola (not in original MS) and basso continuo]. Realized and ed. by Felice Boghen. Milan: Ricordi, c1928. Full score ed.; and piano-vocal ed.: arr. for 2-part chorus of women's voices with soprano and contralto soloists and piano or string orchestra. 61 pp.

Te Deum. "Hymn of Praise" [SSATB with 2 ob., strings and org.]. Ed. by John Castellini. Bryn Mawr, PA: T. Presser, 1954.

Tu es Petrus [SATB SATB with org.]. Ed. by G. Nava. Milan: Lucca.

_____. Ed. by F. Commer. Berlin: Bote & Bock, 1843. (Musica Sacra, 3, no. 18). Score.

_____. Ed. by F. Damrosch. N.Y.: Schirmer, 1900.

_____. N.Y.: Musical Art Society.

_____. Ed. [freely adapted] by G. Piccioli. Milan: Curci, 1960. Score.

**Valerianus in cubiculo* [contralto solo with ob., 2 violins, viola and basso continuo]. Ed. by H. J. Jans.

MASSES AND MASS MOVEMENTS

*Credo concertato (B flat major) [SATB with 2 ob., 2 horns, strings, and org.]. Rielaborazione in partitura moderna dal manoscritto del 1776 di J. Napoli. Milan: Curci, 1960. [NG lists as *Credo].

Missa Clementina in C (1705) [i] [SSATB with "Agnus Dei" for 7 voices]. Sanctus & Agnus Dei only. Ed. by F. Rochlitz. Mainz: Schott, [c1840]. (Collection de morceaux de chant tires des maitres, 2) pp. 48-55.

_____. Sanctus [5 voices], Gloria Patri [5 voices with org.]. Ed. by F. Rochlitz. Mainz: Schott's Sohne, [1840]. (Sammlung vorzuglicher Gesang-Stücke, 2) p. 44.

_____. Sanctus and Agnus Dei only. Realization for org. by G. Ramous. Score. Milan: Curci, 1960. .

_____. Sanctus only. Eng. and Lat. text. Ed. by Ehret. N.Y.: G. Schirmer.

Messa a quattro voci (Messa Ottoboniana in e minor 1706) [SATB]. Ed. by Otto Braune and T. Trautwein. Berlin (Caecilia, Sammlung von Kompositionen alter ital. Meister, 1) p. 1.

_____. Missa quatuor vocum (1706). Ed. by Karl Proske. Regensburg: G. J. Manz, [1841].

_____. Ed. by F. Commer. Berlin: Bote & Bock, 1843. (Musica Sacra, 3).

_____. Première messe a 4 voix. Ed. by C. Vervoitte. Paris: Girod, s.d.

_____. Messa Ottoboniana, per coro a quattro voci. Kyrie and Agnus Dei only. Org. realization by L. Spaggiari. Milan: Curci, 1961. Score.

Missa pro defunctis (in d 1717) [4 voices].

(Oeuvres choisies des meilleurs compositeurs
de musique religieuse classique, 5) Leipzig:
Braun, 1884-85.

_____. Ed. by A. Choron.   Paris,
1827-1830.   (Journal de chant et musique
d'église, 22-28).

Messa di Santa Cecilia. St. Cecilia Mass (1720)
[SSATB soloists, SSATB chorus with strings and
basso continuo].   Ed. by John Steele.   London:
Novello, 1968.   Score 115 pp.

_____.   Ed. and figured bass
realization by Fritz Steffin.   Berlin-
Wiesbaden: Bote & Bock, 1957.   Vocal score
with piano reduction.   76 pp.

Missa ad usum Cappellae Pontificiae (1721) [[SATB]. Ed.
by J. A. Bank. Amsterdam: A. Bank, 1951.
[Lacking the Credo].   [*NGIBM* cites only 1721
mass by this name. Bank article: (item 149: #
2, p. 4) cites earlier version "Missa a 4 voci
alla Palestrina 1710 in d;"   Rostirolla (item
435) cites 1710 mass MS incomplete located in
Naples Cons.and London BM and Paris Cons.]

_____. (1721).   Ed. by
Julius Bas and Franciscus Nekes. Dusseldorf:
Schwann, 1907.   (pub. pl. # 682).   v and 39
pp.

Missa ad canonem; Messa a 4 voci alla Palestrina
[4 voices].   Ed. by O. Braune.   Berlin-
Potsdam.   In: *Caecilia,* 1 (a third above the
original).

LARGE SACRED WORKS

Passio D. N. Jesu Christi secundum Johannem. See **Oratorios
and Large Sacred Works** in this section.

Supplement: Unpublished Church Music Editions
in Dissertations

MOTETS

Ad Dominum cum tribularer (1707), Brandvik, pp. 190–193

Ad te Domine (1705), Brandvik, pp. 194–196

Beatus vir qui timet Dominum, Shaffer, pp. 51–96

Confitebor tibi Domine, Shaffer, pp. 273–323

Constitues eos principes (1716), Brandvik, pp. 303–307

+*Dixit Dominus Domino meo* [5 vc, organ] basso continuo, realized, Shaffer, pp. 118–170

+*Dixit Dominus Domino meo* [5 vc, ob, 2vn, va, bc], Shaffer, pp. 177–211

Domine in auxillum meum (1705), Brandvik, pp. 197–200

Domine vivifica me (1705), Brandvik, pp. 201–202

+*Exaltabo te Domino* (1705), Brandvik, pp. 203–206

+*Exurge Domine* (1705), Brandvik, pp. 207–210

+*Intellige clamorem meum* (1705), Brandvik, pp. 211–213

+*Laudate Dominum omnes gentes*, Shaffer, pp. 17–42

Laudate pueri Dominum (c1715), Brandvik, pp. 271–302 and Shaffer, pp. 219–264

Memento Domine David (1722), Brandvik, pp. 229–247

Miserere mei Deus, secundum [i] (1680), Owens, pp. 109–124

Miserere mei Deus, secundum [ii: *NGIBM*; iii: Owens]

in e minor (*NGIBM* date: 1705; Owens and
Brandvik date: 1714), Brandvik, pp.331-388 and
Owens, pp. 128-135

Miserere mei Deus, secundum [iii: *NGIBM*;
iv: Owens] in c minor [1715], Brandvik, pp.
389-436 and Owens, pp. 229-290

Miserere mei Deus, secundum [Owens: ii; NG:iv in a
minor (1721) same?], Owens, pp. 128-135

+*O magnum mysterium* (1707), Brandvik, pp. 217-228

Properate fideles, Rye, pp. 152-231

Rorate ceoli dulcem, Rye, pp. 101-151

Salvum fac (1705), Brandvik, pp. 214-216

+*Tu es Petrus* (c1707), Brandvik, pp. 248-270

Veritas mea, Shaffer, pp. 101-109

Vexilla regis prodeunt (c1680), Brandvik, pp.
308-330

Madrigals

Jürgens, Jürgen, ed. *Acht Madrigale*. Frankfurt:
H. Litolff and N.Y.: C .F. Peters, c1980.
Score 59 pp. Ed. Peters 8243 (pub. pl.
#308557). Reviews in: *Die Musikforschung* 37
(1984): 169-171 by Wolfgang Osthoff; *Musical
Times* 123 (1982): 38-39 by Malcolm Boyd [of
madrigals issued separately]; *Musica* 36 (1982):
375 by G. Wilhelms; *Musical Times* 122 (1981): 253
by Malcolm Boyd

Complete edition intended for the performer.
Clear where editorial additions made. Brief
introduction discusses sources with reference
to the editor's more extensive article in the
Ronga Festschrift (see item 172). English
translations. Errors in printing in some
copies. Includes piano reduction and continuo
realization. Also issued without piano

reduction. Preface in German and English. Italian text with German translation, pp. 58-59. Few performance suggestions.

Operas

La caduta de' Decemviri. Ed. by Hermine Weigel Williams. Cambridge: Harvard University Press, 1980. Score 224 pp. (The Operas of Alessandro Scarlatti, 6; Harvard Publications in Music, 11) ISBN 0-674-64032-2.

Edition includes comic scenes between Flacco & Servilia. Reviews in *Music Review* 42 (1981): 296-297, by Malcolm Boyd; and *Music & Letters* 63 (1982): 156-158 and 64 (1983): 301-302 by Winton Dean. See also item 235.

Dafni, favola boschereccia. Ed. by John H. Roberts. N.Y.: Garland Publishing, 1986 (Handel Sources: Materials for the Study of Handel's Borrowing, 7) Facs. ed. ISBN 0-8240-6481-X. See also item 238.

Gli equivoci in amore o vero La Rosaura. Acts 1 & 2. Ed. by Robert Eitner. In: Publikation älterer praktischer und theoretischer Musikwerke. Leipzig: Breitkopf & Härtel, [c1885]. Facs.

Gli equivoci nel sembiante. Ed. by Frank A. D'Accone. Cambridge: Harvard University Press, 1982. 200 pp. (Operas of Alessandro Scarlatti, 7; Harvard Publications in Music, 12) ISBN 0-674-64033-0. Eng. trans. of libretto by Charles Speroni and editor, pp. 165-178. Review in *Music Review* 43 (1982): 286.

Full score of Scarlatti's earliest known opera, the first from his Roman period (to 1684) to be published. Clear, accurate edition. Introduction recounts in fascinating detail the history of this work so popular in its own time. See also item 240.

L'Eraclea. Ed. by Donald J. Grout. Cambridge: Harvard University Press, 1974. 192 pp. (Operas of Alessandro Scarlatti, 1; Harvard University Publications in Music, 6) ISBN 0-674-64026-8. Facs. of the Italian libretto by S. Stampiglia with Eng. trans.

Reviews in *Die Musikforschung* 31 (1978): 113-115 by R. Strohm; *Musical Quarterly* 63 (1977): 268-272 by S. Hansell; *Early Music* 3 (1975): 407 *American Musicological Society. Journal* 32 (1979): 352-356 by Owen Jander. See also item 242.

La Griselda. Ed. by Donald J. Grout and Elizabeth B. Hughes. Cambridge: Harvard University Press, 1975. Score 290 pp. (Operas of Alessandro Scarlatti, 3; Harvard Publications in Music, 8) ISBN 0-674-64029-2.

Reviews in *Early Music* 6 (1978): 117 by Colin Timms; *Musical Quarterly* 63 (1977): 268-272 by S. Hansell; *American Musicological Society. Journal* 32 (1979): 352-356 by O. Jander; *Music & Letters* 58 (1977): 365-367 by M. F. Robinson; *Die Musikforschung* 36 (1983): 106 by W. Osthoff. See also item 246.

_____. Ed. by Otto Drechsler. Kassel: [Bärenreiter Verlag], 1960.

Marco Attilio Regolo. Ed. by Joscelyn Godwin. Cambridge: Harvard University Press, 1975. 224 pp. (Operas of Alessandro Scarlatti 2; Harvard Publications in Music, 7) ISBN 0-674-64028-4

Reviews in *Early Music* 6 (1978): 117+ , by C. Timms; *Musical Quarterly* 63 (1977): 268-272 by S. Hansell; *American Musicological Society. Journal* 32 (1979): 352-356 by O. Jander. See also item 253.

Massimo Puppieno. Ed. by H. Colin Slim.

Cambridge: Harvard University Press, 1979. 163 pp. (Operas of Alessandro Scarlatti, 5; Harvard Publications in Music, 10) ISBN 0-674-64031-4

Reviews in *Opera Journal* 12/2 (1979): 43; *Musical Times* 121 (1980): 113-114 by Malcolm Boyd; *Music Review* 41 (1980) by M. F. Robinson. Review of series, 1-5 by Charles Rosen in *New York Review of Books* 26/9 (1979): 14. See also item 254.

Il Mitridate Eupatore. Ed. by Giovanni Morelli, Reinhard Strohm, and Thomas Walker. Milan: Ricordi, forthcoming (Drammaturgia musicale veneta, 11).

Facs. edition with critical essay. Series to be a collection of 30 facs. scores with critical essays in 3 periods. Issued to date nos. 4, 6, 12, 18, 24, 26.

——————————. ...ricostruzione scenica e strumentale... [by] Giuseppe Piccioli. Milan: Curci, 1953. 185 pp. Vocal score with piano reduction. (Full score, rental). Abbrev. to 3 acts.

No indication of what was added or deleted from Scarlatti's original. No editorial comment and no indication of cuts, changes in orchestration, etc. For critique and detailed comparison of this edition with the MS copy Paris Conservatory 22410 in the BN, see item 256.

Il Pompeo. Ed. by John H. Roberts. N.Y.: Garland Publishing, 1986. Facs. ed. (Handel Sources: Materials for the Study of Handel's Borrowing, 6) ISBN 0-8240-6480-1. See also item 260.

La principessa fedele. *The Faithful Princess*. Ed. by Donald J. Grout. Cambridge, MA: Harvard

University Press, 1977.   Score 208 pp.
(Operas of Alessandro Scarlatti, 4; Harvard
Publications in Music, 9). ISBN 0-674-64030-6

Reviews in *Die Musikforschung* 33 (1980): 397–
398, by R. Strohm; *Musical Times* 119 (1978): 53–
by M. Boyd. See also item 261.

La Rosaura. See *Gli equivoci in amore*

La Statira.   Ed. by William Holmes. Cambridge,
MA: Harvard University Press, 1985 (Operas of
Alessandro Scarlatti, 9; Harvard Publications
in Music, 15) ISBN 0-674-64035-7. ix and 199
pp. See also item 265.

Telemaco.   Ed. by Howard Mayer Brown.   N.Y.:
Garland Publishing, 1978.   Facs. edition.
Score.   (Italian Opera 1640–1770, 23)   ISBN
0-8240-2622-5.   Photoreproduction of the
holograph MS 16487 [Libretto facs. cited as
item 198]. See also item 267.

Tigrane. Ed. by Michael Collins. Cambridge,
MA: Harvard University Press, 1983. (Operas
of   Alessandro   Scarlatti,   8;   Harvard
Publications in Music, 13)   ISBN   0-674-
64034-9.

Includes comic scenes with Dorilla and
Oronte. See also item 268.

Il trionfo dell'onore. The Triumph of Honor. Full score,
orch. parts, and piano-vocal score with It.
and Eng. lyrics. Ed. by Hermine W. Williams.
Eng. lyrics by Charles Kondek. St. Louis: MMB
Music, Inc., [1988]. For rental only.

—————————.   *Il Trionfo dell'onore ovvero Il
dissoluto   pentito.*   "...riduzione   scenica,
elaborazione e adattamento" [by] Virgilio

Mortari. Piano-vocal score. Milan: Carisch, 1954. vi and 102 pp.

Based on somewhat altered and abbreviated edition used for performance in Siena in 1941 at Teatro dei Rozzi during the Scarlatti week celebration.

Operas, Selections: Arias, Duets, Overtures (Sinfonias), etc.**

L'Amazzone guerriera [corsara] (1689). "Sinfonia," arias (8) and duets (2) in Lorenz, vol. 2. See item 205.

L'Anacreonte tiranno (1689). Arias (13) and duet (1) in Lorenz, vol. 2. See item 205.

Il Cambise (1719). "Introduzione," ed. by Douglass M. Green in *The Symphony 1720-1840*. Editor-in-chief, Barry S. Brook. Ser. A I. "Antecedents of the Symphony," pp. 7-12 (45-50). N.Y.: Garland Publishing, 1983. ixv and 258 pp. ISBN 0-8240-3828-2. See also item 201.

Il Clearco in Negroponte (1686). Arias (3) in Lorenz, vol. 2. See item 205. Aria "Vengo, vengo a stringerti" in *Arie Antiche*, ed. by Toni.

La Didone delirante (1696). Aria (1) in Lorenz, vol. 2. See item 205.

La donna ancora è fedele (1698). Arias (4) in Lorenz, vol. 2. See item 205. "Son tutto duolo" in *Gesänge altitalienischer Meister* (Vienna, s.d.); "Se Florindo è fedele" in *Suite altitalienischer Arien*. Both of above also in *Arie antiche*, ed. by A. Parisotti (Milan: Ricordi, s.d.).

L'Emireno (1697). Duets (2) in Lorenz, vol. 2. See item 205.

"Sinfonia" and Act 1 scene 2: "Son si dolci le catene (Climene) in *Florilegium Musicum*, pp. 255-260, ed. by Erwin Leuchter (Buenos Aires: Ricordi Americana, 1964).

Il Flavio. "Chi vuole innamorarsi" in *Alte Meister des Bel Canto*, ed. by L. Landschoff (Leipzig: C.F. Peters, s.d.).

L'honestà negli amori (1680). Arias (4) in Lorenz, vol. 2. See item 205. "Già il sole dal Gange" in *Arie antiche*, ed. by A. Parisotti (Milan: Ricordi, s.d.).

Nerone fatto Cesare (1695). Aria (1) in Lorenz, vol. 2. See item 205.

Le nozze con l'inimico (1695). Arias (2) and echo-aria (1) in Lorenz, vol. 2. See item 205.

Olimpia vendicata (1685). "Sinfonia" in *Music History in Examples...*, ed. by Otto Hamburg (N.Y.: C. F. Peters, 1978), pp. 107-110.

Penelope la casta (1696?). Arias (4) in Lorenz, vol. 2. See item 205.

Il Pirro e Demetrio (1694). Arias (5) in Lorenz, vol. 2. See item 205. "Le violette: Rugiadose odorose" in *Gesänge altitalienischer Meister* (Vienna, s.d.). "Le violette" in *Suite antiker Arietten und Kanzonen*.

Il Pompeo (1683).

"O cessate de piagarmi" in *Music in Opera; a Historical Anthology*, ed. by Elaine Brody (Englewood Cliffs, New Jersey: Prentice-Hall, 1970), pp. 77-78. Also in *La flora, arie e cantate antiche italiane*, ed. by K. Jeppesen (Copenhagen: W. Hansen, 1949); *Italian Songs of the XVII and XVIII Centuries*, vol. 2 (N.Y.: International Music Co., 1961); *Musica scelta d'antichi maestri italiani*, ed. by G. W. Teschner (Berlin: T. Trautwein, [1866]) and (Milan: Carisch, s.d.); *Zwei Liebeslieder für eine Singstimme von Alessandro Scarlatti*, ed. by C. Banck (Leipzig: Senff, s.d.).

(Leipzig: Senff, s.d.).

"Toglietemi la vita ancor" in *Arie antiche*, ed. by A. Parisotti (Milan: Ricordi, s.d.); *Italian Songs of the XVII and XVIII Centuries*, vol. 2; *Tres arias*, ed. by Parisotti; *Zwei Liebeslieder für eine Singstimme von Alessandro Scarlatti*, ed. by C. Banck.

Il prigioniero fortunato (1698). "Povera pellegrina suele helas" in *Les gloires de l'Italie"* 1/4, ed. by F. A. Gevaert (Paris, 1868).

La Rosaura.   See *Gli equivoci in amore.*

La Rosmene (1686).   Arias (14) in Lorenz, vol. 2. See item 205.

La santa Genuinda (1694).   Arias (6) in Lorenz, vol. 2.   See item 205.

La Teodora Augusta (1692).   Arias (2) in Lorenz, vol. 2.   See item 205.

Tutto il male non vien per nuocere (1681).   Arias (21), duets (2), trio (1), quartet (1) in Lorenz, vol. 2.   See item 205.

**Only works for which no complete modern edition was located have been included in this list.

Aria Collections and Single Aria Editions

Airs et cantates baroque inédits [solo voice with basso continuo].   Vol. 4: Alessandro Scarlatti.   Ed. by Roger Blanchard. Paris: Bois.   Vol. 2 also contains works by A. Scarlatti.

Alte Meister des Bel Canto.   Ed. by L. Landshoff. Leipzig: C. F. Peters, s.d.   Includes: "Chi vuole innamorarsi" (from *Il Flavio*) [sop. with pianoforte].

Antiche gemme italiane.   Ed. by V. Ricci.   Milan: Ricordi, 1959.   Includes "Tu lo sai," [arietta for sop. with basso continuo].

Arie antiche. Ed. by Alessandro Parisotti. Milan:
Ricordi,   s.d.   Includes: "Se   Florindo   è
fedele"; Son tutta duolo"; Se tu della mia
morte"; Spesso vibra per suo gioco"; "Sento
nel core"; "Su venite a consiglio"; "Già il
sole dal Gange" (from *L'honestà negli amori*;
"All'acquisto di gloria" (from *Il Tigrane*);
"Toglietemi la vita ancor" (from *Il Pompeo*); "Se
delitto è l'adorarvi."

Arie antiche. Ed. by A. Toni. Milan: Carisch.
Includes aria from *Clearco in Negroponte*: "Vengo,
vengo a stringerti."

Ariette [high solo with 2 violins and basso
continuo]. N.Y.: E. C. Schirmer.

Ariette a una voce con e senza strumenti [solo voice with
optional instruments].   Score.   Lausanne:
Foetisch Frères Ed., 1958.

Bel canto [arias for solo voice with basso
continuo].   Ed. by A. Fuchs.   Braunschweig,
s.d.   Includes: "Nevi intatte"; "Per formare
la bella"; "Va per lo mare."

10 [Dieci] arie del sei e settecento. Ed. by Vittorio
Negri Bryks. Milan: Ricordi, 1955. Includes:
"Armati" [aria for sop. with pianoforte].

Echos d'Italie, vol. 4.   Paris: Durand &
Schönewerk,   s.d.   Includes   "Già   mai,"
[siciliana for sop. with pianoforte].

Eleganti canzoni ed arie italiane del secolo XVII. Ed. by L.
Torchi.   Milan: Ricordi, s.d.   Includes: "Ma
prima ch'io mora" [aria for sop. with
pianoforte].

La flora, arie e cantate antiche italiane. Ed by K.
Jeppesen.   Copenhagen: W.   Hansen,   1949.
Includes: " Io dissi," "La tua gradita fe,'"
"O cessate de pagarmi" (from *Il Pompeo*), "O
dolce speranza," "Difesa non ha," "La
speranza" [arias for solo voice with basso
continuo].

"Fortunati miei martiri" [aria for solo voice with basso continuo]. In: *Gluck und die Oper* by A. B. Marx, vol. 2. Berlin, 1863.

Gesänge altitalienischer Meister. Vienna, s.d. Includes: "Son tutto duolo" (from *La donna ancora è fedele*); *Le violette*: "Rugiadose odorose" (from *Il Pirro e Demetrio*).

Les gloires de l'Italie, vol. 1, part 4. Ed. by F. A. Gevaert. Paris: Heugel, 1868. Includes "Povera pellegrina suele helas" (from *Il prigioniero fortunato*).

Italian Songs of the XVII and XVIII Centuries, vol. 2. N.Y.: International Music Co., 1961. Includes: "O cessate di piagarmi" and "Toglietemi la vita ancor" (from *Il Pompeo*).

Lira Partenopea; celebri melodie del ... Alessandro Scarlatti. Realization of the basso continuo by Salvatore Palumbo. Naples: T. Cottrau, s.d.

Musica scelta d'antichi maestri italiani. Ed. by G. W. Teschner. Berlin: T. Trautwein, [1866]. Includes: "Ah barbari sensi," Così amor fa languir," "O cessate di piagarmi" (from *Il Pompeo*).

"O cessate di piagarmi" (from *Il Pompeo*) [solo voice with piano]. Milan: Carisch, s.d.

"Recitative ed aria" [solo voice with piano]. Milan: Carisch.

Sette arie con tromba sola [sop. with tpt. in D, keyboard, optional violoncello]. Ed. by Henry Meredith. Nashville, TN: Brass Press. Includes "Con voce festiva," "Faro la vendetta," "In terra la guerra," "Mio tesoro," "Rompe sprezza," "Si riscaldi il Tebro," "Si suoni la tromba."

Suite altitalienischer Arien. Ed. by Erich F. Wolff von Gudenberg. Frankfurt am Main: Wilhelm Zimmermann Musikverlag. Incl.: "Se Florindo è fedele" (from *La donna ancora è fedele*). It. and

Ger. text.

Suite antiker Arietten und Kanzonen. Ed. by Erich F. Wolff von Gudenberg. Frankfurt am Main: Wilhelm Zimmermann Musikverlag. Incl.: "Le violette" (from *Pirro e Demetrio*). It. and Ger. text.

Theoretisch-praktische Harmonielehre. Ed. by S. W. Dehn. Berlin: Schlesinger, 1860. Includes: "Non so chi è più felice" [aria for solo voice and basso continuo].

Ten Arias for High Voice. Ed. by Michael F. Robinson. N.Y.: G. Schirmer, 1967.

[Trente] 30 arie antiche della scuola napoletana. Milan: Ricordi, 1943. Includes "Pupille belle," "Spiega l'ali il mio pensiero" [cantata], "Ecco, sì, vengo anch'io," "Farfalla che s'aggira" [cantata], "Rosignolo che volando," "Onde belle, voi correte," "La pace del mio core."

Tres arias [solo voice with pianoforte]. Ed. by Parisotti. [Milan]: Ricordi. Includes "Se delitto e l'adorarti," "Toglietemi la vita," and "Tu lo sai." It. text.

"Vaga rosa" [medium solo voice with viola d'amore or viola and pianoforte]. Ed. by L. Van Waffelghem. Score and parts. N.Y.: McGinnis & Marx.

Zwei Liebeslieder für eine Singstimme von Alessandro Scarlatti. Ed. by C. Banck. Leipzig: Senff, s.d. Includes "Toglietemi la vita ancor," O cessate di piagarmi" (from *Il Pompeo*).

Oratorios and Large Sacred Works

Agar et Ismaele esiliati. Ed. by Lino Bianchi. Rome: De Santis, 1965 (Oratorii, 2).

Cain ovvero il primo omicidio. Ed. by Bruno Rigacci and Mario Fabbri.

Used for the first modern performance of the work in Siena, Italy, Sept 3, 1966.

_____. *Il primo omicidio.* Ed. by Lino Bianchi. Rome: De Santis, 1968 (Oratorii, 4).

La colpa, il pentimento e la grazia. See *Oratorio per la passione di Nostro Signore Gesu Criste.*

Davidis pugna et victoria. Il David (Davidis...). Ed. by Lino Bianchi. Rome, De Santis, 1969 (Oratorii, 5). Review in *Music and Letters* 52 (1971): 92-94 by Malcolm Boyd.

La Giuditta (i) [solo voices and chorus with instruments]. Ed. by Lino Bianchi. Rome: De Santis, 1964 (Oratorii, 1).

Text attributed variously to either B. Pamphili or Pietro Ottoboni. MSS: Naples Conservatory and Morristown, NJ. This edition gives date as 1695; *NGIBM* gives date of 1st performance as 1693 in Naples.

La Giuditta (ii) (Cambridge) [3 solo voices with string orchestra and basso continuo]. Ed. by Lino Bianchi. Rome: De Santis, 1966 (Oratorii, 3).

Text by Antonio Ottoboni. First performance c1697-1700. MS location: GB, Kings College.

Il martirio di S. Orsola [arias and a duet with piano reduction]. Ed. by E. Trillat. In *Le Luth.* Lyon: Béal, 1944.

****Il martirio di Santa Teodosia.* Ed. by G. Piccioli.

Oratorio per la Passione di Nostro Signore Gesu Criste. Ed. by Lino Bianchi. Rome: De Santis.

_____. Excerpts: [recitative and duet for women's chorus with ob. and horn]. Ed. by E. Gubitosi. Milan: Carisch. Rental version also includes "O Soave conforto."

_____. Excerpts: "O soave
conforto."   Ed. by C. Banck.   In: *Duette alter
Meister*, 4. (1873).

Passio Domini Nostri. Jesu Christi secundum Joannem.   Ed.
by Edwin C. Hanley. New Haven: Yale University
Dept. of Music, 1955.   Score vii and 136 pp.
(Collegium musicum, 1)   currently available
from [Madison, Wisc.]: A-R Editions. Reviews
in: *American Musicological Society. Journal* 9 (1956):
225-228; *Music Review* 18 (1957): 167-168; *Music
and Letters* 37 (1956): 308-309; *Music Library
Association. Notes* 13 (1955): 129-130.

_____. *Johannespassion*... Ed. by
Oskar Deffner.   Stuttgart: Hänssler-Verlag,
1960.   Lat. and Ger. text. Score   58 pp.
(Die Kantate, 7)   Unfig. bass realized for
org.

_____. Ed.by Reinhold Kubik.
Hannsler Verlag. 70 pp.

Il primo omicidio.   See *Cain ovvero il primo omicidio*.

San Filippo Neri.   Ed. by R. Giazotto and G.
Piccioli. Milan: Curci, 1960.

La Ss. Trinità.   Ed. by G. Piccioli. Bologna: A
Bonfiguoli, 1953.

Il Sedecia, Re di Gerusalemme.   Ed. by G. Guerrini.
Milan: Curci, 1961.

**La Vergine addolorata*.   Ed. by G. Pannain.

Serenatas

Amore e virtù ossia il trionfo della virtù (*No, che non voglio più*)
[Cantata for two voices with instruments].
Ed. by Antonio Tirabassi. Brussels: Schott,
1923. v and 76 pp.

Endimione e Cintia (*Sento un'aura che dolce*) [2 sop.
solos with strings].   Ed. by Otto Drechsler.

It. text.   Kassel: Bärenreiter.

Erminia (Ove smarrita, e sola); for the wedding of the Prince of Stigliano.   [Part 1; part 2, MS lost].   Ed. by Thomas E. Griffin.   M.A. thesis.   Los   Angeles: University   of California, Los Angeles, 1975.

Pace, Amore e Providenza (Al fragor di lieta tromba) [sop., alto, bass and chorus with 2 obs., 2 tpts., timpani, 2 violins, viola and basso continuo]. In Boyd #25, pp. 187-222.

Serenata [sop. and ten. solos with strings and keyboard continuo]. Paris: Bureau de Musique Mario Bois.

Venere, Amore e Ragione: Il ballo delle ninfe (Cerco Amore, Amor che fa?).   Ed. by Hermine W. Williams (Clinton, N.Y., 1982).   Unpublished edition located in the Archives of the Chamber Opera Theater of New York City.   [Information from the editor].

Venere e Adone: Il giardino d'amore (Care selve, amati orrori). Ed.   by   Otto   Drechsler   and   M.   Seidel. Frankfurt am Main: Edition Wilhelm Hansen, 1963.

Venere e Amore (Del mar Tirreno in su l'amena sponda) [for two voices with fl., violins and violoncello]. "Harmonisation de A. Toussaint."   Brussels: Institut Belge de Musicologie; Maison Chester, 1921.   74 pp.   Preface signed by Antonio Tirabassi.

2. Instrumental Music

Orchestral and Chamber Music

12 SINFONIE DI CONCERTO GROSSO

[*No. 1, F major*] *Sinfonien für Kammerorchester*; Nr. 1, F-dur.   Ed.   by Raymond Meylan.   Kassel: Bärenreiter, [1954] (Hortus Musicus, 125) Score 18 pp.

[_____]   *Sinfonia prima.*   Ed. by Layton
Ring. London: Schott.

[*No. 2, D major*] *Sinfonien für Kammerorchester*; Nr. 2, D-
dur.   Ed.   by   Raymond   Meylan.   Kassel:
Bärenreiter, [c1968]   (Hortus Musicus, 146)
Score 18 pp.

[*No. 3, d minor*] *Sinfonia terza di concerto grosso*, 1715, for
treble recorder, 2 violins, viola, violoncello
and   basso   continuo.   Ed.   with   continuo
realization for harpsichord by Layton Ring.
London: Schott, [1955].   Score 15 pp.   Ed.
Schott #10462.

[*No. 4, e minor*]   *Sinfonien für Kammerorchester*; Nr.4, E-
moll.   Ed.   by   Raymond   Meylan.   Kassel:
Bärenreiter, 1955   (Hortus Musicus, 48) Score
19 pp. and parts.

[*No. 5, d minor*] *Sinfonien für Kammerorchester*; Nr. 5, D-
moll.   Ed.   by   Raymond   Meylan.   Kassel:
Bärenreiter, 1954 (Hortus Musicus, 116) Score
19 pp.

[*No. 6, a minor*] *Sinfonia Nr. 6: für Flöte, Streicher und Basso
Continuo*, A-moll.   Ed.   by   Rolf-Julius   Koch.
Frankfurt: H. Litolff, c1972.   Score, 23 pp.
Ed. Peters #8092.

[*No. 7, g minor*] *Sinfonia Nr. 7: für Flöte, Streicher und Basso
Continuo*, G-moll.   Ed.   by   Rolf-Julius   Koch.
Frankfurt: H. Litolff, [c1972].   Score 16 pp.
Edition Peters #8093.

[*No. 8, G major*] *Sinfonia Nr. 8: für Flote, Streicher und Basso
Continuo*, G dur.   Ed.   by   Rolf-Julius   Koch.
Frankfurt: H. Litolff, [c1972].   Score 15 pp.
Ed. Peters #8094.

[*No. 9, g minor*] *Sinfonia Nr. 9: für Flöte, Streicher und Basso continuo*, G- moll. Ed. by Rolf-Julius Koch. Frankfurt: H. Litolff, [c1972]. Score 17 pp. Ed. Peters #8095.

[*No. 10, a minor*] *Sinfonia Nr. 10: für Flöte, Streicher und Basso continuo*, A-moll. Ed. by Rolf-Julius Koch. Frankfurt: H. Litolff, [c1972]. Score 17 pp. Ed. Peters #8096.

[*No. 11, C major*] *Sinfonia Nr. 11: für Flöte, Streicher und Basso continuo*, C dur. Ed. with "Generalbass" realization by Rolf-Julius Koch. Frankfurt: H. Litolff, [c1972]. Score 18 pp. Ed. Peters #8097.

[*No. 12, c minor*]. *Sinfonien für Kammerorchester*, Nr. 12, C moll. Ed. by Raymond Meylan. Kassel: Bärenreiter, c1960 (Hortus Musicus, 168). Score 16 pp.

VI CONCERTOS IN 7 PARTS [nos. 1, 2, 4, 5: Italian overtures with occasional solo passages and cadenzas; no. 3: solo concerto; no. 6: concerto grosso]

[*No. 1, f minor*] *Concerto grosso (F-Moll) für 2 Violinen, Viola, Violoncello (Kontrabass) u. Klavier*. Ed. by Arnold Schering. Leipzig: C. F. Kahnt. [c1928]. Score 11 pp. and parts. (Perlenalter Kammermusik). Fig. bass realiz. for piano.

[*Nos. 1-2, f minor and c minor*]. *6 [Sechs] Concerti grossi*. Berlin: C. F. Vieweg, 1939. Plate no. D. 1939.

[*No. 3, F major*]. *Concerto per orchestra d'archi e cembalo, No. 3, F major*. Ed. by F. M. Napolitano. Padua: G. Zanibon, 1956. Review in *Die Musikforschung* 10 (1957): 581- .

_____. ...*Drittes Konzert in F-dur für*
Streichorchester mit cembalo. Ed. by Gustav
Lenzewski. Berlin: C. F. Vieweg, 1927. 13
pp. Pub. plate no. V1706.

_____. In *A Historical Anthology of Music 2*,
pp. 158-162. Ed. by Willi Apel and Archibald
Davison. Cambridge, MA.: Harvard University
Press, 1950.

[*No. 6, E major*]. *6 [Sesto] concerto in mi, per due violini di
concertino, archi e cembalo di ripieno.* Ed. by Renato
Fasano. Milan: Ricordi, c1959. Score 19 pp.
(Antica strumentale italiana) Fig. bass
realiz.

6 CONCERTOS FOR KEYBOARD & ORCHESTRA

[*No. 4, c minor*]. *Concerto, Harpsichord and String Orchestra,
no. 4, c minor.* Attr. to Alessandro Scarlatti.
Arr. by Lionel Salter. London: Oxford, 1969.
Score 14 pp. and parts.

QUATTRO SONATE A QUATTRO   [f, c, g, d]

Sonata a quattro, no. 3, g minor. N.Y.: New York
Public Library, 1938. Score 8 pp. Unrealiz.
fig. bass and 4 string pts. Pub. pl. no.
NN35.

_____. In: *Eighteenth-
Century Imitative Counterpoint: Music for Analysis*, pp. 41-
46. Ed. by Wallace Berry and Edward
Chudacoff. N.Y.: Appleton-Century-Crofts,
1969. Full score.

Sonata a quattro, no. 4, d minor. Ed. by Hans T.
David. N.Y.: Music Press, c1940. 4 parts.

SETTE SONATE PER FLAUTO E ARCHI   [D, a, c, a, A, C, g]

[*Sonatas, flute, 2 violins & continuo*]. *Sette sonate per flauto, archi e basso continuo*. Ed. and realized by Luciano Bettarini. Milan: Casa Editrice Nazionalmusic, c1969. Score xiv and 109 pp. (Collezione settecentesca Bettarini, 1). Review in *American Recorder* 13/2 (1972): 61-62 by Dale Higbee.

[*Sonatas, flute, 2 violins and continuo, no. 4, a minor*]. *4a [Quarta] sonata in la min*., *per flauto, violini, violoncelli, contrabassi e clavicembalo*. Elaboraz. di Alfredo Casella. Milan: Ricordi, [c1959]. Score 23 pp. Fig. bass realiz.

SONATA (F) [FOR FLUTE, 2 VIOLINS, BASSO CONTINUO]

Quartet in F Major for Recorder (or Flute), 2 Violins, and Figured Bass, With Cello Ad Lib. Ed. by Waldemar Woehl. Frankfurt and N.Y.: C. F. Peters, [c1939? or 1951]. Urtext. Score 10 pp. and parts. Fig. bass realiz.

Review in *Musical America* 71 (Oct. 1951): 29.

SONATA (A) [FOR 2 FLUTES, 2 VIOLINS, BASSO CONTINUO]

Sonata in A major for 2 Flutes, 2 Violins and Basso Continuo. Moeck.

SONATA (F) [3 FLUTES, BASSO CONTINUO]

Quartettino für 3 Alt-Blockflöten oder andere Melodieinstrumente und Basso Continuo. Score and 4 parts. [Frankfurt]: Moeck and Edition Peters, c1939.

SUITES IN G & F FOR FLUTE & BASSO CONTINUO

Zwei Sonaten für Alt-Blockflöte.   Heidelberg: Willy
Müller.

SONATAS , VIOLONCELLO & CONTINUO

*Tre sonate...   Ed. by Giuseppe Zanaboni.
Violoncello ed. by Renzo Brancaleon.   Padua:
G. Zanibon, 1967.   Score 12 pp. and part.
Unfig. bass realiz. for harpsichord or piano.

*Three Sonatas for Cello and Piano. Ed. and bass
realized by Analee Bacon. N.Y.: G. Schirmer,
[1967].   Score 14 pp. and part (Schirmer's
Library of Musical Classics, 1851) [eds. of d
minor, c minor, C major]

*Three Sonatas for Double Bass and Piano. Solo pt. ed.
by Lucas Drew.   Continuo realized by Analee
Bacon.   N.Y.: G. Schirmer, [1969].   Score 14
pp. and pt. (Schirmer's Library of Musical
Classics, 1873)

*Three Sonatas for Two Violoncellos.   Greenwich, CT:
Grancino, 1982.   2 performing scores.

     Reviews in Music Library Association. *Notes*
40: 880-882 by Peter Farrell; *Strad* 94 (1983):
41-43 by Robin Stowell. [No MS source given;
"attributed to Scarlatti." Possibly written
for Franciscello c1700.

Keyboard Music

TOCCATE PER CEMBALO

Sieben Tokkaten für Cembalo.   Ed. by Rio Nardi.
Kassel: Bärenreiter, 1964 [1948].   44 pp.
(Bärenreiter-Ausg., 341)

Toccata prima. Ed. and abridged by Mark Lindley.
In *Early Music* 10 (1982): 335-337.   MS sources

include: BM Add. 32161 and Milan Cons. Noseda
22.9. See also ed. by R. Nardi cited above.

Toccate per cembalo. Per ben principiare a sonare, et al nobile portamento delle mani... (7): MS sources I-MC
[contains all the pieces in the Higgs MS: US-NH which includes the above 7 toccatas along with 22 others among them all of the toccatas in the *Primo e secondo libro...*, see ed. by Gerlin cited below]. No. 7 has title "Toccata per cembalo d'ottava stesa" rather than ..."primo tono" as in the MS at I-Nc; 3 fugues; and the set of variations entitled *Varie partite obbligate al basso* (also MS at I-MC). Ed. by J. S. Shedlock. London: Bach & Co., 1908. Reprint of 1908 ed.: Brescia: Paideia; Kassel: Bärenreiter, c1981. 2 vols. (Biblioteca classica dell'organista, 6-7).

Primo e secondo libro di toccate (1 in G; 2 in a; 3 in G; 4 in a; 5 in G; 6 in d; 7 in d - Primo tono containing the *Variazioni sopra La follia,* 1723; 8 in a; 9 in G; 10 in F). MS sources Nc, MS 34.6.31; I-MC, MS 126.D.3 and 126.D.4 (with simpler version of no. 7 "La follia"); US-NH in Higgs MS; A-Wn 18681. Ed. by Ruggero Gerlin (with bio-bibliographical study by Claudio Sartori, pp. 133-154) (I classici musicali italiani, 13) Milan: La Musicografica Lombarda, 1943. [iii and 153 pp].

Toccata [no. 7] nel primo tono. Ed. by Michael Radulescu (Biblioteca classica dell' organista) Brescia: Paideia, c1969. 31 pp. For organ. Preludio-fuga-partite sull'aria della follia.

_____. *Toccata primi toni, für Orgel.* Ed. by Theodor Klein. Wiesbaden: Breitkopf & Härtel, 1972. 43 pp. (Breitkopf ed., 6598).

Tre Toccate (1716).   MS source I-Nc 22.1.22.
Each followed by a fugue and a minuet.   Ed. by
Guido Pannain.   Naples: Izzo.

Other Collections:

Boghen, F., ed.   *Toccate per clavicembalo o pianoforte*.
Milan: Ricordi, 1918.

Longo, A., ed.   *Composizioni per clavicembalo*.   Milan:
Ricordi, 1922.

N.B.   See **Operas, Selections** above   for
editions of opera sinfonias or selections not
available in more complete editions.

+ Indicates works previously only available in
dissertations   now   available   in   published
editions

* Indicates works of uncertain attribution

** Indicates unpublished modern editions of
these works   located in the RAI Archives.   See
Rostirolla (item 435).

Ha in the list of cantatas above indicates
either the number in Hanley's thematic catalog
(item 134) or the setting number indicated in
the list of Scarlatti's cantatas in *NGIBM*,
(item 430), pp. 253-259.

VI

DISCOGRAPHY

ALESSANDRO SCARLATTI ON RECORD

Introduction

To date, only Giancarlo Rostirolla has
published an extensive list of Alessandro
Scarlatti's works on record (*Catalogo*, pp. 569-
573; see item 435). As useful as his
discography is, its rarity has put it out of
reach of many researchers; in any case, it is
now outdated, since a number of new or
reissued recordings (among them those in the
new CD format) have appeared subsequent to
1972. Thus, to obtain a more complete picture
of the composer's recorded works one must make
a cumbersome search through various journals,
catalogs, and indexes. For this reason, the
following list of recordings (which owes much
to the above-mentioned sources) is included
here.

I have included as many recordings of
entire works as I was able to find reference
to but only selected recordings of excerpts
(e.g., individual arias). The latter
emphasize more recent recordings when
possible. The repertoire of Scarlatti on
record is not vast; in fact, as is true in
regard to modern editions of the composer's
works, what strikes one is the paucity of
works available in complete form. Yet, there
has been slow progress on both fronts during
the last decade.

Both "in-print" and "out-of-print"
recordings are included here since the serious
researcher will want to locate both (in
libraries or sound archives) in order to study

performance practice, etc. To learn which recordings are currently available (and in what format) one should consult the commercial catalogs. The amount of detail provided below for each individual citation reflects the combined information obtained from the various sources consulted. The recordings cited below are either LPs, CDs, or tape cassettes with few exceptions and are identified as such in brackets. Asterisked items indicate works of doubtful authenticity. Arias known to be from specific cantatas, operas, etc., are cited under the title of the complete work.

1. Vocal Music

Arias

Arias with trumpet solo (7). [Fr] Harmonia Mundi HM40.5.137 [cass]; HM5.137 [LP]; [US] HMA190.5137 [CD]. Nelson, sop.; Ferry tpt., Ensemble.

_____ (7). [Ger] Chr CD 74 599 [CD]; Chr SCGLX 74 021. Wirtz, Basch, Jacob.

_____ (2). Crystal CD-952 [CD]; C-952 [cass]. B. Norden, sop.; Bob Haley, tpt., Alexander String Quartet, D. Foster, hpschd.

_____ (2). FSM (Fr. Schott) 68.908 [LP]. Shelton, Carroll, Brewer, Lutzke, Palma, Obrien.

_____ (4). [Ger]: RBM 3 095 [LP]. Trio Con Voce.

_____ (1). [Ger]: IMS Amo 30 [CD]. Clarion-Ensbl.

Bellezza che s'ama. See under *Opera*: *Il Pompeo.*

* *Cara e dolce.* [by Cesti]. Etcetera (Harmonia Mundi) 2-ETC 4-2.002 [cass]; KTC 2.002 [CD]; ETC 2.002 [LP]. R. Scotto.

Con voce festiva. See *Arias with trumpet solo* (7). Also Crystal CD-952 [CD]; C-952 [cass]. B. Norden, sop.; Bob Haley, tpt., Alexander String Quartet, D. Foster, hpschd.; [Ger]: RBM 3 095 [LP]. Trio Con Voce.

Faro la vendetta. See *Arias with trumpet solo* (7). Also [Ger]: RBM 3 095 [LP]. Trio Con Voce.

In terra la guerra. See *Arias with trumpet solo* (7). Also [Ger & Fr] FSM 68 9 08 [LP]; FSM PD 10 729 [CD]. Shelton, Carroll, Brewer, Lutzke, Palma, Obrien.

Mio tesoro, per te moro. See *Arias with trumpet solo* (7). Also Crystal CD-952 [CD]; C-952 [cass]. B. Norden, sop.; Bob Haley, tpt., Alexander String Quartet, D. Foster, hpschd. and [Ger]: RBM 3 095 [LP]. Trio Con Voce and FSM 68 9 08 [LP]; FSM PD 10 729 [CD]. Shelton, Carroll, Brewer, Lutzke, Palma, Obrien.

Rompe sprezza con un sospir. See *Arias with trumpet solo* (7). Also [Ger]: RBM 3 095 [LP]. Trio Con Voce.

Si riscaldi il Tebro. See *Arias with trumpet solo* (7).

Si suoni la tromba. See *Arias with trumpet solo* (7). Also [Ger]: IMS Amo 30 [CD]. Clarion-Ensemble.

Cantatas

Ahi che sarà di me? See *Floro e Tirsi.*

Al fin m'ucciderete. Pleiades Records S-103 [LP]. Sylvia Stahlman, sop.; Albert Fuller, hpschd. [1971]

Ammore, brutto figlio de pottana. Cantata in lingua napoletana. Eurodisc S 70903 MK [LP]. H. Handt, ten.; L. Sgrizzi, hpschd.; E. Roveda, violoncello.

Andate o miei sospiri (in idea inhumana). Musical Heritage Society 1479 [LP]. Neva Pilgrim, sop.; Louis Bagger, hpschd.; Barbara Mueser, viola da gamba.

Andate o miei sospiri (in idea humana). Musical Heritage Society 1479 [LP]. Neva Pilgrim, sop.; Louis Bagger, hpschd; Barbara Mueser, viola da gamba.

Bella madre dei fiori. RI FI Record Company, RFL ST 14050 [LP]. Revisione di L. Bettarini.

_____. (Paris) Auvidis AV4.815 [LP]. Toczyska Ensemble instr. Capella Arcis Varsoviensis, C. Sewen.

_____. Fono Schallplatten Gesellschaft FSM Tac CD 6701 2001 [CD]. Gatti, Banditelli, Ensemble Aurora.

Cantata in lingua napoletana. See *Ammore, brutto figlio de pottana.*

Cantata pastorale per la nascita di Nostro Signore. See *Oh di Betlemme.*

Clori e Lisa compagne (Lisa, del foco mio). L'Oiseau-Lyre OL 50154 [1957] & reissued as OLS 154 [LP], [1972]. Jennifer Vyvyan, sop.; Elsie Morison, sop.; Desmond Dupré, viola da gamba; Thurston Dart, hpschd.

Clori e Mirtillo. See *Mentre sul carro aurato.*

Clori vezzosa e bella. L'Oiseau-Lyre OL 50173 [LP]. Helen Watts, contralto; Desmond Dupré, viola da gamba; Thurston Dart, hpschd.

Correa nel seno amato: "Ombre opache." Telefunken SAWT 9525 B [LP]. M. von Egmond,, bass; Leonhardt Consort.

_____. Hyperion KA66254 [cass] & Hyperion CDA 66254 [CD]. L. Dawson, Purcell Quartet.

_____. Pier PV 7900 13 [CD]. J. Nicolas, S. Deeks, X. Julien-Laferriere, A.

Verzier, M. Bothwell, P Ramin.

Del faretrato nume. Musical Heritage Society 1479 [LP]. Neva Pilgrim, sop.; Louis Bagger, hpschd.; Barbara Mueser, viola da gamba.

Ebra d'amor fuggia; L'Arianna. Harmonia Mundi 30591 [LP]. Ensemble Ricercare di Zurigo; Graf.

Elitropio d'amor. Euro S 70903 MK [LP]. H. Handt, tenor; L. Sgrizzi, hpschd.; E. Roveda, violoncello.

_____. Decca Ace of Diamonds SDD206 [LP]. T. Berganza, mezzo-sop.; F. Lavilla, pianoforte.

_____. Lyrinx CD 062 [CD]. Nascimento, male sop.; Foulon, baroque cello; Hasler, hpschd.

E pur vuole il cielo e amore. Italia ITL 70065 [LP]. Five Centuries Ensemble.

Farfalla che s'aggira. (*La pazzia ovvero La stravaganza*). Musical Heritage Society 1479 [LP]. Neva Pilgrim, sop.; Louis Bagger, hpschd.; Barbara Mueser, viola da gamba.

Floro e Tirsi. L'Oiseau-Lyre OL50154 [LP] [1957] & OLS154 [LP] [1972]. J. Vyvyan, sop.; E. Morison, sop.; Desmond Dupré, viola da gamba; Thurston Dart, hpschd.

Già lusingato appieno. Hyperion KA66254 [cass] & Hyperion CDA 66254 [CD]. L. Dawson, Purcell Quartet.

Il rossignuolo. Oiseau-Lyre TT246 [LP]. L'Oiseau-Lyre OL 50173 [LP]. Helen Watts, contralto; Desmond Dupré, viola da gamba; Thurston Dart, hpschd.

Io morirei contento. Euro S 70903 MK [LP]. H. Handt, ten.; L. Sgrizzi, hpschd.; E. Roveda, violoncello.

_____. Lyrinx CD 062 [CD].
Nascimento, male sop.; Foulon, baroque cello;
Hasler, hpschd.

La pazzia ovvero La stravaganza. See *Farfalla che s'aggira*

L'Arianna. See *Ebra d'amor fuggia.*

Leandro anima mia (Ero ed Leandro). [Eng] Pier PV
790013 [CD].   A. Aubin, A. Verzier, M.
Bothwell, P. Ramin.

Lisa, del foco mio. See *Clori e Lisa compagne.*

Mentre sul carro aurato (Clori e Mirtillo). Italia ITL
70065 [LP]. Five Centuries Ensemble.

_____. Fy (Paris) FYCD 123
[CD]. H.& M. Ledroit, solo instr.

Mitilde mio tesor. Eurodisc 80607 PK [LP]. H.J.
Rotzsch, ten.; Capella Fidicina, dir. by H.
Grüss.

Nacqui a'sospiri e al pianto. RI FI Record Company,
RFL ST 14050 [LP]. Revisione di L. Bettarini.

_____. (Paris) Auvidis.
AV4.815 [LP]. Toczyska Ensemble; instr.
Capella Arcis Varsoviensis, C. Sewen.

No, non ti voglio Cupido. Italia ITL 70065 [LP].
Five Centuries Ensemble.

*Oh di Betlemme (Cantata pastorale per la nascita di Nostro
Signore).* Turnabout TV 34180 [LP]. Vox CT2286
[cass].   Gertraut Stoklassa, sop.; Mainz
Chamber Orchestra, Günter Kehr, conductor.

_____. Lumen LD2-120 [LP]. Jean-Paul
Jeannotte, ten.; Jacques Parrénin, violin;
Marcelle Charbonnier, hpschd.

_____. Electrola, H.M.V. ASD 2615, I C
02058.   Janet Baker, mezzo-sop.; English
Chamber Orchestra, dir. by R. Leppard.

_____. Abbey LPB 761 [LP].

_____. Hungaraton U4-12.561 [cass]; UC
12.561 [CD]; U 12.561 [LP]. Zadori, sop.;
Lax, ct. ten. Capella Savaria, Nemeth.

Pensieri, oh Dio, qual pena?. Euro S 70903 MK. H.
Handt, ten.; L. Sgrizzi, hpschd.; E. Roveda,
violoncello.

Questo silenzio ombroso. Italia ITL 70065 [LP].
Five Centuries Ensemble.

Sento nel core certo dolore: arietta. Angel COLH 117
[LP]. Tito Schipa, La Scala Orch., C.
Sabajno. C1932. Reissue (Eng) 1986. VDP
1009 16-1 [LP]. EMI EX 290948-3 [LP]; EX
290948-5 [cass].

_____. Oiseau-Lyre SOL 323
[LP]. Stuart Burrowes.

_____. Coronet 2818 [LP].
Dicran Jamgochian.

_____. Jerusalem CATD 8702
[CD]. Kohn, bar.; English Chamber Orch.,
Halstead.

_____. [Ger] Hek Ac 23310
[LP]. Bruson.

Solitudini amene, apriche collinette. RCA Italiana
ML20025 [LP]. M. Laszlo, sop.; S. Gazzelloni,
flute; M. De Robertis, hpschd.

_____. Electrecord
ECD 1044. A. Tuccari, sop.; K. Klemm, flute;
L. Franceschini, hpschd.

_____. Claves CLA
P604 [LP]; Claves CD 50-604 [CD]. K. Graf,
sop.; P. Graf, flute; Altwegg, violoncello;
Kobayashi, hpschd.

Speranze mie, addio. Euro S 70903 MK . H. Handt,

ten.;   L.   Sgrizzi,   hpschd.;   E.   Roveda,
violoncello.

_____.   Lyrinx   CD   062   [CD].
Nascimento, male sop.; Foulon, baroque cello;
Hasler, hpschd.

Splendeano in bel sembiante.   Antony Ransome, bar.
Wren Consort.

Su le sponde del Tebro.   Cambridge CRS 2710 [LP].
Bogard;   Ghitalla;   Moriarty;   Copenhagen
Chamber Orchestra   [1970]

_____.   Deutsche   Grammophon
Gesellschaft 2530023 [LP].   [1971]

_____.   Deutsche   Grammophon
Gesellschaft 136291 [LP].   M. Stader, sop.;
Orchestra Bach di Monaco, dir. by Karl
Richter.

_____.   Deutsche   Grammophon
Gesellschaft Archiv APM 14024.   Teresa Stich-
Randall, sop.; H. Wobisch, tpt.; Camerata
Academica des Salzburger Mozarteums, dir. by
B. Paumgartner.

_____.   Electrola/Erato I C 063-
28265 [LP].   Adriana Maliponte, sop.; L.
Sgrizzi, hpschd.   Orchestra della Società
Cameristica di Lugano, dir. by E. Loehrer.
Musical Heritage Society MHS 1148 [LP] an
apparent reissue; with Maurice André, tpt.

_____.   Colosseum   CLPS   1035
[LP]. Teresa Stich-Randall, sop; Orchestra
della Associazione Alessandro Scarlatti di
Napoli, dir. by B. Paumgartner.

_____.   FSM/Pantheon FSM-68-908
[LP].   Shelton, Carroll, Figueroa, How
Ensemble.   Also FSM PD 10 729 [CD]: Shelton
with NY Trumpet Ensemble.

_____.   (Ger) EMI 067-270 175-1
[LP] & EMI 567 749 461-2 [CD].   Donath, André,

Academy of St. Martin-in-the-fields, Neville
Marriner, cond.

_____. [Eng] Nimbus NI 5123
[CD]. Field, sop.; Philharmonia Orch.,
Wright.

_____. Capriccio 10221 [CD] &
[Ger] Del 10 221 [CD]. Schreier, ten.,
Virtuosi Saxonia, Güttler.

Tirsi e Fileno. Cited under **Oratorios and Large Sacred Works**.

Church Music

MASSES

Messa di Santa Cecilia (1720). Musical Heritage
Society 4076H stereo [LP] and 6076K [cass].
c1979. Klebl, sop.; Aks, sop.; Malafonte,
mezzo-sop.; Becker, ct. ten.; Solem, ten.;
Shannon; ten.; Murray, bass; Brewer, org.
Schola Cantorum of St. Mary the Virgin, New
York City. Robinson, cond.

_____. Bach Guild 621 [LP] and
Bach 5044 [LP]. Preston, sop.; B. Christensen,
sop.; Smiley, contralto; R. Christensen, ten.,
Wood, bass; University of Utah Alumni Chorus
and Utah Symphony Orchestra, dir. by Maurice
Abravanel.

_____. Argo ZRG 903 [LP]; KZRC
903 [cass]. Elizabeth Harwood, sop.; Wendy
Eathorne, sop.; Margaret Cable, contralto;
Wynford Evans, ten.; Christopher Keyte, bass;
St. John's College Chapel Choir; Wren
Orchestra, dir. by George Guest.

Missa ad usum cappellae pontificiae. Musical Heritage
Society 721S [LP]. Ensemble Vocale di
Losanne, dir. by Korboz. [1966]

MOTETS

Ad te Domine levavi. Musical Heritage Society 721S [LP]. [1966]

_____. RCA Italiana ML 20207[LP]. Coro Vallicelliano, dir. by P. Antonio Sartori.

_____. Studio SM 30 A 139 [LP]. Ensemble Vocale Turellier.

Caligaverunt oculi mei. Tudor 73 0 29 [LP]. Jans, Luzerner Vokalsolisten.

Cantantibus organis Cecilia. Nonesuch H 71398 [LP]. See *Vespers of Saint Cecilia.*

Completi sunt [not cited in *NGIBM*]; Tudor 73 0 29 [LP]. Jans, Luzerner Vokalsolisten.

De tenebroso lacu. Allegro AL 87 [LP]. [1965]

Dixit Dominus. DG Archiv 423386-2 AH [CD]. Trevor Pinnock, English Consort and Choir.

Domine refugium factus est nobis. Tudor 73 0 29 [LP]. Jans, Luzerner Vokalsolisten.

Domine vivifica me. Erato STV 70287 [LP]. Ensemble Vocale di Losanne, dir. by [M.] Korboz.

Est dies trophaei. Chorus: Miraculis in coelo fulget. RCA Victor E4RP-8566 [LP]. S.3 bd.2.

_____. History of Music in Sound HLP 12 [LP]. London Chamber Orchestra and Singers, dir. by A. Bernard.

Exultabo te. Erato STV 70287 [LP]. Ensemble Vocale di Losanne, dir. by [M.] Korboz.

Exultate Deo. [Ger] BR 680 01 036 [LP]; BR 690 01 036[CD]. Beringer, Windsbacher Knabenchor.

_____. [Ger] Mag AV 2100 116 [CD]; Mag

Lu 2153 113 [CD]. Flämig, Dresdner Kreuzchor.

_____. [Ger] Tho ATH 317 [LP]. Richter,
Knabenchor St. Nikolai Hamburg.

_____. [Ger] RCA GD 69 093 QH [CD]; RCA
GK 69 093 SF [cass]. Schrems, Regensburger
Domspatzen.

_____. [Ger] Ko Ap 86 025 [LP].
Stuligrosz, Posener Nachtigallen.

_____. [Eng] ALPH APS 374 [LP].
Warwick St. Mary's Collegiate Church, T.
Peters, S. Lole

_____. Erato STV 70287 [LP]. Ensemble
Vocale di Losanne, dir. by [M.] Korboz.

_____. Columbia ML 4873 [LP]. Vienna
Choir Boys, dir. by F. Brenn and P. Lacovich.

Infirmata vulnerata. La Voce del Padrone ASD 615
[LP]. Dietrich Fischer-Dieskau, bar. with
orchestra.

_____. Harmonia Mundi HMC40-254/56
[3-cass]; HMC 254/56 [3-LPs].

Intellige clamorem.   Erato STV 70287 [LP].
Ensemble Vocale di Losanne, dir. by [M.]
Korboz.

Jesu corona Virginum. Nonesuch H 71398 [LP]. See
Vespers of Saint Cecilia.

Lauda Jerusalem Dominum. Nonesuch H 71398 [LP].
See *Vespers of Saint Cecilia.*

Magnificat. Nonesuch H 71398 [LP]. See *Vespers of
Saint Cecilia.*

Motetto di Requiem.   Allegro ALL 87 [LP].   Y.
Tinayre, bar.; Allegro Chamber Society, dir.
by Sam Morgenstern. Also Bell-disc 206 [LP].

Nisi Dominus aedificaverat. Nonesuch H 71398 [LP].

See *Vespers of Saint Cecilia*.

Offertorio. Plaisir Musical CPTPM 130549 [LP]. Coro Nazionale Bulgaro.

O magnum mysterium. [Ger] FSM 33 2 07 [LP]; Harmonia Mundi 25162 [LP]. H. Leiwering, Münster Domchor, Bläser.

_____. Tudor 73 0 29 [LP]. Jans, Luzerner Vokalsolisten.

Passio Domini Nostri Jesu Christi Secundum Joannem (St. John Passion). Cited under *ORATORIOS AND LARGE SACRED WORKS*.

Responsori per la Settimana Santa. See *Caligaverunt oculi mei* and *Tenebrae factae sunt*.

Salve Regina [i] for SA, 2 vln., bc (Milan MS). ADDA 581046 [CD]. V. Dietschy, Gradiva Ensemble, A. Zaepffel, alto & dir. [issued 3-90]

Salve Regina. Tudor 73 0 29 [LP]. Jans, Luzerner Vokalsolisten.

Salvum me fac. Erato STV 70287 [LP]. Ensemble Vocale di Losanne, dir. by [M.] Korboz.

Stabat Mater. Lyrichord LL88 [LP]; previously issued as Vox PL 7970 [LP]. R. Giancola, sop.; M. Truccato Pace, contralto; Scuola Veneziana Orchestra, dir. by A. Ephrikian. [1959].

_____. Philips A 02290 L [LP]. Van der Horst, Coro Soc. Bach.

_____. Deutsche Grammophon Gesellschaft Archiv 2533 324 (Int). [LP]. Mirella Freni, sop.; Teresa Berganza, mezzo-sop.; Paul Keuntz Chamber Orchestra, dir. by Charles Mackerras.

_____. Hungaraton SLPD 12732 [LP]; HCD 12732 [LP]. Zádori, sop.; Esswood, ct. ten.; P. Nemeth, Capella Savaria (period instruments).

_____. ADDA 581046 [CD]. V. Dietschy,
Gradiva Ens., A. Zaepffel, alto & dir.
[issued 3-90]

Te Deum. Tudor 73 0 29 [LP]. Jans, Luzerner
Vokalsolisten.

Tenebrae factae sunt. [Ger] Tudor 73 0 29 [LP].
Jans, Luzerne Vocalsoloists

Valerianus in cubiculo. Nonesuch H 71398 [LP]. See
Vespers of Saint

Cecilia. Vespers of Saint Cecilia. Nonesuch H 71398
[LP]; H 4-71398 [cass]. Patricia Clark, sop.;
Ursula Connors, sop.; Shirley Minty,
contralto; Ian Partridge, ten.; John Noble,
bar.; Accademia Monteverdiana Orchestra and
Chorus, Denis Stevens. [1981]. Also Schwann
ANS-3543 [LP].

Madrigals

Madrigals. Deutsche Gramophon Archiv 2533 300
[LP]. Hamburg Monteverdi Choir, Jürgen
Jürgens, cond. Complete [8]; based on
Jürgens' edition.

_____. Selections [7]. [Fr] DHM 7491892
[CD]. Rooley, Consort of Musicke.

_____. Selections [4]. [Fr] REM 10.984
[LP]. Correa, Monteverdi Consort.

Operas

Clearco in Negroponte: "Vengo a stringerti".
Nimbus NI 5102 [CD]. A. Kraus, J.
Tordesillas.

La dama spagnola e il cavaliere romano. See *Scipione nelle
Spagne.*

La donna ancora è fedele: "Se Florindo è fedele."
EMI EX 29 1054-3 [LP]. c1929. H. Spani, Orch.
cond. by G. Nastrucci.

_____ :   "Son   tutto   duolo."
L'Oiseau Lyre SOL323 [LP]. Stuart Burrowes,
ten.; John Constable, piano.

_____ :   "Son   tutto   duolo."
[Ger] EMI 1555-73 200-2 [CD]. Schipa.

Gli equivoci in amore, overa la Rosaura: "Un cor da voi
ferito."   Decca Ace of Diamonds SDD206 [LP];
Teresa Berganza, mezzo-sop; F. Lavilla, piano.

Flavio Cuniberto: "Chi vuolo innamorarsi Rosaura."
Decca Ace of Diamonds SDD206.   Teresa
Berganza, mezzo-sop.; Felix Lavilla, piano.
[Reiss.: Decca 6.48 274DM].

_____ :   "Chi   vuolo   innamorarsi
Rosaura."   Nimbus NI 5102 [CD].   A. Kraus, J.
Tordesillas.

La Griselda. Memories 2 HR 4154/55 [CD]   Freni;
Alva; Luchetti, Panerai; Bruscantini, N.
Sanzogno, Naples "A. Scarlatti" Radio Orch. &
Cho. (Rec. live 10/29/70; issued 7-90).

La Griselda: selections.   Cambridge CRS 2903
[LP].   C. Bogard, sop.; Windingstad, sop.;
Collins, ct. ten.; Cascio, ten.; University
Orchestra, University of California, Berkeley,
cond. by Moe. [1976]

L'honestà negli amore: "Già il sole da Gange", arr.
London OS 26391 [LP].   Luciano Pavorotti.
[Eng] Decca SXL 6650 [LP]; Decca KSXC 6650
[cass]. Also [Eng] Decca 417 006-2DH [CD].

_____ : "Già il sole da Gange."
Qualiton LPX 1289 [LP].

_____ : "Già il sole da Gange."
Cantilena 6236 [LP]. John Stratton.

_____ : "Già il sole da Gange."

Jerusalem CATD 8702 [CD]. Kohn, bar.; Eng.
Ch. Orch., Halstead.

_____ : "Già il sole da Gange."
Del 10 295 [CD]; Del 27 295 CC [cass].

Lesbina e Adolfo (intermezzos in 5 scenes; from
Odoardo, 1700). Bongiovanni 2 GB2063/64-2
[CD]. Uccello, Gatti, D. Sanfilippo, Boemia
del Nord Orch. & Cho. (Rec. live 7/86).

Pericca e Varrone. See *Scipione nelle Spagne*.

Pirro e Demetrio: "Rugiadose, odorose, violette
graziosa." L'Oiseau-Lyre SOL323 [LP]. Stuart
Burrowes, ten.

_____ : "Rugiadose, odorose, violette
graziosa." Telefunken SLT 43116 [LP]. Peter
Schreier.

_____ : "Rugiadose, odorose, violette
graziosa." Con Pol 321 [LP]. N. Gedda.

_____ : "Rugiadose, odorose, violette
graziosa." [Eng] EMI CDH7 63200-2 [CD]. T.
Schipa. (Rec. 1939; iss. 4/90).

_____ : "Rugiadose, odorose, violette
graziosa." [Ger] Decca 421 526 2 ZK [CD]; Dec
2894 21 526 1 AZ [cass]. Pavarotti, Wustman.

_____ : "Le Violette." See
"Rugiadose, odorose, violette graziosa."

Il Pompeo: "Bellezza che s'ama." Etcetera
(Harmonia Mundi) 2-ETC 4-2.002 [cass]; KTC
2.002 [CD]; ETC 2.002 [LP]. R. Scotto.

_____ : "O cessate di piagarmi." (Eng)
Decca SXL6579 [LP]. (USA) London 26303 [LP].
Renata Tebaldi, sop.

_____ : "O cessate di piagarmi." Jerusalem
CATD 8702 [CD]. Kohn, bar.; Eng. Ch. Orch.,
Halstead.

_____: "O cessate de piagarmi."   [Eng]
Nimbus   NI   5102   [CD].   A. Kraus,   J.
Tordesillas.

_____: "Toglietemi la vita ancor."   [Eng]
Nimbus   NI   5102   [CD].   A. Kraus,   J.
Tordesillas.

Il prigionier fortunato: "Sinfonia."   Nimbus NI 5123
[CD]. Philharmonia Orch., Wright.

La Psiche: "Fermate omai fermate."   Lyrinx CD
062 [CD].   Nascimento, male sop.; Foulon,
baroque cello; Hasler, hpschd.

Scipione nelle Spagne: Intermezzos, *Pericca e Varrone* or
*The Spanish Lady and the Roman Cavalier (La dama spagnola e il
cavaliere romano)*.   Decca Met/ Set 230 [LP].
Fiorenza Cossotto; Lorenz Alvary; Complesso
Strumentale   Italiano,   dir.   by   Giulio
Confalonieri.

Tito Sempronio Gracco: "Idolo mio, ti chiamo."   RCA
Victor E4 RP-8564 [LP].

_____: "Idolo mio, ti chiamo."
History of Music in Sound HLP 11 [LP].   M.
Ritchie, sop.; N. Evans, contralto; D. Bondo,
sop.; Joung Orch., dir. by J.A. Westrup.

Il Trionfo dell'onore.   Cetra LPC 1223 [LP] and
Cetera XTV 14511-14 [LP].   Teatro Nuovo di
Milano. Cast of Singers and Orchestra di Radio
Italiana,   dir.   by   Carlo   Maria   Giulini.
[1950/1951].

Oratorios and Large Sacred Works

Il giardino di rose.   Overture.   New   York
Philharmonic,   dir.   by   Raymond   Leppard.
Philips 802 901 LY [LP].

_____.   Overture.   Nimbus NI 5079
[CD]. Anon. orch. & cond.

_____.   Overture.   [Ger] Ar Aris

880 431 909 [CD]. Wright, Philh. Orch. London.

La Giuditta. Harmonia Mundi HMO 30575 [LP];
stereo HMS 30575 [LP]. L. Arséguet, sop.; H.
Boulangeot, sop.; A. Kendall, ct. ten.; M.
Hamel, ten.; A. Vessières, bass. Orchestre de
la Société des Concerts du Conservatoire de
Paris, dir. by Roger Blanchard. Revisione di
Lino Bianchi.

La Giuditta. Hungaraton HCD 12910 [CD]. Zádori,
Gémes, Gregor, Minter, de Mey. Capella
Savaria, cond. McGegan.

*Passio Domini Nostri Jesu Christi secundum Joannem (St. John
Passion)*. [Ger]: EMI 069-99 927T [LP]; RCA GD
77111QH [CD]; RCA GK 77111SF [cass]. [US]:
Editio Classica 77111-2RG [CD] [1990]. René
Jacobs, ct. ten., Graham Pushee, ct.ten.; Kurt
Widmer, bar.; Schola Cantorum Basiliensis,
Näf.

_____. Overtone 1. Stern,
ten.; Laurent, bass; Borden, ten.; George,
org.; Choir of St. Thomas' Church, New Haven;
Yale University Orchestra, H. Boatwright,
cond.

_____. Arion ARN 38.290
(France) Reissue: Musical Heritage
Society MHS-3529. c1976. Musica Polyphonica
Ensemble, dir. by Louis Devos, ten.

Qual di lieti concenti. See *Tirsi e Fileno*.

San Filippo Neri. Music Guild S-12. Italian
releases: Angel LPA 5924; Ars Nova VST 6128.
Reissue, Musical Heritage Society MHS 1866
(stereo). Bruna Rizzoli, sop.; Biancamaria
Casoni, mezzo-sop.; Anna Maria Rota,
contralto; Petre Munteanu, ten.; Milan
Angelicum Orchestra, cond. by Franco
Caracciolo. Based on Piccioli/Giazotto
edition.

_____. EMI CD 7-49255-2 [CD]. Näf,

cond.   Rev. in *Fanfare* 5-6/89 248.

Il Sedecia, Re di Gerusalemme: "Caldo sangue; Col tuo
velo i lumi miei; O del morto mio figlio."
RCA Italiana DSM 227b.   L. Rossi, sop.;   I.
Mancini, sop.;   A.M. Romagnoli, contralto.

_____.   "Caldo   sangue."
Decca LXT 5410.   Renata Tebaldi, sop.; G,
Faveretto, piano.

_____.   "Caldo   sangue."
Erato   70533 and Erato ERA 9509.   Adriana
Maliponte; Società cameristica di Lugano, dir.
by E. Loehrer.

_____.   "Caldo   sangue;
Venite   a   concilio."   Supraphon DM 5256.
Wladimir Ruzdjak, ten.; Alfréd Holecek, piano.

_____.   "Caldo   sangue."
Tappy,   Pache.   Lausanne College Orch.   Gallo
30-265.

Tirsi   e   Fileno,   Christmas   Cantata.
Weinachtspastorale.   Unisono   Tontechnik   UNS
22781/82   2 LPs.   Koch/Eder,   Reichardt.
Unisono-Kammerorch, Pfeifer-Koch.

Serenatas

Clori e Zeffiro.   Musical Heritage Society 1057
(stereo).   Wendy   Eathorne,   sop.;   Maureen
Morrelle,   mezzo-sop.;   English   Chamber
Orchestra, dir. by Frederick Storfer; Geoffrey
Prattley, hpschd.   [1970]

Diana ed Endimione (Voi solitarie piante).   Nicolas,
Aubin/ Deeks, Julien-LaFerriere, Williams,
Verzer, Bothwell, Ramin. PIER PV 790013.

Endimione e Cintia. Deutsche Gramophon Archiv 2533
061 (stereo).   Reri Grist, sop.;   Tatiana
Troyanos, mezzo-sop.; Peter Schreier, ten.
Hamburg   Philharmonic   Orchestra,   dir.   by
[Mathieu] Hans-Jurge Lange. [1971]. Recorded

in 1964.

_____: "Mi sembra di sognar"; "Vaga
Cintia adorata"; "Se geloso é il mio core."
[Ger] Mot 20 090. Fischer/ Haas, Wisskirchen.

_____. "Mi sembra di sognar"; "Vaga
Cintia adorata anima mia." [Ger] Wirtz/
Basch, Jacob. Chr CD 74 599 [CD]; Chr SCGLX
74 021 [LP].

Il giardino d'amore. See *Venere e adone*.

Venere e adone; Il giardino d'amore. Deutsche Gramophon
Archiv ARC 73244. [1965]

_____. Deutsche
Grammophon Archiv 198 344; Reissue: DGG
Privilege 2535.361 (s). Earlier issue ARC
73244. C. Gayer, sop.; B. Fassbänder, mezzo-
sop.; Munich Chamber Orchestra, dir. by H.
Stadlmaier.

_____. Accord 200 082
[CD]. Akerlund, sop.; Ragin, ct.ten.;
Clemencic Consort, Clemencic, cond.

Venere e Amore. Fy (Paris) FYCD 123 [CD]. H.and
M. Ledroit and solo instrumentalists: Cuiller,
Sauve, Simpson, Suzanne, Spieth, Spaeter.

Voi solitarie piante. See *Diana ed Endimione*.

2. INSTRUMENTAL MUSIC

Concertos

VI Concertos in 7 Parts (1740). Numbers 1-6.
Philips 9500 603. I Musici. [c1979].

_____. Numbers 1-6. Deutsche
Gramophon Archiv ARC 2547 020 [LP]. Scarlatti
Orchestra of Naples, dir. by Ettore Gracis.
Nos. 1, 3, 5 available also on DG 427 123-2
[CD] and DG 427 123-4 [cass].

_____. Numbers 1, 2, 3, 6.
Arion ARN 38 402 (France). Reissue: Peters
International PLE-086 (S), c1979. La Follia
Instrumental Ensemble. Miguel de la Fuente,
cond. and violin soloist. [See *Fanfare* 3/4
1979 p.107]

_____. Number 1, f minor.
L'Oiseau-Lyre OL 50129. Boyd Neel Orchestra;
Thurston Dart conducting from the hpschd.
[1956]

_____. Number 1, f minor.
Concert Hall Limited Edition E-15. Winterthur
Symphony Orchestra, Clemens Kahinden, cond.

_____. Number 1, f minor.
(France) Harmonia Mundi HM 596 (stereo disc);
cassette HM 40-596. Banziger, Meylan, Saar
Chamber Orchestra, Karl Ristenpart, cond.

_____. Number 3, F major.
Nonesuch 71052. London Soloists.

12 Sinfonie di Concerto Grosso (1720). Complete. (Ger)
Thorofon Schallplatten ATH 331/2 K, 2 LPs.
Tschupp, Sudwestdt. Kammerorch, Pforzheim.

_____. Complete.
Musical Heritage Society 827429A [LPs] and
229429Z [cassettes].

_____: Nos. 1-6.
Philips 6769066 [2-LP]; Philips 400 017-2
[CD] 2 discs. I Musici. Bennett, flute; L.
Smith, flute; Soustrot, tpt; Elhorst, ob.
Review in *Fanfare* 3/4 (1982) p. 238.

_____: Nos. 1-6.
Musical Heritage Society 11162W [CD].

_____: Nos. 1-2, 4-
5, 9, 12. [Ger] DC Bmu 4209 [LP]. Ravier,
Larde, Franz. Instr. Ensemble. Also Marion ,
flute, Coueffe, tpt., Maisonneuve, ob.

_____: No. 3, for

flute, strings & continuo in d minor.
ASV/Gaudeamus CD GAU 111R [CD]. Harvey,
recorders; London Vivaldi Orch., Huggett.

_____: No. 3, for
treble recorder and strings. Musical Heritage
Society 4857W [LP] and 6857X [cass].

_____: No. 4, for
flute,. ob., strings with basso continuo.
[Ger] FSM CB 12 003 [LP]. Lukas, Lukas
Consort.

_____: No. 8, for
flute with basso continuo. [Ger] DC Pel PSRD
40 704. Joss, Vollenweider.

Keyboard Music

Cinq toccatas. Erato ERA 9089. Luciano Sgrizzi,
hpschd. Includes *Toccata sul primo tono* (d); and
Toccatas in C major, d minor, and A major. Prog. notes
in Fr/Eng by G. Pestelli.

Toccatas. Nos. 1-4. [Ger] Con Dy CD 65 [CD].
Calcagno.

_____: No. 2. [Ger] FSM 56 504. Götz.

_____: No. 6. Sine Qua Non Superba SA 2018
[LP] and C 2018 [cass]. [1978]. Title on
disc *Partita in d*. Judith Norell, hpschd.

_____: No. 6. Musical Heritage Society MHS
1443 [LP]. Bengt Johnnson, hpschd.

_____: No. 7 (arr). [Ger] CVS Spi 5595 XB
[LP]. Burscheider Bläserensemble,
Wisskirchen.

_____: No. 7 (arr). [Ger] DG 419 245-2 [CD];
DG 419 245-4 IMS [cass]. Trompetentrio Läubin,
Preston, Schmitt.

_____: No. 7. See also *Toccata sul primo tono* (in
Cinq toccatas and *Toccata per cembalo d'ottava stesa*).

_____: No. 11. [Ger]   Tudor 73 0 33 [cass].
Bovet.

_____: No. 11.   [Ger]. Org 90 002 F [LP].
Wisskirchen.

Toccata per cembalo d'ottava stesa (1723). [Eng] Hyperion
CDA 66254 [CD]; Hyperion KA66254 [cass].   R.
Wooley, hpschd.

Variations on "La Follia" (1715).   [Eng] Hyperion CDA
66254 [CD]; Hyperion KA66254 [cass].   R.
Wooley, hpschd.

Chamber Music

Sonatas for flute, strings, and continuo: No. 3 in c
minor.   EMI   CDS7 4 7985-2 [CD].   Linde,
recorders; Linde-Consort.

_____: No. 3.
Hungaraton SLPD 12732 [LP]; HCD 12732 [CD].
P. Nemeth, flute and cond., Capella Savaria.

Sonata for flute, 2 violins and continuo in a. Bis LP-8 [LP];
Bis   CD-8   [CD].   Pehrsson,   alto   recorder,
Drottingham Baroque Ensemble.

_____.   Cla 50-
8912 [CD]. Steinmann, London Baroque.

Sonata for recorder, oboe, violins & b.c. in F major. [Ger]
FSM 93 0 09 [3-LP] Dt. Barocksolisten.   3
recorders play violin parts.

* *Sonatas for cello and continuo, nos. 1 and 3*. Lyrinx CD
062 [CD].   Foulon, baroque cello.

* Indicates works of uncertain attribution

BOOK I: INDEX OF AUTHORS

Abert, Anna Amalie, 173
Abraham, Gerald, 325
Ademollo, Alessandro, 84
Alaleona, Domenico, 272
Aldrich, Putnam, 343
Allenson, Stephen Mark, 120
Alton, Edwin H., 326
Anderson, Nicholas, 327
Andrieux, Maurice, 85
Apel, Willi, 314
Arnold, Frank Thomas, 344
Atterberg, Kurt, 401

Badura-Skoda, Eva, 1
Baillie, Lauren, 443
Ballola, Giovanni Carli, 2
Bank, Jan A., 149
Barcham, William L., 345
Barnett, Dene, 346
Basso, Alberto, 219
Benary, Peter, 387
Benton, Rita, 439
Berry, Corre, 121
Bettarini, Luciano, 328
Bjirström, Per, 176
Bianchi, Lino, 273, 274, 275, 293, 295, 298, 299, 301
Bianconi, Lorenzo, 66, 174, 175, 219b
Bland, Leland Dye, 276
Blanks, Fred R., 389
Bollert, Werner, 413
Bonaventura, Arnaldo, 150
Borgir, Tharald, 347
Bosanquet, Caroline, 304

Bossa, Renato, 66, 86, 103
Bowen, Meirion, 409
Bowles, Kenneth Eugene, 171
Boyd, Malcolm, 3, 122, 123, 264, 277, 430, 440
Boyden, David D., 348
Brandvik, Paul Allen, 151
Brook, Barry, 444
Brown, Howard Mayer, 198, 267, 338, 349, 350
Buchau, Stephanie von, 395
Buelow, George J., 40, 41, 351, 352
Burgess, C., 384
Burney, Charles, 42, 43, 445
Burt, Nathaniel, 177

Cafiero, Rosa, 278
Cametti, Alberto, 87, 88, 178
Caraci, Maria, 124
Careri, Enrico, 279
Carse, Adam, 353, 354
Cecchi, Emilio, 44
Celletti, Rodolfo, 104, 355
Ciapparelli, Pier Luigi, 67
Cochrane, Eric, 62
Collins, Leo Wilkie Jr., 125
Collins, Michael, 179, 268, 269, 356, 378, 412
Compagnino, Gaetano, 89

Confalonieri, Giulio,
   68, 262
Confuorto, Domenico, 69
Coniglio, Giuseppe, 70
Corte, Andrea della, 45
Covell, Roger, 357
Cowart, Georgia, 46
Crain, Gordon Ferris,
   105
Croce, Benedetto, 71,
   180
Cyr, Mary, 358

D'Accone, Frank A.,
   240, 241
D'Alessandro, Domenico
   Antonio, 77
Damuth, Laura, 126
Davies, Margaret E.,
   403
Daw, Brian Allan, 127,
   359
Day, Thomas Charles,
   152
Dean, Winton, 181, 360,
   396, 410
De Angelis, Marcello,
   63, 64
Degrada, Francesco,
   182, 183
De Lage, Joseph Ovide,
   Jr., 329
Della Seta, Fabrizio,
   90
Dent, Edward J., 6, 7,
   25, 128, 184, 185,
   186, 244, 245, 330,
   431, 446
Dibb, F., 404
Dietz, Hanns-Bertold,
   26, 72
Dixon, Graham, 153
Doderer, Gerhard, 315

Donadoni, Eugenio, 47
Donato, Giuseppe, 73
Donington, Robert, 361,
   362, 363, 364
Doria, Gino, 74
Dotto, Paolo, 8
Downes, Edward O. D.,
   187
Durante, Sergio, 91

Edmunds, John, 129
Eitner, Robert, 447
Esteban, Julio, 316

Fabbri, Mario, 19, 65,
   154, 155, 296
Fabris, Dinko, 75
Faravelli, Danilo, 156
Ferand, Ernest T., 365,
   366
Ferrari-Barassi, Elena,
   188
Ferrero, Mercedes
   Viale, 189, 190, 191
Fienga, Pasquale, 9, 27
Filippis, Felice de, 10
Florimo, Francesco, 76
Foreman, Edward Vaught,
   367
Freeman, Robert S., 192
Freund, Cecilia Kathryn
   Van de Kamp, 130,
   131

Gallo, Franco, 448
Garbelotto, Antonio,
   294, 432
Gasparini, Francesco,
   368
Gasperini, Guido, 448
Gaye, Vera M., 92
Gervaso, Roberto, 51

Gialdroni, Teresa M.,
    132
Gianturco, Carolyn,
    107, 193
Godwin, Joscelyn, 253
Green, Douglass M., 201
Greenhalgh, Michael,
    392
Griffin, Thomas Edward,
    305, 306, 307, 308,
    309, 310
Grossi, Genaro, 11
Grout, Donald J., 12,
    194, 195, 242, 243,
    246, 247, 248, 261

Haböck, Franz, 369, 370
Hanley, Edwin, 13, 14,
    133, 134, 157, 158,
    427
Hansell, Sven Hostrup,
    331, 371
Harris, Ellen T., 108,
    109
Hearder, Harry, 48
Hell, Helmut, 332
Helm, Everett, 263
Henry, Oscar Mervine,
    135
Heriot, Angus, 372
Hicks, Anthony, 422
Holmes, William C., 15,
    265, 266
Hucke, Helmuth, 196,
    197
Hughes, Elizabeth B.,
    246
Hughes-Hughes,
    Augustus, 441
Humber, Ingrid, 317

Inkeles, Maryann
    Teresa, 136

Jackson, Roland, 339
Jacobs, Arthur, 411
Jannaco, Carmine, 49
Jones, Gaynor G., 236
Junker, Hermann, 249
Jürgens, Jürgen, 172

Kaplan, A., 414
King, Alec Hyatt, 445,
    449
Kinsky, Georg, 137
Kirk, Elise K., 378
Kirkendale, Ursula, 110
Kirnberger, Johann
    Philipp, 20
Kirsch, Winfried, 199
Knapp, J. Merrill, 159
Koch, Heinz W., 415
Koch, Louis, 138
Krist, Esther, 160

Labroca, Mario, 28
Lake, Mary Beth, 138
Lanfranchi, Ariella,
    279
Lattes, Sergio, 450
La Via, Stefano, 333
Lazarevich, Gordana,
    200, 201
Lee, Patricia Ann
    Taylor, 318
Lee, Vernon, 50
Leich, Karl, 202
Leppert, Richard, 257
Lewinski, W.E. von, 416
Liess, Andreas, 280,
    281
Ligi, Bramante, 29
Limmert, Erich, 402,
    417, 418
Lincoln, Stoddard, 258
Lindgren Lowell, 111,
    203, 259

Lindley, Mark, 319
Lionnet, Jean, 204
Livingston, Herbert
  Stanton, 334
Llorens Cisteró,
  José M., 21
López-Calo, José, 22
Lorenz, Alfred, 205,
  206
Lowenberg, Alfred, 207
Luciani, Sebastiano A.,
  35

Mamczarz, Irene, 208
Mancini, Franco, 209,
  311
Marchesi, Gustavo, 373
Marino, Marina, 278
Marx, Hans Joachim, 93,
  94
Marx-Weber, Magda, 161
Masson, Renée M., 433
Mayo, John Stanford
  Miles, 112, 113
Mayrhofer, Marina, 139
McClymonds, Marita P.,
  374, 112, 451
McCredie, Andrew D.,
  397
Mendel, Arthur, 375
Mioli, Piero, 250
Mischiati, Oscar, 452
Mitchell, Donald, 386
Moberg, Carl-Allan, 95
Montalto, Lina, 96, 97,
  98
Montanelli, Indro, 51
Montesi Festa, Hilda,
  99
Morelli, Arnaldo, 282
Morey, Carl Reginald,
  210
Morris, Robert Bower,

  140, 141
Mortari, Virgilio, 271
Müller, Paul, 398
Muraro, Maria Teresa,
  175, 211
Murray, David Colden,
  142
Muscetta, Carlo, 89

Neumann, Frederick, 376
Nicolini, Fausto, 78,
  79
North, Nigel, 377

Owens, Samuel Battie,
  162

Pagano, Roberto, 16,
  17, 30
Paget, Violet, see Lee,
  Vernon
Paoli, Domenico de',
  312
Pasquetti, Guido, 283
Pastore, G. A., 143
Pauly, Reinhard G., 270
Pecman, Rudolf, 335
Perrúcci, Andréa, 80
Pestelli, Giorgio,
  219b, 320, 321, 322
Piersall, Paul Richard,
  144
Piperno, Franco, 213
Porter, Andrew, 393,
  399
Poultney, David George,
  284, 285
Povoledo, Elena, 313
Prota Giurleo, Ulisse,
  31, 32, 33, 214,
  434
Pruett, James, 341

Quazza, Guido, 52

Raguenet, Francois, 53, 54
Rangel-Ribeiro, Victor, 379
Roberts, John H., 238, 260
Robinson, Michael, 81, 215
Rolandi, Ugo, 35
Rolandi, Ulderico, 297
Ronga, Luigi, 18, 35
Rose, Gloria, 145, 237
Rostand, Claude, 407
Rostirolla, Giancarlo, 435
Ruile-Dronke, Jutta, 216
Russo, Rosario, 100
Rye, Charles Stanton, 163

Sadie, Stanley, 338, 408, 419, 420
Salazar, Adolfo, 34
Salvatorelli, Luigi, 55
Sapegno, Natalino, 44
Sartori, Claudio, 217, 234, 239, 255, 323, 438, 455, 455a
Savoca, Giuseppe, 89
Schering, Arnold, 286, 287
Schmitz, Eugen, 146
Schumann, Reinhold, 56
Seebass, Tilman, 23
Seelman-Eggebert, U., 388
Segal, L., 394
Selden, Margery Stomne, 300
Selfridge-Field,

Eleanor, 302
Shaffer, Jeanne
Ellison, 164
Shedlock, James S., 324
Simi Bonini, Eleonora, 165
Slavens, Thomas P., 341
Slim, H. Colin, 254
Smith, Peter, 166
Smither, Howard E., 288, 289
Solar Quintes, N. A., 36
Sonneck, Oscar G. T., 456
Springer, Hermann, 37
Staffieri, Gloria, 290
Stalnaker, William Park, Jr., 218
Steele, John, 167
Stevens, Denis, 390
Stowell, Robin, 336
Strohm, Reinhard, 114-117, 220, 221, 436, 437
Strongin, Theodore, 426
Strüver, Paul, 147
Swale, David, 303

Tagliavini, Luigi Ferdinando, 380
Talbot, Michael, 101, 337
Tellini, Enrico, 400
Terni, Clementi, 168
Testi, Flavio, 57
Tiby, Ottavio, 38
Timms, Colin, 101
Tosi, Pier Francesco, 381
Trowell, Brian, 251
Troy, Charles E., 222

Valesio, Francesco, 102
Valsecchi, Franco, 58,
    59
Van den Borren,
    Charles, 223
Vinquist, Mary, 342
Viviani, Vittorio, 82,
    83

Waley, Daniel Phillip,
    48
Walker, Diane Parr, 451
Walker, Frank, 39
Weaver, Norma Wright,
    226
Weaver, Robert Lamar,
    224, 225, 226
Webber, Nicholas, 421
Westrup, Jack Allan,
    256, 382
Wilier, Stephen A., 457
Wilkins, Ernest Hatch,
    60

Willets, Pamela, 442
Williams, Hermine
    Weigel, 169, 195,
    235
Winternitz, Emanuel, 24
Wirth, Helmut, 227
Witzenmann, Wolfgang,
    170
Wolff, Hellmuth
    Christian, 228, 229,
    230, 231, 291
Worsthorne, Simon
    Towneley, 232
Wright, Peter, 424
Wynne, Shirley, 383

Zanetti, Emilia, 118,
    119, 252, 438
Zanetti, Roberto, 61,
    148, 233, 292
Zazlaw, Neal, 342, 391
Ziino, Agostino, 77

INDEX OF NAMES

Abert, Anna Amalie,
227
Addison, Adele, 428
Adimari, Lodovico,
45
Adkins, Cecil, 126
Agricola, Johann F.,
375
Alaleona, Domenico,
281
Allegri, Gregorio,
161
Alvary, Lorenzo, 263
Amadei, Filippo, 333
Amico, Sandro d', 65
Amico, Silvio d', 65
Appoloni, Apollonio,
177, 234
Aprile, Giuseppe, 367
Archi, Antonio, 270
Arckenholz, J.99
Arles, Oreste d', 234
Arlt, Wulf, 145
Astorga, Emanuel d',
124
Austin, William W.,
256
Avitrano, G. A., 103

Bach, Johann Sebastien,
375
Bailey, Dee, 131
Balsano, Maria Antonella,
5
Barbapiccola, Nicola, 32
Barbapiccola, Giuseppina,
32
Becatelli, Giovanfrances-
co, 154
Beethoven, Ludwig van,
330
Bellis, Frank V. de, 296
Benati, Carlo Antonio,

365
Benthaak, Bernd, 389
Berberian, Ara, 428
Bergamo, da, 248
Bergin, Thomas G., 60
Bernini, Gian Lorenzo,
313
Bernstein, Martin, 351
Biancardi, Sebastiano
(Domenico Lalli),
78
Bianchi, Lino, 285,
300, 436
Bildt, Carlo de, 99
Bitter, Christof, 398
Blackwell, David, 325
Boccaccio, Giovanni,
248
Bogard, Carole, 395
Boghen, Felice, 150,
158
Bononcini, Giovanni
[Battista], 91,
230, 365, 366, 440
Bononcini, Marc, 198
Antonio, 220, 230
Bordoni, Fausta, 349,
351
Bovicelli, Giovanni
Battista, 367
Boyd, Malcolm, 175,
433
Bragaglia, Anton
Giulio, 80
Bremner, Anthony,
421, 424
Bressler, Charles,
385
Brook, Barry S., 201
Brook, Claire, 351
Broschi, Carlo (see
Farinelli)
Buckel, Ursula, 388

Bulifon, 78
Burney, Charles, 187,
    437
Burrows, David L., 368
Bush, Michael, 304
Busse, Wanda, 397

Caccini, Giulio, 367
Cagli, B., 203
Caldara, Antonio, 189,
    276
Capeci, Carlo Sigismondo,
    178, 198
Capelli, Giovanni Maria,
    440
Carissimi, Giacomo, 159,
    273
Carpio, del, Marquis,
    309
Cerda, Luigi Francesco
    de la (duke of Medina-
    celi), 70
Cesti, Pietro Antonio,
    177, 193
Chaucer, Geoffrey, 248
Clement XI, 21
Clinkscale, Edward H.,
    351
Colebrooke, Janet, 393
Confalonieri, Giulio, 263
Conforto, Giovanni Luca,
    367
Confuorto, Domenico, 78
Corelli, Arcangelo, 86,
    87, 90, 91, 94, 96,
    116, 118, 321, 324,
    330, 336, 366
Cossotto, Fiorenza, 263
Covell, Roger, 389
Crescimbeni, Giovanni M.,
    50, 92
Croce, Benedetto, 78
Crowther, Victor, 277

Curiel, Glauco, 403
Curtis, Allen, 374

D'Accone, Frank, 394
Dali, Salvador, 263
Damerini, Adelmo, 155
David, D., 177
Davison, Archibald
    Thompson, 343
Dean, Winton, 277,
    371, 382
Debussy, Claude, 292
DeGaetani, Jan, 426
Degrada, Francesco,
    302
De Los Angeles,
    Victoria, 405
Dent, Edward J., 34,
    39, 109, 122, 125,
    131, 134, 136, 147,
    182, 312, 433
Doni, Giovanni
    Battista, 375
Donington, Robert,
    136, 376
Dorati, Antal, 263
Doria-Pamphili family,
    93, 98
Dotti, Bartolomeo, 45
Dunn, Geoffrey, 419,
    420
Durante, Francesco,
    166, 365, 366, 367
Dziebowska, Elzbieta,
    243

Eitner, Robert, 281,
    312, 393, 457
Elder, Mark, 419
Esswood, Paul, 400,
    412

Fabbri, Mario, 297

Fanna, Antonio, 250
Farinelli (Carlo
    Broschi), 349, 369
Fellerer, Karl Gustav,
    164
Fétis, Francois Joseph
    9, 22, 34
Fienga, Pasquale, 34
Fitton, Mary, 85
Florimo, Francesco, 9
Fortune, Nigel, 166,
    230
Fox, Charles Warren,
    269
Frenaye, Frances, 71
Freni, Mirella, 400
Frescobaldi, Girolamo,
    162
Freund, Cecilia
    Kathryn Van de Kamp
    122
Friend, Lionel, 410
Frigimelica-Roberti
    Girolamo, 202
Fux, Johann Joseph,
    152

Galliard, John Ernest,
    53, 54, 258, 381
Galloway, Brian, 393
Gasparini, Francesco,
    106, 111, 116,
    119, 189, 195, 302,
    356, 371, 380
Geiringer, Karl, 229
Gerber, Rudolf, 197
Gerlin, R., 318, 322,
    323
Gigli, G., 45
Gluck, Christoph
    Willibald von, 227
Goldoni, Carlo, 250
Gottlieb, Peter, 403

Graglia, Giuseppe, 102
Graue, Jerald C., 269
Greig, Patricia, 422
Gress, Theodore, 397
Grimaldi, Nicola, 269,
    270
Grout, Donald J., 192,
    256, 391, 394, 399,
    430

Hager, Paul, 405
Handel, George F., 93,
    104, 108, 109, 110,
    112, 113, 114, 115,
    116, 118, 124, 153,
    159, 167, 175, 178,
    179, 181, 213, 260,
    274, 300, 324, 333,
    355, 360
Hanley, Edwin, 122,
    130, 131, 147, 163,
    328, 437
Harris, Ellen T., 109
Hasse, Johann Adolph,
    43, 114, 117, 197,
    349, 355, 440
Haydn, Joseph, 227,
    335
Haym, Nicola, 258, 259,
    333
Heinichen, Johann
    David, 352, 356,
    366
Henney, Jeanne, 392
Hickok, Robert, 385
Higgs, C. M., 314,
    318, 324
Hansell, Sven, 94, 356
Hanson, Geoffrey, 422
Harman, Alec, 251
Haro, Gaspar de
    (marchese del
    Carpio), 70

Hjelmborg, Bjorn, 382
Hortschansky, Klaus,
    227
Hughes, H. Stuart, 71
Husa, Karel, 391
Hutchings, Arthur, 337

Jans, Hans Jörg, 387,
    400
Jenkins, Newell, 425,
    426, 428
Jennens, Charles, 300
Jeppesen, Knud, 382
Jomelli, Nicola, 43
Juvarra, Filippo, 189,
    190, 212

Kehm, Heinrich, 415
King Louis XIV of
    France, 86
Kirnberger, Johann
    Philipp, 22
Knapp, J. Merrill, 109
Koch, Louis, 137
Kolneder, Walter, 202
Kondek, Charles, 414

Lalande, Roger, 407
Lalli, Domenico (see
    Biancardi, Sebas-
    tiano)
Landon, H.C. Robbins,
    229
Larsen, Jens Peter,
    335
LaRue, Jan, 187, 197
Legrenzi, Giovanni,
    200, 217
Leo, Giacomo, 26
Leo, Leonardo, 26,
    146, 197
Leopold and Empress
    Eleonora of Austria,

1
Lewis, Anthony, 166,
    230
Lissa, Zofia, 243
Livy, Titus, 235
Lonz, Bernhard, 398
Lorenz, Alfred, 244

Maag, Peter, 388
Mackworth, Herbert Sir,
    440
Maffei, Francesco
    Scipione, 367
Mainwaring, John, 320
Mancini, Giambattista
    [Giovanni Battista],
    367
Manfredini, G. B.,367
Manzella, Salvatore,
    211
Marcello, Benedetto,
    179, 302
Marini, Giovanni
    Battista, 47
Martens, Mason, 385
Martuscelli, Domenico,
    11
Marx, Hans Joachim,
    236
Marx-Weber, Magda, 236
Medici, Ferdinando de',
    2, 19, 63, 64, 155,
    203, 226
Melani, Jacopo, 107
Mercer, Frank, 42
Metastasio, Pietro,
    177
Miall, Bernard, 55
Moe, Lawrence, 395
Monges, Richard, 47
Montalto, Lina, 86
Monteverdi, Claudio,
    230, 332, 402

Morelli, Arnaldo, 300
Morelli, Giovanni, 250
Morosini, Alvise, 19
Mortari, Virgilio, 413
Mozart, Wolfgang
    Amadeus, 227, 334
Muraro, Maria Teresa,
    183, 189, 191
Muscetta, Carlo, 89

Nagel, Robert, 428
Neumann, Frederick,
    364
Newman, William S.,
    289
Nicolini, N., 69

Oberlin, Russell, 428
Oesch, Hans, 412
Operti, Giovanni
    Battista, 307
Ortolani, Giuseppe,
    297
Ottoboni, Antonio, 101,
    189, 244, 296, 301,
    303
Ottoboni, Pietro, 23,
    91, 94, 189, 212,
    244, 264, 265, 266,
    282, 287, 300, 301,
    331

Pagano, Roberto, 275,
    300, 436
Paglia, Abate, 209
Paglia, Francesco
    Maria, 237
Palestrina, Giovanni
    Pierluigi, 152, 170
Pallavicino, Carlo,
    276
Pamphili, Benedetto,
    86, 93, 97, 98, 282,
    300, 301, 302, 303

Pariati, Pietro, 236
Parker, Ian, 346
Pasquini, Bernardo, 87,
    91, 105, 107, 152,
    193, 324
Pears, Peter, 129
Pergolesi, Giovanni
    Battista, 150, 156,
    169
Perrucci, Andrea, 83
Perti, Giacomo Antonio,
    64, 91, 153
Petrarch, Francesco,
    248
Petzold, Friedrich,
    397
Piccioli, Giuseppe,
    255, 256, 403, 405
Pitoni, Giuseppe
    Ottavio, 91
Poch, Wolfgang, 415
Pollarolo, Carlo
    Francesco, 114, 177
Pope Innocent XII, 84
Porpora, Niccolo, 166,
    177, 355
Pountney, David, 419
Prota-Giurleo, Ulisse,
    25
Provenzale, Francesco,
    68, 72, 132
Pruett, James W., 225,
    342

Quantz, Johann J., 43,
    328
Queen Christina (of
    Sweden), 87, 89, 95,
    99, 100, 105
Queen (of Spain)
    Donn'Anna, 67

Raguenet, Francois,
    258

Ricci, Marco, 257
Riemann, Hugo, 197
Rolandi, Ugo, 35
Rolli, Paolo Antonio,
    117
Ronga, Luigi, 154, 172
Rose, Gloria, 273, 362
Rossini, Giochino, 150
Rostirolla, Giancarlo,
    131, 149, 236, 285,
    336, 430, 436, 454
Ruspoli, Prince
    Francesco Maria, 284

Sadie, Stanley, 41,
    133, 310, 350
Sandberger, Adolf, 249
Santini, Fortunato, 23,
    147, 446, 450
Sarno, Jania, 77
Sartori, Claudio, 13,
    35, 322
Scano, Gaetana, 102
Scarlatti [unidenti-
    fied], 444
Scarlatti, Abate, 102
Scarlatti, Anna Maria,
    32, 33, 39
Scarlatti, Domenico,
    19, 30, 34, 35, 36,
    39, 42, 45,102, 110,
    115, 147, 153, 161,
    165, 175, 178, 185,
    217, 320, 321, 324,
    339, 364, 368, 380,
    444, 445, 456
Scarlatti, Eduardo, 36
Scarlatti, Flaminia, 4
Scarlatti, Francesco,
    32, 35, 39, 217
Scarlatti, Giuseppe,
    27, 32, 35, 37, 226,

    444, 456
Scarlatti, Melchiorra,
    32
Scarlatti, Pietro, 9,
    38, 39, 279
Scarlatti, Pietro
    Filippo, 26, 29,
    35, 153
Scarlatti, Tommaso, 32,
    217
Schering, Arnold, 216,
    352
Schmitz, Eugen, 125,
    146, 148
Scholes, Percy A., 43
Schrade, Leo, 145
Shedlock, John, 318,
    437
Siegmund-Schultze,
    Walther, 113
Smither, Howard E.,
    277, 285
Söderstrom, Elisabeth,
    401
Solimena, Francesco, 4,
    11
Sorensen, Soren, 382
Spagna, Arcangelo, 274,
    287
Speroni, Charles, 394
Sportonio, Marc
    'Antonio, 73
Stampiglia, Silvio,
    235
Steele, John, 159
Steffani, Agostino,
    104, 276
Steffin, F., 157
Stevens, Denis, 344
Stillings, Frank S.,
    368

Stradella, Alessandro,
91, 107, 193, 273,
333
Stravinsky, Igor, 137
Strohm, Reinhard, 318,
454
Strunk, Oliver, 53
Strüver, Paul, 131

Tangeman, Nell, 129
Tarr, Edward, 388
Tessin, Nicodemus, 175
Thibault, Geneviève,
237
Tiepolo, Giovanni
Battista, 345
Todis, Giuseppe de,
294
Torri, Pietro, 249
Tosi, Pier Francesco,
258, 355, 356, 367,
375, 381
Trillat, Ennemond, 428
Tullio, Francesco
Antonio, 78

Uffenbach, Johann
Friedrich Armand

von, 284

Valls, Franz, 22
Veneziano, Gaetano, 72
Verdi, Giuseppe, 407
Vignati, Giuseppe, 351
Vinci, Leonardo, 146,
197, 221
Vinchioni, Curzio, 153
Vivaldi, Antonio, 179,
198, 203, 216, 250,
302, 345, 349, 356,
357, 358, 374, 378,
383

Walker, Frank, 214
Weaver, Norma, 65
Weaver, Robert, 65
Westrup, Sir Jack, 247
Williams, Hermine W.,
414, 430
Wolf, Ilse, 129

Zacconi, Lodovico, 367
Zanetti, Roberto, 300
Zelter, Paul, 412
Zeno, Apostolo, 192,
230, 248, 249, 250

INDEX OF COMPOSITIONS

Agar et Ismael esilia-
ti, 276, 293, 294
Ah che purtroppo è
vero, 113
Ahi, che sarà di me,
121
Al furor che ti con-
siglia, 430
L'Aldimiro, 191
Ammore, brutto figlio,
148
Amor non vuol inganni.
See Gli equivoci nel
sembinate.
Andate o miei sospiri,
106, 135
Arias, 179, 181, 216,
217, 221, 325, 351,
438
L'Arione, arias, 234
Arminio, 430, 437
L'Arsate, arias, 91
L'assunzione della Be-
ata Vergine Maria,
282

La caduta de' Decem-
veri, 194, 205,
235, 334
Cain, overo Il primo
omicidio, 101, 276,
295-297, 421, 430
Il Cambise, 194
Cantatas, 3, 6, 7, 14,
18, 35, 42, 53, 101,
108, 109, 112, 120,
122-131, 133-136,
139, 141, 143-148,
365, 435-437, 440
"Cerca, cerca nel cor,"
24
Ch'io scoprì il mio

affetto, 139
Il Ciro, 176, 189,
190, 212, 213, 236,
334
Clearco in Negroponte,
186
La Clotolda, arias,
54, 106, 258
Comodo Antonio, 237
Concerti sacri (op.
2), 163
Contentati mio core,
440

Da sventura a sven-
tura, 139
Il Dafni, 238, 239
Dal mio brando al chi-
are lampo, 430
La dama spagnola ed il
cavaliere romano.
See Varrone e
Perricca.
Davidis pugna et vic-
toria, 276, 298,
422-424
Di cipresso funesto,
139
Di dolore in dolor, 430
Diana ed Endimione,
312
La Dirinda, 45
Dixit Dominus (NGIBM
[iv]), 159, 167
[Dodici] 12 sinfoni di
concerto grosso,
337, 449
La Dori, 234

Eliotrope d'amore, 148
L'Emireno, 191

Gli equivoci nel amore,
    258 (arias), 392,
    393
Gli equivoci nel sem-
    biante, 1, 4, 132,
    194, 204-206, 216,
    240, 241, 394
Era un giorno Fileno,
    430
L'Eraclea, 230, 242,
    243, 334, 389, 390,
    391
Erminia, Tancredi,
    Polidoro e Pasto-
    re, 306

Fate, O Cieli, 430
La fede riconosciuta,
    244, 245
Fidalba e Oreste,
    arias, 237, 430
Filli adorata e cara,
    113
Flute music, 326
Fra tante pene, 113

Il Germanico or Già
    di trionfi onusto,
    139
Gerone tiranno di
    Siracusa, arias,
    252, 307
Il giardino d'amore,
    327
La Giuditta [i], 23,
    282, 299, 300, 302,
    425, 426, 430
La Giuditta [ii],
    301-303
La Giuditta, 206
Giunio Bruto, Act 3,
    189
Il Giustino, [pro-
    logue], 200

Il gran Tamerlano, 64
La Griselda, 24, 117,
    194, 203, 220, 246-
    251, 334, 351, 395-
    400, 449
La guerriera costan-
    te, arias, 430

L'honestà negli amori,
    401, 402
(H)or che spunta nel
    prato, 430
Humanità e Lucifero,
    279

Gli inganni felici, 252
Instrumental music, 3,6
Intermezzos, 208, 222
Io morirei contento,
    148

Johannespassion, 291,
    292, 427

Keyboard music, 6, 314,
    320, 321, 323, 437

Laodice e Berenice, 348
Lascia deh lascia al
    fino di tormentarmi
    più, 352
Lisa del foco mio, 121
[Il Lismaco], 430
Lontananza crudele, deh
    perché, 127
Lontanza e gelosia,
    430
Luci vaghe, se mirate,
    430
Lungi dal Tebro in ri-
    va, 430

La Maddalena pentita,
    206

Madrigali spirituali
  (1690), 75
Madrigals, 171, 172,
  226, 436
Marco Attilio Regno,
  194, 253, 334
Il martirio di Sant'Or-
  sola, 428, 430, 437
Masses, 149, 157, 166,
  435, 436
Massimo Puppieno, 254
Mentre Eurillo fedele
  or Su le rive del
  Tebro, 139
Messe e Credo a 4 ad
  Canones (Missa ad
  canonem in G), 152
Messa Clementina, 21
Messa di Santa Cecilia,
  157, 160, 384-386
Messa per il natale di
  Nostro Signore Gesù
  Cristo, 165
Miserere mei Deus,
  secundum (1680),
  161, 162
Miserere mei Deus,
  secundum (in E
  minor), 162
Miserere mei Deus,
  secundum (in C
  minor), 162
Miserere mei Deus,
  secundum (in A
  minor), 162
Il Mitridate Eupatore,
  45, 175, 181, 194,
  202, 220, 255, 256,
  334, 403-408
Motets, 151, 162-164,
  436

Narciso, 35
Ne' tuoi lumi, 113
Nel dolce tempo, 113
Nel silentio comune,
  138

Nella febbre d'amor,
  430
Non ha un giorno di
  contento, 430

Odoacre, arias, 189
Odoardo, 186
Ombre tacite e sole,
  449
Operas, 3, 6, 7, 35,
  61, 78, 105, 107,
  108, 126, 179, 184,
  195, 205, 206, 210,
  221, 226-228, 230,
  233, 434, 436, 438,
  449, 456
Oratorio per la Passi-
  one di Nostro
  Signore Gesù Cristo,
  277
Oratorios, 35, 61, 101,
  105, 273-275, 278,
  285, 289, 291, 292,
  434, 436
Organ music, 315
Overtures, 329, 334

Parti l'idolo mio, 430
Il pastor di Corinto,
  230
Un pensier dice alla
  mente, 430
Pensieri, oh Dio, 148
Per dare pace al vostro
  core, 430
Per il tempo di peni-
  tenza e di tenebre,
  19, 155
Il Pirro e Demetrio,
  53, 54, 189, 194,
  257-259
Il Pompeo, 194, 260
Il prigioniero fortuna-
  to, 334
La principessa fedele,
  194, 261
Properate fideles, 163

Qualor l'egre pupille,
113
Quando il fato un cor
bersaglia, 430
Quante le grazie son,
24, 137
Quattro sonate a quat-
tro, 312, 330, 335

Recorder music, 326
Responsori per la Set-
timana Santa, 154,
168
Restava al mesto Amin-
ta, 430
Rorate coeli dulcem,
163
La Rosaura. See Gli
equivoci nel amore.
La Rosmene o vero l'In-
fedeltà fedele, 73

Sacred music, 3, 149,
170
Salve Regina (c1720),
114
Salve Regina in G mi-
nor, 103
San Casimiro, 206
San Filippo Neri, 304
Scipione nelle Spagne,
262
Il Sedecia, 206
S'en parte sdegnato,
430
Serenatas, 78, 148,
305, 308, 434, 436
Sette sonate per flauto
e archi, 326, 328
Siete belle ancor
piangenti, 430
Sinfonias, 201, 325,
337
[Six] VI Concertos in
VII Parts, 330

"Solo il dolore," 127
Son contento, non
m'amate, 430
Sonata in F for flute,
2 violins and basso
continuo, 326
[Sonata in D for flute,
2 violins and basso
continuo], 326
Sonata in A for 2
flutes, 2 violins
and basso continuo,
326
Sonata in F for 3
flutes and basso
continuo, 326
Sonatas, keyboard, 317
[Sonate per organo] (MS
MM60 Reservados,
Coimbra, Portugal),
315
Sopra le verdi sponde
che la Brenta super-
ba, 139
The Spanish Lady and
the Roman Cavalier.
See Varrone e Per-
ricca.
Speranze mie (1694),
148
Stabat Mater, 150, 156,
158, 166, 169, 430
La Statira, 264-266,
409-411, 440
Su la sponda del mare,
23
Sul margine d'un rio
cui facean, 430

Telemaco, 198, 199, 267
Teodora Augusta, 252,
307
Thomyris Queen of
Scythia, arias, 54,
106

[Three Sonatas for Two
    Cellos], 336
Il Tigrane, 194, 268-
    270, 387, 400, 412
Tito Sempronio Gracco,
    186
Toccatas, 314, 316-320,
    322, 324, 437
Tra speranza e timore,
    142
Il trionfo della
    gratia, 284
Il trionfo della liber-
    tà, 175, 202
Il trionfo delle
    stagioni, 209

Il trionfo dell'onore,
    35, 184, 194, 196,
    199, 221, 271, 334,
    413, 414-420
Turno Aricino, arias,
    221

Varrone e Perricca, in-
    termezzo, 262, 263
Venere, Adone et Amore,
    307
Vespro di Santa Ce-
    cilia, 387, 388
[Una villa de Tuscolo],
    204

Book II
Domenico Scarlatti

BOOK II

CONTENTS

Preface   vii

Introduction   ix

I.   Life and Works   3

    1.   Biographies, Comprehensive
        Studies, Essay Collections   3

    2.   Anniversary Publications;
        Foundation Information   14

    3.   Cultural Milieu   19

    4.   Relationship of Scarlatti to
        Other Composers and to Spanish
        Folk Music   24

II. Studies of the Music   35

    1.   Vocal Music   35

        Choral Works   35
        Operatic Works, Serenatas
        Cantatas   39

    2.   Keyboard Sonatas and Solo/
        Continuo Pieces   47

III. Performance Background   65

    1.   Performance Practice   65

        Teaching and Interpretation   65
        Instruments   70

2. Editions   77

3. Modern Performances   81

        Performance Reviews   83
        Festival Performances   83
        Choral Music   84
        Opera   84
        Sonatas for Keyboard
          (or Violin and Continuo)   85

IV. Sources   87

V. Modern Editions or Facsimiles   97

        Selected Bibliography of Worklists
        and Catalogs   98

        Domenico Scarlatti Worklist   101

        1. Vocal Music   101

                Chamber Cantatas   101
                Operas; Sinfonias   101
                Sacred Music   103
                Serenatas   106
                Vocal Collections   107

        2. Instrumental Music   107

                Keyboard Works   107
                    Sonatas for Organ   111
                "Melo-Bass" or "Violin
                    Sonatas"   111

VI. Discography   113

        Chamber Cantatas   113
        Keyboard Works   115
        Operas   118
        Sacred Works   119
        Serenatas   121
        Sinfonias   121

Contents

Index of Authors   123

Index of Names   127

Index of Compositions   131

PREFACE

Like Book I, this guide cites the principal literature on the composer--here, Domenico Scarlatti--including books, articles, and dissertations. A special effort has been made to include the most recent publications, a number of which appeared in conjunction with conferences held during 1985, the year of the 300th anniversary of Domenico's birth. Earlier studies of importance are also included. The author examined all but a few of the items cited; those not seen are so indicated and references to published abstracts are identified when it was possible to locate them.

Instead of providing yet another worklist here, references to selected published worklists are given; these have been chosen either because they were the most up to date, accurate, informative, historically important, or a combination of these factors. As was true of Book I, in place of a worklist, the author has tried to provide a list of Scarlatti's works available in modern edition or facsimile (among them the previously neglected vocal works); a list of recordings which includes a number of important new releases or reissues has also been prepared.

INTRODUCTION

The known biography of Domenico Scarlatti, the sixth child of Alessandro Scarlatti (see Book I) and Antonia Anzalone, is like a picture in which only the barest outlines have been drawn and to which over several centuries only a handful of fine details have been added, these, the small rewards of years of archival research by committed scholars. It is a biography in which hearsay has often filled the void left by a paucity of surviving historical documentation. What other major composer can one recall for whom only one known musical autograph (the parts of a *Miserere* in g minor from among his early Italian choral compositions) and one autograph letter survive? (For English translations of this letter to the Duke of Alba see item 3, pp. 143-144 and item 13, p. 121 [American ed. 1983]). If other letters existed, as seems likely, the number would probably still not have matched those by his now famous contemporaries, J.S. Bach and G. F. Handel. The major encyclopedia accounts of Scarlatti's life and works all differ from one another in certain details. Even the most recent (item 27), reduced to include only data considered verifiable, may err in locating Domenico in Portugal by September 1720 (see item 22).

Ralph Kirkpatrick's monumental biography and study of Domenico's works--with its subsequent revisions (item 13)--remained unchallenged for almost two decades except by a few scholars, e.g., Gerstenberg (item 132) as the foremost contribution to Scarlatti scholarship. Joel Sheveloff has more recently pointed out that the lack of other comprehensive studies coupled with Kirkpatrick's ability to write convincingly even in the absence of concrete evidence led

many scholars to overlook the flaws in that
book (see items 162 & 44). Sheveloff's
dissertation (item 162) and an earlier one by
Pestelli (item 157) which criticized
Kirkpatrick's work extensively for the first
time so provoked the elder scholar that he
wrote an ironic article which attempted to
belittle their complaints (item 236).
Certainly Kirkpatrick's classic work is a *tour
de force*; however, it must now be read in the
light of the new criticisms, its statements
weighed against those made by a new generation
of scholars dedicated to presenting the life
and works in a factually more accurate if
sparer way.

Sheveloff, of course, is in the forefront
of the new scholarship, having propelled
research on the composer into new territory
with the above-mentioned thesis. His two-part
article in the *Musical Quarterly* (item 44) is one
of the best to appear during the anniversary
year (1985). It can be regarded as a
blueprint for the directions research on
Domenico might take in the following decades.
Other scholars who have contributed
significantly to our knowledge of the composer
include Roberto Pagano, whose investigations
have led to a better understanding of
Scarlatti's milieu and revealed pertinent new
biographical details (see items 22, 23, and
Book I, item 34); Francesco Degrada, who has
illuminated a wholly new aspect of the
composer's output which has important
implications for our understanding of the
keyboard works, through his discovery,
edition, and performance of the comic opera *La
Dirinda* (see items 110, 216 and Section V, 1);
and Malcolm Boyd, whose recent book on the
composer and his works (item 3) provides a new
appraisal of the previously neglected and
underrated vocal works and cogently summarizes
the achievements of the most recent Scarlatti
researches. The work of a number of other
fine Scarlatti researchers was revealed in
important papers given at several conferences
which commemorated the 300th anniversary of

the composer's birth (see Section I, 2 for
published proceedings). Sheveloff (item 44)
and Boyd (items 3 & 30) give excellent
summaries of some of these presentations .

Domenico Scarlatti

I

LIFE AND WORKS OF DOMENICO SCARLATTI

1. Biographies, Comprehensive Studies, Essay Collections

1. Basso, Alberto. "Domenico Scarlatti." In *La Musica; enciclopedia storica* Turin: UTET, 1966. Vol. 4 (1966), pp. 159-177; pp. 168-176, catalog of works; pp. 176-177, editions and bibl. Facs., port.

    A scholarly discussion of the life, vocal works and keyboard compositions. Includes a clearly laid out and carefully prepared catalog of works; however, if used, one must also consult the more recent and correct Sheveloff worklist in item 27.

2. Bauer, Luise. "Die Tätigkeit Domenico Scarlattis und der italienischen Meister in der ersten Hälfte des 18. Jahrhunderts in Spanien." Ph.D. dissertation, Univ. of Munich, 1933.

    An early thesis of major importance which quotes from documents now lost or destroyed including information on Scarlatti's domicile from c1750 on. Author proved for the first time that Scarlatti died in Madrid, not in Naples as many authors had previously claimed. References in Kirkpatrick (item 13, American edition, 1983, pp. 343-344 and pp. 134-135). Not seen.

3. Boyd, Malcolm. *Domenico Scarlatti--Master of Music*. N.Y.: Schirmer Books (Macmillan, Inc.), 1986. xi and 302 pp. 4 apps., bibl., notes, index. ISBN 0-02-870291-3.

The most important book on the composer in
English since Kirkpatrick's (item 13). Draws
upon and summarizes the major Scarlatti
research including the most recent (e.g.,
unpublished conference papers) and examines
the previously unknown or neglected vocal
works in some detail and from a fresh
perspective. Appendix IV is a "List of
Compositions" (see item 243); pp. 253-275
provide the most up to date, accurate, and
inclusive catalog of the composer's works to
date. Appendix I discusses some of the major
Scarlatti arrangements (by other composers);
Appendix II gives Scarlatti's will in Eng.
transl.; and Appendix III prints two hitherto
unpublished sonatas attributed to Scarlatti.

4.   Boydell, Brian. "Domenico Scarlatti and his
       Irish Connection." In *European Music Yearbook*
       (1985). Dublin, 1985.

       Not seen.

5.   Burney, Charles. *A General History of Music*.
       (London, 1776-89). Ed. by F. Mercer. N.Y.:
       Dover, 1957. Reprint of London ed., 1935. 2
       vols. Vol. 2 contains apps. and index to
       names in Vols. 1 and 2. Vol. 2: 1098 pp.

       Vol. 2 is a major early source of
       information on Domenico. The now famous
       story about his encounter with Thomas
       Roseingrave at the keyboard is contained in it
       as are Burney's comments on such things as his
       opera *Narciso* as performed in London, the aria
       "Sparge al mare" from the pasticcio *Alessandro in
       Persia*, and the English Scarlatti cult.

6.   _____. *Memoirs of the Life and Writings of the Abate
       Metastasio...* (1st ed.: London, 1796) Reprint:
       N.Y.: Da Capo, 1971. 3 vols. xlviii and
       407 pp.; xxxii and 420 pp.; xxvi and 414 pp.
       ISBN-306-71110-9.

Contains Burney's commentary on and translations of the correspondence of Metastasio including numerous letters from the librettist to Farinelli. Provides a glimpse of the theatrical activities, cultural milieu, and political goings-on at the Spanish court during the Scarlatti years and Metastasio's close relationship with Farinelli. Vol. 2, pp. 205-206 contains a note by Burney regarding Domenico.

7.   _____. *Present State of Music in France and Italy*.
Reprinted as Vol. 1 of *Dr. Burney's Musical Tours in Europe* with title *An Eighteenth-Century Musical Tour in France and Italy*. Ed. by Percy A. Scholes. London: Oxford University Press, 1959. (Original ed.: London, 1771; 2nd ed., 1773).

Vol. 1 contains allusions to the composer in relation to Farinelli, Vol. 2, Hasse's and Quantz's comments on Domenico's harpsichord playing and Burney's discussion of his visit with L'Augier who told him of Scarlatti's views on composition.

8.   Degrada, Francesco. "Domenico Scarlatti." In *Enciclopedia della Musica*, vol.4, pp. 137-140. Ed. by Claudio Sartori. Milan: G. Ricordi, 1964. Worklist and bibl.

One of the most detailed encyclopedia articles on the composer's life and works published a year before Degrada learned of the existence of a MS of the score to Domenico's *La Dirindina*. Includes references to Scarlatti's contemporaries who may have influenced his early compositions. Generally author's statements cautious and linked to identified sources; however, repeats Mainwaring's account of the keyboard competition between Handel and Scarlatti without documentation. Supports the idea that Scarlatti may have returned to Portugal from Rome some years after the death of his father. Critical of attempts to credit Domenico with the advent of the classical sonata form.

9.   Dent, Edward J., and Frank Walker.
      "(Giuseppe) Domenico Scarlatti." In *Grove's
      Dictionary of Music and Musicians*, 5th ed., vol. 7,
      pp. 456-460. Ed. by Eric Blom. London:
      Macmillan, 1954. Worklist, pp. 458-460;
      bibl., p. 458.

      An intelligent and detailed account of
      Domenico's life. Accepted the idea that
      Gasparini was the composer's teacher in Venice
      and that Handel accompanied Scarlatti to Rome
      [in 1709]. While skeptical of certain early
      stories regarding Domenico's life, Dent cites
      information from Mainwaring, Sacchi, and
      Burney without criticizing their historical
      accuracy.

*   Dixon, Graham. "Handel's Music for the Feast
      of Our Lady of Mount Carmel." Cited as
      item 153 in Book I.

*   *Domenico Scarlatti: 13 [treize] récherches.* Cited as item
      37.

*   Fabbri, Mario. *Alessandro Scarlatti e il Principe
      Ferdinando de' Medici.* Cited as item 19 in Book
      I.

      Contains transcriptions of the
      correspondence of Alessandro, the Prince, and
      Alvise Morosini (Venice), respectively. Pages
      58-61 include references to Domenico.

*   Fienga, Pasquale. "La veritable patrie...."
      Cited as item 9 in Book I.

10.   Flood, W. H. Grattan. "Domenico Scarlatti's
      Visit to Dublin, 1740-1..." *Musical Antiquary* 1
      (Apr. 1910): 178-181.

Author suggests that Domenico may have gone to Dublin in October, 1740 at the suggestion of Roseingrave's brother to try to alleviate his financial problems and to London in 1741. Based on advertisements for two benefit concerts for a "Signor Scarlatti" in *Faulkner's Journal* of Feb. 1740. This view generally discredited (e.g., see item 19).

*   *Gli Scarlatti*. Cited as item 35 in Book I.

11. Ife, E. W. (Barry). *Domenico Scarlatti*. Sevenoaks: Novello, 1985. 23 pp. List of principal works; bibl. ISBN 0-85360-123-2.

A concise, well-written account of the composer's life and works intended to provide a general background to students and concertgoers. Lacking notes, though it contains an abbreviated worklist and very brief bibliography. Doesn't include information from the most recent scholarly investigations.

12. Karpáti, János. *Domenico Scarlatti*. Budapest: Gondolat, 1959. 210 pp. illus. (Kis zenei könyvtár, 10).

Not seen.

*   Keller, Hermann. *Domenico Scarlatti, ein Meister des Klaviers*. Cited as item 140.

*   Kenyon de Pascual, Beryl. See Pascual, Beryl Kenyon de.

13. Kirkpatrick, Ralph. *Domenico Scarlatti*. Princeton: Princeton University Press, 1953. 486 pp. ISBN-0-691-091013.   3rd rev. ed., Princeton: Princeton University Press, 1983. xviii and 491 pp. ISBN 0691 027080. Italian ed.:   Turin: Edizioni RAI Radiotelevisione

Italiana (ERI), 1984. 494 pp.; Ger. ed. in
2 vols. Munich: Ellermann, 1972. Sp. ed:
Madrid: Alianza, 1986. 470 pp. Fr. ed:
Paris: Lattès, 1982. 494 pp.

Kirkpatrick's book with its many revisions
is still the principal study of Domenico's
life and works although a number of his
assumptions have been challenged by several
Italian scholars and especially by Joel
Sheveloff (see items 44 and 161). Boyd's book
(item 3) is now essential in order to
understand the contributions of more recent
scholars and to put past writings and research
into perspective. European editions seen
(German and Italian) include a thematic index
of the keyboard sonatas which is lacking in
the American editions. All editions include
Kirkpatrick's catalog of Scarlatti's works,
musical examples, illustrations, portraits,
documents (e.g., his will), etc.

14.   _____. " Scarlatti, Domenico." In *Die
      Musik und Geschichte in Gegenwart*, Bd. 11, cols.
      1506-1518. Ed. by F. Blume. Kassel:
      Bärenreiter Verlag, 1963. Mus. facs.;
      worklist (col. 1510-1514); eds. (col. 1517);
      and bibl. (col. 1518).

A scholarly summary of Domenico's life and a
discussion of his compositions. The latter
reflects the author's views expressed in
greater detail in his book (item 13), e.g.,
regarding the chronology and pairing of
sonatas.

15.   Lippmann, Friedrich. "Gaetano Greco un
      maestro di Domenico Scarlatti." Cited in
      item 33.

16.   Longo, Alessandro. *Domenico Scarlatti e la sua figura
      nella storia della musica*. Naples: Bideri, 1913.

The pioneering monograph by this Italian

scholar whose "complete works" of the composer were for decades the only published source of most of Scarlatti's sonatas. See Section V, 2 for notes on the edition.

17. _____. "Domenico Scarlatti." *L'arte pianistica* 1/8 (Apr. 15, 1914): 1-3.

Discussion of Scarlatti's keyboard works in relation to those of J.S. Bach, Clementi, the French school, etc. Author gives his perceptions of Scarlatti's unique contributions to the sonata and to keyboard technique. The biographical details cannot, of course, be relied upon at this early date. Longo's emphasis on the significance of Scarlatti's reiteration of the tonic tonality at the conclusion of his sonatas as a new feature which led to the tonal pattern of the pre-classic sonata was perhaps, the source of later writers' misstatements that D. Scarlatti initiated the classical sonata (1st movement) form.

18. Luciani, Sebastiano Arturo. *Domenico Scarlatti*. Turin: Arione, 1939. 32 pp.

A short sketch. Included are 24 illustrative plates relating to the composer's life including an autograph letter from Scarlatti to the Duke of Alba and the frontispiece to "Festeggio armonico musicato" by the composer written for the marriage of Ferdinand of Spain and Maria of Portugal (1728).

19. _____. "Postilla Scarlattiana." *Rassegna Musicale* 44 (1940): 200-203.

Intended to complement the author's biographical and bibliographical notes published in this journal Dec. 1938 and Jan. and Feb. 1939. Disputes Flood's hypothesis (see item 10) that Scarlatti was in London; suggests that the "Signor Scarlatti" he took to be Alessandro was   probably Francesco.

20. Mainwaring, John. *Memoirs of the Life of the Late George Frederic Handel*. (London, 1760). Reprint: Buren: Frits Knuf, 1975. 208 pp.

Source of one of the few surviving stories about Domenico often used to flesh out his biography. The familiar account of his keyboard competition with Handel appears on pp. 59-62 of this facsimile reprint.

21. Malipiero, G. Francesco. "Domenico Scarlatti." *Musical Quarterly* 13 (1947): 476-488.

Malipiero's article reflects some of the approaches and attitudes of his time and place; he sees connections between Scarlatti's sonatas and those of Clementi and Beethoven, views Longo's edition as a faithful reproduction of the original, and emphasizes Domenico's Italian heritage.

22. Pagano, Roberto. "Alessandro et Domenico Scarlatti. Biographie assortie de quelques considérations musicales." In *Domenico Scarlatti: 13 récherches* (item 37), pp. 8-15.

Sheds new light on the question of when Domenico actually arrived in Portugal and on the period of his life between his departure from Rome and his Iberian years. Suggests that Emanuel d'Astorga whose arrival in Lisbon preceded Domenico's, may have substituted for Domenico in the preparation of the latter's works in Lisbon. Cites two additional documents of the Unione dei Musici of Palermo which reinforce the view that Domenico was in Palermo after he left Rome and may have remained there for a longer period than previously thought. Continues to explore the relationship between Domenico and his father begun in the author's books (items 16 and 30 in Book I).

23. _____. "Le origini ed il primo statuto dell'Unione dei Musici intitolata a Santa Cecilia in Palermo." *Rivista italiana di musicologia* 10 (1975): 545-563.

Discusses the Unione... of Palermo (1679-1680) which was a mutual aid society and organization of all the professional musicians in the city; Domenicus Scarlatti became a member in 1720, which suggests that Domenico was in Palermo between the time he resigned from the Capella Giulia, Vatican, and the time he began his service in Portugal; this would account for the total lack of information regarding his supposed London visit.

* _____. *Scarlatti; Alessandro e Domenico: due vite in una.* Cited as item 30 in Book I.

24. Pascual, Beryl Kenyon de. "Domenico Scarlatti and His Son Alexandro's Inheritance." *Music and Letters* 69 (1988): 23-29. Notes, app.

Details regarding the secret marriage and early demise of Domenico's son Alexandro and a legal suit threatened by Domenico over his daughter-in-law's dowry which she and her family attempted to reclaim. Appendix includes transcriptions of the pertinent documents. Author provides interesting financial information relating to Domenico's estate and income.

25. Pestelli, Giorgio. "L'opera musicale di Domenico Scarlatti." In *Domenico Scarlatti. I grandi centenari dell'anno europeo della musica* (item 36), pp. 79-94.

Interesting discussion of Scarlatti's stylistic evolution which takes into consideration the recently discovered MS scores of *La Dirindina* and the *17 Sinfonie* (Bibliothèque Nationale, Paris) and illuminates the composer's unique contributions to eighteenth-century keyboard music. Includes a number of facsimile reproductions (e.g., of the frontispiece and a page from the MS of *Alla caccia di tiranna beltà*, cantata for alto and basso continuo).

* Salazar, Adolfo. "Los Scarlatti (una ilustre familia musical); Domenico Scarlatti, un Napolitano en la Corte de Espana." Cited as item 34 in Book I.

* *Gli Scarlatti.* Cited as item 35 in Book I.

26. Sheveloff, Joel. "(Giuseppe) Domenico Scarlatti." In *The New Grove Dictionary of Music and Musicians*, vol. 6, pp. 568-578. Ed. by Stanley Sadie. London: Macmillan, 1981. Pp. 574-578, list of works; p. 578, bibl.

   The best and most current encyclopedia article about the composer. Biographical information only includes data that the author believed to be factually verifiable. Excellent discussions of Scarlatti's keyboard style and techniques, performance practice, sources and influences which go beyond those in any other dictionary article.

27. Sheveloff, Joel (with Malcolm Boyd). "Domenico Scarlatti." In *The New Grove Italian Baroque Masters*, pp. 327-363. N.Y.: W. W. Norton, 1984. Pp. 351-361, worklist; pp. 362-363, bibl.

   Based on item 26; modified by Malcolm Boyd. Updated worklist and bibliography, however, worklist not as up to date or complete as the one in Boyd's book (item 3).

*   Simi Bonini, Eleonora. "L'attività degli
      Scarlatti nella Basilica Liberiana." Cited as
      item 103.

28.   Sitwell, Sacheverell. *A Background for Domenico
      Scarlatti*. London: Faber & Faber, 1935. 168
      pp. Facs. ed.: Salem, N.H.: Ayer Co. Pubs.,
      [1974]. ISBN 0-8369-51972. Reprint:
      Greenwood, 1971. ISBN 0-8371-43357, SIDS.

      This first book on Scarlatti in English
      attempted to fill the gaps in his biography by
      elaborating upon his milieu and the historical
      and artistic figures who surrounded him.
      Contains a number of errors regarding
      Scarlatti's life and a great deal of
      speculation; therefore, it must be used with
      caution.

29.   Solar-Quintes, Nicolas Antonio. "Domenico
      Scarlatti," subsection of "Músicos de
      Mariana de Neoburgo y de la Real Capella de
      Napoles." *Anuario musical* 11 (1956): 20-24.

      Contains quotation from document contained
      in the church of San Martin, Madrid which
      confirmed that Domenico died in Madrid rather
      than Naples (see item 2). Author's source for
      this information was the *Diccionario de la Música* of
      H. Anglés and J. Pena. Some other
      biographical data given not accurate.

*   _____."Documentos sobra la famiglia de
      Domenico Scarlatti." *Anuario musical* 4 (1949):
      137-154. Cited as item 40 in Book I.

*   Valabrega, Cesare. *Il clavicembalista Domenico Scarlatti,
      il suo secolo, la sua opera*. Cited as item 168.

*   Walker, Frank. "(Giuseppe) Domenico
      Scarlatti." See item 9.

2. Anniversary Publications; Foundation Information

30.   Boyd, Malcolm.   "Nova Scarlattiana."   *Musical*
      Times 76 (1985): 589-593.

      An excellent introduction to the newest
      literature and important scholarly
      contributions on the composer, especially
      those studies which appeared after all the
      various reprints and corrected editions of
      Kirkpatrick's book. Author examines 8 "new"
      sonatas attributed to Scarlatti and eliminates
      some.

31.   Clark,Jane. "'His Own Worst Enemy': Scar-
      latti: Some Unanswered Questions." *Early Music*
      13 (1985): 542-547.

      Explores and hypothesizes about some
      puzzling aspects of the Scarlatti biography,
      the relationship of his keyboard technique to
      Rameau's, the two rival London publications of
      the *Essercizi*, etc.

32.   Dent, Edward J.   "Domenico Scarlatti."
      Monthly Musical Record 65 (Oct. 1935): 176-177.

      A brief commemorative article. Speculates
      that Roseingrave's compositions may have
      influenced Scarlatti and that Beethoven may
      have known (through Czerny, his teacher) and
      been influenced to a degree by Scarlatti's
      keyboard music.

33.   *Domenico Scarlatti e il suo tempo*. [Atti del Convegno
      internazionale di studi...].   Conference in
      Siena on Sept. 2-4, 1985. Sponsored by the
      Accademia Musicale Chigiana Musicologia and
      the Università degli Studi in conjunction
      with the Società Italiana di Napoli.

      Papers to be published in issue of *Chigiana*
      include Roberto Pagano's "Piena utilizzazione
      delle dieci dita, o una singolare applicazione

pratica della parabola dei talenti;" Manuel Carlos de Brito's "Domenico Scarlatti e la musica alla corte di Giovanni V di Portogallo;" Eva Badura-Skoda's "Il significato dei manoscritti scarlattiani recentemente scoperti a Vienna;" Boyd's "Scarlatti Sonatas in Some Recently Discovered Spanish Sources;" Sheveloff's "Uncertainties in Scarlatti's Musical Language;" Fadini's "Problemi e osservazioni sulla grafia scarlattiana;" Hautus' "Insistenza e doppio fondo nelle sonate di Domenico Scarlatti;" Talbot's "Spostamenti fra maggiore e minore nelle sonate di Domenico Scarlatti;" Gianfranco Vinay's "Domenico Scarlatti e il neoclassicismo italiano';" Friedrich Lippmann's "Gaetano Greco un maestro di Domenico Scarlatti;" Georg Doderer's "Osservazioni sul temperamento degli strumento a tastiera nel Portogallo del XVIII secolo."

34. *Domenico Scarlatti en Espana*. Instituto Nacional de las Artes Escénicas y de la Música. Madrid: Ministerio Cultura, [1985?].

   Not seen.

35. Domenico Scarlatti Foundation. [Information about performances of the composer's music scheduled to be performed on Oct. 21-27, 1985 sponsored by the Foundation]. *Early Music* 13 (1985): 422.

   Performances by the Concertgebouw of Amsterdam and the Sweelinck Conservatory. All the sonatas to be performed on both harpsichord and piano. Workshops, lectures, and special concerts (including the Avison arrangements) scheduled. Address: Domenico Scarlatti Foundation, Postbox 15005, 1001 M A Amsterdam, Holland. tel 31.20.27 4679.

36. *Domenico Scarlatti: I grandi centenari dell'anno europeo della*

*musica/ Les grands jubilés de l'année européenne de la
musique: esposizione, 24 augusto- 30 ottobre 1985,
Ascona*. Centro culturale beato Pietro Berno:
Ente turistico Ascona e Losone. Locarno,
Switz.: Edizioni Pedrazzini, c1985. 201 pp.
illus., mus., ports., bibl. refs. ISBN
8874040024. Also Ger./Eng. ed., 208 pp.

A collection of papers by 10 noted
musicologists (with introduction by Francesco
Degrada) on aspects of the European musical
scene in the first part of the eighteenth
century with a focus on Domenico Scarlatti.
See items 25, 106, 107, 204, and Book I, items
211 and 175 for individual papers of
particular relevance to Scarlatti.

37. *Domenico Scarlatti: 13 récherches*. Nice: Société du
     musique ancienne de Nice, 1985. 127 pp.
     Illus., bibl. refs. (Cahiers de la
     Société du musique ancienne de Nice, 1)
     ISBN 290613600X.

     Contains papers read at the first meeting of
     the Société held Dec. 11-15, 1985. Among the
     contributors were music, art, and architecture
     historians; performers; music editors; and a
     harpsichord builder. Areas of focus were
     "Situations" (biographical items); "Les
     sonates"; and "La musique vocale." The volume
     contains introductory remarks by Nicole
     Janicaud, Jacques Charpentier, and Scott Ross
     and a "Postlude" by Kenneth Gilbert as well as
     biographical   information   about   the
     contributors. Individual papers have been
     cited as items 53, 225, 230, 132, 65, 157, 91,
     171, 90, 126, 48, 189, 193, and 22.

38. *Händel e gli Scarlatti a Roma: atti del convegno internazionale di
     studi (Roma, 12-14 giugno 1985)*. Ed. by Nino
     Pirotta and Agostino Ziino. Florence:
     Olschki, 1987. vi and 439 pp. [14] pp. of
     plates; illus.; bibl. refs., index. It. and
     Eng. ISBN 88-222-352-90.

Papers from the conference sponsored by the Accademia Nazionale di Santa Cecilia, Rome. Of greatest relevance to Domenico are those by Reinhard Strohm, E. Simi Bonini, M. Viale Ferrero, G. Rostirolla, M. Boyd, and R. Pagano cited as items 241; 103; 105; 101; 104; 56, respectively; G. Dixon's article (item 153, Book I) is also of interest. Other articles with pertinent information on Alessandro are cited in Book I of this research guide.

39. Lang, Paul Henry. "Scarlatti: 300 Years On." *Musical Times* 76 (1985): 584-589.

Includes background on the politics and atmosphere of the Spanish court during the eighteenth century, a biographical summary, and a discussion of Scarlatti's sonatas (their structure, etc.).

40. Palmer, Larry. "In Search of Scarlatti." *Diapason* 76/12 (Dec. 1985): 13.

Cites quotes from various musicians' writings on Scarlatti (including excerpts from Chopin's letters to Delfina Potocka, and comments of Wanda Landowska and Wilfred Mellers) from secondary sources which are noted. Includes a review of Kenneth Gilbert's recital at London's Wigmore Hall on Jan. 22/24, 1985, etc. Refers the reader to a few major books and editions.

41. Petech, Diana. "Notiziario: Il Convegno di Nizza su Domenico Scarlatti." *Nuova rivista musicale italiana* 19 (1985): 760-761.

Report on the conference dedicated to Domenico held at Nice, Dec. 11-15, 1985 by the Society of Ancient Music of Nice. Participants included: Scott Ross (honorary president) who recorded the complete sonatas for ERATO; Kenneth Gilbert; Emilia Fadini; Roberto Pagano; Laura Alvini; Jane Clark et

al. and performances, including one on
videotape of the *Messa de Arànzazu* edited by
Miguel Alonzo Gomez. See also item 37.

42.   Roncaglia, Gino. "Domenico Scarlatti nel
      secondo centenario della sua morte." In
      Immagini esotiche della musica italiana, pp. 63-69.
      Accademia Musicale Chigiana. Siena: Ticci,
      1957.

      Not seen.

43.   Salter, Lionel. "In Search of Scarlatti."
      Consort 41 (1985): 47-51.

      Calls for a complete edition of all the
      composer's works, discusses the various
      editions of the collected keyboard works,
      points out research problems still to be
      investigated and advocates revival of some of
      the vocal works which the author argues are
      unjustly neglected.

44.   Sheveloff, Joel. "Domenico Scarlatti:
      Tercentenary Frustrations." [Part I] *Musical
      Quarterly* 71 (1985): 399-436 and Part II:
      Musical Quarterly 72 (1986): 90-117.

      Summarizes much of the author's research
      into sources and his criticism of
      Kirkpatrick's work which appeared in his
      earlier dissertation (item 161).
          Part I: Critical review of Scarlatti
      research covering the biography, modern
      editions, recent specialized research
      contributions, the works' authenticity and
      chronology, their textual authenticity, and
      the grouping of sonatas.
          Part II: A fascinating new look at many
      aspects of Scarlatti's music and its
      performance including discussions of the
      following topics: the Queen's instruments
      concerning which the author proposes that a
      great many sonatas may, in fact, have been

written for the early pianoforte and several others for the clavichord (as well as the organ); Scarlatti's ornamentation, in which extemporization of ornaments in repeats is advocated; and a number of other topics pertinent to an understanding of the composer's musical style, such as folk and popular music influences, acciaccaturas, fingering, connections with Bach and Handel, specific contributions to the development of musical style, problems with recent editions and performances (live and recorded).

45. Williams, Peter, ed. *Bach, Handel, Scarlatti: Tercentenary Essays*. Cambridge: Cambridge University Press, 1985. xiv and 363 pp. ISBN 0-521-25217-2.

An anniversary collection of very fine essays, all of them thought provoking. The six contributions by Stephen Daw, David Fuller, Mark Lindley, Giorgio Pestelli, Luigi Ferdinando Tagliavini, and Peter Williams are cited individually in this book as items 208, 173, 175, 154, 165, 170, respectively. An index of the works by Scarlatti cited in the volume is included (pp. 354-355). Reviews include: *Central Opera Service. Bulletin* 26/3 (1985-86): 67-68.

3. Cultural Milieu

46. Black, Jeremy. "Lisbon in 1730: the Account of a British Traveller." *Bulletin of the British Society for Eighteenth-Century Studies* 7-8 (1985): 11-14.

Quotes from a letter of Jan. 1730 by George Hay in which he describes the city and capital of Portugal as it appeared to him in very negative terms. (Compare with Almeida's description in Kirkpatrick, item 13, p. 67).

47. Brito, Manuel Carlos de. "Domenico Scarlatti e la musica alla corte di Giovanni V di

Portogallo."   Cited in item 33.

48. _____. *Opera in Portugal in the Eighteenth Century.*
    Cambridge, Eng.: Cambridge University Press,
    1989. ISBN 0-521-35312-2. Review by Robert
    Stevenson in *Music Library Association. Notes* 47
    (1991): 740-742.

    The first accurate and in-depth published
    history of musical theater in Portugal during
    the eighteenth century.   Also of major
    importance for its chronological list of
    operas, serenatas, and oratorios performed
    during the period in which the author
    identifies copies of the librettos and scores
    preserved in Portuguese libraries. Background
    information on the serenata and on
    performances of serenatas by Domenico in
    Portugal.   Identifies serenata performed Dec.
    27, 1722, for the nameday of Joao V as
    Scarlatti's *Le nozze di Baco e d'Arianna* (libretto
    anonymous).

49. _____. "Le role de l'opéra dans le lutte
    entre l'obscurantisme et les lumières au
    Portugal (1731-1742)." *Informacao musical*
    (1983): 32-43. In Fr. and Pt. Illus.

    A study of Italian opera in Portugal during
    Domenico Scarlatti's tenure as chapel master
    for John V (c1721-29) with sociological
    information from contemporary diaries.   Not
    seen. Abstract in *RILM* 1983 # 454.

*   Cametti, Alberto. "Carlo Sigismondo Capeci
     (1652-1728), Alessandro e Domenico Scarlatti
     e la Regina de Polonia in Roma." Cited in
     Book I as item 178.

50. Chase, Gilbert. *The Music of Spain.* N.Y.: W. W.
    Norton, 1941. 375 pp. 2nd rev. ed. N.Y.:
    W. W. Norton, 1959.

    Chapter 7: "In the Orbit of Scarlatti" (pp.

106-120) includes background on the politics that lead to Italian influence in Spain and Domenico's relationship to Spain, its popular music, and Soler.

51. Clemessy, Nelly. "L'Espagne de Domenico Scarlatti." In *Domenico Scarlatti: 13 récherches* (item 37), pp. 16-23. Notes.

Historical and cultural background on the courts of Portugal and Spain and the milieu in which Domenico worked. Draws heavily on Yves Bottineau's *L'art de cour dans l'Espagne de Philippe V, 1700-1746* (Bordeaux: Féret, 1960).

52. Coxe, William. *Memoirs of the Kings of Spain*. London, 1813. 2nd ed., 1815.

Includes descriptions of Maria Barbara on pp. 111, 18-19. Partially reprinted in Boyd (item 3).

53. Foussard, Dominique, and Michel Foussard. "Filippo Juvarra et Domenico Scarlatti. Questions sur quelques affinités de composition." In *Domenico Scarlatti: 13 récherches* (item 37), pp. 24-35. Illus., notes.

Departing from a statement of Kirkpatrick comparing the structural ideals of Scarlatti and Juvarra, the authors attempt to find a parallel in the works of the architect and the musician but conclude that such a parallel doesn't work and is fundamentally false. The major part of the article goes on to discuss motifs from the work of Juvarra, their diffusion as models in the field of the Piedmont Baroque, and the formation of a national and universal "language" from a local language (or style).

54.   Hamilton, Mary Neal. *Music in Eighteenth-Century*
      Spain. N.Y.: Da Capo Press, 1971. Reprint
      of 1st ed. published in Urbana, Illinois, in
      1937 as Volume 22/1-2 of the *Illinois Studies in*
      Language and Literature. SBN 306-70279-7. Mus.,
      bibl., apps. 283 pp.

      An early history of the music and cultural
      milieu in Spain during the eighteenth century
      with references to Scarlatti. Provides useful
      background but must be used with caution. The
      only book of its time on this subject written
      in English.

55.   Hargreaves-Mawdsley, William Norman. *Eighteenth*
      Century Spain, 1700-1788: A Political, Diplomatic and
      Institutional History. London: Macmillan, 1979.
      xii and 181 pp. Maps, notes, bibl., index.
      ISBN 0-333-14612-3.

      Part Two (pp. 85-98) discusses the reign of
      Fernando VI and includes information on him
      and his wife Maria Barbara, Scarlatti's pupil.
      Useful maps and bibliographic notes.

*   Kastner, Macario Santiago. *Contribución al estudio de*
      la música espanola y portuguesa.
      Cited as item 71.

*   Malinowski, Wladyslaw. "O teatrze Królowej
      Marii Kazimiery, Domenico Scarlattim i Kilku
      innych sprawach z Michalem Bristigerem."
      Cited as item 119.

*   Pagano, Roberto. "Le origini ed il primo
      statuto dell'Unione dei Musici intitolata a
      Santa Cecilia in Palermo." Cited as item 23.

56.   _____. "Venni a Roma cristiana e non
      Cristina..." In *Händel e gli Scarlatti a Roma* (item
      38), pp. 265-284.

A historical review of the literature (diaries, memoirs, biographies, etc.) which discusses Scarlatti's Roman patroness Maria Casimira as well as a fascinating look into the cultural, political, economic, and social factors which combined to form the world in which the exiled Polish queen moved.

57. Russell, Peter Edward, ed. *Spain; a Companion to Spanish Studies.* London: Methuen & Co. Ltd., 1973. Tables, maps, index.

Provides background on "Spanish Literature after 1700" (Chapter 9); "The Visual Arts in Spain" (Chapter 11); and "Spanish Music" (Chapter 12) by noted scholars.

58. Sitwell, Sacheverell. *Baroque and Rococo.* N.Y.: Putnam, 1967.

Chapters 9 and 10 are entitled : "The Castrati, and Others" and "Music-master to the Infanta Barbara: Domenico Scarlatti," respectively. Includes a discussion of the careers of the famous castrati and their milieu as well as a biography of Scarlatti in which information on twentieth- century English keyboardist and interpreter of Scarlatti's sonatas Violet Gordon Woodhouse (1871-1946) is given.

*   Solar-Quintes, Nicolas Antonio. "Domenico Scarlatti," subsection of "Músicos de Mariana de Neoburgo y de la Real Capilla de Napoles." Cited as item 29.

59. Vinay, Gianfranco. "Domenico Scarlatti e il neoclassicismo italiano." Forthcoming in *Chigiana* (cited as item 33).

60. Waliszewski, Kazimierz. *Marysienka: Marie de la Grange d'Arquien, Queen of Poland, and Wife of Sobieski 1641-*

1716. (Paris, 1896). Eng. trans. by Lady
Mary Lloyd. London: William Heinemann,
1898. xviii and 297 pp. "List of
Authorities Consulted: Documents, Authors."
Index.

A literary biography of the Queen based on
early documents and histories. Contains only
minimal information on the Queen's stay in
Rome.

4. Relationship of Scarlatti to Other Composers and to Spanish Folk Music

61.   Allison, Brian Jerome. "Carlos Seixas: the
Development of the Keyboard Sonata in
Eighteenth-century Portugal...." D.M.A.
dissertation. North Texas State University,
1982. 38 pp. UMI order # DA 822 8018

Relationship between Seixas and Domenico
Scarlatti examined. Particular styles and
techniques thought to be innovations of
Domenico shown to exist in works of Seixas
that probably predate Scarlatti's.

62.   Allorto, Riccardo. "Clementi non ha plagiato
Scarlatti." *Musica d'oggi* n.s. 2 (Feb. 1959):
66-67.

Responds to Gerstenberg's view that Clementi
plagiarized Scarlatti by reissuing his London
Scarlatti edition (c1791) in Paris several
years later with the title *Douze sonates...composées
dans le stile du celèbre Scarlati*. Clarifies the
circumstances surrounding the publication.
Sheveloff (item 161) was not convinced by
Allorto's argument that Clementi's Parisian
publisher formulated the title page without
the composer's approval.

63.   Cassingham, Jack Lee. "The Twelve Scarlatti-
Avison Concertos for String Orchestra of

1744." 2 vols. Vol. 1: ix and 119 pp.
Tables, illus., figs., bibl. 3 apps.
(including in app. 1 a facs. reprt. of pp.
106-152 from the 2nd ed. of Avison's "Essay
on Musical Expression as it Relates to the
Performer"). Vol. 2: iii and 354 pp. D.M.A.
dissertation. University of Missouri,
Kansas City, 1968. University Microfilms
order #68-6127.

Author's object to provide a study score of
the 12 Scarlatti-Avison transcriptions (vol.
2), to discuss their historical background, to
examine performance practice with respect to
Avison's writings, and to "briefly summarize
the transcription procedures used by Avison in
making the concertos." The 48 keyboard
pieces (all but 9 known to be by Scarlatti)
transcribed by Avison into 12 four-movement
concertos are given in a modern edition based
on a microfiche of the orchestral parts from
MSS in the Library of Congress and British
Library. The figured bass is unrealized.
Sheveloff states in item 44, pt 1, p. 419, n.
58 that this score "contains so many errors as
to be unuseable." [An edition by Sidney Beck
published by New York Public Library exists in
that collection].

64. Clark, Jane. "Domenico Scarlatti and Spanish
Folk Music: A Performer's Re-appraisal."
Early Music 4 (1976): 19-21.

Relates Scarlatti's sonatas to Andalusian
folk music; sees influences of the latter in
Scarlatti's use of harmony, Phrygian mode,
forms, etc. Boyd (item 3) finds the author's
arguments unconvincing.

65. _____. "La portée de l'influence andalouse
chez Scarlatti." In *Domenico Scarlatti: 13
récherches* (cited as item 37), pp. 63-67. Mus.
exs.

Author restates her position that Scarlatti

was directly influenced by the forms of
Andalusian folk music. Mus. exs. include K.
490 (spirit shows influence of the *saeta*); K.
491 (*seguidilla sevillana*); K. 492 (*buleria*); K. 116
(eighteenth-century *flamenco*); K. 450 (*tango*).
Note cites recording of flamenco music
currently available which is useful .for
obtaining an understanding of these ideas.

66.   Edwards, Donna O'Steen. "Iberian Elements in
      the Sonatas of Domenico Scarlatti." D.M.A.
      dissertation. North Texas State University,
      1980. 92 pp. UMI Order # 8100066

      Compares Kirkpatrick's facsimile edition of
      Scarlatti's 555 sonatas with printed
      anthologies of Spanish folk music edited by
      Kurt Schindler and Felipe Pedrell and to
      recordings of authentic Spanish folk music.
      Discusses Scarlatti's use of folk elements in
      four categories: instrumental imagery as a
      link to Spanish popular music; Spanish folk
      songs with examples from the sonatas showing
      characteristics of cante jondo and fragments
      of folk tunes; elements of Spanish folk dances
      used; Spanish sound achieved through harmonic
      idiom.

67.   Eppstein, Hans. "Henrik Philip Johnsens
      "valtemperade" sonater." *Svens Tidskrift för*
      Musikforskning 59/2 (1977): 79-80. In Swedish.

      Discusses *Sei sonate per il cembalo* by Johnsen
      (1717-79), which are all in one movement and
      possibly modeled after the sonatas of Domenico
      Scarlatti. May have been part of a cycle in
      24 keys. Not seen. Abstract in *RILM* (1977)
      #2599.

68.   Gifford, Gerald. "Viscount Fitzwilliam and
      the English 'Scarlatti sect'." In *Italian Music*
      at the Fitzwilliam. Cambridge: Fitzwilliam Museum,
      1976. 47 pp.

One of several essays prepared on the occasion of an exhibition of Italian music in the museum in May 1976; four concerts of Italian music were given during the exhibition.

69. Goebels, Franzpeter. "Scarlattiana: Bemerkungen zur Scarlatti-Rezeption von Johannes Brahms." *Musica* 40 (1986): 320-328.

Not seen.

70. Huizstee, Theodore van. "Naar aanleiding van Mozarts KV 331: Scarlatti's K 513." *Mens en melodie* 33 (May 1978): 148-156. Mus. exs., notes.

Analyzes and compares motives in Domenico Scarlatti's pastorale *Sonata K 513* and Mozart's *Piano Variations, KV 331*. Discusses the pastoral melodic type in *siciliano* rhythm with references to compositions by A. Scarlatti (his aria "La Siciliana" from *La donna ancora è fedele*), J. S. Bach, G. F. Handel, et al.

71. Kastner, Macario Santiago. *Contribución al estudio de la música espanola y portuguesa*. Lisbon: Éditorial Atica, 1941. 405 pp. Addenda, index, bibl.

A fascinating and important study of the history of Portuguese and Spanish keyboard music from the fifteenth to the twentieth century. The chapter on the eighteenth century includes a detailed examination of the relationship between the works of Scarlatti and his contemporaries in Portugal and Spain, among them Carlos Seixas and Antonio Soler.

72. Klimovickij, Abram. "Ob odnoj neizvestnoj rukopisi Bramsa." [Concerning an unknown MS by Brahms]. In *Pamjatniki kul'tury: novye otkrytija, pis'mennost', iskusstvo, arheologija*, pp. 211-218. Ezegodnik, 1978. (Leningrad: Nauka, 1979).

Illus. In Russian.

Examines Brahm's attitude toward Scarlatti's
music. Includes a facsimile of the MS copy of
Sonata K 394 made by Brahms located in the
Leningrad State Library. Not seen. Abstract
in *RILM* (1979) #2793.

73. Lippmann, Friedrich. "Sulle composizioni per
     cembalo di Gaetano Greco." In *La musica a
     Napoli durante il Seicento* (Book I, item 77), pp.
     285-306. Mus. exs. including facsimiles.

Examines the keyboard style of Greco who may
have studied with, among others, Alessandro
Scarlatti and whose own pupils may have
included Domenico Scarlatti (before 1705).
Greco identified as one of the most
significant Neopolitan masters active between
the seventeenth and eighteenth centuries.
Author gives examples to show that Greco's
style seems to have influenced Domenico's own
keyboard style even though the latter's music
was much more virtuosic.

74. McKay, Elizabeth. "Brahms and Scarlatti."
     Musical Times 130 (1989) 586-588. Facs.

Discussion of the Scarlatti MSS and editions
owned by Brahms now in the collection of the
Gesellschaft der Musikfreunde, Vienna. Focuses
on his copy of the first edition of the *Essercizi*
(Nachlass VII-30133) acquired in his early
twenties; speculates that it could have been
"along with Clara Schumann's influence... a
primary source of his affection for...
[Scarlatti's music] which was to play some
small part in his own development as a
composer of piano music."

75. Marshall, Robert L. "Bach the Progressive."
     Musical Quarterly 62 (1976) 313-357 (see
     especially pp. 347-349).

Challenges Kirkpatrick's contention that
Scarlatti could not have influenced Bach
because Scarlatti's keyboard works were little
known in Germany during Bach's lifetime.
Points to various channels through which Bach
may have become aquainted with these works.
Suggests that the *Goldberg Variations* bear a
resemblance to Scarlatti's *Essercizi* in their
number (30) and technical demands, etc.

76. Mast, Paul. "Brahms' Study, Octaven u.
    Quinten u. A: With Schenker's *Commentary*
    Translated." *Music Forum* 5 (1980): 2-196.

A study of Brahms the theorist/musicologist
which includes examples of Domenico
Scarlatti's works (among others) with Heinrich
Schenker's commentaries translated into
English. 140 exs. of successive octaves and
5ths and related progressions Brahms had found
in works of composers from Clemens to Bizet
cited from the MS in Vienna, Gesellschaft der
Musikfreunde.

77. Newman, William S. "Keyboard Sonatas of
    Benedetto Marcello." *Acta Musicologica* 29
    (1957): 38-39.

Author sees many similarities between
Scarlatti's and Marcello's style, e.g., the
splitting apart of one note into two;
reiteration of short phrases; spiral ascents
and wide leaps; repetition and double notes;
hand-crossing; long trills while line
continues in same hand. Poses question as to
who influenced whom since the two probably
knew each other in Venice for several years
(between 1705 and 1708).

*   Newton, Richard. "The English Cult of
    Domenico Scarlatti." Cited as item 213.

78.   Paterson, Scott.   "The Crossing Paths of
      Handel and Scarlatti."   *Music Magazine (Toronto)*
      8/2 (1985) 15-19.

      Not seen.

79.   Pecman, Rudolph.   "Zum Begriff des Rokokostils
      in der Musik." *Muzikoloski Zbornik* (Yugoslavia) 9
      (1973): 5-34.   Mus.   Summary in Slovenian.

      Discusses the emergence of the rococo style
      and the roles Domenico Scarlatti, G.B.
      Pergolesi, and G.B. Sammartini played in its
      development.   Not seen.   Abstract in *RILM*
      (1974) #333.

80.   Pestelli, Giorgio.   "Contributi alla storia
      della forma-sonata: *Sei Sonate per Cembalo* di
      Girolamo Sertori (1758)." *Rivista italiana di
      musicologia* 2 (1967): 131-139.

      Compares Sertori's sonatas (MS in Biblioteca
      Nacional de Madrid) to those of Scarlatti to
      see if there are characteristics in common
      (folk, technical, formal, etc).   Finds little
      resemblance; author concludes that Scarlatti
      probably knew the works and was familiar with
      the tripartite form but found the bipartite
      form more suitable to his own artistic
      expression.

*   --------.   "Corelli e il suo influsso sulla
      musica per cembalo del suo tempo."   Cited in
      Book I as item 321.

81.   Petrov, Jurij. ["Spanish genres in the clavier
      works of Domenico Scarlatti."]   In *Istoriko-
      teoreticeskie problemy zapadnoevropejskoj muzyki (ot
      Vozrozdenija do romantizma)*.   [Historical and
      theoretical topics of Western European Music
      from the Renaissance to Romanticism.]
      Comp. by Ruzanna Sirinjan.   *Sbornik trudov* 40.
      Moscow: Gosudarstvennyj muzykal'no-

pedagogicesky institut imeni Gnesinyh, 1978.
231 pp. Music, bibl.

Not seen. Cited in *RILM* 1978 #2432 but no
abstract of this article given.

82. Pinchukov, Evgenij. "Cherty stilja v garmonii
     [D. Skarlatti]." *Sovetskaia Muzyka* [Contours of
     Style and Harmony in Domenico Scarlatti].
     Music. (Aug. 1981): 65-68.

     Relates   Spanish   folk   music   in   Kurt
     Schindler's *Folk Music and Poetry of Spain and Portugal*
     (N.Y.: Hispanic   Institute   in   the   United
     States,   1941) to various Scarlatti sonatas.
     Musical examples cited include K 402, 116,
     141,   247,   119.   Analyzes   the   harmonic
     language of the sonatas and the "expressive
     use of the dominant in his part writing...."
     See abstract in *RILM* 1981 #2515.

83. Poniatowska, Irena. "O muzyce fortepianowej
     Muzio Clementiego i jego *Méthode pour le piano
     forte*." In: Bristiger, Michal, ed. *Pagine.
     Polskowloskie materialy muzyczne* 3 [Pages. Polish-
     Italian music topics, 3].   Cracow and
     Warsaw: Polskie Wydawnictwo Muzyczne, 1979.
     In Polish and Italian.

     An analysis of the piano music of Clementi
     and comparison with the music of Domenico
     Scarlatti and others. Not seen. Abstract in
     RILM (1979) #2690 and #2323.

84. Powell, Linton E. "The Keyboard Music of
     Sebastian de Albero: An Astonishing
     Literature from the Orbit of Scarlatti."
     Early Keyboard Journal 5 (1986-1987): 9-28.

     An interesting and important article which
     examines   form,   harmony,   hand   crossing,
     figuration, etc., in Albero's keyboard works
     and   explores   their   relationships   to   the
     keyboard   pieces   of   D.   Scarlatti,   Antonio

Soler, and José Elías. Compares Scarlatti's
fugues with those of Albero.

85. _____. *A History of Spanish Piano Music*. Bloomington,
    Indiana: Indiana University Press, 1980.
    vii and 213 pp. ISBN 0-253-18114-3

    Chapter 1: "Early Spanish Piano Music, 1740-
    1840," pp. 1-46, contains a discussion of
    Scarlatti and Spanish composers the author
    believes he influenced, including Albero and
    Soler. Like Kirkpatrick, Powell believes
    Scarlatti wrote almost exclusively for the
    harpsichord. Author repeats the now generally
    discredited story that Scarlatti wrote fewer
    pieces requiring handcrossing later in life
    because his fingers were too fat to execute
    the passages skillfully.

86. Pozniak, Piotr. "I momenti dell'estetica
    barocca nell'opera liutistica di Sylvius
    Leopold Weiss." *Il "Fronimo." Rivista trimestrale di
    chitarra e luito I* 7/26 (Jan. 1979): 20-23.

    Compares the lute suites of Weiss (1680-
    1760) with the sonatas of Domenico Scarlatti.
    Boyd (item 3) sees Weiss as a possible link
    between Scarlatti and J.S. Bach. Not seen.
    Abstract in *RILM* (1979) #429.

87. Russell, Craig H. "An Investigation into
    Arcangelo Corelli's Influence on 18th-
    century Spain." *Current Musicology* 34 (1982):
    42-52.

    Calls attention to Corelli's popularity in
    eighteenth-century Spain. His works were
    contained in many contemporary MSS, were often
    mentioned by Spanish theorists, and were very
    frequently transcribed for guitar and
    keyboard.

88. Sams, Eric. "Zwei Brahms-Rätsel." *Osterreichische Musikzeitschrift* 27 (1972): 83-84. Mus. ex.

Contains a brief commentary on the reason for Brahms' use of a theme by D. Scarlatti (K 223) in his *Lied* "Unüberwindlich," op. 72/3 (text by Goethe). Makes the connection between its use and Robert Schumann's review of an edition of 200 Scarlatti sonatas in the *Neue Zeitschrift für Musik* in which he said that use of Scarlatti sparingly and at the appropriate time could create a fresh effect.

89. Silbiger, Alexander. "Scarlatti Borrowings in Handel's Grand Concertos." *Musical Times* 125 (1984): 93-95.

Includes a discussion of Handel's use of material from Scarlatti's *Essercizi* (1738-1739) in his *Concerti Op. 6* (1739). Comparison of the two composers' styles reveals the differences in their musical language.

II

STUDIES OF THE MUSIC

1. Vocal Music

Choral Works

90. Alonso-Gomez, Miguel. "La Messe en ré majeur pour choeurs et orchestre dite de Aránzazu." In *Domenico Scarlatti: 13 récherches* (item 37), pp. 109-111.

Discusses questions of this Mass' origin, copyist, links to various composers, and the differences between the surviving score and parts. The author of Radio Nationale Espagnole arranged the showing of the video of the world premiere of the Mass which took place Nov. 29, 1985, at the Cathédrale de Sainte Marie de Vitoria.

91. Andreani, Eveline. "Autour de la musique sacrée de Domenico Scarlatti." In *Domenico Scarlatti: 13 récherches* (item 37), pp. 96-108. Mus. exs.

Emphasizes the role Domenico's contrapuntal background played in his use of brusque shifts in tonalities, avoidance of resolutions, unexpected dropping out of parts, etc., in some of his choral works.

92. Borton, Bruce Erol. "The Sacred Choral Works of Domenico Scarlatti." D.M.A. dissertation, University of Cincinnati, 1983. iv and 370 pp. App., bibl. UMI order #174-363.

Includes detailed analyses of the "nine

surviving sacred choral works," descriptions
of MS sources, and critical commentary and
transcriptions of the 7 not then available in
modern editions: 2 *Miserere* settings; *Iste
confessor à 4; Magnificat à 4; Te gloriosus à
4; Te Deum* for double chorus; *Laetatus sum*
for soprano, alto soloists and four-voice
chorus. Borton's list was made before the
discovery in 1985 by Simi-Bonini of several
other choral works (cited in Boyd, item 3).

93. Casella, Alfredo, ed. "Preface." In Domenico
     Scarlatti's *Stabat Mater*. Rome: De Santis,
     1941. i [p.]. (Includes part of his article
     for *Gli Scarlatti*, item 35, Book I).

     Mentions works (a mass and the motet *Nisi quia
     Dominus*) in the collection of the Basilica
     Liberiana which have only recently brought to
     light again through the research of Eleonora
     Simi Bonini (see item 104).

94. _____. "Le musiche vocali e strumentali."
     In *Gli Scarlatti* (item 35, Book I), pp. 19-21.

     Author's introduction to the works performed
     at the *settimana celebrativa* arranged by the
     Accademia Musicale Chigiana (Siena, Italy) in
     Sept. 1940. Chief among them was Domenico's
     Stabat Mater.

95. DeVenney, David. "The Choral Music of
     Domenico Scarlatti." *Choral Journal* 25/3
     (1984): 13-16. Mus. ex., table (structural
     outline of the *Stabat Mater*).

     Brief discussion of the *Stabat Mater* and *Contesa
     delle stagioni* which urges that more of Scarlatti's
     works be published.

96. _____. "The Sacred Choral Music of
     Domenico Scarlatti." *American Organist* (Oct.
     1985): 98-102. Mus. exs., tables

(structural outlines).

A brief survey of the sacred music excluding the two *Salve Reginas* for solo voices. Introductory background material must be used with caution.

97. Grosse-Boymann, Gilbert. "Studien zur neopolitanischen Kirchenmusik in der 1. Halfte des 18. Jahrhunderts unter besonderer Berücksichtigung von Domenico Scarlatti und Francesco Durante." Ph.D. dissertation. University of Münster.

* Hautus, Loek. "Zu dem Domenico Scarlatti zugeschriebenen *Capriccio fugato a docidi*." Cited as item 210.

98. Jürgens, Jurgen, ed. "Foreword." In Domenico Scarlatti's *Stabat Mater*. Mainz: Universal Eds., 1973. pp. [v-vii]. German "Vorwort": pp.[i-iii].

A brief discussion of the work, its MS sources, and editorial policy. Jürgens used the Santini MS as his primary source.

99. Kirkpatrick, Ralph. "Domenico Scarlatti's Choral Music." In *Essays on Music in Honor of Archibald Thompson Davison*, pp. 243-246. Ed. by R. Thompson. Cambridge, MA: 1957.

Brief discussion which groups the choral music into two basic styles (chordal and neopolyphonic). Emphasizes relationship between the composer's training in polyphonic writing and the skillful ways he handled keyboard textures and rhythms. *Stabat Mater* considered his greatest choral work; has striking harmonic shifts. Further discussion of choral works in item 13.

* Marx-Weber, Magda. "Römische Vertonungen des

Psalms *Miserere* im 18. und frühen 19.
Jahrhundert." Cited in Book I as item 161.

100. _____. "Domenico Scarlatti's *Stabat Mater*."
Kirchenmusikalisches Jahrbuch 71 (1987): 13-22.
Anhang: *Stabat Mater* text set by Scarlatti and
Notenbeispiele: comparison of examples from
the *Stabat Mater* settings of Durante, Caldara,
Steffani, Clari, and Domenico Scarlatti.

Identifies and examines extant MSS of the
work including the one used by Jürgen Jürgens
for his modern edition.

101. Rostirolla, Giancarlo. "Domenico Scarlatti e
la Congregazione dei Musici di Santa
Cecilia." In *Händel e gli Scarlatti a Roma* (item
38), pp. 191-250.

A detailed examination of the surviving
documents of the Archivio storico
dell'Accademia Nazionale di Santa Cecilia
which relate to the period in which Domenico
Scarlatti was active in Rome (1708-19). Gives
excellent picture of the cultural ambience,
the role played by the Cecilia society in
providing music for important occasions during
the liturgical year, Alessandro and Domenico
Scarlatti's participation in these events,
etc. Found that Domenico's participation was
probably limited to 9 events from Mar. 13,
1715 - Jan. 8, 1719.

102. Scandrett, Robert. "Preface" and "Critical
Remarks." In Domenico Scarlatti's *Stabat
Mater*, pp. 6-7 and p. 103, respectively.
Stuttgart: Carus-Verlag, 1986. Mus. exs.,
notes. Pref. also given in German and
French.

Brief discussion of the sacred choral works,
MS sources, and editorial policy for this
projected complete edition of the known sacred
choral works. Edition of the *Stabat* based on

the Venice and Bologna MSS.

103. Simi Bonini, Eleonora. "L'attività degli
     Scarlatti nella Basilica Liberiana." In
     Händel e gli Scarlatti a Roma (item 38), pp. 153-
     173. 2 apps.

     Includes important new research discoveries
     regarding the Scarlattis' activities at the
     Basilica di Santa Maria Maggiore, Rome (or
     Basilica Liberiana) including new biographical
     facts about Domenico's participation in the
     Basilica's performances during his father's
     tenure there and four newly discovered or
     rediscovered choral works: the psalm *Nisi quia
     Dominus*; an A minor setting of the ordinary of
     the mass for soprano, alto, tenor, & bass "*con
     ripieno*" (see Section V, 1 for author's
     edition); a *Pange lingua*, and a *Cibavit nos Dominus*.
     App. 1 contains quotations from relevant
     documents in the Archivio di S. Maria
     Maggiore, and App. 2 lists music by Alessandro
     and Domenico Scarlatti in the same archive.

Operatic Works, Serenatas, Cantatas

*   Bianconi, Lorenzo, and Maria Teresa Muraro.
    "Il teatro di San Giovanni Grisostomo dal
    Diario di Nicodemus Tessin." Cited as item
    175 in Book I.

104. Boyd, Malcolm. "Domenico Scarlatti's *Cantate da
     Camera* and their Connexions with Rome." In
     Händel e gli Scarlatti a Roma (item 38), pp. 251-
     264.

     Provides a revised list of Domenico's
     chamber cantatas and examines problems of
     attribution, provenance, dating, etc., in
     relation to his compositions in this genre.
     Suggests that the eighteen cantatas included
     in the MS volumes located in the
     Nationalbibliothek, Vienna, and the Royal
     Music Library, London, may be of Iberian

origin (whether or not composed there); both
display a calligraphic characteristic (a
backward-pointing hook on the downward stems
of eighth and 16th notes) which consistently
occurs in Iberian MSS of the composer's music
but not in any known Italian sources.

*   Brito, Manuel Carlos de. *Opera in Portugal in the
        Eighteenth Century.* Cited as item 48.

*   Cametti, Alberto. "Carlo Sigismondo Capeci
        (1652-1728), Alessandro e Domenico Scarlatti
        e la Regina de Polonia in Roma." Cited as
        item 178 in Book I.

*   Ferrero, Mercedes Viale. *Filippo Juvarra scenografo e
        architetto teatrale.* Cited as item 190 in Book I.

105. _____. "Juvarra tra i due Scarlatti." In
        Händel e gli Scarlatti a Roma (item 38), 175-190.
        Notes, illus. (stage designs).

Examines the relationship of Filippo Juvarra
to both Alessandro and Domenico Scarlatti and
discusses his innovative designs for *Il Colombo*,
Costantino Pio and *Il Ciro* (all with texts by Pietro
Ottoboni, the last with music by Alessandro
Scarlatti) and the series of operas by
Domenico on texts of Capeci performed at the
Palazzo Zuccari. Compares the two librettists'
approaches.

106. _____. "Scene e teatre a Roma al tempo di
        Alessandro e Domenico Scarlatti." In
        *Domenico Scarlatti. I grandi centenari dell'anno europeo della
        musica* (item 36), pp. 95-108. Illus.

Author illustrates how the smallness of the
stage in Maria Casimira's Palazzo Zuccari and
the impossibility of lowering stage machinery
from above (deduced from Juvarra's surviving
sketches) limited the choice of subjects and

created the problem of scenes too visually similar. Discusses how Juvarra coped with this challenge in Domenico's operas written for that theater including *L'Orlando*, *Tolomeo e Alessandro*, *Tetide in Sciro*, *Ifigenia in Aulide* and *Ifigenia in Tauri*.

107. _____. "Il teatro del Cardinale Ottoboni nel palazzo della Cancelleria a Roma e la sua riproduzione in scala ridotta per la mostra." In *Domenico Scarlatti. I grandi centenari dell'anno europeo della musica* (item 36), pp. 109-120.

Illustrates how, based on the author's research, Prof. Salvatore Manzella utilized Juvarra's scenic designs for Ottoboni's Teatro Piccola and for the theater of Maria Casimira's Palazzo Zuccari to reconstruct in scale idealized scenes from Domenico's operas including *Ifigenia in Tauri*, etc. Discusses the problems Manzella confronted and his solutions.

* Foussard, Dominique, and Michel Foussard. "Filippo Juvarra et Domenico Scarlatti: Questions sur quelques affinités de composition." Cited as item 53.

108. Hoffman, Andreas. "Die Geschichte der Oper *Il Giustino* von Legrenzi bis Händel." Ph.D. dissertation in progress. University of Cologne.

* Muraro, Maria Teresa. "Il teatro Grimani a San Giovanni Grisostomo. Storia e documenti per la costruzione di un modello." Cited as item 211 in Book I.

* Strohm, Reinhard. "Scarlattiana at Yale." Cited as item 241.

*   Viale Ferrero, Mercedes. See Ferrero,
     Mercedes Viale.

CANTATAS

*   **E pur per mia sventura.** See item 113.

*   **Piangete occhi dolenti.** See item 113.

*   **Scritte con falso inganno.** See item 113.

*   **Tinte a note di sangue.** See item 113.

OPERAS

La Dirindina

*   Corte, Andrea della, ed. *Satire e grotteschi di
     musiche....* Cited as item 45 in Book I.

109. Degrada, Francesco. "Una sconosciuta
     esperienza teatrale di Domenico Scarlatti:
     La Dirindina." In *Memorie e contributi alla musica
     dal medioevo all'èta moderna. Offerti a Federico Ghisi nel
     settantesimo compleanno (1901-71).* Ed. by Giuseppe
     Vecchi. Bologna: Istituto di Filologia
     Latina e Medioevale, U. degli Studi di
     Bologna, 1971. Issued in *Quadrivium* 12
     (1971): 229-264.

     Detailed study of Domenico Scarlatti's only
     surviving comic theatrical work (with libretto
     by Girolamo Gigli): *La Dirindina "farsetta per musica"*
     written as an intermezzo to be performed with
     the composer's melodramma *L'Ambleto* during
     Carnival in Rome, 1715.   Illuminating
     discussion of the circumstances which
     prevented its performance and their
     implications, the work as a source of
     inspiration for many succeeding eighteenth-

century comic intermezzi, the polemics of
theatrical reform in the 1700s, and the new
relationship between music and text evident in
the work. See item 216 for Colin Timms'
review of Degrada's ed. (Milan: Ricordi,
1985). See also Section V, 1.

*   Pestelli, Giorgio. "L'opera musicale di
      Domenico Scarlatti." Cited as item 25.

Il Giustino

*   Sartori, Claudio. "Gli Scarlatti a Napoli."
      Cited as item 217 in Book I.

Irene

110. Termini, Olga. "*L'Irene* in Venice and Naples:
      Tyrant and Victim, or the *rifacimento* Process
      Examined." In *Antonio Caldara; Essays on His Life and
      Times*, pp. 365-407. Ed. by Brian Pritchard.
      Aldershot, Eng.: Scolar Press, 1987. App.:
      pp. 401-407.

An extensive discussion of the changes made
by Pollarolo (the composer of the original
Venice score) and Domenico Scarlatti for the
Naples performance. Maintains that some
changes were made to appeal to local tastes,
others to accommodate different singers, etc.

Narciso

*   Malinowski, Wladyslaw and Michal Bristiger.
      "O teatrze Królowej Marii Kazimiery,
      Domenico Scarlattim...." Cited as item 119.

111. McCredie, Andrew D. "Domenico Scarlatti and
      His Opera "Narciso." *Acta musicologica* 33

(1961): 19-29. Mus. exs.

The major article on this opera. Surveys
the sources and the differences between them,
the plot, style, and Roseingrave's additions.
Author groups it with the works of the "1st
Neopolitan school."

112. _____. "Domenico Scarlatti's *Narciso*." *Musical
     Times* 101 (1960): 700.

Full score identified by author in untitled
seventeenth- and eighteenth-century MSS in
Chrysander Collection, Hamburg State
University Library. First known complete
score of this early work. Brief description
of the MS and its history.

113. Sacher, Josephine Pettit. "Selected solo
     vocal music of Domenico Scarlatti (1685-
     1757)." Ed.D. Teachers College of Columbia
     University, 1966. iii and 197 pp. Bibl. 3
     apps. UMI order #66-10315.

Analyses of five arias from *Narciso*, of the
cantatas *V'adoro o luci belle* and *E pur per mia sventura*
and of three arias (one each) from the
cantatas *Scritte con falso inganno*, *Piangete occhi dolenti*,
and *Tinte a note di sangue*, as well as arias from the
Salve Regina. Includes edition of the music with
texts in the original and English translation,
and continuo realizations. Discusses
performance considerations and reconstruction
problems. Finds "many aspects of the style of
the music which recall the more familiar
sonatas."

Tetide in Sciro

114. Corte, Andrea Della. "*Tetide in Sciro*: l'opera di
     Domenico Scarlatti ritrovata." *Rassegna
     musicale* 27 (1957): 281-289.

Describes full score with recitatives found at Venice (Biblioteca del Convento San Francesco della Vigna) in 1953 by Terenzio Zardini who prepared an edition for a concert performance in 1956.

*   Della Corte, Andrea. See Corte, Andrea Della.

*   Malinowski, Wladyslaw, and Michal Bristiger. "O teatrze Królowej Marii Kazimiery, Domenico Scarlattim...." Cited as item 119.

115. Ochlewski, Tadeusz. "Opera Domenica Scarlattiego *Tetyda na Skyros*." *Ruch Muzyczny* 6/14 (1962): 25. In Polish.

Not seen.

116. Sierpinski, Zdzislaw. "*Tetyda* w Leopoldinie." *Ruch Muzyczny* 21/12 (1977): 2-3 and 8-9. In Polish.

A report on the performance of this opera in Wroclaw, Poland. Brief history of the rediscovery of the work, etc. List of performers and 2 photos of the performance included.

Tolomeo et Alessandro

117. Luciani, Sebastiano Arturo. "Un'opera inedita di Domenico Scarlatti." *Rivista musicale italiana* 48 (1946): 433-445.

Author discovered the first act of this opera in MS in what is the only music for this work known to survive (except for the overture found by Strohm; see item 119). Discusses its plot, characters, and settings in detail. Comments that it represents pre-Metastasian opera later thought to be inferior but to which Calzabigi's reforms returned.

118. Strohm, Reinhard. "Werkverzeichnisse:
     Domenico Scarlatti." In "Italienische
     Opernarien des frühen Settecento (1720-
     1730)" (item 221, Book I), p. 226.

     Supplements   Kirkpatrick's   catalog   of
     Domenico's works as published in the German
     2nd rev. ed. (Munich, 1972) of his book (see
     item 13). Strohm discovered a MS copy of the
     overture to *Tolomeo* (dated 1724) in the
     Bibliothèque Nationale, Paris.

SERENATAS

Il consiglio degli dei

119. Malinowski, Wladyslaw, and Bristiger, Michal.
     "O teatrze Królowej Marii Kazimiery,
     Domenico Scarlattim..." [Concerning the
     opera theater of Maria Casimira, queen of
     Poland; Domenico Scarlatti; and several
     other items]. *Ruch Muzyczny* 20/13 (1976): 2-
     6. Illus. In Polish.

     Discusses the opera theater of Maria
     Casimira in Rome and several works by D.
     Scarlatti, one of its chief composers,
     including the serenata *Il consiglio degli dei* the
     libretto of which was recently discovered
     though the music remains lost; the opera *Tetide
     in Sciro*, the fragments of which were discovered
     20 years previously and which were published
     by Panstwowe Wydawnictwo Naukowe; and the
     opera *Narciso*, which has been performed in
     Polish. Not seen. Abstract in *RILM* 1976
     #5394.

Contesa delle stagioni

*   De Venney, David. "The Choral Music of
       Domenico Scarlatti." Cited as item 95.

2. Keyboard Sonatas and Violin/Continuo Pieces

*   Alvarez Martínez, , Maria del Rosario. "Dos
     obras inéditas de Domenico Scarlatti."
     Cited as item 224.

*   Andriessen, Caecilia. "Notities bij de
     klaviermuziek van Domenico Scarlatti."
     Cited as item 205.

*   Baciero, Antonio, ed. "Siete Sonatas; una
     nueva fuente para el estudio y la obra de
     Domenico Scarlatti." Cited as item 226.

120. Basso. Alberto. "La formazione storica ed
     estetica della sonata di Domenico
     Scarlatti." Ph.D. dissertation, Univ. of
     Turin, 1957.

     Not seen.

121. Benton, Rita B. "Form in the Sonatas of
     Domenico Scarlatti." *Music Review* 13 (1952):
     264-273.

     An overview of the formal characteristics of
     all the Scarlatti sonatas with references to
     the editions of Longo, Newton (see Section V,
     2) and Oesterle (*Early Keyboard Music* 2. N.Y., G.
     Schirmer, 1904). Based on the author's M.A.
     thesis, State University of Iowa, 1951, 1v and
     127 pp. (item 122). Reveals that Scarlatti's
     key schemes were varied and did not fit into
     the categories propounded by some writers on
     the sonata form (e.g., R. O. Morris and W. H.
     Hadow).

122. _____. [*Form in the Sonatas of Domenico Scarlatti*].
     Rochester, N.Y.: Univ. of Rochester Press,
     1958. Microcard of Master's thesis.

123. Bogianckino, Massimo. *L'arte clavicembalista di Domenico Scarlatti*. Rome: De Santis, 1956. 83 pp. Bibl., 81-83. 45 mus. exs. *Harpisichord Music of Domenico Scarlatti*. Rome: De Santis, 1967. Eng. trans. by John Tickner. 138 pp. Bibl. pp. 133-138. New preface to the Eng. ed. by the author, pp. 9-10. Reviews in *Musica d'oggi* 1 (1958): 204-205 and *Rassegna Musicale* 27 (1957): 75-77.

Relates Scarlatti's life and the artistry of the keyboard works to the artistic, aesthetic, and sociological milieu. Emphasizes the differing influences that the Latin counter-reformation and the Protestant reformation had upon Scarlatti and the German composers (e.g., J.S. Bach), respectively. Translation awkward at times and text a bit wordy.

124. Bonucci, Rodolfo. "Le sonate per violino e cembalo di Domenico Scarlatti." *Studi musicali* 11 (1982): 249-259.

Analyses the 8 sonatas with figured bass from the Venice MS which have been regarded as keyboard works by some and violin works by others. Chiefly on the basis of numerous passages which illustrate violin techniques, the author narrows the number of sonatas actually intended for the violin to 4.

125. Cerulli-Irelli, Giuseppe. "Domenico Scarlatti ed i suoi trenta *Esercizi per gravicembalo* dedicati al Re Joao V di Portugallo." *Estudos italianos em Portugal* 4/37 (1974): 11-24.

A summary of Scarlatti's career in Portugal and Spain and the cultural milieu in which he worked, as well as a brief discussion of the *Essercizi*. Draws on previously published (known) material.

126. Chambure, Alain de. "Les formes des sonates; compléments   aux   analyses   de   Ralph

Kirkpatrick." In *Domenico Scarlatti: 13 récherches* (item 37), pp. 52-56.

Calls for further structural analysis of Scarlatti's sonatas utilizing the language and techniques of modern analysis. Departs from Kirkpatrick's analyses and concept of pairing and makes some additional suggestions for a system of analysis. Emphasizes the need to work on the correlations that might exist between the dominant characteristics and the particular characteristics of each sonata.

* Choi, Seunghyun. "Newly Found Eighteenth-Century Manuscripts of Domenico Scarlatti's Sonatas and Their Relationship to other Eighteenth and Early Nineteenth-Century Sources." Cited as item 229.

127. Dale, Kathleen. "Domenico Scarlatti: His Unique Contribution to Keyboard Literature." *Proceedings of the Royal Musical Association* 74 (1948): 33-44.

Text of a lecture-recital by Dale. Contains interesting comments on the sonatas (their diversity, style characteristics, possible influences, etc.). Author refers to specific sonatas to illustrate her points.

128. ____. "Hours with Domenico Scarlatti." *Music and Letters* 22 (1941): 115-122.

Author divides Scarlatti's keyboard opus (as represented in the Longo and Newton eds. (see Section V, 2) into 2 main categories: brilliant and expressive, and further subdivides them into various groups of which she gives "a few of the most representative" here and a "short table of reference...[to] enable a reader to find quickly, by number, the sonatas... belonging to any particular category." Subjective yet intelligent insights into the character of various sonatas

from the point of view of a performer and
member of the English cult.

*   De Chambure, Alain. See under Chambure, Alain
        de.

129. Doderer, Georg. "Algunos aspectos nuevos de
      la musica para clavecin en la corte Lisboeta
      de Juan V."   *Musica antiqua* (Cordoba) 8 (Mar.
      1987): 26-31. Bibl., cover port., illus.,
      mus. exs..

      Not seen.

130. Foster, Barbara Rainwater. "Dramatic Contrast
      in the Keyboard Sonatas of Domenico
      Scarlatti to 1746." D.M.A. dissertation,
      University of Illinois, 1970. 173 pp. UMI
      order #70-20, 965

      Examines and classifies the 93 sonatas
      written before 1746 (according to
      Kirkpatrick's chronology) on the basis of
      their use of dramatic or non-dramatic thematic
      contrast. Eight pieces characterized as
      dramatic show more contrast in keys, rhythms,
      thematic structure, character, etc. Author
      assumes that if dramatic contrast exists in
      the pre-1746 sonatas (as it does in the post-
      1746 repertoire), it can be regarded as one of
      Scarlatti's basic compositional procedures
      rather than a development of his late style.

131. Gerstenberg, Walter. *Die Klavier-Kompositionen
      Domenico Scarlattis*. (Forschungsbeitrage zur
      Musikwissenschaft, 22) Regensburg: Gustav
      Bosse, 1969. 2nd reprint of the 1st ed. of
      1933. 158 pp. Pp. 151-158: "Thematischer
      Katalog." Suppl., 22 pp. Review in *Organ
      Yearbook* 2 (1971): 105.

      First basic study of the Scarlatti sonatas
      and their MS sources (including the Parma set

unknown to Longo when he published his complete edition, 1906-1908). Classifies the sonatas according to three types: monothematic; those with more or less equal thematic groups; those in which a thematic group(s) is subordinated to another (others). Technical analyses included. See also item 246 and Section V, 2.

*   Gilbert, Kenneth. "Preface." In *D. Scarlatti Sonates*, Vol. 1, pp. vii-x. Cited as item 192.

*   _____. "Scarlatti et la France..." Cited as item 193.

132. Haas, Arthur. "La pratique de la modulation dans les sonates de Domenico Scarlatti." In *Domenico Scarlatti: 13 récherches* (item 37), pp. 57-62. Mus. exs.

Scarlatti's harmonic practice identified as the principal element of construction in the sonatas. Explores sections of extreme modulation from the diatonic harmony which basically dominates. Illustrative examples include K. 124, K. 518, K. 268. Relates Scarlatti's use of these extreme modulations to the *modulacion lenta* discussed by Soler in his *Llave de la modulacion* (1762).

133. Hashimoto, Eiji. "Domenico Scarlatti 1685-1757." *American Music Teacher* 28/6 (1979): 12-15.

A general introduction to the composer and his keyboard works with references to some of the works and suggestions regarding performance. A former Kirkpatrick student, he accepts his ideas on pairing, chronology, organology, etc. (For author's edition of selected sonatas, see Section V, 2).

134. _____. "Keyboard works of Domenico
     Scarlatti." *American Music Teacher* 35/1
     (Sept.-Oct. 1985): 14-15, 32.

     An introduction to the virtuoso techniques,
     harmony,   rhythms,   ornaments,   dynamics
     pertinent to the performance of the sonatas.
     Accepts Kirkpatrick's premise that over half
     the sonatas were written during the last 5
     years of the composer's life.

*   Hautus, Loek. "Beitrag zur Datierung der
     Klavierwerke Domenico Scarlattis." Cited as
     item 232.

135. _____. "Insistenz und doppelter Boden in den
     Sonaten Domenico Scarlattis." *Musiktheorie*
     2/2 (1987): 137-144.   Score.

     Not seen.

136. _____. "Insistenza e doppio fondo nelle
     sonate di Domenico Scarlatti." Forthcoming
     in *Chigiana* (item 33).

*   Hopkinson, Cecil. "Eighteenth-Century
     Editions of the Keyboard Compositions of
     Domenico Scarlatti." Cited as item 212.

*   Johnsson, Bengt. "Eine unbekannte Sonate von
     Domenico Scarlatti." Cited as item 234.

137. _____. "Omkring nyudgivelse af Scarlatti-
     sonater. *Dansk Musiktidsskrift* 61/1 (1986-
     7): 33.   Facs., mus., port.

     Not seen.

138. _____. "Romersk tastienstrumentmusik; det
     17. arhundrede. Studieri Vatikanbibliotekets

samlinger. [Roman Keyboard Music of the 17th Century. Studies of the Vatican Library Collections]." *Daansk Aarbog Musikforschung* 10 (1979): 5-66. In Danish with Eng. summary.

Examines and partially reorganizes the Vatican catalog of the collections of c.273 keyboard pieces (toccatas, ricercars, correntos, etc.) contained in Biblioteca Apostolica Vaticana Chigiana Q. IV 24-29 and Q. VIII 205-06, Barberini lat. 4288, and Vat. Mus. 569. Reveals the distinction made around the middle of the seventeenth century when these works were copied between organ and harpsichord style. Some pieces anticipate the Italian keyboard style of the late seventeenth- and early eighteenth-centuries as represented in the music of Pasquini and Domenico Scarlatti. Not seen. Abstract in *RILM* 1979 #4603.

139. _____. "Tre faser i klaviermusikkens stil og teknik: 1. De engelske virginalister 2. De franske clavecinister 3. Domeni Scarlatti." *Norsk Musiktidsskrift* 8/2,3,4 (June, Oct., Dec. 1971): 39-46; 93-99; 153-161.

Part 3 examines the question of the use of harpsichord or piano in the performance of Scarlatti's *Essercizi*. Studies characteristics of the keyboard style in relation to the instrument and examples of fingering found in texts and printed editions of the time. Not seen. Abstract in *RILM* [1971].

* Kastner, Macario Santiago. *The Interpretation of 16th and 17th Century Iberian Keyboard Music*. Cited as item 174.

140. Keller, Hermann. *Domenico Scarlatti ein Meister des Klaviers*. Leipzig: Peters, 1957. 95 pp. Mus. exs.

Examines the possible relationship between

the keyboard works of Domenico and Alessandro
Scarlatti, briefly discusses the life, MSS,
etc. Proposes a chronology similar to
Pestelli's. Study of the musical language.
Errors in information on editions noted in
Newman (see item 149, p. 264, notes 23 and 32)
who states that Keller's book "adds no new
material [to Kirkpatrick's] other than an
occasional difference of concept."

141. Kirkpatrick, Ralph. "Domenico Scarlatti's
     Early Keyboard Works." *Musical Quarterly* 37
     (1951): 145-160.

A detailed study of the pieces Kirkpatrick
considered early based upon dates of MS
copies, early printings, and stylistic
characteristics. Includes the *Essercizi* (1738)
and approximately 30 other pieces including 5
fugues and various sonatas. (Reprinted in
Kirkpatrick's *Domenico Scarlatti* [1953], item 13,
pp. 145-161, without the three introductory
pages and footnotes, but with the Kirkpatrick
nos. and Longo nos. in parentheses).

142. _____. "Domenico Scarlatti's Harmony."
     The Score 5 (1951): 33-52, and 6 (1952): 44-
     52.

Major study. Includes discussion of
alterations by Longo. Essentially the same as
pp. 207-233 and 233-241 in Kirkpatrick's book
(item 13); however, the latter includes new
discussions of Scarlatti's sonatas in relation
to equal temperament and Soler's treatise on
modulation. Article includes footnotes
omitted in book and uses Longo nos. instead
of K. nos.

143. Klimovickij, Abram. " The Rise and Development
     of Sonata Form in the Work of Domenico
     Scarlatti." M.A. dissertation. Leningrad
     Conservatory, 1972. 137 pp. In Russian.

Discussion of Scarlatti's sonatas in terms of their national character, the influence of particular genres, their themes, harmonies, instrumental style, texture, etc., and the 2 movement and 3 movement formal types. Not seen. Abstract in *RILM* 73 #340.

144. Lindley, Mark. "Tecnica della tastiera e articolazione: testimonianze della practica esecutiva di Scarlatti, Bach,.. Handel." *Nuova rivista musicale italiana* 19 (1985): 20-61.

Article based on item 175.

* _____. "Keyboard Technique and Articulation: Evidence for the Performance Practices of Bach, Handel and Scarlatti." Cited as item 175.

* Lippmann, Friedrich. "Sulle composizioni per cembalo di Gaetano Greco." Cited as item 73.

145. Longo, Alessandro. "Domenico Scarlatti." *L'arte pianistica* 1/8 (Apr. 15, 1914): 1-3.

Discussion of Scarlatti's keyboard works in relation to those of J.S. Bach, Clementi, the French school, etc. Author gives his perceptions of Scarlatti's unique contributions to the sonata and to keyboard technique. Sees nothing similar to Scarlatti's use of virtuosic effects in earlier composers' works (see Siccardi, item 164, for a different view). The biographical details cannot, of course, be relied upon at this early date.

146. Longyear, Rey M. "Binary Variants of Early Classic Sonata Form." *Journal of Music Theory* 13/2 (winter 1969): 162-185.

Studies binary structures in the sonatas of,

among others, Domenico Scarlatti.

147. Luciani, Sebastiano Arturo. "Domenico
     Scarlatti creatore del sinfonismo." *Musica
     d'oggi* 8/2 (1926): 43-44.

     Author sees the continuous dialogue and
     opposition of parts in Scarlatti's keyboard
     pieces as being at the heart of modern
     symphonic style and maintains that, in view of
     this, his importance, not only as a
     harpsichord composer but as a creator of the
     dramatic symphonic style, must be
     acknowledged.

*   Maxwell, Carolyn, ed. *Scarlatti: Solo Piano Literature*.
     Cited as item 178.

148. Moroni, Federico. "Il settecento clavicemba-
     listico italiano e suoi rapporti con il
     movimento musicale europeo." M.A. disserta-
     tion. U. Cattolica del Sacro Cuore, Milan,
     1977. 283 pp.

     Studies style of Italian harpsichord compo-
     sers and results of their interaction with
     eighteenth-century composers of other European
     countries. Contains detailed analyses of
     Longo nos. 1, 6, 27, 338, 415, 422, 428 and
     495. Not seen. Abstract in *RILM* 1977 #470.

149. Newman, William S. *The Sonata in the Classic Era*.
     Chapel Hill: University of North Carolina
     Press, 1963. 3rd ed, 1983.

     Pages 258-288 give an excellent summary and
     evaluation of previous studies and editions of
     the composer's works and a lucid presentation
     of the author's ideas about the composer's
     style.

150. Okrainec, Inna. "Instrumentalizm kak faktor

stilja i formoobrazovanija." *Sovetskaia Musyka*
7 (Jul. 1980): 103-109. Illus., mus. exs.

"Analyzes the functional links between
Domenico Scarlatti's compositional style and
his keyboard techniques. Includes discussion
of texture, expressive content and technique
from point of view of Baroque aesthetics...."
Abstract in *RILM* 1980 #2728.

151. Pagano, Roberto. "Piena utilizzazione delle
dieci dita, o una singolare applicazione
practica della parabola dei talenti."
Forthcoming in *Chigiana* (item 33).

Discusses Scarlatti in the context of
European stylistic awareness and change.

152. Pannain, Guido. "L'arte pianistica di
Domenico Scarlatti." *Studi musicali* 1 (1972):
133-145. Mus. exs.

Emphasizes that in Scarlatti's sonatas the
technique is one with and inseparable from the
composer's musical conception, and discusses
his "pianistic" style.

153. _____. "Scarlatti junior e la sonata." In
Scritti in onore di Luigi Ronga, pp. 511-513. Milan
and Naples: Riccardo Ricciardi, 1973.

A much abbreviated version of item 152 with
slightly different wording.

154. Pestelli, Giorgio. "Bach, Handel, Domenico
Scarlatti and the Toccata of the Late
Baroque." In *Tercentenary Essays....* (item 45),
pp.277-291.

Scarlatti's Sonata K. 85 is discussed and
characterized; it contains 49 bars of
perpetual motion and departs from the more
typical binary form with a central cadence in

the dominant. The style is at least in a
fragmentary way similar to that of virtuosic
Italian violin music of the Baroque period.

155. _____. "Il mito di Domenico Scarlatti
nella cultura italiana del novecento."
Quaderni della Rassegna musicale 3 (1965):
101-123.

A major review article which examines the
attitudes about Domenico Scarlatti and his
sonatas held and promoted by authors and
musicians (especially Italian) during the
twentieth century (from the early years
through the Futurist period to the present.)

156. _____. *Le Sonate di Domenico Scarlatti; proposta di un
ordinamento cronologico* (Archeologia e storia
dell'arte, 2) Turin: Giappichelli, 1967.
294 pp. Bibl., name index and index to
sonatas with page references.

One of the two most important studies of
Scarlatti's sonatas since Kirkpatrick's book.
Author attempts to establish the approximate
chronology of the sonatas based on the style
of the pieces in the Spanish MS copies made
during Scarlatti's lifetime rather than by
means of the chronology of the MSS (as
Kirkpatrick did) since the latter bear the
dates of copying, not of composition, of the
individual sonatas. Longo edition rather
than the MSS or films of the MSS used as the
basis for this study. Only 1 of the sonatas
in Longo's edition is rejected as falsely
attributed; sonatas author believes to be by
Scarlatti from early and recent printed
editions and other MS sources he discovered
included. See Section V, "Thematic Catalogs"
for a discussion of Pestelli's catalog, which
appears in this book. Reviews: *Music and Letters*
49 (1968): 183-187; *Rivista italiana di musicologia* 3
(1968): 198-200.

157. Rousset, Christophe.   "Approche statistique
     des sonates."   In *Domenico Scarlatti: 13
     récherches* (item 37), pp. 68-87.   Notes, 5
     apps.

     Author (who stresses that he is a performer,
     not a musicologist and that his paper is
     directed primarily to other performers)
     attempts to make an inventory of
     characteristics found in Scarlatti's sonatas
     and through the aid of statistics to "give a
     new complexion to the problems" that confront
     those who strive to better understand the
     composer's works. Appendices group the sonatas
     according to: 1) those for which pairing or
     grouping in three movements is effective and
     those which are clearly single movements; 2)
     range (corresponding to the ranges of the
     various *clavecins*); 3) types of ornaments which
     occur; 4) degree of difficulty; and 5) nature
     of the difficulty.

158. Salter, Lionel.   "Scarlatti's Violin Sonatas."
     The Listener (London) (1947): 116.

     Author discusses 8 sonatas in the Venice MS
     in which he sees a different style and which
     were copied out with bowing indications and
     figured basses in the manner of violin pieces
     with harpsichord accompaniment.   Points out
     that Avison based his string arrangements of
     Scarlatti's sonatas solely on these and, thus,
     was probably aware that these pieces were
     intended for a stringed instrument, a fact
     which made his task easier.   Mentions the
     first BBC broadcast of a performance of all
     the violin pieces.

159. Schachter, Carl.   "Rhythm and Linear Analysis:
     Aspects of Meter."   *Music Forum* 6 (1987): 1-
     59.   Diag., mus. ex.

     Pages 45-49 analyse Scarlatti's Sonata K. 78
     (L. 75), a minuet.

160. Schenker, Heinrich. *Das Meisterwerk in der Musik*.
     Munich: Drei Masken Verlag, A.G., 1925-30.
     3 vols. Reprint: Hildesheim: G. Olms, 1974.
     Vol. 1: trans. into English and ed. by I.
     Bent as "Essays from *Das Meisterwerk*, vol. 1
     (1925)." *Music Analysis* (Oxford) 5 (1986):
     151-185.

     Vol. 1 contains an analysis of Scarlatti's
     Sonatas in D minor (L. 413) and G major (L.
     486).

161. Sheveloff, Joel Leonard. "The Keyboard Music
     of Domenico Scarlatti: A Re-evaluation of
     the Present State of Knowledge in the Light
     of the Sources." Ph.D. dissertation.
     Brandeis University, 1970. 3 vols. 688 pp.
     List of works, thematic catalog, mus. exs.,
     bibl., index.

     One of the most significant studies of the
     keyboard music since Kirkpatrick's book. The
     author has reexamined the original sources,
     called into doubt the authenticity of 39
     works, examined the accuracy and editorial
     policies of extant major editions, questioned
     the   credibility   of   Kirkpatrick's   and
     Pestelli's   chronologies,   and   explored
     questions of performance practice (pairing,
     performance on the harpsichord vs. other
     keyboard instruments, improvisation etc.).
     Major examination of the characteristics of
     form, harmony, phrase structure and style.
     Review by W. S. Newman: *Piano Quarterly* (fall
     1972): 19-20.

*   _____. "Domenico Scarlatti: Tercentenary
     Frustrations." [Part I]. Cited as item 44.

162. _____. "Uncertainties in Scarlatti's
     Musical Language." Forthcoming in *Chigiana*
     (item 33).

     Examines "elements of imbalance" or "the

ways in which supposedly parallel places do
not function or behave in parallel manners" in
Scarlatti's keyboard sonatas. (See item 44,
Pt. 2, p. 103).

163. Siccardi, Honorio M. *Domenico Scarlatti a
     traves de sus sonatas*. Buenos Aires, 1945. 100 pp.

     Not seen.

164. _____. "Los sonatas de Scarlatti."
     Revista musical chilena (Nov.-Dec. 1945): 16-18.

     Points out that Scarlatti's predecessors
     including Rameau and other French clavecinists
     used certain keyboard techniques in their
     compositions much before Scarlatti though
     various writers have claimed they were
     Scarlatti's innovations.

165. Tagliavini, Luigi Ferdinando. "Remarks on the
     Compositions for Organ of Domenico
     Scarlatti." In *Tercentenary Essays...* (item
     45), pp. 321-325.

     Discusses the Sonatas Kk287-288 for organ as
     well as Kk328 (comments on type of organ and
     registration probably used) and states that
     Kk254-55 are probably not for organ [as Loek
     Hautus' edition indicates].

166. Talbot, Michael. "Spostamenti fra maggiore e
     minore nelle sonate di Domenico Scarlatti."
     Forthcoming in *Chigiana* (item 33).

*   Timbrell, Charles. "A Look at Recent
     Scarlatti Editions." Cited as item 215.

167. Unger, James Dale. "Domenico Scarlatti: The
     Methods and Incidence of Preparation for the
     Tonal Plateau, the Crux, and the Apex."
     Ph.D. dissertation. Univ. of Port

Elizabeth, 1976. 468 pp.

Examines 575 sonatas and the varied means
Scarlatti used to emphasize the onset of
contrasting tonal and thematic areas. Not
seen. Abstract in *RILM*.

168. Valabrega, Cesare. *Il clavicembelista Domenico Scarlatti,
      il suo secolo, la sua opera*. Modena: Guanda, 1937.
      2nd ed. rev.: Parma: Guanda, 1955. 224 pp.
      Bibl.: pp. 215-216; discog.: 217-218.

The first major study of Scarlatti's
keyboard works in Italian. Part One gives
cultural background including a discussion of
the instrumental reforms of the Neopolitan
composers, the literature, music, etc.
Analyzes Scarlatti's keyboard pieces in terms
of technique, rhythm, and harmony. Viewpoint
influenced by Futurist interpretations of the
composer in vogue in Italy when the book first
written. Review by Eric Blom in *Music and Letters*
18 (1937): 421-423.

169. Valenti, Fernando. *The Harpsichord: a Dialogue for
      Beginners*. Hackensack, N.J.: Jerona Music
      Corp., 1982. 92 pp.

Final chapter (10): "Music of Domenico
Scarlatti, Twenty Questions," pp. 77-92, is an
insightful commentary on the composer's
technical and stylistic innovations; also
includes performance suggestions by one of the
twentieth century's foremost Scarlatti
interpreters.

170. Williams, Peter. "*Figurae* in the Keyboard
      Works of Scarlatti, Handel and Bach: An
      Introduction." In *Tercentenary Essays* (item 45),
      327-346.

Examines types of motives in keyboard music
of the three composers and considers the
question of whether the works illustrate the

"rules" of the theorists (mainly German).
Considers whether performance of similar types
of motives should be the same for the three and
states that any hypothetical chronology of the
Scarlatti   Sonatas   should   take   into
consideration some analysis of his use of
figurae.

*   _____. "Harpsichord Acciaccatura: Theory
      and Practice in Harmony, 1650-1750." Cited
      as item 184.

III

PERFORMANCE BACKGROUND

1. Performance Practice

Teaching and Interpretation

171. Anfuso, Nella. "La vocalité italienne au temps de Scarlatti." In *Domenico Scarlatti: 13 récherches* (item 37), pp. 112-118. Notes.

Discussion of the "golden age" of Italian singing as reflected in treatises from Maffei (mid-sixteenth century) to Mancini (end of the eighteenth century). Emphasis on modern performers' lack of understanding of the vocal techniques and characteristics of the period (e.g., equality and homogeneity of ranges, understanding of and skill in implementing ornamentation and improvisation, vocal suppleness, etc.). Calls for singers to recreate the performance style of the epoch.

172. Avison, Charles. *An Essay on Musical Expression*. (London: C. Davis, 1752. 2nd ed., 1753). Facs. of 1753 ed.: N.Y.: Broude Bros., [1967] (Monuments of Music and Music Literature in Facsimile, 2nd series, 55) *Essay....*, 152 pp.; "Letter to Author", 43 pp.; "Mr. Avison's Reply", 53 pp.

Valuable source of information regarding mid-eighteenth-century music printed in England and the then prevalent ideas on the function of music (criticized by Burney, Hawkins, et al.). The author was the composer/arranger of twelve well-known string concertos (1744) based on a number of Scarlatti sonatas. Fundamental source for Avison's ideas on performance methods.

* Brown, Howard Mayer and Stanley Sadie, eds. *Performance Practice*. 2 vols. Cited as item 338 in Book I.

* Donington, Robert. *The Interpretation of Early Music*. (New Version). Cited as item 362 in Book I.

* _____. "A Problem of Inequality." Cited as item 364 in Book I.

173. Fuller, David. "The Dotted Style in Bach, Handel and Scarlatti." In *Bach, Handel, Scarlatti Tercentenary Essays* (item 45), pp. 99-117. Ed. by Peter Williams.

   Article explores the question of "what persistent dotting meant to the three composers" and whether the French overture or practice of *notes inegales* influenced them. Useful comparison of variant versions of some sonatas, e.g., Kk 8.

* Gasparini, Francesco. *The Practical Harmonist at the Harpsichord*. Cited as item 368 in Book I.

* Gilbert, Kenneth. "Preface." Cited as item 192.

* _____. "Scarlatti e la France..." Cited as item 193.

* Jackson, Roland. *Performance Practice, Medieval to Contemporary: A Bibliographic Guide*. Cited as item 339 in Book I.

174. Kastner, Macario Santiago. *The Interpretation of 16th and 17th Century Iberian Keyboard Music* (Monographs in Musicology, 4) Trans. of "Interpretación de la música hispana para

tecla de los siglos XVI y XVIIo."
Stuyvesant, N.Y.: Pendragon Press, 1987.
ISBN 0 918728 53 3.

Interesting background on the performance
practice of keyboard music in Spain and
Portugal in the centuries preceding
Scarlatti's compositions by one of the leading
Hispanicists and specialists on Iberian music
of the present century.

*   Lindley, Mark. "An Introduction to Alessandro
Scarlatti's *Toccata prima*." Cited as item 319
in Book I.

175. _____. "Keyboard Technique and Articulation:
Evidence for the Performance Practices of
Bach, Handel and Scarlatti." In *Bach, Handel,
Scarlatti Tercentenary Essays* (item 45), pp. 207-243.
Ed. by Peter Williams.

A discussion of the fingering most practical
in the performance of Domenico and Alessandro
Scarlatti's keyboard pieces. Concludes that
the fingering of the period more adaptable
than fingerings based on general principles.
Alessandro Scarlatti's *Toccata prima* composed
c1720 of unique value because fingerings given
throughout.

176. Lister, Craig L. George. "Traditions of
Keyboard Technique from 1650 to 1750."
Ph.D. dissertation. University of North
Carolina, Chapel Hill, 1979. 362 pp. App.
UMI order #8005051

Compares and contrasts treatises written for
clavier players during the period. Includes
original texts and English translations of
relevant sections on keyboard instruction
including a number not available in other
secondary sources. Contains an annotated
bibliography of primary sources including "all
currently known sources on keyboard technique

prior to 1750" with references to English
translations and modern commentaries.

177. MacClintock, Carol.   *Readings in the History of Music in
     Performance*.   Bloomington, Indiana: Indiana
     University Press, 1979.   xii and 432 pp.
     Mus. exs.   ISBN 0 253 14495 7.

     Part IV contains the author's translations
     of selections from eighteenth- and early
     nineteenth-century writings relevant to the
     history of performance.   Includes excerpts
     from Burney, de Brosses, Geminiani, Quantz,
     and Avison, among others.   No index.

178. Maxwell, Carolyn, ed.   *Scarlatti: Solo Piano Literature*.
     Boulder, CO.: Maxwell Music Evaluation,
     1985.   ii and 410 pp.   Bibl., apps. (5).

     A guide for piano teachers based on the
     Kalmus reprint of the "complete" Longo
     edition (cited because of its more reasonable
     price and wider availability).   Includes
     remarks concerning the musical and technical
     requirements of each sonata.   Grades them
     according to difficulty; gives metronome and
     tempo markings (from the Kalmus reprint) and
     the number of measures for each piece. Lists
     approximately 15 other modern editions for
     each sonata, excluding Gilbert's complete
     edition (cited at the end) and Fadini's (for
     which see Section V, 2 of this book).

   * Neumann, Frederick.   *Essays in Performance Practice*.
     Cited in Book I as item 376.

179. _____.   *Ornamentation in Baroque and Post-Baroque
     Music*.   3rd ed.   Princeton: Princeton
     University Press, 1983.   630 pp.

     Author criticizes the rigidity that has
     dominated Baroque performance practice, for
     example, in the insistence upon beginning

trills on the upper note (Putnam Aldrich, Ralph Kirkpatrick.) Documents French, Italian, and German approaches to one-note graces, slides, trills, compound trills, mordents, and "other small ornaments" as well as free ornamentation. Emphasis on J.S. Bach.

180. Newman, William S. "Four Baroque Keyboard Practices and What Became of Them." *Piano Quarterly* 33 (1985): 19-25.

Discusses certain aspects of the following four keyboard practices: the use of non-legato as the "normal" touch; use of terrace dynamics; use of upper notes as the usual starting notes in trills; and use of poetic feet as guides to expressive rhythmic grouping. Revision of the keynote address prepared for the tercentenary celebration of Bach, Handel, and Scarlatti at Sweet Briar College, Virginia.

*   Pagano, Roberto. "Piena utilizzazione delle dieci dita, o una singolare applicazione pratica della parabola dei talenti." Cited as item 151.

181. Parkins, Robert. "Keyboard Fingering in Early Spanish Sources." *Early Music* 11 (1983): 323-331.

Interesting article on keyboard fingering in an earlier period as discussed by 6 Spanish writers from Juan Bermudo to Pablo Nassarre.

*   *Performance Practice Review*. Vol. 1- 1988- Cited as item 340 in Book I.

182. Petrov, Jurij. "On the Cyclic Principle of Performing Domenico Scarlatti's Sonatas." In Alekseev, Aleksandr, comp. *Sovremennye voprosy muzykal'nogo ispolnitel'stva i pedagogiki* (Sbornik

trudov, 26)   [Contemporary problems in
performance practice and pedagogy.
Transactions, 26]   Moscow: Gosudarstvennyi
muzykal'no-pedagogiceskij institut imemi
Gnesinyh, 1976. 224 pp. Mus. exs., index.
In Russ.

Not seen.

183. Schenkman, Walter. "Rhythmic Patterns of the
     Baroque, I and II." *Bach* 5/3-4 (July, Oct.
     1974): 21-28 and 9-16, respectively.

     Proposes that certain recurrent rhythmic
     patterns in Baroque music form a
     characteristic structure and suggests
     particular ways of interpreting music by
     composers of the period including Scarlatti.
     Selections from his sonatas are examined from
     this standpoint.

*   Sheveloff, Joel. "Domenico Scarlatti:
     Tercentenary Frustrations." Cited as item
     44.

*   Tagliavini, Luigi Ferdinando. "L'armonico
     pratico al cimbalo." Cited as item 380 in
     Book I.

184. Williams, Peter. "Harpsichord Acciaccatura:
     Theory and Practice in Harmony, 1650-1750."
     Musical Quarterly 54 (1968): 505-523.

     Pages 518ff. cite various sonatas by
     Scarlatti as examples of the "percussive use
     of acciaccatura."

Instruments

185. Badura-Skoda, Eva. "Domenico Scarlatti und
     das Hammerklavier." *Österreichisches Musikzeitung*
     40 (1985): 524-529.

Includes a discussion of Scarlatti's awareness of the new pianoforte as early as his sixteenth year, reasons for Kirkpatrick's negative comments regarding performance of the sonatas on the piano rather than the harpsichord, various factors which lead more recent researchers to believe that some of the sonatas were intended for the pianoforte, the necessity of learning more about the eighteenth-century pianos appropriate for a performance of his music and the need to build accurate restorations of these.

186. Boalch, Donald Howard. *Makers of the Harpsichord and Clavichord, 1440-1840.* Oxford: Clarendon Press, 1974. xxi and 225 pp. Plates, illus., bibl., index.

A dictionary of harpsichord and clavichord makers for the period with locations of surviving instruments. Contains a list of the chief collections of early keyboard instruments and their catalogs. Includes name of Giovanni Ferrini who supposedly made a pianoforte for Farinelli.

187. Bordas Ibáñez, Cristina. "Instrumentos españoles de los siglos XVII y XVIII en el Museo del Pueblo Español de Madrid." *Revista de musicología* 7/2 (1984): 301-333. Apps., illus. (photos).

Describes some of the instruments of major interest in the Museo including two fortepianos, one by Juan del Marmol of Seville dated 1784 and one by a nineteenth-century maker, Ferrer. Gives biographical information on the makers in the notes and describes the instruments.

188. Doderer, Georg. "Osservazioni sul temperamento degli strumento a tastiera nel Portogallo del XVIII secolo." Forthcoming in *Chigiana* (item 33).

189. Dowd, William. "Le clavecin de Domenico
     Scarlatti." In *Domenico Scarlatti: 13 récherches*
     (item 37), pp. 88-95. Notes.

     Attempt   by   a   noted   twentieth-century
     harpsichord builder to discover what types of
     keyboard instruments Scarlatti knew and used.
     Describes the technical characteristics of a
     number of keyboards including five eighteenth-
     century   instruments   which   survive   at   the
     Conservatoire National of Lisbon and two
     others which resemble them.   Also discusses
     the almost total absence of surviving Spanish
     keyboards and the consequent lack of knowledge
     about   them.   Points   out   that   most   modern
     harpsichords   are   constructed   on   eighteenth-
     century French models and suggests performing
     Scarlatti   on   such   keyboards   may   not   be
     inappropriate since Maria Barbara herself
     played on similar instruments as evidenced by
     a   portrait   in   the   Hermitage   depicting   a
     concert at the Spanish court painted by Louis
     Michel Van Loo, an artist known for his
     attention to details.

190. Fabbri, Mario. "Nuova luce sull'attivita
     fiorentina di Giacomo Antonio Perti,
     Bartolomeo Cristofori e Giorgio F. Handel;
     valore storico e critico di una *Memoria* di
     Francesco M. Mannucci." Subsection: "Il
     primo pianoforte di Bartolomeo Cristofori."
     Chigiana (n.s. 1) 21 (1964): 162-172.

     Discusses   references   to   Cristofori   in
     Francesco Mannucci's diary.   Shows that
     Cristofori had already begun construction of
     the first pianoforte which he called *Arpicimbalo
     che fà il piano e forte* in 1698 and that it was
     finished and in the Medici family's inventory
     by 1700, a year before Domenico visited there
     with his father.

191. Gai, Vinicio.   *Gli strumenti musicale della corte Medicea e
     il museo del Conservatorio Luigi Cherubini di Firenze*.
     Florence: Licosa, 1969.

Publishes the 1700 Medici instrument inventory which includes the first Cristofori pianoforte.

192. Gilbert, Kenneth. "Preface." In *Domenico Scarlatti Sonates*, vol. 1, vii-x (Eng. version). See also Section V, 2.

Discusses editorial policy, instruments, ornaments, Spanish elements, and Kirkpatrick's catalog (which the author believes gives "a rational account of the sources as they have survived to our time" though he feels that the problems of chronology and style should be considered completely separately). Unlike Boyd (item 64), Gilbert views Jane Clark's ideas regarding the influence of Spanish folk music (see, 'for example, items 64-65) as "brilliantly argued."

193. _____. "Scarlatti et la France; postface pour l'édition du tricentennaire." In *Domenico Scarlatti: 13 récherches* (item 37), pp. 119-124. Notes.

A reduced version of the "Preface" to Gilbert's Scarlatti edition (see item 192).

194. Harding, Rosamund Evelyn Mary. "The Earliest Pianoforte Music." *Music and Letters* 13 (1932): 194-199.

Describes Giustini's *Sonate da Cimbalo di piano e forte....* Translates excerpts from Maffei's *Giornale* (1711) regarding Cristofori's new fortepiano.

195. _____. *The Piano-forte; Its History Traced to the Great Exhibition of 1851.* Cambridge, Eng.: Cambridge University Press, 1933. xviii and 432 pp.

Includes the original and English translation of Maffei's description of Cristofori's new pianoforte. Frontispiece is a photo of the Cristofori pianoforte built in 1726 which survives in Leipzig. Also gives Maffei's diagram of the Cristofori action and a page of the first known piano music by Giustini (see item 194).

196. Howell, Almonte. "Organos, Organeros and Organistas of Spain During the Scarlatti Years." *American Organist* (Dec. 1985): 91-97.

Informative, detailed discussion of music thought to be for organ by Domenico Scarlatti and of the characteristics of eighteenth-century Spanish organs.

197. Hubbard, Frank. *Three Centuries of Harpsichord Making*. Cambridge, MA: Harvard University Press, 1965. 373 pp. and 41 pl., each with page of notes appended. ISBN 0 674 888 45 6.

Major study of harpsichord making in Italy, Flanders, France, England, and Germany. Based on contemporary documents, some of which are translated and presented in part as appendices. Includes descriptions of instruments, technical processes, and instrument workship inventories. Glossary, pp. 351-363. Bibl. 343-349.

198. Pascual, Beryl Kenyon de. "Diego Fernandez-- Harpsichord-Maker to the Spanish Royal Family from 1722 to 1775--and His Nephew Julian Fernandez." *Galpin Society Journal* 38 (Apr. 1985): 35-47.

Brief biographical information about Diego "one of the few eighteenth-century Portuguese harpsichord makers known by name" and tuner/builder during three reigns to various Spanish royal families including Maria Barbara's. Information regarding the instruments he built or rebuilt from documentary records. Appendices 43-46 include possibly Spanish-built instruments in the inventory of Maria Barbara.

199. _____. "Harpsichords, Clavichords and
     Similar Instruments in Madrid in the Second
     Half of the Eighteenth Century." *Royal Musical
     Association, London. Research Chronicle* 18 (1982): 66-
     84.

     Information on and scholarly discussion of
     harpsichords, clavichords, and hybrid keyboard
     instruments of Spanish or foreign manufacture
     advertised in the Madrid daily newspaper from
     Feb. 1758-Dec. 1799.   2 appendices include
     selected descriptions of the instruments from
     the paper. Brief but useful bibliography.

200. Pollens, Stewart. "The Early Portuguese
     Piano." *Early Music* 13 (1985): 18-27.

     Important study of the early Portuguese
     piano; comparison with the instruments of
     Cristofori (1720), whose design it was modeled
     after. The fact that the earliest known music
     written specifically for piano (Lodovico
     Giustini's sonatas) was dedicated to Don
     Antonio of Portugal and that there were 5
     pianos in Maria Barbara's 1758 instrument
     inventory indicates that Scarlatti must have
     been acquainted with the piano.

201. Russell, Raymond. *The Harpsichord and the Clavichord*.
     2nd ed. rev. by Howard Schott. N.Y.: W. W.
     Norton, [1973].   208 pp.   Illus., plates,
     app., bibl.

     Appendix I contains documents from the
     Medici files including the 1716 musical
     instrument inventory, Appendix 18, an English
     translation of Queen Maria Barbara's inventory
     of musical instruments (given in the original
     Spanish in Kirkpatrick's book [see item 13]).
     See also Sheveloff (item 44, Pt. 2) for that
     author's English translation of the latter
     inventory.

202. Schott, Howard. "From Harpsichord to
     Pianoforte." *Early Music* 13 (1985): 28-38.

     A chronological summary of the "principal
     events in the history of the rise of the
     pianoforte" and of less significant events
     which assume greater importance within the
     total context. Suggests that performers
     interchanged keyboard instruments far more
     frequently than present day musicologists
     think and poses some interesting questions.
     Pascual challenges his conclusion that there
     were no Spanish makers of the pianoforte
     before the late 1780s in *Early Music* 13 (1985):
     469-470.

*   Sheveloff, Joel. "Domenico Scarlatti:
     Tercentenary Frustrations." Cited as item
     44.

203. Sloane, Carl. "A Note on Scarlatti's
     Harpsichord Temperament." *Diapason* 79/4
     (1988): 15.

     Suggests that Scarlatti used a "somewhat
     different temperament than those used by his
     contemporaries" perhaps based on Werckmeister,
     a temperament of North German origin which he
     may have learned from Handel. (Ref. to Andrea
     Werckmeister's *Musikalische Temperatur* (1691).
     Reprint, Utrecht: Diapason Press, 1983).

204. Tiella, Marco. "Simbolo e strumento." In
     *Domenico Scarlatti. I grandi centenari dell'anno europeo della
     musica* (item 36), pp. 153-188.

     Author has identified in the characteristics
     of the keyboard instrument a symbol and
     unifying element of European musical thought
     in the seventeenth and eighteenth centuries.
     Includes a discussion of the keyboard
     instruments with which Domenico may have been
     familiar, with an emphasis on the Medici
     collection. Discusses the friendship between

Giovanni Casini (from 1708 chapelmaster for
the Grand Princess Violante and organist for
Grand Duke Cosimo III) and Alessandro
Scarlatti. Notes the use in Florence of a
chromatic-enharmonic keyboard instrument based
on the plans of Nicola Vicentino during the
period when Alessandro and Domenico Scarlatti
visited there.

2. Editions

* Allorto, Riccardo. "Clementi non ha plagiato
  Scarlatti." Cited as item 62.

205. Andriessen, Caecilia. "Notities bij de
     klaviermuziek van Domenico Scarlatti." *Mens
     en Melodie* 11/6 (1956): 181-184. Mus. exs.

     Discusses tempo markings in the sonata MSS
     at the Biblioteca Marciana, Venice, and
     compares them with the treatment in various
     published editions.

206. Banowetz, Joseph. "A Close Look at Scarlatti
     Sonatas." *Clavier* 17/8 (1978): 18-19, 19-
     24. Pages 21-24, author's ed. of
     Scarlatti's Sonata in F# minor, K.447.

     Comments on the early editions (von Bülow,
     Tausig, von Sauer, etc.) and their distortions
     of Scarlatti's original text. Criticizes the
     11v. Longo edition which added, deleted, and
     changed notes. Also comments on Kirkpatrick's
     facsimile edition, the Gilbert set and the
     Hermann Keller and Wilhelm Weismann edition of
     150 sonatas. Interpretive suggestions for
     Performance of K. 447 (L. 294) on the piano.
     Errs in assumption that all of the *Sonatas*
     written originally for the harpsichord (no one
     can know this with absolute certainty) and in
     suggestion that C. P. E. Bach's idea that it
     is useful to sing instrumental melodies to
     understand how they should be rendered is
     pertinent to the performance of Scarlatti's

keyboard works.

*   Benton, Rita B. "Form in the Sonatas of
     Domenico Scarlatti." Cited as item 121.

207. Crowder, Louis L. "Domenico Scarlatti, Some
     Facts, Some Opinions, and a Belated Book
     Review." *Clavier* 4/1 (1965): 16-20.

     Written in a popular vein; contains a
     summary review of editions of the keyboard
     sonatas from Clementi to Weismann-Keller
     (1956). Criticizes Kirkpatrick's belief that
     all trills must begin on the upper note. Never
     identifies the problem of establishing the
     chronology of the sonatas, apparently
     accepting Kirkpatrick's hypothesis that the
     copy dates are acceptable indications of
     composition dates.

208. Daw, Stephen. "Muzio Clementi as an Original
     Advocate, Collector and Performer, in
     Particular of J.S. Bach and Domenico
     Scarlatti." In *Bach, Handel, Scarlatti
     Tercentenary Essays* (item 45), pp. 61-74.
     Ed. by Peter Williams.

     Includes a calendar of Clementi's
     performances, including those of the music of
     Domenico Scarlatti. Comments on Clementi's
     edition of Scarlatti sonatas. An objective,
     appreciative study of Clementi's advocacy of
     these composers.

209. Dent, Edward J. "Randbemerkungen zu Domenico
     Scarlatti." *Der Auftakt* (1922): 325-328

     Criticizes the early keyboard editions
     (Longo, von Bülow, Tausig), discusses the MSS
     known to the author (including those in Vienna
     bequeathed by Brahms). Believes that
     Scarlatti composed over a wide period for
     diverse keyboard instruments. Includes

discussion of the keyboard ranges represented
in the works.

210. Hautus, Loek. "Zu dem Domenico Scarlatti
     zugeschriebenen *Capriccio fugato a dodici*." *Die
     Musikforschung* 24 (1971): 294-295.

     Discusses a work published by Paul Winter
     (Cologne, 1969) and attributed to Domenico
     Scarlatti. Doubts authorship. Identifies as
     originally a sacred vocal work for 2 choirs,
     strings, and continuo.

211. Hopkinson, Cecil.   "Domenico Scarlatti--a
     Postcript to the Eighteenth-Century Editions
     of the Keyboard Compositions...." *Brio* 7/1
     (1970): 9-10.

     Supplements   the   author's   earlier   article
     (item 212) with newly discovered information
     and responds to Ralph Kirkpatrick's criticism
     (in item 13) of that study.

212. _____. "Eighteenth-Century Editions of
     the Keyboard Compositions of Domenico
     Scarlatti." *Edinburgh Bibliographical Society.
     Transactions* 3/1 (1952): 47-71. "Volumes
     Consisting Entirely of Works by Scarlatti
     (arranged chronologically)," pp. 58-66;
     "Volumes Consisting Partly of Works by
     Scarlatti," pp. 67-68; "Thematic Index of
     Sonatas Attributed to Scarlatti and
     Unidentified by the Present Writer," p. 69;
     and "Table Showing the First Appearances of
     the Different Sonatas," pp. 70-71.

     Major   bibliographical   study   of   c27
     eighteenth-century   editions   of   Scarlatti's
     sonatas published in various countries, among
     which 8 appeared in France, 6 with the imprint
     of Boivin and the two Le Clercs (Jean and
     Charles Nicolas). Detailed investigation of
     the possible dating of these including a
     discussion of the problems resulting from a

lack of specific information in publishers'
catalogs, etc.

*   Kirkpatrick, Ralph. "Scarlatti Revisited in
       Parma and Venice." Cited as item 235.

213. Newton, Richard. "The English Cult of
     Domenico Scarlatti." *Music and Letters* 20
     (1939): 138-156.

     A major review of Scarlatti's advocates,
     MSS, and editions in England during the
     eighteenth century. Important article though
     it must be used with caution as the author's
     conclusions often based on sources and methods
     now generally discredited.

214. Schott, Howard. "Early Music for
     Harpsichord." *Early Music* 4 (1976): 27-30.

     A critical review article which examines
     available modern editions of eighteenth-
     century harpsichord music by major composers
     including Domenico Scarlatti.

*   Sheveloff, Joel. "The Keyboard Music of
       Domenico Scarlatti...." Cited as item 161.

*   _____. "Domenico Scarlatti: Tercentenary
       Frustrations." Cited as item 44.

215. Timbrell, Charles. "A Look at Recent
     Scarlatti Editions." *Piano Quarterly* No.
     131 (1985): 54-56.

     Critical examination of, among others, the
     Gilbert, Fadini, Hashimoto, Balla, Kite, and
     Valenti editions of the Scarlatti sonatas.

216. Timms, Colin. [Review of Domenico Scarlatti's

La Dirindina, score ed. by F. Degrada (Milan: Ricordi, 1985)]. *Early Music* 14 (1986): 99, 101.

Brief discussion of this first edition which is based upon the only known surviving MS of the work thought, until recently, to be lost. Notes the importance of the work as a prototype for other operas which satirize the opera and musical life of the times. Praises the edition for the most part but is critical of some of Degrada's decisions regarding the assignment of voice types to certain roles. Notes premiere performance in autumn 1968 in Naples [presumably based on a then-unpublished edition by Degrada].

217. Tonegutti, Marta. "La fortuna de Domenico Scarlatti nell'Ottocento. Da Clementi a Longo." Ph.D. dissertation. Università degli Studi, Venice, 1986-1987. 2 vols. 560 pp. Texts, mus. exs.

Not seen.

3. Modern Performances

Domenico Scarlatti's most popular keyboard sonatas have been performed and recorded many times; however, they represent only a small part of the total opus (c.555). In the eighteenth century his works were especially admired in England where Thomas Roseingrave revised, published, and directed performances of various compositions (including the *Essercizi* and the opera *Narciso*). He had his advocates in the nineteenth century as well (Clementi, Czerny, Brahms, etc.), though Schumann could not abide him.

While in the latter century the sonatas were performed on the piano using editions now discredited, by the mid-1930s Wanda Landowska had performed and recorded some of them on the harpsichord, the instrument for which many, if not most, of the sonatas were intended (although to this day we don't know much about the actual instruments used by the Spanish court; it appears that a number of different types of harpsichords and early pianos were used). Though overshadowed in the 300th anniversary year of his birth (1985) by festivals featuring the works of his more famous contemporaries Bach and Handel, performances of the Scarlatti sonatas were undoubtedly quite numerous. Notable events included the issuance of the first recording of all (555) of the sonatas (performed by Scott Ross), and an eight-hour "Scarlatti Saturday" held in Symphony Space, New York City, on the composer's birthday in which (among other works) the sonatas were played by some 25 keyboard artists.

The vocal compositions, especially the secular works, have not fared as well. With few exceptions they have not been heard since the eighteenth century until several revivals in the recent tercentenary year. Ralph Kirkpatrick viewed them for the most part as inferior and lacking interest. A new assessment of these works made possible in part by the rediscovery of some of the scores previously thought to be lost has led to a greater appreciation of the composer's vocal works and provided some new insights into the relationship between certain of them and the keyboard pieces.

What follows is a selection of reviews of some of the most important recent performances of Domenico Scarlatti's music based in part on citations given in the *Music Index*. References have also been made to various articles or announcements which note additional performances held in conjunction with conferences celebrating the tercentenary of the composer's birth.

Performance Reviews

Festival Performances (Various)

NEW YORK

218. Page, Tim. "A Scarlatti Birthday Bash." *New York Times*, July 28, 1985, p. 17, 23.

    Announcement and description of the plans for the 8-hour Scarlatti tribute "Scarlatti Saturday: the Top 100," to be held in New York's Symphony Space. Program produced by Sara Fishko and Teresa Sterne and hosted by Fernando Valenti.

219. Porter, Andrew. ["Concert Review"]. *New Yorker* 61 (Nov. 11, 1985): 137-139.

    Includes a discussion of the 8-hour-long free concert held on Oct. 26, 1985, at Symphony Space in New York City to celebrate the composer's birth. The program was broadcast on WNYC. Participants performed many of the sonatas (Porter indicates c. 90) on various keyboard instruments including a modern Steinway piano, two harpsichords (a Franco-Flemish model built by William Dowd and an Italian type built by Carl Fudge), as well as a Yamaha synthesizer. Among them were Valenti, Brewer, Tilney, and Cooper, harpsichordists; Ivan Davis, R. Taub, pianists; and John Van Buskirk, who performed on the synthesizer.

SIENA

*   Sheveloff, Joel. "Domenico Scarlatti: Tercentenary Frustrations." Cited as item 44.

    Pt. 2, note 114 mentions vocal performances based on editions of Degrada at the Siena conference (see item 33 for proceedings).

Choral Music

*Messa de Arà

nzazu in D major*

* Alonso-Gomez, Miguel. "La Messe en ré majeur
  pour choeurs et orchestre dite de Aránzazu."
  Cited as item 90.

* Petech, Diana. "Notiziario: Il Convegno di
  Nizza su Domenico Scarlatti." Cited as item
  41.

Stabat Mater

* Casella, Alfredo. "Le musiche vocali e
  strumentali." Cited as item 94.

Operas

La Dirindina

220. Reininghaus, F.   "Hinter den *Suendenfall* der
     bürgerlichen Musik zurück? Aus Anlass des
     Scarlatti-Festes in Berlin." *Neue Zeitschrift für
     Musikwissenschaft* 10 (1985): 4-7. Illus., port.

     Review of the first performance in German of
     this comic intermezzo.

221. Tellini, Enrico. "Naples." *Opera (Eng.)* 36
     (1985): 1024-1025.

     Reviews a performance on May 18 staged by
     the San Carlo in the Sannazzaro Theatre,
     Naples. Produced by Roberto De Simone, with
     Antonella Manotti in the title role, Andrea
     Snarsky as Don Carissimo, and Daniela
     Mazzuccato and Max-Rene Cosotti as Liscione.
     A filmed parody of *Ambleto* (the *opera seria* with
     which *La Dirindina* was originally intended to be
     performed) was inserted as an intermezzo   in
     this performance.

* Timms, Colin. [Review of Domenico Scarlatti's
  La Dirindina]. Cited as item 216.

Mentions premiere of this work which took place in autumn 1968 in Naples (presumably based on a then-unpublished edition by Francesco Degrada). Riccardo Muti conducted at the 11th *Autunno Musicale Napoletano*.

Narciso

* Malinowski, Wladyslaw, and Bristiger, Michal. "O teatrze Królowej Marii Kazimiery, Domenico Scarlattim..." Cited as item 119.

222. Molina-Foix, V. "Scarlatti to Hindemith (1985-86 Season)." *Opera (Eng.)* 37 (1986): 700-701.

Review of the Clemencic Consort's performance of this work at the Teatro la Zarzuela, Madrid in conjunction with Madrid's Autumn Festival. Clemencic's revision used the title but not the additional music of Thomas Roseingrave (who produced the work in 1720 in London, Haymarket). Countertenor, Gerard Lesne.

223. Stegemann, Michael. "Sucht mich nicht wo ich nicht bin: Internationales Musikfest und Internationaler Musikwissenschaftlicher Kongress in Stuttgart." *Neue Zeitschrift für Musikwissenschaft* 11 (1985): 33. Port.

Tetide in Sciro

* Corte, Andrea Della. "*Tetide in Sciro*: l'opera di Domenico Scarlatti ritrovata." Cited as item 114.

* Sierpinski, Zdzislaw. "*Tetyda* w Leopoldinie." Cited as item 116.

Sonatas for Keyboard (or Violin and Continuo)

* Domenico Scarlatti Foundation. [Information about performances of the composer's music

scheduled to be performed on Oct. 21-27,
1985 sponsored by the Foundation]. Cited as
item 35.

Performances   by   the   Concertgebouw   of
Amsterdam and the Sweelinck Conservatory. All
the sonatas performed on both harpsichord and
piano.   Workshops,   lectures,   and   special
concerts (including the Avison arrangements)
scheduled.

*   Palmer, Larry. "In search of Scarlatti."
      Cited as item 40 in Book I.

*   Porter, Andrew. ["Concert Review"]. Cited as
      item 219.

*   Salter, Lionel. "Scarlatti's Violin Sonatas."
      The Listener (London) (1947): 116. Cited as
      item 158.

IV

SOURCES

It is well known that no autograph MSS of Domenico Scarlatti's keyboard pieces have yet been found, if indeed, any exist. The primary sources for the majority of his sonatas are contained in two MS copies brought back to Italy from Spain in 1759 by Farinelli. At least one was compiled for Queen Maria Barbara, his employer. The two sets are now located in Venice (Biblioteca Nazionale Marciana MSS 9770-84) and Parma (Conservatorio Arrigo Boito MSS AG 31406-20). Most editions of the sonatas (including Longo's complete edition (1906-8) and Gilbert's (1971-84) are based on the former MS as is Kirkpatrick's numbering of the sonatas; however, recently Joel Sheveloff in a exhaustive examination of the sources (item 161) found evidence that led him to believe that the Parma MS was the earlier, and therefore, more reliable of the two sources.

Two other important collections of the sonatas, both incorporating part of the private library of the Roman collector Fortunato Santini (b. 1778-d. 1861), are located in Münster (Diözesan-Bibliothek) and Vienna (Gesellschaft der Musikfreunde MSS VII 28011/A-F; MS VII 28011/G). The Vienna volumes were once owned by Johannes Brahms who made a thematic index for each of them. In 1971 Eva Badura-Skoda discovered 12 overlooked MSS volumes of the sonatas in the same collection. Of these, 11 volumes (MSS Q.15112-20, Q.11432 and Q.15126) containing 98 individual sonatas by D. Scarlatti have been studied by Seunghyun Choi (item 229). Their contents are summarized by Boyd (item 3, p. 152) in his excellent overview and evaluation of all the extant sources.

Locations of other works in MS by
Domenico Scarlatti are cited most recently by
Boyd (in item 3, pp. 253-264 and p. 272).
Published catalogs exist for some of these
libraries (see Vincent Duckles' and Michael
Keller's *Music Reference and Research Materials: An
Annotated Bibliography*, 4th ed. (N.Y.: Schirmer
Books, 1988). The latter book also describes
other reference tools helpful in identifying
MSS and early editions.

Descriptive Articles

224. Alvarez Martínez, Maria del Rosario. "Dos
     obras inéditas de Domenico Scarlatti."
     Revista de musicologia 8 (1985): 51-56.

     Author describes the private collection in
     Tenerife (Canary Islands) which contains 2
     previously unknown eighteenth-century keyboard
     works attributed to Domenico: a sonata and a
     fandango. Article includes facsimiles of the
     incipit of the sonata and the first page of
     the fandango. Both have been published in an
     edition by the author (see Section V, 1).
     Boyd (item 3) agrees with Kastner, that the
     sonata (in G) is by Seixas, not Scarlatti.

225. Alvini, Laura. "Les certitudes ambiguës;
     Farinelli et les manuscrits italiens des
     Sonates." In *Domenico Scarlatti: 13 récherches* (item
     37), pp. 36-42. Notes.

     Attempts to trace the MSS of Scarlatti in
     Farinelli's possession which were "lost" and,
     thus, unknown to Kirkpatrick. Author believes
     it is possible that the missing 3rd MS book
     exists today as the collection of 7 sonatas
     bound (in a modern binding) with a ballet of
     Gluck in the Naples Conservatory Library.

226. Baciero, Antonio, ed. "Siete Sonatas; una nueva fuente para el estudio y la obra de Domenico Scarlatti." In *Nueva biblioteca española de musica de teclado*, 3, pp. ix-x. Madrid, 1978.

Discusses the MS located in Valladolid, Metropolitan Cathedral which contains 9 sonatas by Scarlatti including 3 previously unknown sonatas (in G, d, and A) which Baciero attributes to Scarlatti. Boyd catagorizes these as doubtful works (item 3, p. 191).

227. Badura-Skoda, Eva. "Il significato dei manoscritti scarlattiani recentemente scoperti a Vienna." Forthcoming in *Chigiana* (item 33).

Reports on the latest status of the sources evaluated in Choi's thesis (item 229).

228. Boyd, Malcolm. "Scarlatti Sonatas in Some Recently Discovered Spanish Sources." Forthcoming in *Chigiana* (item 33).

An important new study of sources; discoveries seem to corroborate the arguments of those who disagree with Kirkpatrick's ideas on pairing.

229. Choi, Seunghyun. "Newly Found Eighteenth-Century Manuscripts of Domenico Scarlatti's Sonatas and their Relationship to other Eighteenth- and Early Nineteenth-Century Sources." Ph.D. dissertation. University of Wisconsin, Madison, 1974. xi and 221 pp. Apps., bibl. UMI order #74-26, 484.

An important, careful study of the 12 previously unknown MS volumes of Domenico Scarlatti's sonatas discovered by Eva Badura-Skoda in the Gesellschaft der Musikfreunde, Vienna. Purpose was to learn whether any "stem directly from sources other than the known Parma and Venezia MSS; whether textual

deviations...may be ...authentic versions,"
and to resolve questions of the provenance of
the MSS and their relationship to Vienna and
early Viennese printed editions.

230. Fadini, Emilia. "Hypothèse à propos de
     l'ordre des sonates dans les manuscrits
     vénitiens." In *Domenico Scarlatti: 13 récherches*
     (item 37), pp. 43-51. Mus. exs., notes.

     Critique of the two major arguments for a
     chronology of Scarlatti's sonatas, those of
     Kirkpatrick based on MS copy dates and those
     of Sheveloff based on organology. Concludes
     that no really certain chronology is possible
     and that attempts to arrive at one limit the
     creative options which should always be open
     to performing artists.

231. _____. "Problemi e osservazioni sulla grafia
     scarlattiana." Forthcoming in *Chigiana* (item
     33).

*   Gerstenberg, Walter. *Die Klavier-Kompositionen
     Domenico Scarlattis*. Cited as item 131.

232. Hautus, Loek. "Beitrag zur Datierung der
     Klavierwerke Domenico Scarlattis." *Die
     Musikforschung* 26 (1973): 59-61.

     Concludes that there are grounds for the
     assumption that the Sonatas K 31 and 32 were
     composed before 1714. Not seen. Abstract in
     RILM.

*   Hopkinson, Cecil. "Eighteenth-Century
     Editions of the Keyboard Compositions of
     Domenico Scarlatti." Cited as item 212.

*   _____. "Domenico Scarlatti--a Post-

script..." Cited as item 211.

233. Jaenecke, Joachim. *Die Musikbibliothek des Ludwig Freiherrn von Pretlack (1716-1781)*. Wiesbaden: Breitkopf & Hartel, 1973. 330 pp. (Neue musikgeschictliche Forschungen, 8) Reprint of Ph.D. dissertation, Univ. of Frankfurt am Main, 1973. ISBN 3 7651 0072 2.

Describes the discovery in 1968 of a library established between 1740 and 1770 by Freiherr von Pretlack (for a time an envoy of Maria Theresa of Austria to the Russian court at St. Petersburg) in a castle in Hessen and its transfer to the Staatsbibliothek Preussischer Kulturbesitz in Berlin (West) where it now resides. Contained 727 fascicles in MS and 25 printed works with a total of 1000 pieces by 143 composers including 2 MSS with a total of 19 sonatas attributed to Domenico Scarlatti, and a "Capriccio" in C (incipit given; MS burnt). Not among the 555 sonatas cited in Kirkpatrick's thematic catalog; see item 13) and 18 Sonatas (g, d, g, d, c, d, G, G, B flat, D, c, D, A, f#, b, E, D, g) as well as a number of opera arias, several duets, and a ballet by Giuseppe Scarlatti (1718-1777). Study includes a partial thematic catalog, genealogy of the von Pretlack family, discussion and identification of repertory, unica, paper, watermarks, etc., a description of the MSS and information on copyists, singers, composers, etc. The copyist of Scarlatti's sonatas is identified as K 1 whom Friedrich Noack has classified as the Darmstadt copyist of the second half of the eighteenth century (see Jaenecke, p. 55).

234. Johnsson, Bengt. "Eine unbekannte Sonate von Domenico Scarlatti." *Die Musikforschung* 34 (1981): 309-310.

Discusses a Toccata (probably an eighteenth-century copy) bearing the name Scarlatti found in the archives of the singing school

Escolania in the Benedictine Cloister of Mon-
serrat. The Toccata, in the key of C major, is
not included in Longo's *Opere complete*.... Author
identifies 8 types of motives found in
Scarlatti's sonatas which are also present in
this piece and which, he concludes, clearly
mark it as a composition by Domenico.

235. Kirkpatrick, Ralph. "Scarlatti Revisited in
     Parma and Venice." *Music Library Association. Notes*
     28 (1971): 5-15.

     Account of problems the author encountered
     in the preparation of his facsimile edition of
     the complete sonatas: decay of the MSS,
     difficulty in obtaining legible microfilms,
     problems of access and bureaucracy in Italian
     libraries, etc.

236. _____. "Who Wrote the Scarlatti
     Sonatas? A Study in Reverse Scholarship."
     Music Library Association. Notes 29 (1973): 426-431.

     Advances the thesis (in an ironic manner)
     that Maria Barbara actually composed the
     Scarlatti keyboard sonatas. Illustrates the
     questions and problems that result from the
     total lack of autograph MSS and sparse
     information about Scarlatti's performances,
     etc. Intended to ridicule critics of the
     author's theory that Scarlatti wrote the
     majority of his sonatas in the last five years
     of his life.

237. Luciani, Sebastiano Arturo. "Alla scoperta
     degli autografi di Domenico Scarlatti."
     Archivi (Rome) ser.3, anno 2 (1935): 298-304.

     Discusses the style of handwriting in the
     known autographs (a letter to the Duke of Alba
     and a *Miserere*) and makes the hypothesis based
     on a study of three MS volumes now in the
     Naples Conservatory Library of arias by the
     composer and other contemporaries that the

latter were copies in his hand. Author also proposes that Scarlatti copied some parts from Pergolesi's cantatas and was influenced by them; he cites the resemblance of an aria from Scarlatti's cantata *Dire non voglio* to Pergolesi's aria "Stizzoso mio stizzoso."

*   McKay, Elizabeth. "Brahms and Scarlatti." Cited as item 74.

238. Mondolfi, Arnoldo. "I manoscritti napoletani di Domenico Scarlatti." *Gazzetta Musicale di Napoli* (Mar. 1957).

Not seen.

*   Newton, Richard. The English Cult of Domenico Scarlatti." Cited as item 213.

239. Pestelli, Giorgio. "Contributo per un ordinamento cronologico delle sonate di Domenico Scarlatti." In *Studi di musicologia in onore di Guglielmo Barblan in occasione del LX compleanno* (Historiae Musica Cultores-Biblioteca; Collectanea Historiae Musicae, 4).

Discusses the possibility that Scarlatti wrote some sonatas before the end of his life which appeared in MSS in Italy. Evidence in two MSS of Milan, Giuseppe Verdi Conservatory L. 22.1 - L. 22.9 and L. 24.35, which contain keyboard pieces of Alessandro Scarlatti. Noseda R. 11.4 contains a fugue attributed to Alessandro which is identical to one of Domenico (K. 41). In the Noseda MS it appears as "Andante in re minore." MS Noseda L. 22.8 contains a Toccata in A major which seems, on the basis of style, to be composed by Domenico.

*   _____. *Le Sonate di Domenico Scarlatti; proposta di un ordinamento cronologico*. Cited as item 156.

240. Rey, Juan José. "Manuscritos de música para
      tecla en la Biblioteca del Conservatorio de
      Madrid." *Revista de musicologia* 1 (1978): 221–
      233.

      Bemoans the dreadful state of preservation
      and access to manuscripts in this major
      library and discusses the reasons. Provides
      (pp. 224–233) a catalog of the library's
      keyboard manuscripts, some of which contain
      works by Domenico Scarlatti, Antonio Soler,
      and Sebastián de Albero.

*   Sheveloff, Joel Leonard. "Domenico Scarlatti:
      Tercentenary Frustrations." Cited as item
      44.

*   _____. "The Keyboard Music of Domenico
      Scarlatti: A Reevaluation of the Present
      State of Knowledge in the Light of the
      Sources." Cited as item 161.

*   Simi Bonini, Eleonora. "L'attività degli
      Scarlatti nella Basilica Liberiana." Cited
      as item 103.

*   Strohm, Reinhard. "Italienischen Opernarien
      des frühen Settecento (1720–1730)." Cited
      as item 118.

241. _____. "Scarlattiana at Yale." In *Handel e gli
      Scarlatti a Roma* (item 38), pp. 113–152.

      Pages 113–118 discuss the Domenico Scarlatti
      papers (among which are transcriptions,
      photographic reproductions of sources, etc.)
      donated to the Yale University School of
      Music's John H. Jackson Library in 1976 by
      Ralph Kirkpatrick along with several
      eighteenth-century editions including the
      Essercizi. Page 143 notes a mid-eighteenth-
      century German MS copy of the composer's

"Cat's Fugue" in the Rinck Collection at Yale.

242. Terrayova-Dokulilova, Maria Jana. "Ein
     Dokument zur Geschichte der Orgelmusik in
     der 2. Halfte des 18 Jahrhunderts
     (Sammelhandschrift A XII/220-MS Martin)."
     Sbornik praci fil. fak. Brnenske university 16 (1967):
     107-128.

     Discussion of a MS compiled in 1803-1820
which includes works by Domenico Scarlatti as
well as   W. F. Bach, Handel, many Viennese-
oriented composers and Benedek Istvanffy
(1733-1788). Reflects the musical culture of
the Franciscan monasteries in western Slovakia
during the period. Not seen. Abstract in
RILM.

V

MODERN EDITIONS OR FACSIMILES

This section begins with a selected bibliography of published worklists and catalogs relevant to Domenico Scarlatti; only those considered to have historical importance or to be the most complete, detailed, and/or up to date are included.

Following this is a list of Domenico Scarlatti's compositions. This worklist does not cite Scarlatti's surviving manuscripts or early (eighteenth-century) printed editions with their locations since this task has been admirably accomplished already by Joel Sheveloff (items 161 and 27) and Malcolm Boyd (items 3 and 27). Nor does it include nineteenth-century keyboard editions. For an exhaustive discussion of these, see Sheveloff (item 161). Rather, its purpose is to identify a greater number of modern (primarily twentieth-century) editions of the composer's works than were included in the above-mentioned sources, thereby providing a useful tool for those who seek more recent published scores for study or performance.

The numerous straightforward arrangements that exist of the keyboard works (for guitar, etc.) have been excluded. Their number, variety of types, and greatly disparate quality create problems of control which exceed the scope of this guide. For a discussion of some significant arrangements in which Scarlatti's music has been "recreated" to a greater extent, see the discussion by Boyd in item 3, "Appendix I." All "complete" editions of the keyboard works are included here but only selected editions of the many extant partial collections.

Selected Bibliography of Worklists and Catalogs

Worklists

243. Boyd, Malcolm. "List of Compositions" (Appendix IV). In *Domenico Scarlatti--Master of Music* (item 3), pp. 253-275.

   The most up to date, accurate, and inclusive catalog of the composer's works published to date. Cites the serenata "Le nozze di Baco e d'Arianna" (unidentified by title in *NGIBM*). The list of keyboard works is a useful tool for identifying the sonatas; provides a list by K. (Kirkpatrick) numbers with the keys and corresponding Longo, Fadini, and Pestelli catalog numbers. Cites works not included in Kirkpatrick's catalog with MS locations as well as the 3 major "complete" editions, and gives a cross index from Longo nos. to K. nos.

244. Kirkpatrick, Ralph. "Keyboard Works" (App. V); "Vocal Works" (App. VI); and "Miscellaneous, Doubtful, and Spurious Works" (App. VII). In the author's *Domenico Scarlatti* [Princeton, 1983], (item 13), pp. 399-428.

245. Sheveloff, Joel (with Malcolm Boyd). "Domenico Scarlatti: Works." In *NGIBM* (item 27), pp. 351-361.

Thematic Catalogs

*   Brook, Barry. *Thematic Catalogs in Music*. Cited as item 444 in Book I.

Keyboard Works

246. Gerstenberg, Walter. "Thematischer Katalog:
     (Quellennachweise s. S. 31 und S. 35f.)"
     [12 sonatas]. In *Die Klavierkompositionen Domenico
     Scarlattis* (item 131), pp. 151-158.

     Contains theme of a Sonata in C
     (Gerstenberg, no. 2; tempo 3/8) not cited in
     Kirkpatrick's catalog but, apparently, the
     same as the "Capriccio" in C cited in
     Jaenecke's catalog of the von Pretlack
     collection (item 233).

247. Kirkpatrick, Ralph, comp. "Catalogo delle
     sonate di Scarlatti in ordine
     approssimativamente cronologico con
     riferimenti alle fonti principali." In
     Kirkpatrick's *Domenico Scarlatti*, Italian ed.,
     (item 13), pp. 445-459.

     A complete thematic catalog of the 555
     sonatas in Kirkpatrick's catalog (not included
     in the American edition and its revisions) in
     order of K. number with references to the
     principal manuscript sources and the Longo,
     Fadini and Kirkpatrick (*60 Sonatas*) editions.
     See Section V, 2.

248. Longo, Alessandro. *Indice tematico (in ordine di tonalità
     e di ritmo) delle sonate per clavicembalo contenute nella
     raccolta completa riveduta da ... Longo e nelle altre
     pubblicazioni della casa editrice G. Ricordi & c..* Milan:
     Ricordi, 1937. vii and 36 pp.

249. _____. "Tavole tematiche." In the
     introductory pages of each volume of the
     complete edition cited in Section V, 2.

     Each volume contains the themes for the
     sonatas contained in that volume.

Individual Catalogs of Scarlatti's Keyboard Works

*   Boyd, Malcolm. "Keyboard Works." In "List of
        Compositions" (App. IV). Cited as item 243.

250. Kirkpatrick, Ralph.   "Catalogue of Scarlatti
     Sonatas and Table of Principal Sources in
     Approximately Chronological Order."   In
     Domenico Scarlatti (item 13), pp. 442-456.
     [Princeton, 1983].

     List in K. no. order with references to the
     author's edition of *Sixty Sonatas*; key, time
     and tempo; primary sources (including the
     Parma, Münster, and Vienna MSS); and source
     notes.

*   Longo, Alessandro. See items 248 and 249.
        See also the "Table of Sonatas in the Order
        of Longo's Edition" in Kirkpatrick, item 13,
        pp. 457-459 for a concordance of the Longo
        numbers with the K. numbers.

251. Pestelli, Giorgio. ["Catalogo"]. In *Le sonate di
     Domenico Scarlatti* (item 156), pp. 105-265.

     Book contains within its text Pestelli's
     catalog in which the sonatas are placed in an
     approximately chronological order on the basis
     of style and assigned numbers referred to in
     the literature as P. or Pestelli nos.   They
     are cited in tables which give the
     corresponding Boivin ed. nos., the Longo and
     Kirkpatrick nos., and the principal sources
     for each sonata.   559 sonatas are identified,
     4 more than in Kirkpatrick's catalog. K. 95
     was excluded as Scarlatti's authorship was
     rejected.   Pestelli's analysis was based
     primarily on the Longo complete edition.

252. Sheveloff, Joel.   "Scarlatti Source Control."
     In item 44, Pt. 1, pp. 410-413.

List of manuscripts, eighteenth-century publications, nineteenth- and twentieth-century publications of keyboard music; also identifies works which are "certain, likely, doubtful, spurious, and melo-bass."

Domenico Scarlatti Worklist

1. Vocal Music

CHAMBER CANTATAS

A chi nacque infelice [sop. with pianoforte]. Revisione e elaborazione di Lino Bianchi. Milan: Ricordi, 1958. 8 pp.

Ah, sei troppo infelice [sop. with pianoforte]. Revisione e elaborazione di Lino Bianchi. Milan: Ricordi, 1958. 9 pp.

Amenissimi prati, fiorite piagge. Ed. by Loek Hautus. Cologne: Gerig, 1971.

Pur nel sonno almen tal'ora [sop. with 2 violins and basso continuo]. Trascrizione, revisione e realizzazione del basso di Lino Bianchi. Rome: Edizioni de Santis, 1963. Score. 36 pp.

Selve, caverne e monti [sop. with basso continuo]. Ed. by Loek Hautus. Kassel: Bärenreiter, 1973. 10 pp. and parts (Concerto vocale) 10 pp. and parts. Bärenreiter #6456.

OPERAS

La Dirindina, farsetta. Ed. by Francesco Degrada. Milan: G. Ricordi, 1985 (Intermezzi del settecento) Review by Colin Timms in *Early Music* 14 (1986): 99 and 101.

Tetide in Sciro, selections.   Ed. by Tadeusza
Ochlewskiego.   Cracow: Polskie Wydawn.
Muzyczne, [1963-66].

_____. *Tetyda na Skyros; opera, 2 tercety i duet na
glosy, wiolonczele i klawesyn* (Florilegium musicae
antiquae, 5)   [1963].   score, 23 pp.   Unfig.
bass realized for hpschd. Contains: "Vorrebbe
dal tuo cor," "Amando tacendo," and "Lasciami
piangere."

_____. *Tetyda na Skyros; opera: 8 arii Tetydy na
sopran, skrzypce, wiolonczele i klawesyn* (Florilegium
musicae antiquae, 6) [1964].   score, 37 pp.
and 5 parts. Unfig. bass realized for hpschd.

_____. *Tetyda na Skyros; opera, 5 arii Antiopy na
sopran, skrzypce (flety), wiolonczele i Klawesyn*
(Florilegium musicae antiquae, 7)   [1964].
Score, 30 pp. and 2 parts. Bass realized.

_____. *Tetyda na Skyros; opera. 3 arie Deidamii na
mezzosopran, skrzypee, wielenezele i klawesyn.*   [1965]
(Florilegium musicae antiquae, 8)   Score, 20
pp. and parts.   Contains: "Per credere,"
"Credimi o core," "Io credea." Bass realized.

_____. *Tetyda na Skyros; opera, 7 arii Achillesa na
tenor, skrzypce, wiolonczele i klawesyn.*   [1966]
(Florilegium musicae antiquae, 9)   Score, 43
pp. and parts. Bass realized.

_____. *Tetyda na Skyros;... [Zwei Arien des
Lykomedes].*   [1966]   (Florilegium musicae
antiquae, 10)   Score, 22 pp. and parts.

Sinfonias

Geoffroy-Dechaume, A., ed. *17 Sinfonie.* Paris:
1974. Issued in single fascicles with parts.
[Based on MS Bibliothèque du Conservatoire,
Res. 2634].

Meylan, Raymond, ed. *Drei Sinfonien, für Oboe, Streicher und Cembalo*. Munich: F. E. C. Leuckart, 1969. Score, 28 pp. (Alte Musik für verschiedene Instrumente, 38) [Ed. from MS Cat. Rés. 2634, Nos. 12, 15 and 10 at the B.N., Paris and from the overture to *Narciso* printed in London by Walsh in 1720 which is identical to the first sinfonia].

SACRED MUSIC

*Capriccio fugato a dodici. Arr. by Francis Baines. London and N.Y.: Schott, [c1971]. Score, 9 pp. and parts.

―――――――――――――――. Ed. and harmonization of basso continuo by Paul Winter. Cologne: H. Gerig, 1969. Score, 8 pp. and 15 parts. Edition Gerig 678.

Kirkpatrick believed this piece to be by Durante, but Hautus (see item 210) defended Scarlatti's authorship.

Cibavit eos in F major [SATB a capella]. Forthc. Stuttgart: Carus Verlag (Domenico Scarlatti Musica Sacra. Gesamtausgabe, 2).

Iste confessor. In *Musica sacra*, 3. Milan: 1879.

――――――― in G major. For SATB, Org. Forthc. Stuttgart: Carus Verlag. (*Domenico Scarlatti Musica Sacra. Gesamtausgabe*, 2).

Laetatus sum , Psalm 121 in D major. For SA, SATB, Org. Forthc. Stuttgart: Carus Verlag. (*Domenico Scarlatti Musica Sacra. Gesamtausgabe*, 2).

Magnificat in d minor. For SATB, Org. Forthc. Stuttgart: Carus Verlag. (*Domenico Scarlatti Musica*

Sacra. Gesamtausgabe, 1).

Miserere in e minor. Psalm 50. For SATB. Forthc. Stuttgart: Carus Verlag. (*Domenico Scarlatti Musica Sacra. Gesamtausgabe,* 2).

Miserere in g minor. Psalm 50. For SATB. Forthc. Stuttgart: Carus Verlag. (*Domenico Scarlatti Musica Sacra. Gesamtausgabe,* 2).

Missa breve "La stella." Mass in a minor for 4 voices ... ripieno and basso continuo. Ed. by Eleonora Simi-Bonini. (Studi musicale romani, 3). Rome: Pro Musica Studium, 1985. Score, 58 pp.

The first edition of this work.

————————————. *Messe in A für vierstimmigen gemischten Chor mit Generalbass und Ripienochor....* Ed. by Günther Massenkeil. Frankfurt: Peters, 1987. ii, score, 39 pp. and parts. Review in *Music Library Association. Notes* 46 (1989): 498-499.

————————————. (Rome Mass) in a minor. For SATB, a capella. Forthc. Stuttgart: Carus Verlag. (*Domenico Scarlatti Musica Sacra. Gesamtausgabe,* 1).

Missa quatuor vocum in g minor. (Messa di Madrid). Trascrizione e revisione di Lino Bianchi. Rome: Edizioni de Santis, 1961. 31 pp.

————————————. in g minor. (Madrid Mass). For SATB. Stuttgart: Carus Verlag, 1985. (*Domenico Scarlatti Musica Sacra. Gesamtausgabe,* 1). Ed. 40.699/02.

Nisi quia Dominus. Psalm 123 in d minor. For SATB, Org. Forthc. Stuttgart: Carus Verlag. (*Domenico Scarlatti Musica Sacra. Gesamtausgabe,* 2).

Pange lingua in d minor. For SATB (T part lost; reconstructed). Forthc. Stuttgart: Carus Verlag. (*Domenico Scarlatti Musica Sacra. Gesamtausgabe*, 2).

Salve regina, soprano & string orchestra in A major. Ed. by Rudolph Ewerhart. Cologne: Arno Volk Verlag, 1960. Score, 23 pp. and parts. (Polyphonia sacra). Figured bass realized for keyboard instrument.

_____. For solo mezzo and strings. Forthcoming, Stuttgart: Carus Verlag. (*Domenico Scarlatti Musica Sacra. Gesamtausgabe*, 2).

_____. Cologne: Gerig.

_____. Ed. by Raymond Leppard. London: Faber Music, 1979; N.Y.: G. Schirmer, 1979. 19 pp.

Salve regina, soprano, alto & continuo in a minor. Ed. by Loek Hautus. Kassel: Bärenreiter, 1971. Score, 16 pp. and parts. (Concerto vocale).

_____. Forthc. Stuttgart: Carus Verlag. (*Domenico Scarlatti Musica Sacra. Gesamtausgabe*, 2).

Stabat mater. Ed. by Alfredo Casella. Rome: De Santis, 1941.

Casella was aware of three MSS but doesn't indicate which one(s) he used in preparing this edition. See item 93 for remarks about the preface to this edition.

_____. Ed. by Jürgen Jürgens. Mainz: Universal Edition, 1973. (Accademia Musicale, 27). UE 25 A 027. [xii] and 111 pp. Miniature score, 111 pp.

Sheveloff (see item 44, Part I, p. 407)
calls this "an exemplary edition."

_____.   Ed.   by   Robert   Scandrett.
Stuttgart: Carus   Verlag,   1986.   103   pp.
Edition 40.472/01.   (*Domenico Scarlatti Musica Sacra.*
Gesamtausgabe, 3).

Text   in   Lat./Ger./Eng.,   p.3.   Contains
preface (in German, English, and French), pp.
4-9 and critical remarks for the set (in
English), p. 103.

_____.   Revisione di Bonaventura Somma.
Realizzazione del basso continuo di Riccardo
Nielsen.   Rome: Edizioni   De   Santis,   1941.
(Musiche vocali e strumentali, sacre e profane
sec. xvii, xviii, xix, 1).   Score 58 pp.

Te Deum à 8 in C major. Hymnus Ambrosianus.
For SATB/SATB, Org. Ed. by Wolfgang Horn and
Evelyn Weidel. Stuttgart: Carus Verlag, 1985.
Ed. 40.477/02. 16 pp.   (*Domenico Scarlatti Musica*
Sacra. Gesamtausgabe, 1).

Te gloriosus in C major. For SATB, Org. Forthc.
Stuttgart: Carus Verlag. (*Domenico Scarlatti Musica*
Sacra. Gesamtausgabe, 2).

SERENATAS

Contesa delle stagioni.   Serenata per 4 voci.
Primavera, estate, autunno, inverno.   Coro
misto e orchestra da camera.   Revisione e
realizzazione del basso continuo di Renato
Fasano. [vi], score, 187 pp. (Antica musica
italiana). Milan: G. Ricordi, 1965.

The only serenata for which a surviving MS
score is known.

VOCAL COLLECTIONS

Five Songs (high solo or med. solo). N.Y.: Carl Fischer.

Lebell, L., ed. *Four Arias*. Eng. transl. by Edward J. Dent, etc. London: Oxford University Press, 1927.

2. Instrumental Music

KEYBOARD WORKS

"Complete Works"

+Fadini, Emilia, ed. *Domenico Scarlatti: Sonate per clavicembalo*. Milan: G. Ricordi, 1978- . [10 vols. projected] Pl. no..:E.R. 2749. Intended to replace the Longo ed. of the same publisher (cited below). Rev. of vol. 1 in *Nuova rivista musicale italiana* 14 (1980): 659-662 by Alexander Silbiger; rev. of vol. 5-6 in *NRMI* 23/3 (1989): 461 and of vol. 6 in *Music Library Association. Notes* 44 (1987): 156-157 and *Music and Letters* 69 (1988): 563-565.

+Gilbert, Kenneth, ed. *Domenico Scarlatti: Sonates*. Paris: Heugel, 1971-1984. 11 vols. (Le Pupitre, 31-41).

Based on the Venice edition upon which Kirkpatrick based his K. catalog nos. "Preface" (see item 192) in vol. 1 (1984). A scholarly and clearly printed edition.

Kirkpatrick, Ralph, ed. *Domenico Scarlatti: Complete Keyboard Works in Facsimile*. N.Y.: Johnson Reprint Corp., 1972. 18 vols. [includes ed. of *Essercizi*].

Based primarily on the Parma MS though
Kirkpatrick's catalog corresponds exactly to
the Venice MS (not used because of its fragile
condition); see Kirkpatrick's article (item
235).

Longo, Alessandro, ed.   *Opere complete per
clavicembalo di Domenico Scarlatti*.   Milan: [G.
Ricordi], 1906-10 and Supplement. 11 vols. in
3.

Sonatas Not Included [thus far] in the Complete Editions

Sonata in A major.   In *Nueva biblioteca espanola de música
de teclado* 3; (Heretofore referred to as *NBEMT*),
pp. 47-50.   Ed. by Antonio Baciero.   Madrid,
1978.

Sonata in A major.   (Source: Madrid, Real
Conservatorio Superior de Música, MS Sign.
Roda Leg 35/504).   Ed. by Malcolm Boyd.   In
"Appendix III," pp. 246-252 of his book (item
3).   Notes on p. 239.

Sonata in d minor.   In *NBEMT*, pp. 41-46.   Ed. by
Antonio Baciero.

Sonata in d minor (Fandango).   In *Obras inéditas para tecla*,
no. 3.   Ed. by Maria del Rosario Alvarez
Martínez.   Madrid, 1984.

Sonata in D major.   (Source: Madrid, Real
Conservatorio Superior de Música, MS Sign.
Roda Leg 35/504).   Ed. by Malcolm Boyd.   In
"Appendix III," pp. 239-246 of his book (item
3).

Sonata in E major.   Ed. by Enrique Granados.   In
Domenico Scarlatti: 26 sonatas inéditas.   Madrid: Union
Musical Espanola, 1967 [reissue of 1905 ed.
?].   2 vols.

Sonata in G major.   In *NBEMT*, pp. 37-40.   Ed. by
A. Baciero.

Selected Sonata Editions or Facsimiles not included above

Balla, György, ed.   *200 Sonatas/ Domenico Scarlatti*.
4 vols. Budapest: Editio Musica, c1977-[80?]
[Bryn Mawr, Pa.: T. Presser, c1977-[80?].
Urtext.

   Based on Kirkpatrick's facsimile edition of
the Parma MS. Charles Timbrell calls it "The
best multi-volume performing edition...for
Scarlatti" (see item 215, p. 56), whereas
Sheveloff refers to it as "too haphazardly put
together to take seriously" (see item 44, Pt.
1, p. 407).

Banowetz, Joseph, ed.   *Selected Sonatas*. [15].
Park Ridge, IL: General, 1979.

Bartók, Béla, ed. *Scarlatti/ a darabokat kibálogatta és
jegyzetekkek ellátta*....   2 vols. [1973-74]   (A
Zongorairodalom remekmüveiböl= Meisterwerke
der Klavierliteratur). Pub. no. Z.2632-2633

Essercizi per gravicembalo by Domenico Scarlatti.
Facsimile of the 1739 ed. Farnsborough, Eng.:
Gregg Press, 1967.   110 pp. Frontispiece by
Amiconi. Probably printed in London by
Fortier, the engraver.

_____.   Facsimile of the
1738-9 ed. Intro. by Roy Howat. Fontenay-
sous-Bois: Stil Editions, 1977.   Review by
Howard Schott in *Early Music* 13 (1985): 97-99.

Gerstenberg, Walter, ed.   *5 Klaviersonaten*.
Regensburg: Gustav Bosse, 1933. Pub. pl. no.
G.B. 14.   22 pp. (Leipzig. Universität.
Musikwissenschaftliches Forschungsarbeiten 2:
Notenbeilage). Cited as (Forschungsbeiträge
zur Musikwissenschaft, 22) in 1969 reprint.
Musical supplement to item 131.

Goebels, Franzpeter, ed. *42 Pieces for the Harpsichord;* facsimile of *XLII Suites de Pieces Pour le Clavecin.* (London: Cooke, 1739). Wolfenbuttel & Zurich: Möseler Verlag, 1985.

Volume of the *Essercizi* edited by Thomas Roseingrave with an added piece by him and a fugue by Alessandro Scarlatti. Includes 12 other sonatas by Domenico Scarlatti and a second version of *Essercizi* no. 8. Editorial commentary badly translated into English.

Hashimoto, Eiji. *100 Sonatas.* 3 vols. N.Y.: G. Schirmer, 1975 (by arrangement with Zen-On Music Co., Tokyo).

Keller, Hermann, and Wilhelm Weismann. *Sonaten [von] Domenico Scarlatti.* Leipzig: Edition Peters, c1957. 3 vols. (Edition Peters 4692a-c)

Kirkpatrick Ralph, ed. *Domenico Scarlatti: Sixty Sonatas.* N.Y.: G. Schirmer, 1953. 2 vols.

Lee, Robert Charles, ed. *Three Sonatas.* Wichita, Kansas: [author], [1959-61]. 2 vols. Vol. 2 has title: *A Second Collection of Rare and Unpublished Keyboard Sonatas* and the imprint: Seattle, Wash.: [author], n.d. Vol. 1 contains sonatas in f# minor, K. 142; C major, K. 143; and G major, K. 144. Vol. 2: sonatas in g minor, K. 4; E major (Granados 13), A major (Granados 10), d minor, K. 41; g minor, Bologna; G major, K. 80 with second movement, *Minuet in F,* K. 94. None were included in the Longo, Kirkpatrick (*60 Sonatas*), or Gerstenberg editions.

Valenti, Fernando. *Essercizi: 30 sonatas for keyboard 1738/ Domenico Scarlatti.* N.Y.: G. Schirmer, c1979. 122 pp.

Discrepencies with the Gilbert edition frequent.

Sonatas for Organ

Greene, Douglass, ed. *Five Organ Sonatas*. N.Y.: G. Schirmer, [1962]. 21 pp.

+ Hautus, Loek, ed. *Sonaten und Fugen für Orgel*. Kassel: Bärenreiter, 1968. 31 pp. Bärenreiter, 5485. [Contains: Fuga, K. 41 and Sonatas K. 58, 93, 254, 255, 287, 288, 328].

Tagliavini (item 165) and Gilbert (item 192) only accept the last 3 cited above as being definitely organ works.

Vignanelli, Ferruccio, ed. *Quattro sonate; trascritte per organo*. Rome: Edizioni De Santis, 1941. 14 pp. Contains: B minor, L. 33; G major, not in Longo; f minor, L. 382; and c minor, L. 158. (Musiche vocali e strumentali sacre e profane, sec. xvii, xviii, xix, 3).

+ Indicates modern sonata editions rated most highly by Sheveloff (see item 44, Part I, p. 422).

"Melo-Bass" or "Violin Sonatas"

Bonucci, Rodolfo, ed. *Sonata, mi minore, per violino e cembalo*. Boccaccini & Spada, 1987. 4 pp. Score, 16 pp. and part.

Salter, Lionel, arr. and ed. *Sonatas for Violin and Clavier*. London: Augener, [c1940-1950]. Score. 8 vols. in 1 and parts. [Sheveloff in item 44, Pt. 1, p. 414n says 7 vols.] Bass realized for keyboard instrument. Contains c minor, L.

217 [K. 73]; d minor, L 168 [K. 77]; F major,
L. 75 [K. 78]; e minor, L. 271 [K. 81]; g
minor, L. 36 [K. 88]; d minor, L. 211 [K. 89];
d minor, L. 106 [K.90]; G major, L. 176 [K.
91].

3 sonate per violino e basso continuo (pianoforte o
cembalo con violoncello ad lib.) Kozreadja
Károlyi Pál; a hegeduszólamot kidolgozta Rolla
János. Urtext. Budapest: Editio Musica,
c1978. Score, 44 pp. and 2 parts. Pub. no. Z
8105. Includes K. 77, 81, 89-91.

VI

DISCOGRAPHY

DOMENICO SCARLATTI ON RECORD

Introduction

So far as this author has been able to determine, there is no reasonably complete, current discography of the works of Domenico Scarlatti. Of course, many lists of recordings of the *Sonatas* exist within general discographical sources; however, for more recent recordings, particularly those which reflect the research that has been done in the last 5 years on the vocal works, no single source exists. Thus, the following list is intended to fill a gap; it includes all the recordings of the non-keyboard works it was possible to identify and a very selective list of recordings of the keyboard pieces, the latter consisting principally of recent issues, attempts to record the entire opus (or at least a sizeable number of the sonatas), or items of historical interest. Emphasis has been placed on performances on the harpsichord rather than the modern pianoforte although there are many fine performances on the latter instrument.

CHAMBER CANTATAS

Ah sei troppo infelice. Musical Heritage Society MHS 1443 [LP] C. Lehmann, sop.; B. Johnsson, hpschd.; G. Weiss, viola d'amore; J. Fischer-Larsen, violin; K. Madahl, fl.; L. Strehl, viola da gamba.

_____. Lyrinx CD 062 [CD]. Nascimento, male sop.; Foulon, baroque cello; Hasler, hpschd.

Amenissimi prati. For bass and instr. ensemble.
Bongiovanni GB2026-2 [CD]. R. Girolami, bass;
Ensemble, Maestri. (Rec. live, 1988).

Bella rosa adorata. Schw Au 17 101 [LP] and
International Music Service IMS Auv 6101 [CD].
Anfuso, Gray.

Deh che fate o mie pupille. Schw Au 17 101 [LP] and
International Music Service IMS Auv 6101 [CD].
Anfuso, Gray.

Mi   tormento   il   pensiero.   (Fr)   Rhodanienne
d'Enregistrements Magnetiques REM 10.984 [LP].
Correa, Monteverdi Consort.

Onde della mia Nera.   IMS Auv 6101 [CD]; Schw Au
17 101 [LP]. Anfuso, Gray.

Pur nel sonno almen talora.   RCA Serie Europa ML 75
[LP]. Complesso "ars cantandi", L. Bianchi,
cond.

_____. (Fr) REM 10.984 [LP].
Correa, Monteverdi Consort.

Quando miro il vostro foco. Schw Au 17 101 [LP]; IMS
Auv 6101 [CD]. Anfuso, Gray.

Rimirai la rosa un dì. Schw Au 17 101 [LP]; IMS Auv
6101 [CD]. Anfuso, Gray.

Se fedele tu m'adori.   For sop. and ensemble.
Bongiovanni GB 2026-2 [CD]. A. Rossi, sop.;
Maestri, Ensemble.

Selve, caverne e monti.   Lyrinx CD 062 [CD].
Nascimento, male sop.; Foulon, baroque cello;
Hasler, hpschd.

Tinte a note di sangue. G.DA 5372 [LP]. L. Albanese
and string orch. (Buzzi-Peccia: Colombretta)

Tuo mi chiami; aria only.   G.DA 5372 [LP].   L.
Albanese and string orch. (Buzzi-Peccia:
Colombretta).

KEYBOARD WORKS

Sonatas. Complete Keyboard Works. 34 vols.: (Rec. 1984-85). [Eng] Erato ECD 75400 [CDs] (issued 1989). [USA] Erato 45309-2 [CDs] (issued Mar. 1991). Scott Ross, hpschd. and org. Rev. by Malcolm Boyd in *Early Music* 17 (1989): 267+. Booklet (206 pp.) includes essays on Scarlatti's life and music and an incipit and brief analysis of each sonata.

_____. [Complete]. Keyboard KGR 1001, 1002, 1003, 1004, 1005, 1006, 1007, 1008, 1009, 1010, 1011, 1012, 1013, 1014, 1015, 1016, 1017, 1018, 1019, 1020, 1021, 1022, 1021, 1022, 1023, 1024 [LPs]. KGR 1025 [CD] Gilbert **Rowland**, hpschd.

_____. Complete Works for Harpsichord. Musical Heritage Society MHS 834517 (MHS 4517-4519), MHS 844581 (MHS 4581-MHS 4584). Erato ERA 9222 [4 LPs], ERA 9232 [4 LPs]. Luciano **Sgrizzi**, hpschd.

_____. (299) Sonatas for harpsichord. Vols. 1-26: Westminster 51-06; 51-16; 51-39; 51-86; 52-05; 53-25; 53-59; 18009; 18029; 18068; 18094; 18102; 18112; 18153; 18170; [no v.16?]; XWN18460; XWN18461; XWN18705; XWN18772; XWN18785; XWN18814; XWN18826; XWN18826; XWN18868 & WST-14079 [SD]: SD omits L.88 & MD omits L.113 & 138; XWN18918 & XWN18869[?]; XWN19071 & WST-17071 [SD]. Also XWN19069 & WST-17069 [SD]: issued as vol. 24 though not a reissue of vol. 24: XWN18868 cited above; and XWN19070 & WST17070 issued as vol. 25 though not a reissue of vol. 25: XWN18869 cited above. Fernando **Valenti**, hpschd.

_____. (34) Sonatas. Music Guild MS 830-832. F. **Valenti**. [Previously issued as Westminster WST 17069-17071; see above].

_____. (8) Sonatas. [not included in series cited above]. Music Guild 31. **Valenti**, hpschd.

Sonatas. Selections

Essercizi.... Telefunken 6.35487 EK [2-LPs]. Stil
0809 S76 [2- LPs]. Scott Ross, hpschd.

Sonatas. (24) Sonatas. Vanguard VSD-71201/02.
Kenneth Cooper, hpschd.

_____. (70) Sonatas. Telefunken SBA-25127
[4 LPs]. H. Dreyfus, hpschd.

_____. (17) Sonatas. CBS MK 42410 [CD].
Vladimir Horowitz, piano.

_____. (12) Sonatas. CBS MT 6658 [cass].
Vladimir Horowitz, piano.

_____. (15) Sonatas. Angel CDM 69118 [CD];
Angel SZ 37310 [LP]; 4ZS 37310 [cass]. Igor
Kipnis, clavichord, hpschd.

_____. (60) Best Sonatas.... Columbia SL221;
reissue Odyssey 32.26-0007 [2-LPs], vol. 1;
and 32-26-0012 [2-LPs], vol. 2. Ralph
Kirkpatrick, hpschd.

_____. (18) Sonatas. DGG Archiv 2533 072
[LP]. Ralph Kirkpatrick, hpschd.

_____. Sonatas. Capriccio 10212 [CD] Ton
Koopman, hpschd.

_____. (20) Sonatas. Angel COLH73 [LP]
reissue of Sept. 1934 performance. Wanda
Landowska, hpschd.

_____. (20) Sonatas, v.2. Angel COLH304
[LP] & Odeon QJLP108 [LP]. Seraphim 6139 [2-
LPs]. Reissues from performances in 1939 and
1940. Landowska, hpschd.

_____. Sonatas. London CS 7177 (and Decca
SXL 6949). Alicia de Larrocha, piano.

_____. Sonatas. Harmonia Mundi 065 99615
(from BASF). Also Pro Arte PAL 1022 [LP] and
RCA RL 3-0334 [LP]. Gustav Leonhardt, hpschd.

_____. (12) Sonatas. Titanic Ti-77. Martin **Pearlman**, hpschd.

_____. (13) Sonatas. CRD 1068 [LP]; CD-3368 [CD];CRD C 4068 [cass]. Trevor **Pinnock**, hpschd.

_____. (14) Sonatas. DG ARC-419632-2 AH [CD]. Trevor **Pinnock**, hpschd.

_____. (30) Sonatas . Harmonia Mundi 2-HMC 90 1164/5 [2-CD]. Raphael **Puyana**, hpschd. Rev by T. Hoeft in *Concerto* 6 (Feb. 1989): 24-25.

_____. (15) Sonatas. London 421422-2 LH [CD]. A. **Schiff**, piano.

_____. (12) Sonatas. Hungaraton HCD 11806 [CD]; same selections: Fidelio 3325.   **A. Schiff**, piano.

_____. (19) Sonatas. Oiseau-Lyre DSLO 567 [LP]. Dorian DOR-90103 [CD].   Colin **Tilney**, hpschd.

_____. (18) Sonatas. Angel CDC 49078 [CD]. M. **Tipo**, piano.

_____. (30) Sonatas.   Philips 6770650 [2-LPs]. Blandine **Verlet**, hpschd.

_____. (15) Sonatas. DG 415511-2 GH [CD]. A. **Weissenberg**, piano.

_____. *Hommage à Scarlatti. 27 sonatas performed by same number of artists on harpsichord, piano, cimbalom, and lute...to mark the 300th anniversary....* Hungaraton SLPX 12674-75 [2 stereo LPs].

Sonatas for Organ

Organ music (complete).   Frequenz 061-004 [CD]. *Sacchetti, org.*

Sonatas (5).   K. 254, c minor; K.255, C major; K. 287, d minor; K. 288, D major; K. 328, G major.   Hyperion CDA-66182 [CD]; A-66182 [SD].

Francis Grier, org.

Sonaten für Orgel Nr. 1-3 [D, G, C]. Disco-Center Vereinigte Schallplatten DC Gal 30221. Bovet.

Sonata Nr. 1 in D-dur per organo da camera con 2 tastatura, flauto e trombone. Chr SCK 70 349 [2 LP]. Schuba.

Sonata Nr. 2 in G-dur. Chr SCK 70 349 [2 LP]. Schuba.

Sonatas for Violin and Continuo

Sonatas, violin and continuo (8). Westminster 18113 [LP]. J. Olevsky, violin, Valenti, hpschd.

_____: (4) in e minor, d minor, G major, d minor. Frequenz CAY 1 [CD]. Bonucci, violin., Canino, hpschd.

_____: (2) C. Cornoldi, G. Catalucci. (Rec. live 1988). Bongiovanni GB 2026-2 [CD].

OPERAS

La Dirinda. Bongiovanni GB 2026-2 [CD]. F. Maestri, Gamberucci, Mari, Gatti, Kammerensbl. d. Philh. Umbra.

_____. Videotape made by Televisione della Svizzera Italiana and directed by Filippo Crivelli; Silvia Baleani (Dirinda); Gianfranco Mari (Liscione); Enrico Fissore (Don Carissimo); and the orchestra of the Radio della Svizzera Italiana directed by Marc Andrae, with Francesco Degrada, hpschd. [Not commercially available as far as this author knows].

_____. Nuova Era 2-2253/54 [CD]. Ravaglia, Bonisolli, Bruscantini; Muti, Naples "Alessandro Scarlatti" Radio Orchestra & Chorus. (rec. 1968). In Germany: FSM Nu 2253/4 [CD].

Tetide in Sciro; arr. Zardini. Abridged.
Westminster OPW1305 (3 LP]. Martino, sop;
Franzini, ten.; Meucci, bar.; Ferrein, bass;
Angelicum Orch, Milan; Janes, dir.

_____: selections. [Six arias of
Achilles]. Pye GSGC 14126 [LP]. P. Taylor,
ten.; Northern Sinfonia Orch., J. Snashall,
cond.

SACRED MUSIC

Cibavit nos. Carus Car 83120 [CD]. Scandrett,
Choir of W. Wash. Univ., Bellingham.

Iste confessor. Carus Car 83120 [CD]. Performers
as above.

Laetatus sum. Carus Car 83120 [CD]. Performers
as above.

Magnificat. Carus Car 83120 [CD]. Performers
as above.

Messa de Arazázu. Messe en ré majeur. Videotape
of world premiere. See item 90.

Miserere. Carus Car 83120 [CD]. Performers as
above.

Missa quatuor vocum. Messa in sol min. [g minor].
RCA Serie Europa ML 75 [LP]. Quartetto
polifonico del Centro dell'oratorio musicale,
L. Bianchi, cond.

Salve Regina [in a minor] for sop., contralto, and
basso continuo. Con So 42. [Fr] Solstice
SOKS42 [cass]; SOL42 [SD]. Comoy, Herlido,
Ladrette, Frémont.

_____. Hyperion CDA-66182
[CD] and Hyperion A-66182 [LP]. Harris,
treble; Clapton, alto; Byram-Wigfield, org.

_____. Carus Car 83120 [CD];

CV 68.110.   Scandrett, Choir, W. Wash. Univ.,
Bellingham.

Salve Regina [in A major] (soprano with string
orch.). Vanguard (Bach Guild) BG 683 (70683).
M. Forrester, contralto; Wiener Solisten,
Anton Heiller, cond.

Stabat Mater. Christophorus CD 74534. Deutsche
Bach-Vocalisten; cond, Weinberger.   Rev. in
Fanfare (7-8 1988): 241.

_____. Musical Heritage Society MHS 1148
[LP]. A. Maliponte, sop.; M. André, tpt; L.
Sgrizzi, hpschd.; Società Cameristica di
Lugano; Edward Tarr Brass Ensemble; Edwin
Loehrer, cond. Rev. in ARG 6-72, p. 518. Same
as Erato ERA 9509. Rev. in Gr 7-78, p. 243.

_____. Argo ZRG 768. Heinrich Schütz
Choir (London); Roger Norrington, cond. Rev.
in Gr 7-74, p. 253.

_____. Decca DL710114. Amor Artis
Chorale, Johannes Somary, cond.

_____. CBS Masterworks 76 531. Julie
Kennard, sop.; Paul Taylor, ten.; BBC Singers;
Timothy Farrell, org.; Anthony Pleeth,
violoncello; Francis Baines, double bass; John
Poole, cond.

_____. [in c minor] Matrix E4-KP 1522-
1523. Chamber Chorus of Washington, with
org., violoncello, doub. bass; Paul Callaway,
cond.

_____. Hyperion CDA-66182 [CD] and
Hyperion A-66182 [LP]; Hyperion KA66182
[cass].   Christ Church Cathedral Choir,
Oxford, Grier; Byram-Wigfield, org.

_____. Erato NUM 75172 [LP]; Erato 2292-
452 19-4 [cass]. [Fr]: Erato MCE 75.172
[cass]; ECD 88.087 [CD];   NUM 75.172 [LP].

Monteverdi Choir, English Baroque Soloists,
J.E. Gardiner.

Te Deum. Carus Car 83120 [CD]. Scandrett,
Choir, W. Wash. Univ., Bellingham.

Te gloriosus. Carus Car 83120 [CD]. Scandrett,
Choir, W. Wash. Univ., Bellingham.

SERENATAS

Contesa delle stagioni (Le quattro stagioni). Tudor 500 707
[CD]; Tudor 73014 [LP]. Lövass, Marheineke,
Bollen, Hopfner; Münchener Vokalsolisten;
Münchener Kammerorchester, cond. Hirsch. Rev.
Fanfare (11-12 1988): 269. Also Tudor 73014.
Rev. in Gr 2-81, p. 981 and FF 9-10-82, p.
335.

SINFONIAS

[Based on the MS (Pc, Rés. 2364) of 17
unidentified sinfonias to operas, oratorios,
and/or serenatas now housed in the
Bibliothèque Nationale, Paris].

17 sinfonie. Adès (Paris) 21.003 (21.002-
21.004). Orchestre de Chambre "Les Solistes
de Paris," Henri-Claude Fantaplé, cond.
Réalisation , A. Geoffrey-Dechaume.

Sinfonias for flute, oboe and strings Nos. 1-3 [G, Bb, G].
[Fr] Harmonia Mundi HM 596 [LP]; HM40-596
[cass] and Odyssey 321.60016 (LP) (USA).
Piguet, Banziger, Saar Chamber Orch., dir.,
Karl Ristenpart.

Sinfonias. Selections. Douze sinfonie [Nos. 1, A major;
3, G major; 4, D major; 5, A major [a minor];
6, D major; 9, F major [d minor]; 10, G major;
11, C major; 12, G major; 14, G major; 15, Bb
major; 16, A major]. Réalisation: Antoine
Geoffrey Dechaume. Métropole 2599 004. J.
Vandeville, ob.; Quatuor Arcana; David

Fournier, theorbo; Yannick Le Gaillard,
hpschd.; or Martine Géliot, harp.

Sinfonia in B.   Philips PHS 900-235, 802 901LY.
In *Eighteenth Century Overtures.*

BOOK II

INDEX OF AUTHORS

Allison, Brian Jerome, 61

Allorto, Riccardo, 62

Alonso-Gomez, Miguel, 90

Alvarez Martínez, Maria del Rosario, 224

Alvini, Laura, 225

Andreani, Eveline, 91

Andriessen, Caecilia, 205

Anfuso, Nella, 171

Avison, Charles, 172

Baciero, Antonio, 226

Badura-Skoda, Eva, 185, 227

Banowetz, Joseph, 206

Basso, Alberto, 1, 120

Bauer, Luise, 2

Benton, Rita B., 121, 122

Black, Jeremy, 46

Boalch, Donald Howard, 186

Bogianckino, Massimo, 123

Bonucci, Rodolfo, 124

Bordas Ibáñez, Cristina, 187

Borton, Bruce Erol, 92

Boyd, Malcolm, 3, 27, 30, 104, 228, 243, 245

Boydell, Brian, 4

Bristiger, Michal, 119

Brito, Manuel Carlos de, 47, 48, 49

Burney, Charles, 5, 6, 7

Casella, Alfredo, 93, 94

Cassingham, Jack Lee, 63

Cerulli-Irelli, Giuseppe, 125

Chambure, Alain de, 126

Chase, Gilbert, 50

Charpentier, Jacques, 37

Choi, Seunghyun, 229

Clark, Jane, 31, 64, 65

Clemessy, Nelly, 51

Corte, Andrea Della, 114

Coxe, William, 52

Crowder, Louis L., 207

Dale, Kathleen, 127, 128

Daw, Stephen, 208

Degrada, Francesco, 8, 36, 109

Dent, Edward J., 9, 32, 209

DeVenney, David, 95, 96

Doderer, Georg, 129, 188

Dowd, William, 189

Edwards, Donna O'Steen, 66

Eppstein, Hans, 67

Fabbri, Mario, 190

Fadini, Emilia, 230, 231

Ferrero, Mercedes Viale, 105, 106, 107

Flood, W. H. Grattan,
    10
Foster, Barbara R., 130
Foussard, Dominique, 53
Foussard, Michel, 53
Fuller, David, 173

Gai, Vinicio, 191
Gerstenberg, Walter,
    131, 246
Gifford, Gerald, 68
Gilbert, Kenneth, 37,
    192, 193
Goebels, Franzpeter, 69
Grosse-Boymann, Gilbert,
    97

Haas, Arthur, 132
Hamilton, Mary Neal, 54
Harding, Rosamund
    Evelyn Mary, 193,
    194
Hargreaves-Mawdsley,
    William Norman, 55
Hashimoto, Eiji, 133,
    134
Hautus, Loek, 135, 136,
    210, 232
Hoffman, Andreas, 108
Hopkinson, Cecil, 211,
    212
Howell, Almonte, 196
Hubbard, Frank, 197
Huizstee, Theodore van,
    70

Ife, E. W. (Barry), 11

Jaenecke, Joachim, 233
Janicaud, Nicole, 37
Johnsson, Bengt, 137,
    138, 139, 234
Jürgens, Jurgen, 98

Kárpáti, János, 12
Kastner, Macario
    Santiago, 71, 174
Keller, Hermann, 140
Kirkpatrick, Ralph, 13,
    14, 99, 141, 142,
    235, 236, 244, 247,
    250
Klimovickij, Abram, 72,
    143

Lang, Paul Henry, 39
Lindley, Mark, 144, 175
Lippmann, Friedrich,
    15, 73
Lister, Craig L.George,
    176
Longo, Alessandro, 16,
    17, 145, 248, 249
Longyear, Rey M., 146
Luciani, Sebastiano
    Arturo, 18, 19, 117,
    147, 237

MacClintock, Carol, 177
Mainwaring, John, 20
Malipiero, G. Francesco,
    21
McCredie, Andrew D.,
    111, 112
McKay, Elizabeth, 74
Malinowski, Wladyslaw,
    119
Marshall, Robert L., 75
Marx-Weber, Magda, 100
Mast, Paul, 76
Maxwell, Carolyn, 178
Molina-Foix, V., 222
Mondolfi, Arnoldo, 238
Moroni, Federico, 148

Neumann, Frederick, 179

Newman, William S., 77,
  149, 180
Newton, Richard, 213

Ochlewski, Tadeusz, 115
Okrainec, Inna, 150

Pagano, Roberto, 22,
  23, 56, 151
Page, Tim, 218
Palmer, Larry, 40
Pannain, Guido, 152,
  153
Parkins, Robert, 181
Pascual, Beryl Kenyon
  de, 24, 198, 199
Paterson, Scott, 78
Pecman, Rudolph, 79
Pestelli, Giorgio, 25,
  80, 154, 155, 156,
  239, 251
Petech, Diana, 41
Petrov, Jurij, 81, 182
Pinchukov, Evgenij, 82
Pirotta, Nino, 38
Pollens, Stewart, 200
Poniatowska, Irena, 83
Porter, Andrew, 219
Powell, Linton E., 84,
  85
Pozniak, Piotr, 86

Reininghaus, F., 220
Rey, Juan José, 240
Roncaglia, Gino, 42
Ross, Scott, 37
Rostirolla, Giancarlo,
  101
Rousset, Christophe,
  157
Russell, Craig H., 87
Russell, Peter Edward,
  57

Russell, Raymond, 201

Sacher, Josephine
  Pettit, 113
Salter, Lionel, 43, 158
Sams, Eric, 88
Scandrett, Robert, 102
Schachter, Carl, 159
Schenker, Heinrich, 160
Schenkman, Walter, 183
Schott, Howard, 202,
  214
Sheveloff, Joel, 26,
  27, 44, 161, 162,
  245, 252
Siccardi, Honorio M.,
  163, 164
Sierpinski, Zdzislaw,
  116
Silbiger, Alexander, 89
Simi Bonini, Eleonora,
  103
Sitwell, Sacheverell,
  28, 58
Sloane, Carl, 203
Solar-Quintes, Nicolas
  Antonio A., 29
Stegemann, Michael, 223
Strohm, Reinhard, 118,
  241

Tagliavini, Luigi
  Ferdinando, 165
Talbot, Michael, 166
Tellini, Enrico, 221
Termini, Olga, 110
Terrayova-Dokulilova,
  Maria J., 242
Tiella, Marco, 204
Timbrell, Charles, 215
Timms, Colin, 216
Tonegutti, Marta, 217

Unger, James Dale, 167

Valabrega, Cesare, 168
Valenti, Fernando, 169
Vinay, Gianfranco, 59

Walker, Frank, 9
Waliszewski, Kazimierz,
   60
Williams, Peter, 45,
   170, 184

Ziino, Agostino, 38

INDEX OF NAMES

Alba, Duke of, 18, 237
Albero, Sebastian de,
   84, 85, 240
Aldrich, Putnam, 179
Alekseev, Aleksandr,
   182
Almeida, Fortunato de,
   46
Alvini, Laura, 41
Anglès, Higini, 29
Astorga, Emanuel d', 22
Avison, Charles, 35, 63,
   158, 177

Bach, Carl P. E., 206
Bach, Johann Sebastian,
   17, 44, 45, 70, 75,
   86, 123, 144, 145,
   154, 170, 173, 175,
   179, 180, 208
Bach, Wilhelm F., 242
Badura-Skoda, Eva, 229
Balla, György, 215
Barblan, Guglielmo, 239
Beck, Sidney, 63
Beethoven, Ludwig van,
   21, 32
Bent, Ian D., 160
Bermudo, Juan, 181
Bizet, George, 76
Blom, Eric, 168
Boivin, Madame (la
   Veuve), 212, 251
Bottineau, Yves, 51
Boyd, Malcolm, 13, 52,
   64, 86, 92, 192,
   224, 226
Brahms, Johannes, 69,
   72, 74, 76, 88, 209
Brewer, 219
Bristiger, Michal, 83

Brosses, Charles de,
   177
Bülow, Hans von, 206,
   209
Burney, Charles, 9,
   172, 177

Caldara, Antonio, 100,
   110
Calzabigi, Ranieri de,
   117
Capeci, Carlo Sigis-
   mondo, 105
Casimira, Maria, 56,
   60, 106, 107, 119
Casini, Giovanni, 204
Charpentier, Jacques,
   37
Choi, Seunghyun, 227
Chopin, Frederic, 40
Christina (Queen of
   Sweden), 56
Clari, Giovanni Carlo
   Maria, 100
Clark, Jane, 41, 192
Clemens non Papa, 76
Clementi, Muzio, 17,
   21, 62, 83, 145,
   207, 208, 217
Cooper, Kenneth, 219
Corelli, Arcangelo, 87
Cosotti, Max-Rene, 221
Cristofori, Bartolomeo,
   190, 191, 194, 195,
   200
Czerny, Carl, 32, 160

Davis, Ivan, 219
Davison, Archibald
   Thompson, 99

Degrada, Francesco, 36,
    216
De Simone, Roberto, 221
Dixon, Graham, 38
Dowd, William, 219
Don Antonio of Portu-
    gal, 200
Durante, Francesco, 97,
    100

Elias, José, 84

Fadini, Emilia, 41,
    178, 215, 243, 247
Farinelli (Carlo Bros-
    chi), 6, 7, 186, 225
Ferdinand of Spain, 18
Fernandez, Diego, 198
Fernandez, Julian, 198
Fernando VI of Spain,
    55
Ferrer, 187
Ferrini, Giovanni, 186
Fishko, Sara, 218
Fitzwilliam, Richard,
    Viscount, 68
Flood, H. W. Gratten,
    19
Fudge, Carl, 219

Gasparini, Francesco, 9
Geminiani, Francesco
    S., 177
Gerstenberg, Walter, 62
Ghisi, Federico, 109
Gigli, Girolamo, 109
Gilbert, Kenneth, 37,
    40, 41, 178, 206,
    215
Giustini, Lodovico,
    194, 195, 200
Gluck, Christoph Willi-
    bald von, 225
Goethe, Johann W. von,

    88
Gomez, Miguel Alonzo,
    41
Greco, Gaetano, 33, 73

Hadow, W. H., 121
Handel, George
    Frideric, 8, 9, 20,
    44, 45, 70, 78, 89,
    103, 108, 144, 154,
    170, 173, 175, 180,
    190, 208, 241, 242
Hashimoto, Eiji, 215
Hasse, Johann Adolf, 7
Hautus, Loek, 165
Hawkins, Sir John, 172
Hay, George, 46
Hindemith, Paul, 222

Istvanffy, Benedek, 242

Jaenecke, Joachim, 246
Janicaud, Nicole, 37
John V of Portugal, 33,
    47, 48, 49, 125, 129
Johnsen, Henrik Philip,
    67
Juvarra, Filippo, 53,
    105, 106

Kastner, Macario Santi-
    ago, 224, 225
Keller, Hermann, 206,
    207
Kirkpatrick, Ralph, 2,
    3, 30, 44, 46, 53,
    66, 75, 85, 118, 126,
    130, 133, 134, 140,
    142, 156, 161, 179,
    185, 192, 201, 206,
    207, 211, 225, 228,
    230, 233, 241, 243,
    246, 251
Kite, 215

Landowska, Wanda, 40
L'Augier, 7
Le Clerc, Charles Nico-
    las, 212
Le Clerc, Jean, 212
Legrenzi, Giovanni, 108
Lesne, Gerard, 222
Longo, Alessandro, 17,
    21, 121, 128, 131,
    142, 148, 156, 178,
    206, 209, 217, 234,
    243, 247, 251

Maffei, Francesco Scipi-
    one, Marchese di,
    171, 194, 195
Mainwaring, John, 8, 9
Mancini, 171
Mannucci, Francesco M.,
    190
Manotti, Antonella, 221
Manzella, Salvatore,
    107
Marcello, Benedetto, 77
Maria Barbara, Queen,
    52, 55, 58, 189,
    197, 200, 201, 236
Maria of Portugal, 18
Maria Theresa of
    Austria, 233
Marmol, Juan del, 187
Mazzuccato, Daniela,
    221
Medici, Cosimo III
    (Grand Duke), 204
Medici, Violante (Grand
    Princess), 204
Medici family, 190,
    191, 201, 204
Mellers, Wilfred, 40
Metastasio, Abate, 6
Morris, R. O., 121
Mozart, Wolfgang A., 70

Nassarre, Pablo, 181
Newman, William S.,
    140, 161
Newton, R., 121, 128
Noack, Friedrich, 233

Oesterle, Louis, 121
Ottoboni, Pietro, 105,
    107

Pagano, Roberto, 41
Pasquini, Bernardo, 138
Pedrell, Felipe, 66
Pena, J., 29
Pergolesi, Giovanni B.,
    79, 237
Perti, Giacomo Antonio,
    190
Pestelli, Giorgio, 140,
    156, 161
Pollarolo, Carlo Fran-
    cesco, 110
Potocka, Delfina, 40
Pretlack, Ludwig Frei-
    herrn von, 233, 246
Pritchard, Brian, 110

Quantz, Johann Joachim,
    7, 177

Rameau, Jean-Philippe,
    31, 164
Ronga, Luigi, 153
Roseingrave, Thomas, 5,
    10, 32, 111, 222
Ross, Scott, 37, 41

Sacchi, 9
Sadie, Stanley, 26
Sammartini, Giovanni
    Battista, 79
Santini, Fortunato, 98
Sartori, Claudio, 8

Sauer, Emil von, 206
Scarlatti, Alessandro,
    22, 70, 73, 101,
    103, 105, 106, 140,
    175, 204, 239
Scarlatti, Alexandro,
    24
Scarlatti, Francesco,
    19
Scarlatti, Giuseppe,
    233
Schenker, Heinrich, 76
Schindler, Kurt, 66, 82
Scholes, Percy A., 7
Schumann, Clara, 74
Schumann, Robert, 88
Seixas, Carlos, 61, 71,
    224
Sertori, Girolamo, 80
Sheveloff, Joel, 1, 13,
    62, 201, 230
Simi Bonini, Eleonora,
    92, 93
Sirinjan, Ruzanna, 81
Snarsky, Andrea, 221
Sobieski, King John III
    (Poland), 60
Soler, Antonio, 50, 71,
    84, 85, 132, 142,
    240

Steffani, Agostino, 100
Sterne, Teresa, 218
Stevenson, Robert, 48

Taub, R., 219
Tausig, Carl, 206, 209
Thompson, R., 99
Tickner, John, 123
Tilney, Colin, 219
Timms, Colin, 109

Valenti, Fernando, 215,
    218, 219
Van Buskirk, John, 219
Van Loo, Louis Michel,
    189
Vecchi, Giuseppe, 109
Vicentino, Nicola, 204

Weismann, Wilhelm, 206,
    207
Weiss, Sylvius Leopold,
    86
Werckmeister, Andrea,
    203
Winter, Paul, 210
Woodhouse, Violet
    Gordon, 58

Zardini, Terenzio, 114

INDEX OF COMPOSITIONS

[Alla caccia di tiranna beltà], cantata, 25
L'Ambleto, 109, 221

Cantatas, 104
[Capriccio in C major], keyboard, 233, 246
[Capriccio fugato a dodici], 210
"Cat's Fugue", 241
Cibavit nos Dominus, 103
Il consiglio degli dei, serenata, 119
La contesa delle stagioni, serenata, 95

Dire non voglio, arias, 237
La Dirindina, 8, 25, 109, 216, 220, 221

E pur per mia sventura, 113
Essercizi, 74, 75, 89, 125, 139, 241

Fandango, 224
Festeggio armonico, serenata, 18
Fugues, 84, 141, 239, 241

Il Giustino, 108

Ifigenia in Aulide, 106
Ifigenia in Tauri, 106, 107
L'Irene, 110
Iste confessor, 92

Keyboard music, 1, 3, 17, 25, 26, 32, 43, 71, 73, 77, 81, 83-85, 140, 141, 144, 145, 147, 150, 161, 168-170, 175, 189, 209, 211, 212, 214, 217, 240, 243, 244
Keyboard music, arr., 63, 158, 172

Laetatus sum, 92

Magnificat, 92
Mass in A minor "con ripieno", 93, 103
Messa de Aranzazu (in D major), 41, 90
Miserere (E minor), 92
Miserere (G minor), 92, 237

Narciso, 5, 111, 112, 113 (arias), 119, 222, 223
Nisi quia Dominus, psalm, 93, 103
Le nozze di Baco e d'Arianna, serenata, 48, 243

Operas, 105, 106, 107
Organ music, 165, 196, 242
L'Orlando, 106

Pange lingua, 103
Piangete occhi dolenti, arias, 113

Sacred choral music,
    91, 92, 96, 97, 99,
    102
Salve regina (A major),
    96, 113
Salve regina (A minor),
    96
Scritte con falso
    inganno, arias, 113
Serenatas, 48
17 Sinfonie, 25
Sonata, K. 8, 173
Sonata, K. 31, 232
Sonata, K. 32, 232
Sonata, K. 78, 159
Sonata, K. 85, 154
Sonata, K. 95, 251
Sonata, K. 116, 65, 82
Sonata, K. 119, 82, 148
Sonata, K. 124, 132
Sonata, K. 139, 148
Sonata, K. 141, 82, 148
Sonata, K. 209, 148
Sonata, K. 223, 88
Sonata, K. 238, 148
Sonata, K. 247, 82
Sonata, K. 254, 165
Sonata, K. 255, 165
Sonata, K. 268, 132
Sonata, K. 287, 165
Sonata, K. 288, 165
Sonata, K. 328, 165
Sonata, K. 394, 72
Sonata, K. 402, 82
Sonata, K. 450, 65, 148
Sonata, K. 490, 65
Sonata, K. 491, 65
Sonata, K. 492, 65
Sonata, K. 513, 70
Sonata, K. 514, 148
Sonata, K. 518, 132

[Sonata in A major], 226
[Sonata in D minor], 226
[Sonata in G major],
    224, 226
Sonatas, keyboard, 3,
    13, 14, 16,17, 21,
    30, 33, 35, 39, 41,
    44, 61, 62, 65-67,
    80, 82, 86, 88, 120-
    124, 126-128, 130-
    137, 141-143, 145,
    146, 149, 152, 153,
    155-157, 161-167,
    173, 178, 182-185,
    192, 193, 205-209,
    211, 212, 215, 219,
    225-230, 233, 236,
    239, 243, 246-252
Sonatas, violin and
    continuo, 124, 158
"Sparge al mare", aria,
    5
Stabat Mater, 93-95,
    98-100, 102

Te Deum, 92
Te gloriosus, 92
Tetide in Sciro, 106,
    114-116, 119
Tinte a note di sangue,
    arias, 113
[Toccata in A major],
    239
[Toccata in C major],
    234
Tolomeo e Alessandro,
    106, 117, 118

V'adoro o luci belle,
    113
Vocal music, 1, 3, 244

About the Author

Carole Franklin Vidali worked as Music Librarian at Pennsylvania State University from 1969 to 1982. Most recently, she has been an Adjunct Instructor in music at the Department of Fine Arts, Syracuse University, Syracuse, New York.